Ballet Biographies

Maria Tallchief

in Ballanchine's "Four Temperaments".

Ballet
Biographies

by the author of Stories of the Ballets,
Standard Stories from the Operas, etc.

Gladys Davidson

Werner Laurie ◉ London, W.C.1.

First published in 1952
by T. Werner Laurie Limited
1 Doughty Street London WC1
Revised edition 1954

Printed in Great Britain by
Northumberland Press Limited
Gateshead on Tyne

For
MARY ABBOTT
whose love of Ballet equals my own, and
for whose long and encouraging friendship
I am truly grateful

☙☙☙

Contents

꩜꩜꩜꩜꩜꩜꩜꩜꩜꩜꩜꩜꩜꩜꩜꩜꩜꩜꩜꩜꩜꩜꩜꩜꩜꩜꩜꩜꩜꩜꩜꩜꩜꩜꩜꩜

vi

CONTENTS

vii

CONTENTS

List of Illustrations

Preface

OWING TO THE EVER-INCREASING POPULARITY OF BALLET AND to the constant demand among lovers of this beautiful Art for information about the lives and careers of the seemingly remote beings who delight them from afar—for the ballet stage from the front appears to be a wonderful world apart from those who gaze upon it—this book has been written with the hope of satisfying that demand in some small measure.

Within these pages will be found short biographical sketches —not mere outlines and dates only—of seventy-three artists connected with ballet during the past forty to fifty years. Many of these names are world-famous; others are less renowned; quite a number are quickly becoming distinguished; and some are, as yet, known only in our own country.

Among the several hundreds of fine dancers one would naturally have liked to include in a book of this kind, it has not been easy to make a selection practicable for the size of the volume, nor one likely to please such a vast number of ballet-lovers thirsting for knowledge of their own particular favourites. It was, therefore, necessary to draw lines in various directions. As I wished to include as many as possible of our present-day, firmly established dancers and also some of our most promising "comers-on", I decided not to go back further than the magical days of Madame Adeline Genée—even so, I could not attempt to cover adequately even this chosen period, elastic though I have at times made it.

I have endeavoured, however, to make my list a representative one and to include in it many of the leading artists in most of the well-established ballet companies of modern times, in addition to a number of the famous dancers who were stars during the earlier years of my chosen period, and a sprinkling of the aforesaid "comers-on" of to-day.

Naturally, I have made my final selection from among those artists I have either known personally, have actually seen in frequent performances, or about whom I have been able to secure the most information within a reasonable time. It is not easy to contact dancers who may happen to be on tour in other countries; letters are apt to go astray, and so on. (This, of course, accounts in a measure for the absence of certain distinguished names which might otherwise have appeared in this book.) It is hoped, later on, to issue a second volume of these short biographical sketches of ballet folk in which the famous stars of the Taglioni and earlier periods can be dealt with in similar style, together with additional well-known dancers of the Diaghileff and succeeding Companies, plus a considerably larger number of the outstanding or quickly advancing younger artists of the present day—so many of whom, most reluctantly, I had to omit this time.

Meanwhile, this first selection of *Ballet Biographies* is sent forth in the sincere hope that it may interest not only those whose happy memories, like my own, go back to the great and dazzling Ballet Renaissance of the first and second decades of the present century, but also the enthusiastic audiences who applaud our many brilliant dancing stars of to-day and our "White Hopes" of to-morrow.

G.D.

Note. It is much regretted that it has not been found practicable, as at first intended, to include in this new and revised edition about twenty additional Short Biographies of our young dancers of to-day and a few more world-renowned artists omitted, for lack of space, from the first edition—nor, as also hoped, to add a complete List of New Ballets produced by the various Companies since 1951-52. The book has, however, been brought nearer to date by considerable information about new ballets and the movements of dancers so far as existing space could be found; and a careful revision of the earlier material has also been made.

G.D. 1954.

Author's Acknowledgments

I WISH TO EXPRESS MY GRATEFUL THANKS TO THE FOLLOWING ballet-lovers for the generous assistance they have given me in the preparation of this work, especially in regard to such matters as dates, sources of information required, addresses of artists, books and programmes loaned, etc:

Mr. A. H. Franks (of "The Dancing Times").
Mr. E. G. Derrington } *International Ballet.*
Miss Mona Inglesby
The Secretary, Book Information Department, The National Book League.
The many dancers named in this book who have so kindly supplied me with personal information concerning themselves and their careers, and their helpful secretaries who have passed on to me these essential details.

I likewise wish to thank most sincerely the authors of the books listed in the Bibliography, which I have consulted from time to time for the purpose of checking information received from so many sources.

Bibliography

Ambrose, Kay	*Ballet Impromptu*
Anthony, Gordon	*Studies of Robert Helpmann*
Anthony, Gordon and Sacheverell Sitwell	*Massine*
Beaumont, Cyril	*The Complete Book of Ballets*
	Margot Fonteyn
	The Diaghileff Ballet in London
	Michel Fokine
	Enrico Cecchetti
Benois, Alexandre	*Reminiscences of the Russian Ballet*
Borodin, George	*This Thing Called Ballet*
	Invitation to Ballet
Bradley, Lionel	*Sixteen Years of Ballet Rambert*
Bruce, J. M.	*Thirty Dozen Moons*
	Silken Dalliance
Chappell, William	*Studies in Ballet*
Coton, A. V.	*The New Ballet*
Dandré, Victor	*Anna Pavlova*
Dolin, Anton	*Divertissement*
	Ballet-Go-Round
Franks, A. H.	*Approach to the Ballet*
Gourlay, G. Logan	*Robert Helpmann Album*
Haskell, Arnold	*Ballet. (Penguin Series)*
	Ballet Vignettes
	Balletomania
	Diaghileff
	Ballet Annual, Nos. 1-8
Hall, Fernau	*Modern English Ballet*
Hurok, Sol	*Impresario*
Karsavina, Tamara	*Theatre Street*

xv

Kyasht, Lydia	*Romantic Recollections*
Lawson, J.	*Choreography of Ninette de Valois*
Legat, Nicholas	*Ballet Russe*
Lieven, Prince	*The Birth of Ballet Russes*
Lifar, Serge	*Ballet Traditional to Modern Diaghilev*
Lynham, Deryck	*Ballet Then and Now*
Magriel, Paul	*Vaslav Nijinsky*
Noble, Peter	*British Ballet*
Nijinsky, Romola	*Nijinsky*
Perugini, Mark	*A Pageant of the Ballet and Dance*
Sitwell, Sacheverell and Gordon Anthony	*Massine*
Stage and Screen Press Ltd., Glasgow (with Personal Presentations Ltd., London) (Edited, G. Logan Gourlay)	
Stokes, Adrian	*Robert Helpmann Album* *Russian Ballet* *Tonight the Ballet*
Taylor, Geoffrey Handley	*Mona Inglesby*
Tenent, Rose	*Moira Shearer*
Twysden, A. G.	*Alexandra Danilova*
Valois, Ninette de	*Invitation to the Ballet*
Williamson, Audrey	*Ballet Renaissance*

Ballet Biographies

Algeranoff

SEEING HIM IN ACTION ON THE STAGE, ONE COULD HARDLY IMAGINE this outstanding character dancer to be other than a very Russian of the Russians—or, if not that, then certainly a Latin. Neither is the case, however. Harcourt Algeranoff is proud to acknowledge himself an Englishman, born in London near Charing Cross. He trained with several famous teachers and dancers, among them being Nicholas Legat, Oboukhoff, Tcherni-cheva, Nikolaeva, Idzikovsky, Laurent Novikoff, Petroff, and, later on, Nicolai Sergueeff. He also specialized in Oriental dancing, and studied Indian ballet work with Uday Shan-Kar, and Japanese classical dancing in Tokio with Matsumoto Koshiro VIIIth—the latter being the greatest dancer on the famous Kabuki stage. When Uday Shan-Kar left the Pavlova Company, Algeranoff succeeded to the famous Indian dancer's roles in the Company—with which, by the way, he travelled practically all over the world. He has since lectured on and demonstrated Japanese and Indian dancing in many countries. Algeranoff began his dancing career with Madame Pavlova's Company while still in his teens, making his début in *Die Puppenfee* at the Théâtre St. Denis at Montreal; and he soon began to partner the famous Russian dancer in her *Danse Russe* and *Oriental Impressions*. After the sad death of Anna Pavlova, Algeranoff worked with several other companies, among them being: Opéra Russe de Paris, de Basil's Ballet Russe de Monte Carlo, Les Ballets Russes Classiques, the Markova-Dolin Ballet, Educational Ballets, Covent Garden Ballet Russe. While he was dancing at Covent Garden as a principal in the last pre-war season, Mona Inglesby was also in the Company as one of the *corps de ballet*. They did not meet, however, until Algeranoff came from South America to join the International Ballet Company in 1943.

In the world of "straight" ballet, Algeranoff has been associated with, in addition to Pavlova and her dancers, the following: Danilova, Baronova, Egorova, Markova, Nijinska, Spessiva, Nana Gollner, Nemtchinova, Phyllis Bedells, Sokolova, Tchernicheva; and he has worked with the following choreographers: Massine, Fokine, Lichine, Dolin, Lifar, B. Nijinska, and Mona Inglesby.

Algeranoff is a splendid mime, and it is as a character dancer that he first made his name and has continued to add to his world-wide reputation. Among his most successful roles have been: The Blackamoor in *Petrouchka*, Fate in *Les Présages* (this is likewise his own favourite role), Kotchei in *L'Oiseau de Feu*, Rigadon in *Scuola di Ballo*, the Astrologer in *Le Coq d'Or*, Nicolo the Waiter in *Les Femmes de Bonne Humeur*, Pierrot in *Le Carnaval*, the Prophet Samuel in *David Triomphant*, etc.

After spending some time in South America, Algeranoff returned to England in 1943 and joined International Ballet, with which Company he has remained ever since as principal character dancer. Among the interesting roles he has danced with this Company are: Death in *Everyman*, Carabosse in *The Sleeping Beauty*, Sir Andrew Aguecheek in *Twelfth Night*, the Tutor and Czardas in *Le Lac des Cygnes*; Chinese, Ivan, and Puss-in-Boots in *Aurora's Wedding*, and Dr. Coppélius in *Coppélia*. In the latter role, he is outstanding and is regarded as one of the best living exponents of this would-be magician. He likewise makes a blood-curdling Carabosse in *The Sleeping Beauty*; and his Puss-in-Boots in the latter is a dashing Cat-Cavalier indeed.

Algeranoff is married to one of the principal solo dancers of International Ballet, Claudie Algeranova (*née* Claudie Leonard). Algeranoff's first ballet, *For Love or Money* (set to an original score by Gilbert Vinter, with costumes by John Bainbridge), was presented with much success by International Ballet in July 1951, and had its London *première* during that Company's six weeks' season at the Festival of Britain in the Royal Festival Hall of the South Bank Exhibition.

Claudie Algeranova

○○

BORN IN PARIS, THIS REMARKABLY FINE YOUNG DANCER, AL-
though she did not begin her ballet training until the
rather late age of nineteen, is now dancing leading roles in
all the classical ballets and also in the modern works of International Ballet. She has certainly more than made up for lost
time. She received her first training at the Olive Ripman School;
and then she entered the International Ballet School (of which
the well-known ballerina, Mona Inglesby, is Director). Here she
has studied under Idzikovski, Madame Judith Espinosa, Vera
Volkova, and Madame Egorova; and she has also had the great
advantage of coming under the personal supervision of Nicolai
Sergueeff (for many years *régisseur-general* of the Russian
Imperial Ballet School at St. Petersburg), until 1951 the Supervisor of all the classics in the Company's repertoire.

Claudie Algeranova has been with International Ballet ever
since its foundation in 1941, and she is now the only remaining
member of the original Company, with the exception of its
founder, Mona Inglesby. After training for a time in the School,
she passed into the *corps de ballet*, and gradually was given
small solo parts to perform. Her first solo was that of Prayer
in *Coppélia*; and she is still regarded as a perfect exponent of
that small but exquisite role. She has advanced rapidly and had
already tried many of the important classic roles when Miss
Inglesby, herself the Company's ballerina, met with an accident
in 1948 and was out of action for some considerable time.
During this period, Algeranova appeared as Odette-Odile in
Swan Lake, the Princess Aurora in *The Sleeping Beauty*, *Giselle*,
and Swanilda in *Coppélia*—for all of which roles, fortunately,
she was qualified and had been well-practised in. Later, she
shared these roles with other leading dancers of the Company,
Hélène Armfelt, Anne Suren, Domini Callaghan, Sandra Vane,
Menen Smeta.

She also makes an excellent and dignified Olivia in *Twelfth
Night*; and her performance as the Princess Florisse (the Enchanted Princess) in the Blue-Bird variation in *Sleeping Beauty*
is one of the best to be seen at the present time. In the 1949

3

production of Dorothy Stevenson's ballet, *Sea Legend* (music by Esther Rofe, *décor* and costumes by John Bainbridge), in which she takes the part of a seductive Siren of the Sea, she has proved herself alluring, and an actress of considerable dramatic ability; and the grace of her undulatory arm and body movements enhances the glamorous effect of her classical beauty. During the International Ballet Company's London season at the Coliseum in May 1950, she was particularly successful in the part of the Flower-girl in the revival of Massine's popular ballet *Gaieté Parisienne*.

Claudie Algeranova is an extraordinarily good dancer and may be looked upon as a future ballerina who should go far. She first became known to her always appreciative public as Claudie Leonard; but upon her marriage in 1945 to the famous character-dancer, Algeranoff, she has preferred to continue her ballet career as Claudie Algeranova.

She was extremely successful in a leading role in her husband's first ballet, *For Love or Money*, produced by International Ballet first at Leeds on July 6th, 1951, and then at the South Bank Exhibition of the Festival of Britain, on July 31st, 1951.

She has also done excellent work in Television.

Alicia Alonso

AN AMAZINGLY LIGHT AND GRACEFUL DANCER WITH GOOD ELEVAtion, style and great natural charm, Alicia Alonso has become well known in America and over here as one of the leading dancers of the Ballet Theatre of New York.

She is a native of Cuba; but while still very young she went to New York to receive her training in ballet. She studied there with the School of American Ballet and also at the Vilzak-Shollar School. After dancing for a time with the American Ballet Caravan, she joined Ballet Theatre on its inception in 1940, and remained throughout its first Spring Season of 1941. She then returned to Cuba for some time, to assist in the organizing of the *Pro Arte Musical* in Havana, where she remained and danced for a couple of seasons. After this, she rejoined Ballet Theatre in New York as their principal classical ballerina, though she also danced leading roles in their modern ballets; and she remained with this Company until 1949.

When Alicia Alonso came to London with Ballet Theatre in 1946, she revealed herself as a very delightful dancer—though not so powerfully dramatic as her co-star, Nora Kaye. She showed, however, a charming personality, and reminded many of her London admirers of the famous ballerina, Markova, in the latter's earlier and less maturely perfect days. She made a truly sympathetic Giselle, soft and gentle—especially at the beginning of the first act and in the last scenes as a Wili—the mad episode being less satisfactory at that period of her career. She was also quite brilliant in the *Grand Pas-de-Deux* from Petipa's *Don Quixote,* in which her excellent partner was John Kriza; and she was likewise much admired in *Les Sylphides,* in which André Églevsky was the male dancer. She was outstanding as the Italian Ballerina in *Gala Performance,* and *Apollon Musagète;* and she danced delightfully in *Le Jardin aux Lilas.*

Returning to New York, Alicia Alonso continued to dance these leading roles with Ballet Theatre, this particular season being one of the high-lights of the Company. Her Giselle, in particular, became increasingly individualistic and stronger in every way. In the 1947-48 season, she danced the role of the Puppet Ballerina in *Petrouchka* alternately with Nora Kaye, and was particularly attractive in this part. When Nora Kaye unfortunately became ill for some considerable time, Alonso very successfully took over the latter's other dramatic roles, in addition to continuing her own regular parts. She also danced in Anthony Tudor's new ballet, *Shadow of the Wind,* and in Agnes de Mille's *Fall River Legend.* In the latter she took over the principal role of Lizzie, with but a few days' notice, owing to the sudden illness of Nora Kaye; and she made a tremendous success in this difficult part, thus proving her capability of portraying a strongly dramatic modern character, in addition to being a fine classical dancer—even though as the latter she is more generally admired. She also danced in Balanchine's *Theme and Variations,* which requires special virtuosity on the part of the ballerina and which Miss Alonso carried off with remarkably impressive *éclat*—her likewise excellent partner on this occasion being Igor Youskevitch.

In 1948, Ballet Theatre having been disbanded temporarily— though it reformed again fairly soon—Alicia Alonso left New York to organize in Havana a new Company of her own, which is known as the Ballet Alicia Alonso. Several of the Ballet Theatre artists joined her for a time; and she had a good send-off, with a quite large repertory of ballets, among these being *Giselle, Swan Lake* excerpts, *Les Sylphides, Le Spectre de la Rose, Apollo, Aurora's Wedding, Peter and the Wolf, L'Après-Midi d'un Faune, Petrouchka, Coppélia, Prince Igor Dances, La Valse*, etc. She herself was chief ballerina; and her Company has been very successful. Some months later, she was granted a monthly subsidy by the Cuban Ministry of Education. The latter also aided financially the production of a new all-Cuban ballet, entitled *La Rebambaramba*, with music by Amadeo Roldàn and choreography by Alberto Alonso. The Company will probably visit New York and Europe later on.

In the spring of 1951, Alonso was dancing again with Ballet Theatre (now known as The American National Ballet Theatre) in New York, where her first choreographic work, *Ensayo Sinfonica* (set to Brahms' Variations on a Theme by Haydn) was produced. She also went with that Company on its European tour during the previous year and has gained fresh laurels everywhere as a charmingly sympathetic ballerina in the more romantic vein. She was on temporary guest artist leave from her Cuban Company for this purpose.

Frederick Ashton

◎◎

A S PROBABLY THE MOST POPULAR, AND CERTAINLY THE MOST PROlific of modern choreographers, Frederick Ashton holds an important place in the history of British ballet. He has grown up with it, and he has greatly helped to establish its present high position in the World of Art by the excellence of his own creative work. That he, in his turn, has been helped by the great opportunities that so fortunately came his way, there is no doubt; but it is equally true that, having seized these golden opportunities with both hands, he has made a wonderful use of them and has employed his own natural gifts to the best advantage.

This talented choreographer was born at Guayaquil, Ecuador; and he spent his early youth in South America, receiving a first-class public school education, first in Lima, Peru, and later at Dover College, Kent. Coming to London at the age of eighteen, he determined to make ballet his career; and to this end he studied dancing with Massine, Legat, Nijinska, Craske, Astafieva and Marie Rambert. It was while studying with the latter and dancing in the ballets then being produced by her at the little Mercury Theatre at Notting Hill Gate that he began to turn his thoughts to original choreographic work—his ambitions being encouraged by Madame Rambert herself, always eagerly on the look out for new ballets suitable for her own small theatre and her then very youthful student Company.

Ashton's first chance of public recognition came in 1926 when Sir Nigel Playfair produced *Riverside Nights* at the Lyric Theatre, Hammersmith. Requiring a suitable ballet for inclusion in his revue, he asked Madame Rambert to supply this item and the necessary dancers for it. The result was Frederick Ashton's first ballet, *A Tragedy of Fashion* (music by E. Goossens, *décor* and costumes by Sophie Fedorovich), which proved a great success and brought him into early favourable notice.

After this, Ashton spent a year with the Ida Rubinstein Company. Then, on his return, he created a number of ballets for the Rambert Company, some of which still remain in its repertoire and are likewise performed by other companies. He also created ballets for the Ballet Club and for the Camargo Society. From 1927 to 1929, he produced *Fairy Queen Dances, Les Petits Riens, Leda and the Swan, Mars and Venus*; in 1930 came *Capriol Suite* and *A Florentine Picture*; in 1931 *La Péri, Façade, Mercury, The Lady of Shalott* and *The Tartans*; in 1932 *Foyer de Danse*; in 1933 *Pavane pour une Infante Défunte, High Yellow, Récamier*; in 1934 *Mephisto Valse*; in 1935 *Valentine's Eve*; in 1936 *Passionate Pavane*. The most admired of these are, possibly, *Façade, Capriol Suite* and *Foyer de Danse*. Alicia Markova danced as a guest artist in *La Péri, Mephisto*

Valse, Façade and *Foyer de Danse*; and Karsavina danced, likewise as a guest artist, in his *Mercury*. Pavlova came to see his *Capriol Suite*, and was so impressed with the poetic originality of his work that she asked him, then and there, to create a ballet for her—alas, however, this did not materialize, owing to the great ballerina's untimely death soon afterwards.

Ashton himself danced in many of the ballets with the Rambert Company at the Mercury, and also at the Lyric, Hammersmith; and he danced on several occasions with Karsavina, Lopokova, Ninette de Valois and Markova. In later years, he danced with Margot Fonteyn. In 1927-28, he toured in Europe with Ida Rubinstein and her Company; and then returned to the Rambert Company. In 1935, Ashton joined the Sadler's Wells Company—then the Vic-Wells Ballet—with whom he has remained ever since as chief choreographer and occasional dancer. During the Second World War he joined the R.A.F. and was away for several years; but on his return, he continued the brilliant work he had already begun and has since been untiring in his output. With such a large selection of dancers ever developing and coming into prominence, he has always had ample and varied material to study; and many of his ballets have been created around this rich store of outstanding personalities, whose particular qualities he has been able to set forth to the best advantage in his highly imaginative artistic work. In their turn, they have reciprocated by suggesting ideas, consciously and unconsciously.

The main ballets he has created for the Vic-Wells and The Sadler's Wells Ballet, from 1935—most of which were produced at The Old Vic and the Sadler's Wells theatres, and at the New Theatre—are: *Les Rendezvous* (1933) (with Markova and Idzikovsky as principals, together with Ninette de Valois, Robert Helpmann, and Stanley Judson); *Rio Grande* and *Le Baiser de la Fée* (1935); *Apparitions, Nocturne, Siesta* (1936); *Les Patineurs, A Wedding Bouquet* (1937); *Horoscope* (1938); *Harlequin in the Street* (1938); *Cupid and Psyche, The Judgment of Paris* (1939); *Dante Sonata, The Wise Virgins* (1940); *The Wanderer* (1941); *The Quest* (1943). He also revived several of his earlier ballets, such as *Façade, The Lord of Burleigh* (1931), *Pomona*.

In many of these ballets Ashton danced himself, though

8

gradually taking the less strenuous roles and devoting himself more and more to the creative work of ballet-making, for which he has such a versatile and poetic gift. Most of the principal roles in his Sadler's Wells ballets were created by Margot Fonteyn and Robert Helpmann.

When the Sadler's Wells Ballet went to Covent Garden Opera House as their permanent home, Frederick Ashton arranged new choreographic additions to one or two items in Nicolai Sergueeff's splendid production of the Petipa-Tchaikovsky ballet, *The Sleeping Beauty*, given on the opening night on February 23rd, 1946, in the presence of Their Majesties the King and Queen and a brilliantly distinguished audience, which crowded that historic building to capacity. That same year, also, he created two entirely new and original ballets, *Symphonic Variations* (presented April 24th) and *Les Sirènes* (presented November 12th). The former (set to the music of César Franck's Symphonic Variations, with *décor* and costumes by Sophie Fedorovich) is usually regarded as his most beautiful dance creation; and it was his first example of the abstract ballet of pure movement, devoid of plot or emotional passion, and presenting a continuous pattern of beautiful movements of exquisite grace. It is performed by six dancers only, three youths and three girls; and it is an evocation of the spirit of joyous youth, the dancing being continuous until the ballet ends. *Les Sirènes* has music by Lord Berners and *décor* and costumes by Cecil Beaton, and deals with a gay, light-comedy plot of the Edwardian period, in which Ashton himself took the part of an Eastern potentate. It contains many delightful choreographic items, and provided Margot Fonteyn and Robert Helpmann with excellent comedy roles, plus a remarkable Spanish dance for the former. At Christmas that same year, too, Ashton arranged the choreography for the Company's magnificent production of Purcell's *Fairy Queen* as a Masque-Opera-Ballet, with *décor* and costumes by Michael Ayrton.

For Sadler's Wells Theatre Ballet (the Junior Company of the Covent Garden Sadler's Wells Ballet), Ashton created in 1947 the charming ballet *Valses Nobles et Sentimentales*, with music by Ravel and *décor* and costumes by Sophie Fedorovich; and in 1948 he produced another ballet of the plotless, pure movement type in *Scènes de Ballet* (music by Stravinsky and *décor* by

André Beaurepaire) produced at Covent Garden on February 11th.

On November 25th, 1948, Ashton created a remarkably clever ballet of the plot-and-psychological type on the subject of *Don Juan*, to the music of Richard Strauss' Symphonic Poem of that title and with *décor* and costumes by Edward Burra. This ballet contained some brilliant dancing more suited in its fireworks display to the 5th than the 25th; but critics varied widely in their appreciation of this work, some regarding it as somewhat lacking in period style and atmosphere (scenic as well as choreographic), while others hailed it as approaching the height of the creator's inventive genius.

At Christmas, 1949, came Frederick Ashton's most important work to date—the first three-act, full-evening-length ballet in the traditional style of Tchaikovsky's *The Sleeping Princess* to be created by a British choreographer. On the evergreen subject of *Cinderella*, with music by Prokofiev and designs by Jean-Denis Malclés, it was presented at Covent Garden on December 23rd, most appropriately for the opening of the Christmas Season. This was an historic occasion, and the full-length pantomime-ballet aroused much interest and praise, though naturally it could not avoid comparison with Tchaikovsky's famous work. While some lovely solos are allotted to Cinderella and to the many fairy characters introduced, in this fine work undoubtedly the Ugly Sisters "run away with the ballet". This comical pair, as created by Robert Helpmann and Frederick Ashton himself, provide much fun—even "clowning" at times—though the latter dancer's performance, as the more timid and frustrated of the elderly spinsters, is not without pathos.

Nevertheless, the character of Cinderella (created by Moira Shearer on the first night, owing to the temporary absence of the Company's leading ballerina, Margot Fonteyn, due to an accident) is conceived with real dramatic sentiment, and the whole inventive work for all the dancers is of a remarkably high standard, making this magnificent ballet a high-spot in its gifted creator's brilliant career.

On April 26th, 1949, Roland Petit's Ballets de Paris produced at the Prince's Theatre, London, a new ballet by Ashton, entitled *Le Rêve de Léonor*, on a subject already chosen and partly worked out by Roland Petit and the designer, Madame Fini, on a most extraordinary and *outré* theme. Mainly owing to the latter fact, it did not meet with success, despite the beauty of much of Ashton's choreography and of Benjamin Britten's graceful music.

When the Sadler's Wells Ballet went on its famous first tour to the United States of America in the late autumn of 1949, Ashton went with them, dancing in several of the ballets—and, of course, in his own *Cinderella*. Curiously enough, the New York critics did not at first express much general admiration for the latter, though they warmed up later; but the Metropolitan audiences themselves were extremely enthusiastic. While in New York, Ashton was invited to prepare a new work for the New York City Ballet's repertory at the City Center. This new ballet, *Illuminations*, consists of a sequence of nine "danced pictures", based on certain poems of Rimbaud, to music by Benjamin Britten and *décor* and costumes by Cecil Beaton. Early in 1950, Ashton went to New York to create and rehearse the ballet, which was produced there on March 3rd, 1950, all the dancers being American trained; and it met with a most enthusiastic reception. This ballet was given at Covent Garden in the summer of 1950, when it formed part of the New York City Ballet's programme on the latter's first visit to this country. Ashton returned to London in time to take part in the Grand Gala Performance at Covent Garden on March 9th, 1950, in honour of the State Visit of the French President and Madame Auriol, at which Their Majesties the King and Queen were present.

The ballets of Frederick Ashton can be placed in several types. There is the somewhat satirical type, such as *Les Sirènes*, *A Wedding Bouquet*, *Façade*, etc., in which he indulges in burlesque and pokes fun at various conventions. Then there are his more recent abstract symphonic ballets of pure movement, as exemplified in *Symphonic Variations*, *Scènes de Ballet*, etc. There are the more psychological ballets such as *Dante Sonata* and *The Wanderer*; and the ballets having plots and a definite story to tell, such as *Le Baiser de la Fée*, *Apparitions*, *Nocturne*, *The Quest*, *The Wise Virgins*, etc. Other ballets, again, are more or less a group of *divertissements*, such as *Les Rendezvous*. But several are a mixture of most of these types; and it is not easy to pin down an Ashton ballet thus—a fact which makes his work all the more interesting. He is often elusive.

That he has a strongly religious side to his character is evident in his reverently treated work, *The Wise Virgins*; and that he is intensely musical is revealed by the fact that he has already acted as producer of some Operas, among which may be mentioned Massenet's *Manon* (Covent Garden, 1946), and Benjamin Britten's *Albert Herring* (Glyndebourne, 1948).

On April 5th, 1951, Ashton's new choreography to the Fokine ballet, *Daphnis and Chloe*, was presented at Covent Garden. The original music of Maurice Ravel was used; and in place of the former Bakst *décor* and costumes, the contemporary artist, John Craxton, was chosen. Comparison with the Fokine ballet for Diaghileff was inevitable; but, for the most part, this cleverly modernized presentation was regarded with much favour as a mature and progressive work. For the 1951 Festival of Britain, Ashton was commissioned by the Arts Council of Great Britain to compose a special ballet in celebration. He chose the subject of *Tiresias*, with original music by Constant Lambert and *décor* by Isabel Lambert; and it was presented by Sadler's Wells Ballet at Covent Garden during the Company's July Gala Month at the height of the Festival Season. In 1951, he was choreographer for the dances in the film *The Tales of Hoffmann*.

In the Birthday Honours of 1950, Frederick Ashton received the award of C.B.E. as an acknowledgment of his work as choreographer and dancer.

In 1952, Ashton produced his ballets *Picnic at Tintagel* (Bax—Beaton), *Vision of Marguerite* (Liszt—Bailey) and *Sylvia* (Delibes—C. & R. Ironside); and in 1953, his special Coronation ballet *Homage to the Queen* (Malcolm Arnold—Oliver Messel) was truly brilliant.

Jean Babilée

ALMOST THE ONLY MALE DANCER OF TO-DAY APPROACHING THE brilliant virtuosity and dramatic understanding of a Nijinsky, Jean Babilée has already won fame while still in his early twenties. He is what is often described as a "born natural dancer", and would almost certainly have been an extraordinarily good virtuoso performer even had he never been taught at all—as is also the case with many of the gipsy folk. Fortunately, however, excellent training was provided for him at an early age, in spite of a temperamental aversion to discipline. Thus his work was not always on the same level; and this tendency—though, happily, now in ever-lessening degree—has continued into his adult life.

Jean Babilée spent his early childhood in an atmosphere of comfortable ease in the midst of an intellectual family circle. His father, Dr. Gutmann, was a well-known medical specialist in Paris. The parents soon realized that their small son possessed a natural genius for dancing, his unusual suppleness of limb, his effortless grace and astonishing jumping powers having been noticeable from his earliest years. He was, therefore, sent to the Ballet School of the Opéra in Paris, where he advanced at great speed and soon outstripped his contemporaries. Owing to his charming good looks and poetic grace, he was always noticeable at the various pupils' performances given from time to time.

One of his teachers was Alexandre Volonine, at whose students' shows he was invariably the "star turn". He adopted his mother's name for his dancing career.

At the age of seventeen, during the Second World War, he was sent out of Paris to the South of France; but here, fortunately, he was able to join a small ballet company at Cannes directed by Marika Besobrasova, a former member of the Monte Carlo Ballet. Here he made his dancing début and, quickly attracting attention by his already extreme technical virtuosity, he won great popularity as a star performer in that district.

Later on during the war he served his country with the Maquis; and when, in 1944, he returned to take up his dancing career once more it was found that he had lost practically nothing of his old-time skill during his adventurous absence.

He now developed rapidly, though becoming increasingly impatient at finding himself still compelled to remain for a longer and seemingly indefinite spell in the *corps de ballet* at the Opéra. He began to take special lessons at the studio of Victor Gsovsky; and soon afterwards he obtained an engagement with the recently formed Ballets des Champs-Élysées. Here his obviously unusual talent was quickly recognized, and he was given the role of The Joker in *Jeu des Cartes*, and thus became a star practically overnight, his truly amazing performance in this acrobatic yet subtle part winning him high praises on every side. The young actor-dancer had definitely "arrived" in this new Company of youthful dancers and in this amazing ballet by a twenty-year-old girl choreographer, Janine Charrat, whose reputation, now ever-increasing, was made that same night.

Babilée remained with this virile and enterprising Company of young dancers for several years, dancing most of the classical or virtuoso roles, though his fine miming qualities were likewise made good use of by its discerning Director, Boris Kochno. His performance in the famous *Blue-Bird pas de deux* in *The Sleeping Beauty* is regarded as probably the finest of all present-day exponents, his perfect technique and truly astonishing elevation being executed with the utmost ease. The same may be said of his lovely *Don Quixote pas-de-deux Classique*, in which his partner is usually Nathalie Philippart, now his wife.

With the latter, too, he gives a beautiful and most poetic performance in Roland Petit's *Le Jeune Homme et la Mort*, in which much tragic and even violent miming is required of the two performers and in which the emotional atmosphere is kept at a constantly high pitch. This is a masterpiece of perfect artistry. His rendering of The Don in Milloss' *Le Portrait de Don Quichotte* is also a wonderful creation; and again, in this ballet, he is admirably supported by his remarkably clever and artistic wife.

In Lichine's fantastic *La Rencontre*, Babilée dances the very thrilling role of Oedipus, depicting the visit of the latter to the Sphinx in order to solve her famous riddle; and this gives him scope for some very dramatic movements. In this ballet his whole performance is full of intense and breathless interest and reveals him as a supreme artist in dance and drama. As leading dancer with the Champs-Élysées Company, he had excellent roles in all the ballets in its repertoire. With the Company, too, he has taken leading parts in important Television programmes in Paris and at the B.B.C. Studios in London. At the latter he appeared in *Le Jeune Homme et la Mort* (with Nathalie Philippart) and in the Blue-Bird *pas de deux* (with Hélène Constantine).

In 1948, Jean Babilée made his début as a choreographer,

creating a charming little work entitled *L'Amour et Son Amour*, with music by César Franck and designs by Jean Cocteau, which was produced in Paris at Le Théâtre des Champs-Élysées on December 13th that year, and proved a very successful first venture. It deals with the love of Psyche for Cupid, and the action is developed on most original lines, resulting in a calm and beautiful conception, with Babilée and Philippart as this famous pair of lovers.

Babilée's second creative work was his new and original choreography to Nijinsky's last ballet, *Tyl Eulenspiegel* (music by Richard Strauss, *décor* and costumes Tom Keogh), produced at Le Théâtre des Champs-Élysées, November 9th, 1949. Babilée has treated the subject in an entirely comedy vein, omitting the former Tyl execution finale and giving a happy ending instead; and the amusing and most acrobatic adventures and puckish pranks of his fantastic medieval hero provide him with some amazing and hilarious dancing. For all his rogue-hero's almost diabolic trickery, he yet imbues him with a likeable and fascinating personality; and as he also deals generously from the choreographic point of view with the other characters of the story, this remarkable ballet—once believed to be lost to the present generation—has now taken on a new lease of life.

At the Nijinsky Gala Performances held at the Empress Hall, Earl's Court, in November 1949, Jean Babilée was one of the several Continental dancers who appeared there to do honour to the artist he so closely resembles. Here, too, he danced for the first time in Nijinsky's own famous role as The Faun in *L'Apres-midi d'un Faune*, and gave a truly remarkable performance; as he did also of the Blue-Bird. In 1951, Babilée and his wife, Nathalie Philippart, appeared as guest artists with Ballet Theatre in New York, where they were received with enthusiasm. Here he danced brilliantly in *Tyl Eulenspiegel*, *Le Jeune Homme et La Mort*, and *L'Amour et Son Amour*. In 1953 he was *danseur-étoile* at Paris Opéra, with *début* as Albrecht in *Giselle*, and creating the title-role in Lander's *Hop-Frog*. For television and films he has choreographed *Le Poignard* and *The Dancing Professor*, and has contracts ahead.

Jean Babilée is gaining fresh laurels with every year that passes. He never fails to astonish his audiences with his almost unbelievable elevation and balance, his real theatre-sense, and his intense and ever-increasing dramatic qualities. Though still so young, he is already a great dancer, and may be—he certainly has the latent powers within him—greater still.

George Balanchine

GEORGE BALANCHINE, COMING INTO EARLY PROMINENCE AS AN extremely original creator of ballets during the last few years of the great Diaghileff's meteor-like career, may be regarded as heading the "Big Five" among the leading Russian choreographers of to-day—the other four being Leonide Massine, Serge Lifar, David Lichine and Bronislava Nijinska. He was born at St. Petersburg in 1904 and came of a musical family, his father being a successful composer of high repute.

He entered the Imperial Ballet School at the age of ten, in 1914; and he was soon selected to perform in various ballets at the Maryinsky Theatre. He studied mainly under P. A. Gerdt and S. C. Andreyanov. His original Russian name was Balanchivadze; but, later on, this became shortened to Balanchine for the convenience of his European audiences and colleagues.

Balanchine was already a very promising student at the Imperial Ballet School when the Russian revolution took place. Under the new régime that famous institution became known as the State Ballet School; and after a year's absence during the confusion and hardships of the Civil War, the young dancer returned to the school and remained there a few years longer. In due course he completed his education and his ballet training, and passed out into the Maryinsky Theatre as a full-fledged dancer. Wishing to continue his musical studies, he also now became a regular student at the Conservatoire of Music for three years.

Even at that early period he had definitely modern choreographic ideas, having come into contact with Michael Fokine before the latter left to join Diaghileff. Being a great admirer of Fokine, he quickly became dissatisfied with the old-established repertoire of classical ballets then still the main fare at the Maryinsky; and he determined to strike out for himself.

Even when still a student, he had created and danced in a small original ballet of a then daringly unconventional type. This was strongly disapproved of by the authorities—as was likewise his next balletic adventure, entitled *Enigma*, which, indeed, brought him into considerable official disrepute. Undeterred in his purpose, however, the youthful innovator next gathered a number of young dancers into a group and gave performances in accordance with his own original ideas. This was in 1923.

This still more daring adventure having likewise been stopped, Balanchine decided to leave Russia and to form a little Company of his own to tour in other countries where he would be able to carry out his balletic wishes more easily. Having assembled his group of dancers, he joined forces with M. Dimitriev, one of the singers in the Maryinsky Opera, who managed to get the necessary permits for leaving the country. The party toured first in Germany, where the Balanchine group performed under the name of The Russian State Dancers. Among the latter was a beautiful young dancer named Alexandra Danilova, the future world-famous ballerina.

After a successful tour in Germany and having now cut themselves off from the singers, the little group of dancers appeared at the Empire Theatre, London, where they were remarkably well received—in particular, the glamorous and exquisite dancer, Danilova, being hailed with great acclaim. On proceeding later to Paris to make further plans and to await engagements, they found that their newly won fame had gone before them; and, presently, they received an invitation from the great impresario, Serge Diaghileff, to join his famous Company—which they gladly did.

This was in 1925; and Balanchine now became *maître de ballet* and choreographer of the Company, as well as being one of the dancers. The first ballet he created for Diaghileff was *Barabau* (music by Vittorio Rieto, *décor* by Utrillo), which was produced at the Coliseum, London, on December 11th, 1925. This was followed in 1926 by *La Pastorale* (music by Auric, *décor* Pruna) and *Jack-in-the-Box* (music by Satie, *décor* Derain);

and later that same year came the remarkable ballet, *The Triumph of Neptune*.

The latter was a pantomimic ballet, with music by Lord Berners and *décor* by Prince Schervachidze from designs for the Juvenile Drama Theatres published by B. Pollock and H. J. Webb; the book for the ballet having been written very wittily by Sacheverell Sitwell. This delightfully fantastic work was given a most elaborate production at the Lyceum Theatre, London, on December 3rd, 1926; and it was one of the most amusing and inconsequent ballets ever staged by Diaghileff. It contained some fine group dancing—which included a lovely Flying Ballet—and many exquisite solos for the principals, among whom were Danilova, Sokolova, Tchernicheva, Lifar and Balanchine himself.

In 1947, another clever ballet, *La Chatte* (music by Sauguet, *décor* Gabo and Pevsner) was created by Balanchine and received its *première* at Monte Carlo. That year he also arranged the choreography for a revised version of Stravinsky's *Le Rossignol* for the very youthful new soloist recruit to the Company, Alicia Markova, eventually to become a great ballerina. In 1928, he created his splendid ballet *Apollon Musagète*, presented in Paris (music by Stravinsky, *décor* Bauchant). This beautiful work has been revived several times since, more recently under the title of *Apollo*. In 1928, too, he created his delightful, Watteau-like pastoral ballet *The Gods Go a-Begging*, to a book by Sobeka (Boris Kochno), music by Handel, and *décor* by Bakst and Gris. This charming ballet was first produced at His Majesty's Theatre, London, 1928; and it is one of the most poetic he has ever created. When it was later produced in Paris, its title became *Les Dieux Mendiants.*[1] In 1929, he created two more ballets for the Company. The first on the subject of *The Prodigal Son* (*Le Fils Prodigue*) (music by Prokofiev, *décor* Roualt), in which Serge Lifar made his remarkable début with the Company in Paris. The other ballet was *Le Bal* (music by Rieti, *décor* di Chirico), likewise produced in Paris.

Balanchine always received the greatest encouragement from Diaghileff, who admired his originality and gave him a more or less free hand; but alas the great impresario died in Venice

---

[1] Ninette de Valois arranged new choreography for a revival of this subject at Sadler's Wells in 1936, with *décor* by Hugh Stevenson.

in 1929, and the newly established choreographer was left stunned for a time, as was the whole of the ballet world of that day.

When the moment for recovery came, however, after spending an interval as *maître de ballet* at Copenhagen, he joined the René Blum and Colonel de Basil Ballet Russe de Monte Carlo as choreographer, when it began its good work of carrying on the Diaghileff tradition in 1932. Having discovered in Paris studios, and recruited for this new Company, the famous three "Baby Ballerinas" (or "de Basil Babes" as they also came to be called) —Tamara Toumanova, Irina Baronova and Tatiana Riabouchinska—he created around their individual personalities the special ballets *La Concurrence* (music by Auric, *décor* Derain) and the lovely, dream-like *Cotillon* (music by Chabrier, *décor* Bérard). These were first produced at Monte Carlo in 1932, with the extremely youthful ballerinas as principals (all were under fifteen years of age); and, later on, they were given in London with other ballets at the Alhambra Theatre in 1933, where the "de Basil Babes" made an immense sensation. He also created for this Company in 1932 an amusing ballet on the subject of Molière's *Le Bourgeois Gentilhomme*, with music from Richard Strauss's opera *Ariadne auf Naxos* based on that subject, and with *décor* by Benois.

Before the opening of this great and most successful London season, however, Balanchine left de Basil, after a disagreement, to form a Company of his own, for which he created the ballets *Errante, Songes* (music Milhaud, *décor* Derain), *Mozartiana* (music Mozart's *Suite 4*, *décor* Bérard), and *Les Sept Péchés Capitaux*, all produced in Paris, and afterwards given with other works produced by the Edward James group, Les Ballets, 1933, at the Savoy, London. Toumanova danced with the latter for a short time, but rejoined de Basil at the Alhambra for the remainder of his very successful four-months season. The Les Ballets enterprise was later disbanded.

Not very long after this, Balanchine settled down in New York as his headquarters, working under the auspices of E. M. M. Warburgh and Lincoln Kirstein, with whom he established the American Academy of the Dance and The Ballet Society of New York, training young dancers and producing ballets.

Following upon the various reshuffles of the Russian Ballet Companies, he created for the Ballet Russe de Monte Carlo (under the Directorship of Sergei Denham) in 1940, the ballets *Card Party*, or *Poker Game* (music Stravinsky, *décor* Sharaff), *Sérénade* (music Tchaikovsky, *décor* Lurçat), and *Le Baiser de la Fée*[1] (music Stravinsky, *décor* Kalicka). For the same Director, in 1944, he also created *Danses Concertantes* (music Stravinsky, *décor* Berman); in 1945, a revival of *Mozartiana*, and *Grand Adagio* (music Tchaikovsky, *décor* Bérard); and in 1946, *Night Shadow* (music Rieti after Bellini, *décor* D. Tanning and Robier). He also arranged many revivals. Other ballets he created for this Company, for American Ballet, and for Ballet Caravan, were *Concerto Barocco* (music to Bach's *Concerto* for two violins and orchestra, *décor* Berman), and *Ballet Imperial* (music Tchaikovsky's Second Piano Concerto, *décor* Dobujinsky). For the Original Ballets Russes he created, in 1941, *Balustrade* (music Stravinsky, *décor* Tchelitchev).

For Ballet Theatre in New York, Balanchine created, in 1944, *Waltz Academy* (music Rieti, *décor* Colt and Smith); *Apollo* (a revival of *Apollon Musagète*, with music by Stravinsky and *décor* by Dunkel); and *Theme and Variations* (to Tchaikovsky's *Suite No. 3* and *décor* by Woodman Thompson).

More recently, Balanchine has created for the Ballet Society in New York in 1946, 1947 and 1948 *Symphonie Concertante* (music Mozart, *décor* J. M. Morcom); *The Triumph of Bacchus and Ariadne* (music Rieti, *décor* Cagli); *Four Temperaments* (music Hindemith, *décor* Seligman); *Divertimento* (music Alexei Haieff); *Elégie* (music Stravinsky, *décor* Tchelitchev); *Orpheus* (music Stravinsky, *décor* Isamu Noguchi); a grand revival of *The Spellbound Child* (music Ravel, *décor* Aline Bernstein); revival of *Le Renard* (music Stravinsky, *décor* Esteban Francés).

In 1947, Balanchine created a new ballet for the Paris Opéra, entitled *Le Palais de Cristal* (music to Bizet's Symphony in C, *décor* Léonor Fini), in which Toumanova danced more exquisitely than ever; and the ballet is a fine example of the choreographer's more recent work. This ballet was given as *Symphony in C* by ballet Society in 1948.

[1] Frederick Ashton also created a ballet on this subject to Stravinsky's music and with *décor* by Sophie Fedorovich, produced Sadler's Wells, London, 1935.

An early ballet of Balanchine's, *La Nuit* (music Sauguet, *décor* Bérard) was given in 1930 by the *Cochran 1930 Revue* at the London Pavilion, with Nikitina and Lifar as principals; and this was recently revived by the Ballets des Champs-Élysées in April 1949. His *Night Shadow* has also recently been given by The Marquis de Cuevas' Grand Ballet de Monte Carlo.

On October 11th, 1948, Balanchine launched his New York City Ballet, with which Ballet Society is now merged, and of which he is Artistic Director; and for the opening seasons he revived his *Orpheus, Symphony in C, Sérénade, Concerto Barocco* and *Divertimento*. He also produced several new works by other choreographers. For the 1949-50 seasons he created *Bourrée Fantasque* (music Chabrier, *décor* Karinska), *Pas de Deux Romantique* (music Weber, *décor* Stevenson), and in collaboration with Jerome Robbins, *Jones Beach* (music Andriessen, *décor* Jantzen). In 1950, too, he created new choreography for Fokine's *The Firebird* (music Stravinsky, *décor* Chagall); and he also revived *The Prodigal Son*, etc. In March 1950, he also produced with great success a new ballet by the famous English choreographer, Frederick Ashton, entitled *Les Illuminations* (music by Benjamin Britten, *décor* by Cecil Beaton).

On April 5th, 1950, Balanchine produced his *Ballet Imperial* for the Sadler's Wells Ballet, at Covent Garden, London, where he and his new work received a splendid reception. The ballet is set to the music of Tchaikovsky's *Piano Concerto No. 2 in G Major*; and the scenery and costumes by Eugène Berman are dignified and exquisite. This is a magnificent and even noble ballet of pure movement in perfect accord with the music; and it is a wonderful medium for the famous ballerinas and leading male dancers of the Sadler's Wells Company, for whom it was revived. It is, indeed, a triumphant example of the almost unconscious welding of the purest classical dance tradition with a modern conception, in which Balanchine excels.

In 1950, also, Balanchine was invited to create a new ballet for the Sadler's Wells Theatre Ballet; and, consequently, on September 19th that year, his *Trumpet Concerto* (to Haydn's famous music of that title, and with *décor* and costumes by Vivienne Kernot) was produced at the Sadler's Wells Theatre. Though this is a much less complicated ballet and not intended to compete with the dazzling brilliance of *Ballet Imperial*, it is, nevertheless, a very charming work; and it provides plenty of excellent scope for the more youthful dancers of the junior company.

George Balanchine is justly regarded as one of the greatest choreographers of to-day; and in U.S.A., in particular, he shares with Antony Tudor an immense popularity. Some of his works are brilliant examples of the abstract ballet of pure movement —such as *Symphony in C* and *Symphonie Concertante*; but that he can also deal most successfully with the plot or story ballet is exemplified by the fantastic complications of his witty *Triumph of Neptune*. His *Orpheus* and *Apollo* are regarded by many as his most important works. He has a facile imagination. A great modernist, he likes to employ present everyday subjects, but often treats these in the classic manner—for, having been trained in this fine tradition, he is a natural lover of classicism. He even at times manages to combine the two schools very successfully. Classicism, however, seems to remain his ideal; but, no matter what medium he uses, he never fails to bring to the work in hand the grace of a poetic mind.

In 1938, Balanchine was married to Vera Zorina, from whom he later secured a divorce.

In 1946, he married Maria Tallchief, the brilliant young ballerina who now dances the leading roles in most of his ballets, and whose dazzling performance in his recent revival of *The Firebird* has placed her in the front rank of American ballet artists.

In 1952, Balanchine created for his Company three new works, *À la Françaix* (Françaix—Dufy), *La Valse* (Ravel—Karinska), *Scotch Symphony* (Mendelssohn—Armistead—Ffolkes—Karinska), *Metamorphoses* (Hindermith), and *Caracole* (Mozart—Bérard).

Irina Baronova

AS ONE OF THE FAMOUS "DE BASIL BABES", IRINA BARONOVA, like the other two members of this remarkable trio—Tamara Toumanova and Tatiana Riabouchinska—had to work very much harder and to endure far more fatigue at

a much younger age than is the case with most other leading ballerinas of to-day. This was mainly because she was
launched as a unique performer when scarcely beyond childhood.

During the early days of the Russian revolution, Baronova's
parents managed to escape and made their way with their infant
daughter to Rumania, where they settled for a time. Here the
little Irina, soon showing signs of dancing ability, was able to
secure preliminary dancing lessons that resulted in her determination to adopt ballet as a career. Her parents, eager to
provide the best training possible for their obviously talented
daughter, took her to Paris at the age of nine years, and placed
her in the studio of Madame Olga Preobrajenska. Here she
advanced quickly and became bracketed with the famous
teacher's other brilliant pupil, Tamara Toumanova, as joint stars
of the studio.

When seen in 1932 by George Balanchine—then hunting for
new dancers for de Basil's Ballets Russes de Monte Carlo—this
bright pair of juveniles was eagerly signed-up by him. The pair
became a trio, Tatiana Riabouchinska being recruited at the
same time from another source; and they were an instant and
sensational success.

The uniqueness of the "baby ballerinas'" extreme youth—
none was more than fifteen years of age—together with the
excellence of their early training and their already astonishing
technique and precocious understanding of the important parts
allotted to them, brought them fame and recognition in an
infinitely shorter period than ever before experienced by any
Russian dancers. Had their circumstances been different, and
had de Basil not been eager for some such sensation at that
particular time, they would certainly still have been students
for two or three more years to come, and have thus continued
their training in a more reasonably leisured manner. However,
though thus pushed into such early public prominence, they by
no means remained static as regards progress, but earnestly
continued their training while shining as star performers, each
developing her own individuality and gradually enlarging her
scope and range. Fortunately, though this entailed a considerable amount of overwork and consequent additional fatigue, it
did not prevent them from becoming the brilliant adult baller-

inas they have since been acclaimed—each, too, miraculously preserving her own remarkable individuality.

Irina Baronova remained with de Basil's Ballets Russe for five years, appearing in London first at the Alhambra in 1933, and then each following year until 1937 at Covent Garden. During this period she shared with Toumanova the principal classic roles, many of the leading parts in several of the Fokine masterpieces, and in the modern ballets of Massine, Balanchine and others.

She went with the Company to New York several times; and she danced leading roles in all their European seasons. She developed a great dramatic sense and was remarkable for the easy smoothness of her technique; and as a mime of power and versatility she revealed an amazing quality which matured with each year that passed. During this first dazzling period in her career she danced the Queen of Shemakhan in *Le Coq d'Or*, the Dancer in *Petrouchka*, the Street Dancer in *Le Beau Danube*, and performed also in *Les Cents Baisers*, *Les Présages*, and took other difficult and diversified roles with astonishing brilliance. Her performance as the Queen of Shemakhan was regarded as really dazzling, despite the fact that she was then only in her early teens; indeed, her almost mature conception of the coquettish, heartless, all-triumphant Queen, conscious of the power of her beauty and fascination, even then proved the high-spot of this fantastic ballet, and gave infinite promise of still further latent dramatic qualities awaiting development with successive years—since abundantly fulfilled. Her rendering of Odette-Odile in *Le Lac des Cygnes* was likewise outstanding even at that early period, her extreme youth seeming an almost negligible handicap. She also danced in *Union Pacific*, *Scuola di Ballo*, and in most of the other ballets in the repertoire.

In the reshuffle of the Russian Ballet Companies that took place in 1938, this quickly developing dancer appeared with Educational Ballets that year at Covent Garden. With this Company, too, she appeared in 1939, creating the principal role in Fokine's *Paganini*, produced at Covent Garden on June 30th, her partner then being Rostoff as Paganini.

When the Second World War broke out in 1939, Baronova went to America; and here she had many opportunities for still further improving her technique and developing her personality.

With Ballet Theatre in 1941, she appeared in Fokine's *Bluebeard*, with Dolin and Markova. She was outstanding as Lisette in *La Fille Mal Gardée*. In 1945, she was one of the stars in Massine's Ballet Russe Highlights, and danced in his *divertissements, Contredanses, Polish Festival, Russian Dance* and *Strange Sarabande*. She also went to Hollywood and made several films there; and at the end of the war, when she returned to England, she made more films later on. Her first British film was *Train of Events*, made at the Ealing Studios, in which she did not dance at all but played a gay comedy part.

Before this, however, Baronova had taken part with Massine in *A Bullet in the Ballet*, a stage version of the novel by Caryl Brahms and S. J. Simons. This production was a curious mixture of a more or less "straight" play, a murder mystery thriller, and ballet, in which she and Massine danced. She has danced more recently in other Massine works, notably in *Rêverie Classique*. She has also taken part in various other plays, operettas and musical comedies; and for a time she was inclined to consider giving up ballet in favour of films and "straight" acting.

It is greatly to be hoped, however, that this charming and still young ballerina will soon return to Ballet. As one of our best modern classical dancers alone, it would be a serious loss indeed if she did not return while still young enough to delight us with her serene beauty of form and movement. As a brilliant exponent of modern ballet roles, with her dramatic, yet subtle gift of mime and her wide emotional range, coupled with her fine technique, great opportunities should still be hers for the taking.

Svetlana Beriosova

SVETLANA BERIOSOVA WAS BORN AT KAUMAS IN LITHUANIA; AND she comes of a dancing family; her father, two of her aunts, and an uncle all being professional ballet dancers. Thus, for this very young and most attractive newcomer to the Sadler's

Wells Theatre Ballet, dancing was a *sine quâ non* from her earliest days and her greatest joy. She passed most of her early life in America, where she received her training first from her father, Nicholas Beriosov, a well-known dancer and *maître de ballet*, and with the Vilzak-Schollar School of Ballet. Later, in Paris, she studied with Madame Olga Preobrajenska, and in London with Madame Volkova.

Her first appearance on the stage was at the early age of seven years; but this was an entirely unexpected and unofficial début. One evening, the little girl was standing in the wings at the theatre, watching the performance of her father, who was dancing a solo on the stage. Presently, feeling somewhat bored, she suddenly decided to join him; and, not stopping to remember where she was, she ran to the middle of the stage—then turned to face a laughing audience. She was equal to the occasion, however; and, realizing her mistake, she politely made a deep curtsey and ran off again.

In 1946, the young Svetlana joined the Ottawa Ballet Company in Canada; and with this Company she danced various parts in *Les Sylphides* and in *Casse Noisette*, for her real début dancing the Mazurka in the former.

In 1947, she became a member of the Grand Ballet de Monte Carlo, dancing in *La Fille Mal Gardée*, *Dramma per Musica*, *Constantia*, *Nauteus*, *Petrouchka* and *Noir et Blanc*. The following year, at the age of sixteen, in 1948, she was invited to join, as a principal soloist, the Metropolitan Ballet, of which her father had become *régisseur* and *maître de ballet*; and here she quickly began to dance leading roles with much success. Among these have been the ballets *Les Sylphides*, *Lac des Cygnes* (Act 2), *Giselle* (Act 2), *Fanciulla delle Rose*, *Design with Strings*, *Ballamento*, *Lovers' Gallery*, *Pygmalion*, *Le Beau Danube*, *Spectre de la Rose*, *Blue-Bird pas de deux*, *Casse Noisette* and *Don Quixote pas de deux*. Her dancing of the Enchanted Princess in the Blue-Bird *pas de deux* is full of charm; and for her fine performance as First Hand in *Le Beau Danube* she has been acclaimed as the very first dancer to make this role of real interest since Irina Baronova's perfect performance of it when the ballet was produced in 1933-34. She also gives a delightful rendering, in Frank Staff's *Fanciulla delle Rose*, of the young girl who, bringing an offering of a wreath of roses to the statue of the Virgin in a church, is attacked by the Seven Deadly Sins who steal the blossoms from her one by one; and her performance in this is moving in the extreme.

As Odette in *Lac des Cygnes* (Act 2) her arm movements are particularly graceful, and her wonderful " lifts " are already as light as thistledown and promise an elevation likely to become remarkable. She is also very fine in Andrée Howard's *Ballamento* and in John Taras' *Design with Strings*.

In July 1948, the Metropolitan Company produced *The Pilgrim's Progress* as a Masque-Ballet at Covent Garden for a fortnight. It had choreography by Andrée Howard, to music by Bach, Gluck and Handel (arranged by Sir Malcolm Sargent), and with *décor* and costumes by Joseph Carl. In this not altogether successful presentation, Beriosova, in the Delectable Mountains scena, gave a performance of real charm and sincerity. In May 1949, she took part in a television performance entitled *Stars of the Ballet*, with Alexandra Danilova, Leonide Massine and Frederic Franklin; and in this she danced with Franklin the second valse in *Le Beau Danube*. She also later took part in another successful television performance of John Taras' *Design with Strings*, in which she danced with Eric Hyrst and Frank Schaufuss.

When the Metropolitan Company had to close down towards the end of 1949, Svetlana Beriosova was invited to join Sadler's Wells Theatre Ballet, and made her début there on May 20th, 1950, as Odette in *Swan Lake,* Act 2. Later that year, she danced a leading part in Balanchine's *Trumpet Concerto* with great success. She has now become one of the principal ballerinas of the Sadler's Wells Ballet at Covent Garden. In 1953, she danced in Ashton's fine Coronation ballet, *Homage to the Queen*.

This very young and most attractive dancer shows definite promise of becoming a future really fine ballerina in the grand Russian manner. She already has the true classical line and style, coupled with real artistry, and the assured easy carriage of the Russian School.

June Brae

⦿⦿

THOUGH FORMERLY ONE OF THE LESS GENERALLY CONSISTENT of the leading dancers in the Sadler's Wells Ballet, June Brae has, nevertheless, later established herself among the Company's present ballerina group. At an early age, she began her career quite brilliantly for one so young; then for a period she seemed to remain static and to make no appreciable progress; and finally, on returning to the Company after a five-years' absence, she blossomed forth once more into prominence.

June Brae was born at Ringwood, in the New Forest, Hampshire. Part of her childhood was spent in China, where she first began to study dancing with the former Diaghileff dancer, George Gontcharoff, then teaching in Shanghai. On her family's return to London, she continued her training with Nicholas Legat and Madame Volkova; later on, she went to Paris for lessons with Mesdames Kschesinskaya and Preobranjenska. After joining the Sadler's Wells Ballet School, she studied further under Ninette de Valois, and later passed out into the Company proper. While she did not shine as a classical dancer, she took great personal joy in dancing and revealed a lyrical tendency and great musical sensitivity. She showed keen interest from the beginning, and threw herself into every part she danced with the utmost enthusiasm.

Her first appearances in important roles aroused considerable interest. Among these were the Prelude in *Les Sylphides*, Pas des Patineuses (with Pamela May) in *Les Patineurs*, the Black Queen in *Checkmate*, the Lilac Fairy in *The Sleeping Beauty*, *Giselle*, Josephine in *Wedding Bouquet*, the Woman in *Adam Zero*, etc. For a time she became a guest artist with the Rambert Company, where she danced leading roles in a number of that Company's ballets.

On returning to Sadler's Wells Ballet in 1946, after the absence referred to above, she was loaned as chief ballerina to the latter's newly established Junior Company at Sadler's Wells Theatre, this Junior Company being known as the Sadler's Wells Theatre Ballet. Here she danced leading roles in *The Vagabonds* (Vagabond Girl), *La Fête Étrange* (the Bride), *The*

Haunted Ballroom (Alicia), also dancing in *Façade*, *The Gods Go a-Begging*, *Assembly Ball* and many others. She travelled with the Junior Company, and firmly established herself as a star in their midst.

When, presently, she again returned to the parent Company, she distinguished herself greatly in Helpmann's *Adam Zero*, as the Woman in the latter's life during its various phases—in particular, in her wonderful Dance of Death. Her versatility was revealed in this varied plural role, in which many critics consider she has never been equalled.

Another of her best roles has always been that of the Black Queen in de Valois' *Checkmate*, in which she created a real sensation by her vivid and dramatic rendering of that all-conquering and sinister character. Her lighter side, too, has been plainly revealed in her clever portrayal of the hilarious Josephine in *Wedding Bouquet*.

June Brae went with the Sadler's Wells Company on its first visit to U.S.A. and Canada in the autumn of 1949; and here she earned high praise for her extremely fine miming in such parts as the Prince's mother in *Lac des Cygnes*, the Queen in *The Sleeping Beauty*—small but important roles which, while not concerned with actual dancing, nevertheless require to be presented with dignity and understanding. As Job's Wife in the de Valois biblical ballet *Job,* she revealed great dramatic sincerity and emotional restraint—also much admired by the Company's enthusiastic audiences out West. June Brae has a natural poetic style, real musicality. a spontaneous love of movement, and she is an excellent mime.

Domini Callaghan

A YOUNG DANCER OF EASY FACILITY AND PRECISION, DOMINI Callaghan seems likely to become an artist of considerable attainments. She has had an excellent training and opportunities of advancement are now coming her way.

Domini Callaghan was born in Leeds in 1923, and is of Irish parentage. She was educated at the Notre Dame Convent there, with the idea of becoming a teacher; but her natural love of dancing soon prevailed and she became a member of the Sadler's Wells Ballet School. Here she trained under Ninette de Valois; and she also studied with Idzikovsky, Egorova, Swevesky, Margaret Craske and, later, with Sergueeff.

On finishing her training, she danced for a time as soloist with the Carl Rosa Opera Company and with the Sadler's Wells Opera Company; also with the London Ballet and the London Guild. In 1939, she danced in *The Sleeping Beauty*, with the Vic-Wells Company at the Royal Command Gala Performance in honour of the visit of the French President, Monsieur Lebrun; and subsequently she has danced various roles in this ballet.

Later on, Domini Callaghan joined International Ballet, under the direction of Mona Inglesby, its founder; and she soon began to dance increasingly important parts. Among these were the Mazurka and *pas de deux* in *Les Sylphides* (the first time at His Majesty's Theatre in 1945); Columbine and Chiarina in *Le Carnaval*, and variations in *Giselle*. In *The Masque of Comus*, presented by International Ballet at the Coliseum in 1946, she danced Psyche in the Prologue and afterwards Cotytto alternately with Mona Inglesby, the Company's ballerina. During this successful Coliseum season, too, she danced in *Lac des Cygnes* (Cygnet Quartette), *Everyman* (Kinsman's Wife), *Les Sylphides* (Mazurka), Grand Pas d'Action from *Sleeping Beauty*, *Twelfth Night* (Olivia), *Aurora's Wedding* (Florisse) and *Le Carnaval* (Columbine). She also danced in several of Mona Inglesby's own ballets: *Amoras, Planetomania*, as well as in her production of *Everyman*, in Harold Turner's *Fête Bohème*, and in Dorothy Stevenson's *Sea Legend* (Siren and Mermaid).

In 1949, Domini Callaghan joined the Metropolitan Ballet; and with this Company she danced Swanilda in *Coppélia* for the first time; likewise the Queen of the Wilis in *Giselle*. In John Taras' *Design with Strings*, her neat precision (always one of her good points) and her gracefully expressive hands and arm movements were shown to advantage.

Soon after joining the Metropolitan Ballet, she took part in the Grand Festival of Ballet performance in the Empress Hall at Earls Court that year, in which Danilova, Frederic Franklin and Leonide Massine were the star performers; and when the latter's *Le Beau Danube* was given, she danced the young girl fiancée, with Massine as her partner, and gave a very delightful rendering of this charming part. Earlier that same year, too, she had taken part with the Metropolitan Company in a Television Programme, in which she danced Odette in Act 2 of *Lac des Cygnes*, with Eric Hyrst as her partner. For Television, also, she danced very successfully in *Ballet for Beginners*, with Michel de Lutry, to whom she is now married. On seeing Domini Callaghan's excellent performance as *Giselle* in a television programme, Madame Rambert invited her to dance that role with her Company for three nights at Glasgow. This was practically at a moment's notice, owing to an accident to Margaret Hill, one of the Company's principals, who had been dancing the part on tour. After the collapse of Metropolitan Ballet, she joined the Three Arts Ballet; but she is now dancing mainly for television. This clever young dancer has much charm and should go far. In 1953, she joined the new Walter Gore Ballet.

Enrico Cecchetti

A S THE GREATEST DANCE TEACHER OF MODERN TIMES, ENRICO Cecchetti will always be famous; but the ballet world has good reason to be grateful to him for more than this. He invented an amazingly complete and scientific method of ballet training, which benefited not only his own contemporary pupils but which—owing to the initiative and good offices of his English friend, Mr. Cyril Beaumont—has been preserved for the use of present day and future dancers.

Enrico Cecchetti was born and died literally in the atmosphere of ballet. His birth took place actually in a dressing-room of the Tordinona Theatre, Rome, on June 21st, 1850; and he died while instructing members of the ballet at the famous

Scala Theatre in Milan, November 13th, 1928. In between those two dates, he had passed his childhood, and his early, middle and late manhood in the realms of Terpsichore.

His mother, Serafina Casagli, was a principal ballerina of note; and his father, Cesare Cecchetti, was a *premier danseur* and *maître de ballet*. He had a sister, Pia, and a brother, Guiseppe. The little Enrico was instructed at first by his father, and later on by Giovanni Lepri, pupil of the famous Carlo Blasis. At the age of twenty years, the superlatively trained young dancer made his début at the Scala Theatre, Milan, in one of Borri's ballets, *La Dea del Walhalla*; and after this, he toured in most of the capitals of Europe.

In 1885, Cecchetti came to London to dance at Her Majesty's Theatre in Manzotti's ballet, *Excelsior*, with Adelina Rossi as his ballerina partner, in which he made a great sensation; and he returned to London for many seasons afterwards to dance at the Empire in various elaborate ballets there. This was the time when male dancers were thought but little of; but the advent of Cecchetti entirely reversed this low opinion and he became immensely popular, being hailed as the greatest male dancer ever seen in this country.

In 1887, after dancing with Giovanina Limido in St. Petersburg, he was engaged as principal dancer and teacher at the famous Maryinsky Imperial Theatre there, where he remained until 1902. He created many ballet roles himself as principal dancer, the most famous of these being Carabosse and the Blue-Bird in the Petipa-Tchaikovsky fairy ballet, *The Sleeping Beauty*, produced there on January 1st, 1890. After this he danced most of the principal roles as *danseur noble*, having used his now firmly established influence to gain more important work for the leading male dancer than that of merely supporting partner to the ballerina. In 1896, he became *maître de ballet* at the Maryinsky, where most of the more famous dancers of the coming Diaghileff Russian Ballet passed through his truly magical care.

After spending three years in Warsaw as *maître de ballet* at the Imperial Ballet School there—following a difference of opinion with the Maryinsky authorities—he set up his own ballet school in St. Petersburg, closing this for a short time only in order to accompany Anna Pavlova on one of her tours. The lovely Pavlova was always his favourite pupil; and she continued to take lessons from him when, later on, he came to live in London.

Meanwhile the great impresario, Serge Diaghileff, had formed his famous Russian Ballet Company for touring in Europe; and he persuaded Cecchetti to join him as instructor to his Company and as a leading character dancer therein. As the latter, there has never been anyone superior to Cecchetti. He was a perfect mime; and his psychological understanding of every character he portrayed was truly astonishing. Among the roles he performed for Diaghileff were: The Magician in *Petrouchka*, the Corregidor in *Le Tricorne*, the Astrologer in *Le Coq d'Or*, the Shopkeeper in *La Boutique Fantasque*, the Marquis in *Les Femmes de Bonne Humeur*, the Chief Eunuch in *Schéhérazade*, Kostchei in *L'Oiseau de Feu*, Pantalon in *Le Carnaval*, etc.

In 1918, Cecchetti opened a School of Dancing in London, while continuing to dance his old highly specialized parts with the Diaghileff Company during their seasons at Covent Garden and other theatres in the West End; and here many of his former and now famous pupils continued to visit him for "refresher" courses. He spent many long and happy hours with Pavlova—when resting from her frequent world tours—at her beautiful London home, Ivy House, in Hampstead; and there was nothing he enjoyed more than to help his best-loved pupil to keep that exquisite perfection of grace and lovely movement never since surpassed.

It was about 1920 that Mr. Cyril Beaumont, the well-known writer on ballet, having become one of Cecchetti's warmest London friends, felt that it would be of great value to ballet students of the future if some record could be made of this great master's own system of teaching dancing—a system which was quite unique; and with the assistance of one of Diaghileff's leading dancers, Stanislas Idzikovsky, he began this difficult task. When Idzikovsky presently had to leave London to go on tour, he continued the work alone for a time; and then Cecchetti himself very generously helped him to finish the book—a complete record of the system, which had taken over two years of patient hard work to get down on to paper. The book was given the title of *A Manual of Classical Theatrical Dancing (Cecchetti Method)*; and it has proved an extremely valuable work. In 1922, the Cecchetti Society was formed in order to spread further knowledge of the system now on record.

In 1923, Cecchetti returned to Italy, where he had intended to retire—but, instead, he was persuaded to continue his teaching, this time at the Ballet School of the Scala Theatre in Milan. Here, on November 13th, 1928, he died, literally "in harness" —a splendid dancer and the greatest and best-beloved of ballet teachers.

William Chappell

WILLIAM CHAPPELL IS NOT ONLY ONE OF OUR FOREMOST scenic and costume designers for Ballet, but has also made a name for himself as an excellent and versatile dancer, extremely useful as a reliable all-round ballet company member. He does not, however, dance very much at the present time, as he has been devoting himself more and more during recent years to designing, for which he has very considerable gifts.

He was born in Wolverhampton, Staffordshire, where, on leaving school, he studied at the Art School, soon showing an original gift for scenic and other designing. He soon, also, became greatly interested in ballet, and determined to become a dancer himself. He began his successful career in dancing by training first with Madame Marie Rambert, and later on with Madame Bronislava Nijinska and Leonide Massine. The first ballets in which he danced were in connection with the Ballet Club, these being *Leda and the Swan* and *Capriol Suite*, both early ballets by Frederick Ashton.

While with the Ballet Rambert—with whom he remained until 1934—he danced many leading parts, including, in addition to the above-named, the following: *Les Petits Riens* (Cupidon), *Le Cricket* (Batsman), *Mars and Venus* (Mars), *Les Sylphides* (Mazurka), *Mercury* (Apollo), *The Spectre of the Rose* (Spectre), *Le Boxing* (American Champion), *L'Après-midi d'un*

Faune (Faun), *Façade* (Popular Song), *Lord of Burleigh* (Lord), *Les Masques* (Personage), *The Mermaid* (Prince), *Passionate Pavane* (Dancer) and *Le Rugby* (Player). He was one of the principal dancers in the Camargo Society during its three years' existence (1931-34), dancing with such famous dancers as Karsavina, Lopokova, Massine, Ida Rubinstein, Nijinska, Markova and Pearl Argyle.

In 1931, he danced in Ninette de Valois' *Job* (one of the seven sons) at the Old Vic Theatre. It was also in 1931 that he danced the difficult role of The Faun in Nijinsky's famous ballet *L'Après-midi d'un Faune*, this part having been his favourite role ever since. He was, indeed, the very first English dancer to perform that celebrated Nijinsky role. Another equally famous Nijinsky part he danced was the Dream Spirit in Fokine's lovely *Spectre of the Rose*.

In 1936 and 1937, William Chappell had become a very experienced dancer, and was performing several leading roles with the Sadler's Wells Ballet—to which Company he had transferred in 1934. Among these was the Shepherd in Ninette de Valois' very charming ballet *The Gods Go a-Begging*. In 1937, he danced the Second Red Knight in the same choreographer's *Checkmate* on its first production at the Théâtre des Champs-Élysées, in Paris. He also danced in other ballets by Ninette de Valois: *The Haunted Ballroom* (Stranger Player), *The Rake's Progress* (Rake's friend), *Bar aux Folies-Bergère* (Habitué), *Job* (this time, Elihu) and *La Création du Monde*. In de Valois' *The Emperor's New Clothes,* he danced the Tailor; and in Frederick Ashton's *Les Patineurs*, he danced in the *pas de deux*. He also danced in the famous classics *The Sleeping Princess* (Cavalier), *Casse Noisette* (Danse Chinois), *Swan Lake* (Prince and Benno).

There are few things William Chappell dislikes more than bad dancing; and during the whole of his dancing career he could always be relied upon as an excellent performer—in particular as a most helpful partner. Because of this, therefore, he declares the following disconcerting incident to be his most awkward stage moment: One time, when he was dancing with that exquisite ballerina, Alicia Markova, they were both so completely dazzled by some unusually glaring footlights that, totally unaware of the fact, they just danced past each other, instead of meeting and going into a big "lift" at the beginning of a *Grand Pas de Deux*.

It is, however, as an artist designer for ballet that William Chappell is more particularly admired; and it was while he was dancing with the Ballet Rambert that he first discovered his gifts in this direction and where he was greatly encouraged to use them. For this Company he designed the *décor* and costumes for *Leda and the Swan* (1928); *Capriol Suite* (1930); *Le Boxing, La Péri*—in which Markova danced, *Mercury*—with Karsavina, *The Lady of Shalott* (all in 1931); *Lysistrata* and *Foyer de Danse*—with Markova (1932); *Atalanta of the East* (1933); *Récamier* (1933); *Paramour* and *Bar aux Folies-Bergère* —with Markova (1934); *Passionate Pavane* (1936); *The Tartans* (1938). For the Camargo Society, he designed *The Origin of Design, Mercury, Passionate Pavane* (costumes only) and *High Yellow*. For the London Ballet he designed *The Seasons*. For the Sadler's Wells Ballet he has designed *Les Rendezvous* (1937), *Les Patineurs* (1937), *The Jackdaw and the Pigeons, Narcissus and Echo, Regatta, Cephalus and Procris, Giselle, Coppélia, The Jar, The Judgment of Paris*, etc.

In the Second World War, William Chappell served for six years in H.M. Forces; but in 1943, he found time to design the costumes for International Ballet's remarkable production of *Everyman*—these particular designs being often regarded as possibly his very best creations. They were certainly a worthy complement to the wonderful scenic *décor* for the same production by the late Rex Whistler; the combined work of these two artists for *Everyman* having resulted in one of the most effectively perfect settings of any British Ballet of modern times.

For International Ballet, too, William Chappell was also the designer for Mona Inglesby's *Amoras* and for *Lac des Cygnes* (Act II) and for this Company's revival of *Lac des Cygnes* in its entirety in 1947. He has also done artistic work for the Markova-Dolin Company; *Casse Noisette, Blue-Bird pas de deux*, etc.

William Chappell has designed to a considerable extent for Revues; one of these being *The Shephard Show* of 1946-47.

This versatile artist also finds time to be much interested in writing and book illustration. He has contributed excellent articles to the Penguin New Writing books; has illustrated several books about Ballet; and his own original book, *Studies in Ballet*, was published in 1948, and has aroused very considerable commendation. His delightful book on Margot Fonteyn was published in May 1951. It is entitled *Fonteyn—Impressions of a Ballerina*, and it contains excellent word-pictures of this famous dancer.

Yvette Chauviré

UNIVERSALLY REGARDED AS THE MOST CONSISTENTLY PERFECT classical ballerina in Europe to-day, Yvette Chauviré seems likely to retain this enviable title for several more successful years to come.

She was born in Paris, and is a true Parisienne. At an early age she entered the Ballet School of Le Théâtre National de l'Opéra (until recently known as L'Académie Nationale de Musique et de Danse), where she received her education and complete ballet training. The very elaborate examinations held each year at the Paris Opéra grade the students in several classes. The youngest of all and the new entrants are described as *Les Petits Rats*, and are not allowed to take the examinations until they have been accepted as members of the *corps de ballet*. Then, at the first examination, the dancers are graded as *Second and First Quadrilles, Coryphées, Petits Sujets* and *Grand Sujets*. Having passed successfully through these stages, they become real artists, of which there are two classes, the *Premières Danseuses and the Premiers Danseurs* and *Les Étoiles (or Stars)*, who no longer take examinations.

During her preliminary years of training, Yvette Chauviré passed brilliantly through all these various stages, studying with different teachers, dancing in all the ballets that were staged, and advancing from small to ever-increasingly important roles and the performance of principal parts; and at last she passed the final examination and emerged as an *Étoile* or Ballerina Star of the Paris Opéra.

Always beautiful and full of grace, her dancing, miming and intelligent understanding of every character she portrayed, quickly won for her the envied position of *Première Étoile*. She danced as this in all the classics—*Giselle, Le Lac des Cygnes, The Sleeping Beauty, Don Quichotte*, etc.; and she also danced the leading roles in the Fokine ballets and in the modern works of Balanchine, Lichine and Lifar. She created many of the principal roles in the ballets of Serge Lifar, the Opéra's famous *maître de ballet*, among these being *Noir et Blanc, Le Cantique des Cantiques, Les Mirages, Alexandre le Grand, Le Chevalier et la Damoiselle, Guignol et Pandore, Le Roi Nu, La Mort du Cygne* and many others.

At quite an early period in her career, Chauviré took part with other stars of the Company, Mia Slavenska and Janine Charrat, in a French film on the subject of Serge Lifar's *La Mort du Cygne* (later known in America as *Ballerina*), in which her exquisite work created a real sensation; and this lovely creation—now arranged as a *pas de deux*—still provides one of her most famous roles. Soon after this came her first appearance in London in 1937, when she danced with the Opera Ballet at Covent Garden in connection with the special programmes held there in celebration of King George VI's Coronation.

Chauviré built up a tremendous reputation in France; and then she became restless and desired a wider experience. In 1946, she left the Opéra Company and joined the Ballets des Champs-Élysées for a time, where she danced principal roles in many of the ballets of Boris Kochno and Roland Petit; and in 1947, she was with the Marquis de Cuevas' Grand Ballet de Monte Carlo as chief ballerina for the summer season. Afterwards she returned to the Paris Opéra and continued there as *première danseuse Étoile*. In July 1948, she appeared in a television programme at Alexandra Palace with the Paris Opéra Company, dancing in *Suite en Blanc* and as *The Spirit of France*, the latter created for her specially for this occasion by Serge Lifar. In December the same year, she appeared again with the Company in a second television programme at Alexandra Palace in *Suite en Blanc* and *Divertissement*.

In February 1949, she appeared in a third television programme with the Company in London, in which she created the leading role in a new ballet by Serge Lifar, *L'Ecuyère*, which proved an extremely successful work.

But Chauviré again became restless and desirous of further

change; and, without authorization from the Paris Opéra, she began to accept outside engagements. In 1949, she appeared in a show entitled *Stars of the Dance* at the Princes Theatre, London, where she danced again in *L'Ecuyère*, in *La Mort du Cygne* and the *Aurora pas de deux*, with Alexandre Kalioujny as her partner.

In November 1949, after a short tour in Europe with Vladimir Skouratoff, she came again to London to take part in the Nijinsky Gala Performances held at the Empress Hall. She danced exquisitely in *Les Sylphides* and *La Mort du Cygne*—this time with Skouratoff as her partner, her co-stars in these programmes being Toumanova, Marjorie Tallchief, Massine, Jean Babilée and George Skibine.

Owing to her several unauthorized absences and to her obvious desire for a change, it was announced in November 1949 that Yvette Chauviré had been suspended from the Paris Opéra. This left her free to tour with the Grand Ballet de Monte Carlo for a short time. Very soon after she accepted a contract to appear at the Scala Theatre in Milan; and in January 1950, she departed to Italy to take up this important engagement. In the late spring of 1950, she appeared as guest artist with the Ballet Russe de Monte Carlo during their season in New York, where she danced *Giselle*, *La Mort du Cygne*, *Swan Lake*, *Romeo et Juliette*, and Gsovsky's *Grand Pas Classique* to delighted audiences. Returning to Paris, she danced at a Tchaikovsky Concert there on July 6th, with Anton Dolin as her partner in *pas de deux* from *Swan Lake* and *Casse Noisette*, and with Boris Trailine in another excerpt from *The Sleeping Beauty*. In May 1951, she appeared at the Florence Festival with Vladimir Skouratoff, where she devised the choreography for one of the two works she also directed during that season. She also appeared again as guest artist at La Scala, Milan, in the spring of that year, and she danced twice with Anton Dolin's Festival Ballet at the Stoll Theatre, London, during 1951. Later in 1951, she was again in New York with the Ballet Russe de Monte Carlo, thrilling every audience with the splendour of her classical roles; in 1952, she was back at the Paris Opéra for a short time; and in 1953, she gave a series of delightful recitals in Paris.

The exquisite and delicate grace of Yvette Chauviré in her superb rendering of the wounded Swan in *La Mort du Cygne* caused many people to regard this poignant little ballet for two performers as one of the loveliest items in her vast repertoire to date. Of the larger classical works, *Giselle* is considered to suit her sensitive personality more closely than any of the others. She has always set a very high standard in classical dancing and is one of its finest living exponents—indeed, she is often declared to be the greatest classical ballerina since the Romantic Era.

John Cranko

O NE OF OUR YOUNGER CHOREOGRAPHERS WHO HAS QUICKLY sprung into front-rank appreciation is John Cranko. He hails from South Africa, having been born in Rustenburg. At an early age he gained his first experience of ballet, dancing for several years with the Ballet Club of Cape Town. Later on he joined the University Ballet.

Although, as a good all-round dancer, he danced many leading roles in the repertoire of both these companies, he showed a special gift for choreography from the beginning of his ballet career. Among his early ballets were *Primavera*, to music by Debussy; to Stravinsky's music he devised *Soldier's Tale*; and to music by Grieg he composed *Aus Holberg's Seit*.

In 1946, he left South Africa and, coming to England, joined the Sadler's Wells Theatre Ballet, with which Company he has danced many important roles, and has also created for its youthful members several new and successful ballets. He has danced principal roles in Celia Franca's *Khadra* (The Husband) and *Bailemos*, and in Andrée Howard's *Mardi Gras* and *Assembly Ball*. He soon began to create ballets for this clever young Company, the first of these being *Tritsch-Tratsch* to Johann Strauss's famous polka tune. This was followed by *Children's Tales*, *Beauty and the Beast* (a beautiful ballet with music by Ravel, produced January 1950), *Sea Change* and *Pastorale* (produced December 19th, 1950). He also created *The Witch* for the New York City Ballet, produced on December 12th, 1950. *Sea Change* has music by Sibelius and *décor* and costumes by John Piper; and it was produced by Sadler's Wells Theatre Ballet in Dublin on July 18th, 1949, again revealing Cranko as a gifted choreographer. *Pastorale*, produced at Sadler's Wells on December 19th, 1950, is set to music by Mozart, and has *décor* and costumes by Hugh Stevenson; and it is a very charming ballet of the almost plotless kind. *The Witch* is set to Ravel's Second Piano Concerto, and has *décor* and costumes by Dorothea Tanning.

In 1949, he became a Member of the Sadler's Wells Ballet at Covent Garden.

It was, however, his delightfully humorous ballet *Pineapple Poll*, produced at Sadler's Wells on March 13th, 1951, which brought Cranko such well-deserved praise from the critics and real appreciation from his public. He was the first choreographer to make use of the lapse of copyright in Sullivan's music; and very excellent use he made of it, mostly of the nautical kind in which this famous composer excelled. It is set to one of Gilbert's *Bab Ballads*, and deals with the diverting adventures of a Bum-Boat Woman (Pineapple Poll), a sea captain and a pot-boy. It is a very cleverly devised ballet, which met with an instant success, and the choreography is remarkably well adapted to the gay humour of the music. Costumes and *décor* are by Osbert Lancaster.

John Cranko also created a special ballet for Sadler's Wells as a contribution to the Festival of Britain in 1951, entitled *Harlequin in April*. The music is by Richard Arnell, and the *décor* and costumes are by John Piper; and it was produced at Sadler's Wells Theatre on May 8th, 1951. This ballet was commissioned by The Arts Council of Great Britain.

In 1952, Cranko created *Reflection* (Gardner—New) for Sadler's Wells Theatre Ballet; and that same year his charmingly simple *Dancing* (Shearing—Piper) was given at Henley. On April 4th, 1952, his first work for Sadler's Wells Ballet was produced at Covent Garden, *Bonne Bouche* (Oldham—Lancaster), a most diverting ballet; and his second was *The Shadow* (Dohnanyi —Piper), March 1953. He also choreographed the charming ballet incidents for Benjamin Britten's Coronation Opera *Gloriana*, Covent Garden, June 8, 1953. On June 21, 1954, the Rambert Company produced his ballet, *Variations on a Theme* (Britten—Rowell).

Further work from this versatile choreographer is looked forward to with keen interest.

41

Alexandra Danilova

ALEXANDRA DANILOVA IS ONE OF THE LAST OF THE RUSSIAN IMperial Ballet-School-trained, Maryinsky-Theatre-finished and Diaghileff-produced ballerinas now dancing to-day. She still remains a shining example of the irreproachable perfection of body control and the truly regal dignity always expected and unfailingly exhibited by all outstanding dancers of that almost magical ballet period—plus her own arresting personality, beauty and grace, her magnificently straight and finely sculptured limbs and the glamorous charm with which she was born.

Though it is now over twenty years since she appeared in London as the then very youthful *première danseuse* of the last two years of the Diaghileff Company, and though she had not been seen in this country for quite ten years when she reappeared as guest artist of the Sadler's Wells Ballet at Covent Garden in the spring of 1949, she still held her crowded audiences spellbound and was as breath-taking as of old.

Alexandra Danilova has probably had far more setbacks and major mishaps in her private life and in the continuance of her brilliant career than falls to the lot of most successful ballerinas —such as might have caused an artist with less determination and inborn belief in herself to throw up the sponge and cease struggling at quite an early age.

Born only just before the First World War, in St. Petersburg, of a good aristocratic family and well-to-do parents, she was a very bright and extremely pretty child, with a small face, almost perfect features, big dark eyes, and long, naturally waving dark hair; and life seemed likely enough to be happy for one so seemingly favoured by fortune. Nevertheless, her early life knew little stability, and the charge of this most attractive child fell into many hands. When but two years old, the father of the family died; and a short time after, the mother died also. The little Alexandra and her elder sister, Helen, three years older than herself, were left to be cared for by their grandmother; but, unfortunately for the two little girls, she also died quite suddenly when the younger sister was three years old.

After this third sad death in the family in as many years, the two children went to live with the younger child's godmother—with whom Helen remained, her young sister being presently adopted by a well-to-do lady, Madame Lydia Golovzeva, whom she was taught to regard as an aunt and with whom she lived very happily for several years. She lived in great comfort and was brought up in aristocratic surroundings, such as she would have enjoyed had her parents lived.

Then there came another change. Alexandra's kind "unofficial" aunt married a second time, a certain General Batianov, a well-known figure in military and Court circles in St. Petersburg, a widower with an already large family, but who gladly welcomed his new wife's charming little adopted daughter into his own household circle. Here, one of his daughters, Maria Batianova, became very fond of the orphan, and the pair remained staunch friends for many years.

At that time in Russia it was the custom for children of the upper classes to attend a preparatory school at the age of seven for a year or two, until ready to enter a more important school known as an Institute, where they remained to complete their education to the age of seventeen or eighteen years. The little Alexandra Danilova did well at her preparatory school, and showed there such a special aptitude for dancing, that it was soon decided she should go to the Imperial Ballet School, instead of to any other "Institute". Application to this effect was made at once; and after passing all the usual entrance examinations and tests, Alexandra Danilova, at the age of eight years, was admitted as a student to the Imperial Ballet School, where she remained for nine years, receiving there the best and most famous ballet training known to the civilized world, plus an excellent general education, with special music and language studies.

Strange to say, the kind guardian, Madame Batianova, died within a year after her *protégée* had entered the Ballet School; and the General, her husband, likewise died about half-way through the First World War, just before the Russian Revolution. But the little orphan they had cared for so generously was now already placed in such a position as to ensure for her a safe and brilliant future; and she was still able to visit her beloved Maria at her old home during holiday periods.

When the Revolution broke out in Russia in 1917, the Ballet School continued its work; but though their training and education never ceased, the students, like all the other inhabitants in the capital, suffered from a lack of food. For a time they had to feed out at their own homes, instead of having all their meals provided by the School; and for about a year the young Danilova lived out in a country district with Maria Batianova, returning once more to the School as soon as the German menace grew less. Here, her training went on as usual; for the officials of the new Bolshevik régime determined to retain their famous Russian Ballet School, which now, however, was renamed the Russian State Ballet School. The students still suffered from scarcity of food and the intense cold caused by the non-heating of the School and of the Maryinsky Theatre.

However, despite these hardships, Alexandra Danilova passed safely and brilliantly through all her years of splendid training; and at the age of seventeen years, she was admitted as a member of the Russian State Ballet Company at the Maryinsky Theatre. Here her gay personality, bright beauty, straight limbs, and the excellence of her dancing and good miming quickly brought her to the notice of certain important people. Among them was the Artistic Director and Conductor of Rehearsals, Fédor Lopokov, the brother of Lydia Lopokova (at that time a bright particular star in the Diaghileff Company), who soon recognized that she was outstanding and that a brilliant future undoubtedly awaited her; and he lost no time in including her among his own private little band of "specials", and tried her out in many small parts, gradually using her also in the more important roles. Her first solo part at the Maryinsky was that of "Prayer" in Act 3 of *Coppélia*; and in this she proved so satisfactory that she was included in parties of dancers performing in special shows at various clubs and summer shows—an unusual honour for one so young.

During her second season at the Maryinsky Theatre she attracted the notice of the gifted young choreographer, George Balanchine who, although he also danced at the Maryinsky— he had, indeed, been a co-student with Danilova—was intensely interested in creating new ballets on more modern lines and had many novel ideas for these. He easily interested Danilova in a scheme for a new Company as she now had a great desire for a wider field for her own unusual gifts.

It was about this time that, quite unexpectedly, an opportunity occurred for Danilova to dance the title-role of the Fokine-Stravinsky ballet *The Firebird*; and her truly brilliant perform-ance and quite dazzling appearance in this exciting ballet finally established her as a leading ballerina of great talent. This was in 1924; and that same year, when the holiday season came along, Vladimir Dimitriev, a retired singer, invited Danilova and Balanchine to join a very small troupe of singers and dancers he was taking for a holiday trip to Europe. Only too gladly the already firmly established ballerina and the ambitious and successful choreographer-to-be accepted this most providential and timely invitation.

The visit to Berlin proved so successful that the little party received invitations from other cities and towns in Germany, where they performed with equal success; and presently the dancers in the troupe were engaged to perform at the Empire Theatre in London, where they were billed as "The Russian State Dancers". Again they met with great enthusiasm; and the Empire audiences hailed the glamorous Danilova with much acclaim.

By this time, the quartette of dancers had overstayed their leave of absence from the Maryinsky Theatre; but though Danilova received a message bidding her to return immedi-ately or to forfeit for ever her rights as a Maryinsky ballerina, she was determined, at least, to see Paris first; and with her equally adventurous colleagues she journeyed thither. It was a momentous decision on her part; for it was while waiting in Paris in 1925 for "something to turn up", that she and her friends were invited to join the Diaghileff Company—their fame having preceded them and brought them to the notice of the great impresario himself.

Among the galaxy of famous dancers in this world-renowned Company, during the four years Danilova was a member of it, were Vera Nemtchinova (then the *première ballerina*), Lud-mila Schollar, Bronislava Nijinska, Alice Nikitina, Tamara Karsavina (occasional guest artist), Olga Spessiva, Lydia Lopo-kova, Lydia Sokolova, Lubov Tchernicheva, Alicia Markova, Felia Doubrovska, Anton Dolin, Serge Lifar, Leonide Massine, Leon Woizikovsky, George Balanchine, etc. The latter, with Massine, Nijinska and Lifar, were also choreographers of the Company. Among the famous new ballets then being produced were *Cimarosiana, Le Train Bleu, Les Fâcheux, The Faithful Shepherdess, Les Matelots, Flore et Zéphyr, Barabau, Les Noces, Roméo et Juliette, La Pastorale, Jack-in-the-Box, The Triumph of Neptune, Pas d'Acier, La Chatte, Mercury, Apollo, Ode, Les Deux Mendiants, The Prodigal Son, Le Bal, Renard, Sacre de Printemps, La Boutique Fantasque, Pulcinella, Apollon Musagètes,* etc. There were also revivals of *Lac des Cygnes* and other classics, and of many of the Fokine Ballets.

Although Danilova danced in most of these ballets from time to time, she came only gradually from smaller to more important parts; but in 1926, when Balanchine's *The Triumph of Neptune* was produced, she created the leading ballerina role with such outstanding and brilliant success that, on the departure of Vera Nemtchinova in 1927 to join Anton Dolin in a new enterprise, Diaghileff appointed her to succeed the former as *première danseuse* of his Company. Thus, within five years of completing her training in Russia, this brilliant young dancer attained to the most enviable position in the whole ballet world of that time. From now onwards, she went from success to success; and then, alas! fate yet once again dealt her a terrible blow. With the early death of Serge Diaghileff in 1929, his splendid Russian Ballet Company fell to pieces, and its dancers became scattered far and wide.

There is not space here to describe the eventual formation of the several fresh Russian Ballet companies built up in Europe after the stunning effects of the unexpected death of the great leader had been overcome; but Danilova later became associated with these from time to time. After dancing to enthusiastic audiences for a year in Sir Oswald Stoll's musical play *Waltzes from Vienna*, Colonel de Basil, who had now formed his Ballet Russe de Monte Carlo, invited her to join him as his *prima ballerina* with Massine as his chief choreographer. This she did, receiving a great welcome at the Alhambra in London, where she was the sensation of de Basil's four-months' season there. Among other star members of the Company were Massine, David Lichine, Vera Tchernicheva, Irina Baronova, Tamara Toumanova and Tatiana Riabouchinska. The last three-named were extremely young and were then known as the "de Basil Babes" or as "Baby Ballerinas", having been discovered by Balanchine in the Paris Ballet School of Madame Preobrejenska and, in the case of Riabouchinska, that of Madame Kschesins-kaya. These three very young girls, although not of the Russian State School, had been taught on the Russian principle and were already such excellent dancers that Colonel de Basil had taken them into his Company for early production; and it was partly for the benefit of these "baby ballerinas" that he had been so anxious to have the thoroughly classically trained Danilova in his Company to serve as a constant living example of the high standard up to which he desired them to live.

Danilova's presence in the Company undoubtedly answered this purpose; but she, personally, had many difficulties and disappointments with which to contend while providing such a privilege for these then embryo "Stars". Nevertheless, having the welfare of her beloved Russian Ballet deeply ingrained within her, she continued to work with the Company under its various reorganizations and different titles.

When the Company went to America, she was hailed as the great *prima ballerina* she had already proved herself to be; and it was the same in every other country she visited. She danced with Massine in many of his own ballets, and was the star *par excellence* as the Street Dancer in his famous *Le Beau Danube*, dancing also the leading roles in his *Scuola di Ballo*, *Les Présages*, *La Boutique Fantasque*, *Les Femmes de Bonne Humeur*; and later in his *Gaieté Parisienne*, etc. In the Nijinska ballets, too, she danced leading roles in *Les Biches*, *Danses Slaves*, *Bolero*; in David Lichine ballets, *Nocturne*, *La Pavillon*, *Les Dieux Mendiants*. In the ballets of George Balanchine she danced the lead in *The Triumph of Neptune*, *Jack-in-the-Box*, *Apollon Musagète*, *Le Bal*, *Les Deux Mendiants*, *Baiser de la Fée*, *Sérénade*, *Jeu des Cartes*; in Paul Petrov's ballets, *Opera Ballets*, *Dance of the Seven Veils* (*Salome*). In 1939, she danced in the ballet *Le Diable s'Amuse*, specially composed for her by Frederick Ashton, the well-known choreographer of the Sadler's Wells Ballet. Having during her early years in the Maryinsky Theatre danced in most of the famous Fokine ballets and in the classics throughout her whole career, she has taken part in at least fifty different ballets, and probably in many more.

During the Second World War, Danilova again visited New York and danced at the Metropolitan Theatre with the Ballet Russe de Monte Carlo, afterwards travelling to South America with the Company. Later on, she went to Hollywood, where the filming of *Gaieté Parisienne* and *Cappriccio Espagnol* took place. After a visit to Canada, there was yet another return visit to New York and still further tours; and Danilova met with many real personal triumphs wherever she went.

She remained in America until a few years ago, among her later partners being André Églevsky and Frederic Franklin. It was with the latter as her partner—and later in the same season with Leonide Massine—that she made her reappearance in London, as guest artist with the Sadler's Wells Ballet at Covent Garden, in 1949, after a ten years' absence; and, as stated at the beginning of these notes, she danced as delightfully and looked as beautiful as ever. In May and June, 1951, she danced as guest artist with Anton Dolin's Festival Ballet at the Stoll Theatre, London.

In 1952-53, Danilova danced with the Slavenska-Franklin Company touring America; and she had another brilliant success as *Mlle. Fifi* in Solov's ballet of that name.

The secret of Danilova's continuous success is partly due to the fact that she is constantly learning and seeking to improve herself, always reaching out towards perfection; and partly because of her immensely wide range, not only in classical ballet but likewise in modern roles. She is not especially well suited to the new symphonic ballets, but is at her best in classical roles, and also in character parts of a gay and vivacious type. She is, indeed, a fine example of the finest ballet school in the world.

An excellent Biography of Alexandra Danilova has been written by A. E. Twysden, published in England by Mr. Cyril Beaumont.

Serge Diaghileff

WHEN, IN 1909, SERGE DIAGHILEFF FIRST BLAZED, METEOR-like, a dazzling trail across the artistic sky of civilized Europe with his truly astounding Ballets Russes, he caused so great a sensation that all who were privileged to experi-

Jean Babilée

Melvin

in " Le Jeune Homme et la Mort ".

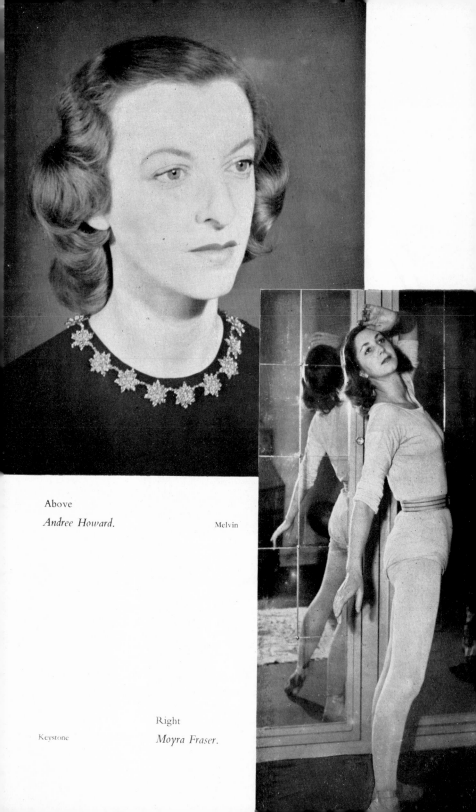

Above

Andree Howard.

Melvin

Right

Moyra Fraser.

Keystone

ence it literally, as well as metaphorically, gasped. What was more, even though one absorbed, admired, and readily enough grasped the idea of this new beauty of the art form it was his mission to reveal, the thrill of it never quite ceased to be breathtaking.

Yet, one might say, here was a man who merely presented other artists to these same eager audiences—and impresarios had been seen and admired before. True; but Diaghileff was no ordinary producer, and there was nothing "mere" about him —without doubt, he was the greatest impresario of our modern times, an artist himself who understood artists and the worthy presentation of artistic beauty in the grand manner.

Serge Pavlovitch Diaghileff was born at Perm (now known as Molotov), Russia, on March 19th, 1872. He came of an aristocratic family belonging to the country nobility. He was accustomed to the exercise of authority; and as a member of the old governing classes he expected to be deferred to. He had, however, a very great personal charm and was much beloved by his friends, even though often aggressive with those who thwarted him in any way.

He was well educated and lived a cultural life from his earliest days; and he quickly developed his natural passion for music and the arts in general. When eighteen years of age he went to St. Petersburg and entered the University, ostensibly to study law. His main interests, however, lay in matters of Art, and he attended concerts and theatres, being particularly attracted by opera. On coming of age, he inherited money from his mother, and this enabled him to travel and to visit the various Art centres in which he had always been interested.

On returning to St. Petersburg, Diaghileff became one of the inner circle of cultured young men who were just then forming an exclusive group interested in the development and advancement of music, painting, literature, opera, the drama and ballet. Among them were Walter Nouvel (musician), D. V. Filosofov (sociologist and art lover, a relative of the Diaghileff family), Alexandre Benois (artist), Leon Bakst (great scenic artist and designer) and others.

Curiously enough, on first becoming one of this group, Diaghileff was not especially attracted by ballet, being at that time mainly interested in music. He even hoped to become a

E

composer, but was discouraged in these efforts by the great Rimsky-Korsakov—then at the height of his operatic glory. His vast knowledge and love of music, however, were to serve him well later on.

He likewise had a real and extensive knowledge of painting and, indeed, of all the plastic arts, and was a sincere critic of these. He soon began to turn his attention to the organization of Art Exhibitions, and met with great success in this direction. In 1899, with the help of interested friends, he founded the famous art review known as *Mir Iskusstva* (*The World of Art*), to which Bakst, Somov, Aubrey Beardsley, Serov, Korovin, Filosofov, Benois, and other members of his advanced group contributed. Through his editorship of this journal, however, he made many enemies, owing to his uncompromising attitude to all whose views were opposed to his own. This art journal remained in existence for about five years, when it ceased publication. But about this time, he became attached as an official to the Imperial Theatres, his friend and supporter there being the new Director, Prince Wolkinsky.

Here, Diaghileff's main interest began to be directed towards opera and ballet. The Academic Russian Ballet had already been at the height of its classical glory for many years under Marius Petipa, Ivanov and Cecchetti; and the Imperial Ballet Schools were just then producing such famous dancers—later to become world-renowned, though then known only to Russia herself—as Gerdt, Pavlova, Karsavina, Trefilova, Preobrajenska, Nikitina, Egorova, Nijinsky, Lopokova, etc. This wonderful galaxy of dancing talent, with its perfection of classical academic training, was there to be used. But to Diaghileff and his group, the ballet art had become static and artificial, with too much emphasis being laid on the principal dancers and with too little regard for the dramatic work as a whole. Their new revolutionary ideas were to alter all this . . . while retaining the great classical training, the ballet was to become unified as one complete whole, with its constituent parts—dance, music, *décor*, costumes, dramatic action and even lighting—to be treated as being of equal importance.

Already the ballet world of St. Petersburg had been shaken to the core by the appearance of Isadora Duncan and her naturalistic Greek type of dancing; and Jacques Dalcroze had likewise flashed on to the scene with his amazing Eurhythmics; and Diaghileff's dream of a ballet renaissance now began to take shape. In the young dancer, Michael Fokine, he found the ideal choreographer of the new ballet he visualized; and the work was begun. Fokine had already produced several ballets at the Maryinsky Theatre; and his ideals were similar to those of his new friend.

But Diaghileff, with his revolutionary ideas, had made many enemies among members of the old régime; and, all too soon, he had to abandon the idea of leading a ballet renaissance in his own country—even though several of the greatest dancers of the Imperial Ballet were interested in his plans and willing enough to collaborate with him. Eventually the antagonism became too strong, and Diaghileff was dismissed. But his ideas and his ambitions remained; and he determined now to introduce the great Russian Ballet to the European capitals for the first time, reinforced with his own ideas and those of his enthusiastic friends, Benois, Bakst, Fokine, Stravinsky and others.

Already in 1908, Diaghileff had introduced Russian Opera into Paris (Moussorgsky's *Boris Godounov*, with the magnificent singer, Chaliapin, in the title-role), where it had been received with tremendous enthusiasm by the elegant and fastidious musical circles there; and in 1909, he brought the first Russian Ballet Company to the Théâtre du Chatélet. For this great initial venture, he produced five ballets, all with choreography by Fokine, *décor* and costumes by Benois, Bakst, Korovin and Roerich, and music by Chopin, Arensky, Taneyev, Moussorgsky, Glazounov, Glinka, Rimsky-Korsakov, Tchaikovsky, Tcherepnine and Borodin. The ballets were *Les Sylphides*, *Cléopâtre*, *Le Festin*, *Le Pavillon d'Armide*, *Prince Igor Polovtsian Dances*. Among the dancers were Pavlova, Nijinsky, Karsavina, Ida Rubinstein, Mordkin, Karalli, Bolm. Two operas were likewise given, *Ivan the Terrible* (with Chaliapin) and *Russlan and Ludmila*.

An immediate furore was created. The sensation and delight caused by this Russian invasion of artistic Paris was so tremendous that Diaghileff was instantly launched as the greatest producer and impresario of the modern theatrical world. His original ideas were now received with enthusiasm all over Europe; and the technical and dramatic perfection of his dancers, the musical precision of his orchestra, the originality of his choreographer, Fokine, and the vivid scenic designs and exotic costume colourings devised by his fine artists were a revelation.

In 1910, he returned to Paris, this time to the Opéra House, with new Fokine ballets, *L'Oiseau de Feu* and *Le Carnaval* and *Giselle* (Coralli), with Lydia Lopokova in the Company. 1911 saw Diaghileff and his Company at Covent Garden, London, for the first time, where, perhaps, the sensation created was almost greater still; and Paris, Monte Carlo, Belgium, Italy and Berlin were likewise visited. New ballets with choreography by Fokine were given during 1911, 1912 and 1914: *Petrouchka, Le Spectre de la Rose, Le Dieu Bleu, Narcisse, Daphnis et Chloe, Thamar, Le Coq d'Or, Papillons, Midas, The Legend of Joseph.*

During the 1914-18 war, the Diaghileff Company travelled in Italy, Switzerland, Spain, Portugal, and made a second American tour (having already made their first visit to South America in 1913). In 1918, they again visited London; and during the following years until Diaghileff's early and lamented death in 1929, they paid regular return visits to London, Paris and most of the European capitals.

The early years of Diaghileff's great enterprise, and the five or six years immediately following the conclusion of hostilities in 1918, were his most brilliant periods, when nothing but perfection would satisfy him; and he would work days and nights on end to gain such perfection. He was the born impresario, who knew what he wanted and had the determination to get it. Nothing must stand in the way of that complete work of art, the Diaghileff Russian Ballet; and nothing did. The expenses were extravagantly tremendous—but money was always forthcoming and difficulties were always surmounted. Even though the Company was at times on the verge of bankruptcy, some rich enthusiast seemed always miraculously to be there and to come to the rescue in the very nick of time. He had the almost unique gift of always being able to find the right person for the particular job in hand, of discovering new talent exactly suitable for every new project of his fertile brain; and he inspired the deepest loyalty and enthusiasm among those who came in contact with him.

But Diaghileff had a restless nature and was never satisfied for long with even the most beautiful creations he produced. He was for ever searching for something new, something different, some novelty never seen before. It was this excessive urge for novelty at almost any price—even at the cost of beauty, at times—that led him during his later years to produce work which, though certainly original, was far from lovely, and which led him to alienate some of his earlier friends and collaborators. He just could not be static.

One of the first of his collaborators to be alienated was the gifted dancer and choreographer, Michael Fokine, whose beautiful dramatic ballets had brought such initial and well-deserved fame to the Company. In most of these wonderful works—*Les Sylphides, Le Carnaval, Petrouchka, The Spectre of the Rose, The Firebird, Schéhérazade, Cléopâtre, Narcisse, Sadko, Le Dieu Bleu, Thamar, Papillons, Le Coq d'Or,* etc.—the very remarkable male dancer, Vaslav Nijinsky, had danced with such amazing technique and natural grace that he was rightly regarded as the greatest male exponent of the dance that the world had ever seen. After his first three phenomenally successful years, Diaghileff now decided to encourage the young Nijinsky to become a choreographer as well, thinking that, in his turn, the latter might bring something new into the ballet as Fokine had done in regard to the old classical ballet—and this regardless of the fact that Nijinsky was totally inexperienced in the art of choreography. The result was that Fokine left the Company (though he returned later for a time to devise *Thamar* and other ballets); and Nijinsky's first choreographical work, *L'Après-midi d'un Faune,* was duly produced. It was presented in Paris in 1912, where, at first, it created a real scandal, mainly because of Nijinsky's somewhat scanty costume and certain of his actions which displeased the audience. Nevertheless, the ballet survived this initial trouble, and was included in the repertoire for a time, though it was never a very popular ballet with the Company in Europe.

However, the *Faune* met Diaghileff's passion for novelty; and a year later, Nijinsky was also the choreographer of *Le Sacre du Printemps* (*The Rite of Spring*) and *Jeux* (*Games*). The former was startlingly grim and stark in subject, and deliberately heavy and even grotesque in treatment; and though again an undoubted novelty, it was by no means a beautiful one. *Jeux* proved to be even less successful. This was in 1913; and when, later that year, the Company went on tour to America (without Diaghileff, who always avoided an ocean journey if possible) Nijinsky married there—this proceeding having been kept secret from Diaghileff. This totally unexpected event was a real shock to Diaghileff, who had been completely wrapped-up in Nijinsky as his own especial *protégé*; and it proved to be the parting of the ways personally between the pair. Nevertheless, Nijinsky again danced with the Company in New York in 1916, on his return from internment in Austria (Diaghileff had worked with his other friends in negotiations for his release); and his last choreographic work *Tyl Eulenspiegel*, was produced that same year for the Company at the Metropolitan Theatre there. But the famous dancer soon afterwards fell a victim to the sad clouding of his brain that caused his brilliant dancing career to end in the tragedy of hallucinations and a lost memory.

The sparkling young dancer and choreographer, Leonide Massine, had already joined the Company, and he now became Diaghileff's new choreographer. He devised many excellent ballets, among the most famous of which were *La Boutique Fantasque, Le Tricorne, Les Femmes de Bonne Humeur, Pulcinella, Contes Russes, Parade, Les Matelots, Zéphyr et Flore, Chant de Rossignol, Le Pas d'Acier, Mercure, Les Jardins d'Aranjuez, Ode* (with Boris Kochno). Massine was also a leading dancer with the Company.

Later on, George Balanchine became a choreographer with Diaghileff, and provided the following ballets: *Barabau, La Pastorale, Jack-in-the-Box, The Triumph of Neptune, La Chatte, Apollon Musagète, Les Dieux Mendiants, Le Fils Prodigue, Le Bal.* Later on came ballets by Bronislava Nijinsky (the sister of Vaslav, and a leading dancer with the Company), *Le Renard, Les Fâcheux, Les Noces, Les Biches, Le Train Bleu, Romeo and Juliet* and *Les Tentations de la Bergère.* A few other smaller ballets were also given by the Company, as well as several of the famous old classics, *Giselle, Lac des Cygnes, The Sleeping Princess.*

Among the famous dancers who performed with the Company, apart from those already mentioned, were Massine, Leon Woizikovsky, Tchernicheva, Adolf Bolm, P. Vladimiroff, Serge

Lifar, Kschesinskaya, Alexandra Danilova, Stanislas Idzikovski, Catherina Geltzer, Bronislava Nijinska, Mia Slavenska, Piltz, Anton Dolin, Doubrovska, Nicolas Zverev, Sokolova, Fokina, Nemtchinova, Schollar, Kremneff, Enrico Cecchetti, V. Trefilova, L. Egorova, Olga Spessivtseva (Spessiva), Nikitina, Petrova, Wilzak, Alicia Markova. The great maestro, Enrico Cecchetti, was with the Company for many years as *maître de ballet* and principal teacher, and also danced many character parts . . . for Diaghileff, despite his revolutionary ideas in art, never ceased to regard the classic training provided by the Imperial Theatre Schools as the one and only training for his own dancers, of which Cecchetti was the greatest living exponent.

Among Diaghileff's artist-designers of *décor* and costumes were Alexandre Benois, C. Korovin, Leon Bakst, Roerich, Serov, N. Gontcharova, Soudeikine, Federovsky, Doboujinsky, Larionov, Sert, Picasso, Balla, R. Delaunay, Derain, Matisse, Survage, Laurencin, Braque, Juan Gris, Laurens, Pruna, O. Messel Masks, Utrillo, Miro and Ernst, Prince Shervachidze, Iakouloff, Gabo and Pevsner, Tchelitchev and Charbonner, Bauchant, Roualt, di Chirico.

The many famous composers who provided the music for his ballets were: Chopin, Arensky, Tchaikovsky, Tcherepnine, Glinka, Borodin, Rimsky-Korsakov, Stravinsky, Schumann, Adam, Weber, Reynaldo Hahn, Ravel, Balakirev, Debussy, Florent Schmitt, Richard Strauss, Steinberg, Albeniz, Fauré, Scarlatti, Liadov, Satie, Chabrier, Rossini, Moussorgsky, Respighi, de Falla, Auric, Prokofiev, Cimarosa, Poulenc, Montclair, Milhaud, Gounod, Dukelsky, Rieti, Lord Berners, Henri Sauget, Nabokoff, Handel (arr. Beecham), Constant Lambert.

Although the critics blame the great impresario for his seeming mania for mere novelty, it may be that his joy in presenting such had something more reasonable behind it than this. So great was his belief that ballet was yet another means of presenting every phase of life to its beholders, that he felt he could not very well refuse to present the modern world in which he found himself. Fashions, ideas, and society conditions were changing; and the new world after the Great War was considerably different from that of the luxurious social world when he first blazed his own dazzling trail across it. If some of these always exquisitely danced "living pictures" revealed characters and characteristics that at times seemed somewhat hard, sophisticated, and even bizarre, they were, at least, the results of his own observations of social aspects revealing themselves to his sensitive vision.

For twenty years Diaghileff and his famous Russian Ballet regularly visited most of the capitals of Europe; and his seasons in London, in particular, never ceased to be hailed as the greatest theatrical and artistic events of the year. Then, during the early part of 1929, after a full life of robust health, he began to be seriously ill with diabetes; and on August 19th that same year, he died in Venice—to the deep and sincere sorrow of the entire artistic world.

That Serge Diaghileff was a real artistic genius where ballet production was concerned—that he was, indeed, the presiding genius of ballet—no one has ever doubted or denied. He was never a practising dancer himself, nor a specially successful practising musician; nor had he any pretensions of being more than an ordinary amateur painter, though his knowledge and appreciation of music, painting and the plastic arts generally were both thorough and very considerable. Yet he was an undoubted connoisseur of all the Arts; and he left the mark of beauty on everything he touched.

He came to ballet as no mere commercial producer—the financial, profit-making side of his stupendous undertakings meant little to him; and he was never a rich man personally. But as an artist-impresario—knowing exactly how he desired to present his unique ideas to the artistic world, regardless of cost and determined to let nothing interfere with his plans or force him to accept a lower standard—he was supreme. In other words, he desired to present to the world the perfection he saw in his own conceptions of beauty; and by the exercise of his own unswerving will power, driving force, and the amazing charm of his dynamic personality, for twenty brilliant years he succeeded in doing this. Every ballet he produced bore the hall-mark of his own magic touch.

An autocrat? Yes; but one who, though he could not fail to make enemies in his search for perfection, could likewise not fail to make many devoted friends. Just as Pavlova was "the one and only Pavlova", so Diaghileff was "the one and only Diaghileff"—the greatest impresario the modern world has known.

Anton Dolin

THIS WORLD-FAMOUS DANCER WAS BORN PATRICK HEALY-KAY in 1904, at Slinfold, Horsham, in Sussex, of well-to-do English parents, though his mother had Irish connections. He had no dancing or ballet antecedents. His father, however, was an excellent amateur county cricketer, so that athletics were regarded as important in the family; and his mother, though not a dancer herself, loved to watch dancing and movement of all kinds.

But the little boy, Patrick, began to dance almost as soon as he could walk, being born with an extraordinary sense of music and rhythm; and he soon became an expert in movement games and exercises. He was an attractive, well-built child, and his bodily strength and muscular powers increased rapidly.

His real dancing training did not begin until he was ten years old, when, his parents having removed to Hove, he was allowed to join the Dancing Academy of Miss Clarice James, where he learned to perform perfectly every kind of dance she taught and was soon even able to dance upon the tips of his toes. In later years, during his ballet training, young Patrick always liked to learn—and to dance, in private, for his own pleasure—as many ballerina parts as he could; with the result that, when eventually launched upon his ballet career, he quickly became the ideal partner he has always been, probably from the knowledge he thus gained of exact ballerina requirements.

After leaving his first dance teacher, he joined the classes of the Cone Sisters in Brighton; and then, after giving outstanding performances at School shows and displays at the Brighton Hippodrome and at the King's Theatre, Hammersmith, it was finally decided that he should take up ballet and stage work as a career and that his general education should be conducted privately, so that his professional training should not be interfered with unduly. For this main purpose, his family now moved to London; and here the youthful dancer joined the Italia Conti School for the Study of Acting and Dancing. Within a short time of joining this well-known School for child actors, he played the part of "Peter, the Black Cat" in the Seymour Hicks and Ellaline Terriss famous production of *Bluebell in Fairyland*; and a year later, he played the part of "John" in *Peter Pan*. Later on, he acted in the musical comedy, *Betty*. He won an elocution prize, presented to him by Ellen Terry; and he acted in several more plays, including *The Man Who Knew the Future* and Sardou's *Fedora* (with Marie Lohr in the latter).

But dancing was always his main objective and in 1917, at the age of thirteen, determined to be trained on the Russian principles, he joined the famous Ballet School of the Princess Seraphine Astafieva, who produced so many famous dancers for the Diaghileff Company and for modern ballet generally. After quite a short time with Astafieva, he was chosen to dance in a special quartet required for one of the ballets in the great impresario's Russian Company, where he was billed as Patrikieff. He was chosen and taught this dance by Nicolai Sergueeff, once *régisseur* of the Maryinsky Theatre; and the Company performed at the Alhambra.

In addition to being a star pupil of Astafieva, Dolin now likewise studied under Nicholas Legat, Bronislava Nijinska, and the great Enrico Cecchetti.

It was while he was a student with Astafieva that he appeared as Pat Kay in 1921 in the third Sunshine Charity Matinée organized by *The Dancing Times*, where he danced with great success in the small ballet *La Chasse*. Two years later, Astafieva again presented him as her star student, this time under his new dancing name of "Anton Dolin"—by which name he has been known ever since. At the Royal Albert Hall his performance was such a brilliant one that the critics immediately began to take serious notice of the elegant young male dancer thus so successfully launched. One of the solo dances he gave on this occasion was his own arrangement of *The Hymn to the Sun* from Rimsky-Korsakov's fantastic opera *Le Coq d'Or*—a beautiful solo for which Anton Dolin has remained famous ever since, and which he still dances. It is full of lovely movements and perfectly suits his magnificent figure and natural grace. Another solo he danced on this occasion was *Danse Russe*—again his own arrangement, and still often danced by him. At another of these Sunshine Matinées some years later, he danced with Adeline Genée.

It was later that same year, 1923, that Dolin, now nineteen years old, joined the Diaghileff Company; and it was owing to the strict and careful training he had received for so many years and to the excellent progress he had made, that he was presently given the leading part of Daphnis in the Fokine ballet *Daphnis and Chloe* at the Opera House, Monte Carlo, in 1923. His first part with the Company in Paris and afterwards in London was Le Beau Gosse in *Le Train Bleu*, by Nijinska.

When the Company had finished their season at Monte Carlo, Dolin travelled with them to Barcelona, Paris, Berlin, Florence and elsewhere, and danced in many ballets, one of his most celebrated performances already being the difficult and famous Blue-Bird *pas de deux* in *The Sleeping Beauty*.

When the Company returned to Monte Carlo, Dolin now danced leading roles in most of the ballets; and he appeared in these parts during the 1924 and 1925 Diaghileff Seasons in London. Amongst these ballets were *Les Matelots, Flore et Zéphyre, Barabau, Cimarosiana, Le Train Bleu, Les Fâcheux, The Faithful Shepherdess, Les Biches (House Party), La Boutique Fantasque* and others. Among his famous partners were Nemtchinova, Sokolova, Nijinska, Danilova, Doubrovska, Nikitina, Markova; and among his male colleagues at this time was Serge Lifar.

Having had a serious disagreement with Diaghileff, Dolin left the Company for several years, and appeared in many London Revues and Music Hall Shows. First, he danced in *The Punch Bowl* at His Majesty's, arranging a solo to the popular song of Leyton and Johnstone, "Alabamy Bound", also dancing *The Hymn to the Sun* and other solo numbers. He likewise appeared in *Charlot's Revue, Piccadilly Revels, Vaudeville Vanities*, etc. In 1926, he danced with Iris Rowe in the Dolin-Doone Ballet *A Flutter in the Dovecot* at the Palladium; and he likewise partnered Phyllis Bedells at the Coliseum. With the latter, he again appeared in 1927, also at the Coliseum; and again at the Coliseum that same year he danced with Nemtchinova in his own ballet, *The Nightingale and the Rose* and in extracts from *Lac des Cygnes*. It was in 1927, too, that he appeared with Ninette de Valois in *Traffic in Souls* in *The White Birds Revue*.

In 1928, he produced his own ballets, *Rhapsody in Blue* (with the popular Gershwin music) and *Revolution* at the Coliseum, with Nemtchinova as his partner.

It was about this time, too, that Dolin realized his life's dream—to dance with Tamara Karsavina. The latter's partner, Wilzak, having had to cancel his engagement, Dolin, to his delight, was invited to take his place at the Coliseum to enable the great ballerina to finish her engagement there. The ballet chosen was *Le Spectre de la Rose*, and thus another of his ambitions was at last fulfilled—to dance Nijinsky's famous role with the great Russian's own equally famous partner. The performance was a brilliant success; and though the pair then danced together but a few times, it has always remained one of his happiest memories.

It was soon after the end of *The White Birds* run that Dolin was invited to join Vera Nemtchinova in a tour of the pleasure resorts of the South of France; and after this tour had ended, the Nemtchinova-Dolin Ballet appeared for a month at the London Coliseum in Dolin's own *Nightingale and the Rose* (music by H. Fraser-Simson, *décor* and costumes by Phyllis Dolton) and *Lac des Cygnes*. This season was a tremendous success; and when it ended, the two dancers visited Paris for a special dance recital, then returned to England and toured the provinces with their ballet, returning yet again for another season in London and another tour in France. After this they gave a season at Le Théâtre des Champs-Élysées in Paris, and on their return to London, Dolin appeared alone at a Royal Command Performance at the Coliseum. After this, further tours took place during 1928; and then the partnership with Nemtchinova came to an end.

In 1929, after a four years' absence, Dolin rejoined the Diaghileff Company, dancing once more with them at Monte Carlo in Nijinska's new ballet, *Le Bal*, and Massine's *Pas d'Acier*. He also danced the Blue-Bird and in other ballets in the repertoire, including Balanchine's *Le Fils Prodigue*. After this came the last Diaghileff season in London at Covent Garden in 1929, the dancers including Spessiva, Markova, Danilova and Sokolova; and Dolin danced with Danilova in *Les Sylphides* and with Markova in *The Blue-Bird* and in *Aurora's Wedding*. He also danced in *Le Bal* and took the American Sailor in *Les Matelots*. He danced again with Karsavina in *Petrouchka*.

After the death of Diaghileff in Venice in 1929 and the consequent disbanding of the Diaghileff Company, Dolin danced with Anna Ludmilla in a short engagement at the Coliseum that same year; and after a visit to America—where he danced in International Revue—he returned to London. Here, in 1931, he joined the newly formed Vic-Wells Ballet, dancing leading roles, mostly with Markova as his partner. In 1932, he danced with Adeline Genée at a special charity matinée performance at the Coliseum, in a series of old French dances; and later that same year he was one of the company of English dancers organized by the Operatic Association to appear four times at the Royal Theatre in Copenhagen before the King and Queen of Denmark and the Prince of Wales whom they were entertaining.

It was in 1935 that the famous Dolin-Markova Ballet was formed and toured in Britain and elsewhere, many ballets being performed—among these being *Giselle*, *Lac des Cygnes*, *Les Sylphides*, *Aurora's Wedding*, *Casse Noisette* extracts, the *House Party* (*Les Biches*), Dolin's own choreographic works *The Nightingale and the Rose*, *Bolero*, etc., in addition to his famous solo, *Hymn to the Sun* and his equally famous rendering of the *Blue-Bird*. This Company lasted until 1937, when the principals parted for a time to take up other engagements; but during later years it was re-formed and proved even more successful than ever.

After 1937, Dolin danced in the Revue *All the Best*; and in 1938 he joined one of the Russian Companies and went with them to Australia. In 1939 he went to America, where he became choreographer, *maître de ballet*, and chief classical dancer to the Ballet Theatre in New York. He produced for this Company the classics *Giselle* and *Lac des Cygnes*; and he also danced the part of Bluebeard in the ballet thus entitled (Fokine's fine ballet), which he produced. He likewise danced the principal role in *Fair at Sorochinsk*, which he also produced.

Since the re-forming of the Markova-Dolin Company in 1945,

Dolin also danced with Ballet Theatre and other companies from time to time. In 1948, Dolin and Markova appeared as guest artists with the Sadler's Wells Ballet at Covent Garden with the utmost success, their long absence of nine years from this country serving only to reveal an additional finish to the perfect technique of both these great artists. In *Giselle* they were particularly satisfying, Dolin functioning once again as the perfect cavalier-partner—very handsome, with the added dignity and perfection of style that only long and continued experience can give to a dancer highly gifted.

Anton Dolin has contributed, and is continuing to contribute, very considerably to the now high prestige enjoyed by British Ballet; and his satisfying and always completely finished performances are a joy to all ballet lovers. He has a specially deep feeling for the classical ballet; and his own favourite roles are still those of Albrecht in *Giselle*, and Bluebeard in Fokine's choreographical work of that name—the latter, though modern compared with the former, still being conceived on the old classical lines in which that famous ballet-maker was trained.

Dolin is intensely keen about his work, and is always on the look-out for new ballet talent, having been instrumental in the discovery of Frederic Franklin, Vera Zorina, Paul Haakon, Belita and others. His main outside interests are travelling and literary work. He has an easy style in writing, and his well-known books *Divertissement* and *Ballet-go-Round* provide much interesting information for ballet lovers. Arnold Haskell, by the way, has written a book about this dancer, entitled *Anton Dolin*.

Dolin's happy partnership with Alicia Markova is regarded as being probably one of the longest on record; and during their more recent tours they have demonstrated the fact that their consecutive and several intermittent periods together have resulted in the most perfect harmony and timing—in addition to the grace and ease of their combined lovely movements—that only an adequately long experience can give. Among their more recently produced ballets—given in contrast to their classical items—may be mentioned the American type *Blue Mountain Ballads*, which shows the clever weaving together of primitive and classical courtly sources in which Dolin himself, with his fine elocutionary and dramatic powers, recites verses descriptive of the action—these words being by Tennessee Williams and the music by Paul Bowles.

During the Festival of Britain year in 1951, Dolin was responsible for the grand Festival Ballet which appeared at the Stoll Theatre, London, and for which—in addition to himself and Markova, with their fine company—he engaged many famous guest artists. The Festival Ballet also appeared in Birmingham, Manchester, Bristol and Monte Carlo before the Festival season began. In addition to giving fine presentations of *Giselle, Swan Lake, Les Sylphides,* there were also excellent revivals of *Petrouchka, The Spectre of the Rose, Prince Igor Dances, Beau Danube, Nutcracker* (complete), *Graduation Ball.* Two new ballets were also produced: *Impressions* (choreography by Lichine, set to Bizet's Symphony in C, costumes and *décor* by Hugh Stevenson); *Harlequinade* (choreography by Lichine, music by Drigo, and *décor* and costumes by Eleanor Watts). Dolin's Festival Ballet has continued since as a most successful Company.

Although Anton Dolin has attained to front rank as one of the finest and most versatile male dancers of the present day, one of his main wishes for the future is to become a producer of straight plays and to act once more in legitimate drama.

Isadora Duncan

ⓄⓄⓄ

ISADORA DUNCAN BECAME FAMOUS IN THE FIRST DECADE OF THE present century as the most successful exponent of a revival of the free-moving natural Greek dance as exemplified by the attitudes of figures to be seen in ancient Grecian friezes and designs on vases, a form of new-old dance which she gradually invented herself.

An American, born at San Francisco in 1878, she very early showed promise of becoming a dancer, though, her parents being poor, she never received any classic ballet training and she always despised the latter as restrictive and unnecessary. But she was always dancing with the natural ease of youth, and would gather her brothers and sisters and their child companions around her and make them dance—with such good effect that she even toured them about the neighbouring districts, where they provided a novel and amusing entertainment.

Then, at the age of seventeen, her attractive looks—for she was tall, graceful, with reddish hair and good features—her definite dancing ability won for her the part of a fairy in *A Midsummer Night's Dream* then being played at Daly's Theatre in New York. Soon the young Isadora, firmly believing in herself and having already formed the idea of reviving the ancient Dancing Art of Greece, persuaded her parents to take her to Europe, where she would have further opportunities for study—which they did, though the family had to travel in a cattle boat, since they were still too poor to pay passenger-vessel fares.

Though suffering many privations and disappointments, Isadora Duncan—who had great determination and tenacity of purpose—managed to overcome them all and at last bring her theories before the dancing world. She studied Greek Art, and gradually learned how to build up her own dance movements from observing and taking sketches of figures shown upon the ancient Grecian vases and sculptures to be seen at the Louvre in Paris and at museums and galleries in Florence, Berlin, Budapest and other art centres she somehow managed to visit; and finally, in Athens itself she perfected her ideas of the dancing movements she intended to use.

Next, she built up her dances and groupings to the lovely music of Chopin, Mendelssohn, Gluck and many other classical composers, and even used the compositions of the more modern operatic works of Wagner and Strauss—she could not tolerate inferior music.

Having thus adopted the old Greek style of dancing, she refused to have anything to do with the conventional classic systems of the Italian, French and Russian Schools, which she considered artificial—likewise she discarded the conventional dress that went with them. She and the young students she gradually gathered around her, wore the Greek type of dancing dress, the *chiton*, and the lightest of draperies and flowing

rgot Fonteyn and Roland Petit in " *Les Demoiselles de la Nuit* ". Melvin

old Turner and Sally Gilmour in " *Orlando's Silver Wedding* " at the Festival Gardens. Keystone

TWO UNUSUAL STUDIES

Above

An early photograph of
Karsavina.

Right

Pavlova in the Garden
of Ivy House,
Hampstead.

scarves, with no distorting or confining under-garments and no shoes or stockings. She insisted upon absolute freedom of movement for every part of the body, believing in a natural development only.

Isadora Duncan established her first School of Naturalistic Greek Dancing near Berlin; and when she and her very youthful students began to dance in public, they created a considerable sensation and rapidly became known and admired in many of the capitals of Europe—though London was not visited until many years later when she appeared at the Prince of Wales Theatre in 1921, in a series of special matinées.

It was soon realized by admirers and critics alike that, despite her entire lack of the conventional ballet training, Isadora Duncan was, nevertheless, a great dancer—a naturally inspired dancer, who had cleverly evolved a dance art form peculiarly and entirely personal to herself alone—a form of dancing that suited her own beauty, personality and temperament. For, though she taught the technique of her art to others and, later on, set up many schools in various parts of Europe and America for this purpose, she could not inspire them—and, without her own natural inspiration and personality, that particular technique lost its main interest.

Nevertheless, Duncanism, as it came to be called, has left its definite mark upon our modern dancing. When Isadora visited St. Petersburg in 1905, she created a real sensation even in that conventional home of the greatest of Ballet Schools. All the principal dancers of the Maryinsky Theatre were thrilled by her ideas, revolutionary though they were. That Michael Fokine, the famous dancer-choreographer, was influenced by her, there has never been any doubt—though certainly not to the extent that some aver. Fokine, himself, was a dance revolutionary, too, and had worked hard to free the old classic Russian Ballet, then ruled over by Marius Petipa, from its hampering dress, over-crowded *décor*, and stereotyped ballet formulae—with the brilliant result that made his own original ballets so acceptable to Diaghileff later on. The simplicity and freedom of movement in Duncan's dancing appealed to him, even though he found it somewhat monotonous and narrow in conception.

Thus, although Duncan had always disliked the conventional ballet, declaring it to be cramping, artificial, and even stilted at

F

times—and, in particular, deprecated point-work and the wearing of block-shoes and tights—her influence was, nevertheless, to be helpful to the established ballet, by introducing into it a free and simple note it had formerly lacked.

What was more, she could and did admire the brilliant dancers she now saw for the first time—Pavlova and her contemporaries; but she always declared that she pitied them because of the many rules and regulations they had to observe and the strict self-discipline they had to exercise in order to retain the high standard expected of them. Isadora, herself, never submitted to discipline of any kind, but was a law unto herself alone. Her dancing, of its kind, was beautiful and full of grace; but it was limited in its scope. Consequently, when seen several times, her performances tended to become monotonous and even tedious; and, in addition, they varied with her own day-to-day moods, for she was highly temperamental.

The naturalistic form of dancing introduced by Isadora Duncan consisted mainly of the dancer taking up first one chosen Greek frieze-like pose after another—all deliberately copied from ancient Grecian vases and sculptures—these being varied by little tripping runs forward with the head flung back and with very graceful arm movements, with or without flowing scarves. Charming and graceful though these movements were, it was the vivid personality and the natural inspiration of Isadora herself that made them so lovely when she performed them; but, even so, they still tended to become monotonous, lacking, as they did, the multiplicity and consequent variety in the steps and positions of the legitimate classical ballet. This fact was quickly realized by Fokine and the modern choreographers who followed him, who, nevertheless, were influenced to a considerable extent by her ideas regarding freedom of movement and dress and her scorn of the more outworn conventional methods.

Having established her ideas firmly in a new School of Dancing in Europe, Isadora Duncan returned on a visit to the country of her birth in 1908, where her reception was, at first, a mixed one; but in 1915, she was in America again, where she brought her European School and danced with her students at the Century Theatre in New York. However, outstanding success still eluded her in New York; and though many rich and influential people helped her from time to time, she fell into debt and had to return to Europe with her School disbanded, making her way, eventually, to London for a time.

In 1921, she was invited to go to Russia by the new Soviet Government, with whom her political sympathies lay; but though she gathered a number of Russian children around her in the confiscated nobleman's palace in Moscow allotted to her and taught them her own form of the dance art, the recently formed political régime was too poor and too full of other projects to help her definitely to establish on firm foundations the School she desired.

Her struggles and disappointments during this much less brilliant visit to Russia were many; but her indomitable spirit and enthusiasm remained. She fell in love with and married a young Russian poet, Sergei Essenine, many years younger than herself, who, however, brought her far more trouble than joy, since he was irresponsible, dissolute and extravagant. With him, in 1922, she came again to New York. This proved to be anything but an easy trip. Her tour in America might, however, have been a tremendous success had Isadora kept solely to dancing, but she could not refrain from making speeches in favour of Bolshevism, Socialism, ultra-Feminism, and freedom from control in every phase of life in most of the places she visited, even waving red scarves and lecturing her audiences for not fighting fiercely against conventions. Outraged members of her audiences, consequently, frequently walked out when she persisted in haranguing them.

On her return to New York at the end of the tour, her domestic troubles caused more scandals; yet, throughout her farewell performances there, she danced more beautifully than ever before and often received terrific ovations, despite the unrestrained character of her famous speeches. And the tour had been a financial success.

Nevertheless, on her return to Europe, she soon fell into debt again. More scandals arose in Paris and Berlin, where she and her unbalanced husband stayed for a time; and finally, on their return to Moscow, tragedy followed on excess, and Essenine committed suicide in a dramatic manner.

The last years of Isadora Duncan's short life were not only sad but continued to be tragic. Although many of her friends rallied around her and helped to keep her Schools going in

Moscow and elsewhere—later on they even raised a fund to establish a Duncan Memorial Dance School at Neuilly—she still passed the remainder of her days struggling with debts and difficulties. Gradually she sank lower and lower—that once lovely and enthusiastic woman who had established and led with success an important new Art movement, had received the high praises of other great artists, had been adored by her several lovers and had enjoyed many brief spells of real joy, as well as suffered stark tragedy. Two of her four children had been drowned accidentally with their nurse in a car which fell into the Seine, and her poet-husband had hanged himself.

Thus, in middle life, worn out by a wild and passionate disposition that could brook no restriction against the free expression of her own original, and often quite unreasonable, views, fighting ever for her convictions against a conventional social period—her turbulent life came to a sad and tragic end. She met her death in Nice, on September 14th, 1927, while driving in a car, when she was accidentally strangled by the flowing ends of her scarf becoming entangled in one of the wheels. The work of her Schools was continued for a time by her sister, Elizabeth, and certain of her students, the best known of the latter being her Russian adopted daughters, Irma and Anna.

There is no doubt that Isadora Duncan contributed very definitely to the development of modern ballet; and she had many followers and imitators, some of the latter, indeed, being her contemporaries. Among these followers may be mentioned Maud Allan, Margaret Morris, Ruby Ginner and Irene Mawer. Later on came Mary Wigman and Kurt Jooss, both of the Central European School of the Dance. Mary Wigman created a great furore in America and established her Schools there; and Kurt Jooss, while accepting Duncanism to a certain extent, developed it on much more dramatic lines. Another modernist is Martha Graham, the American dancer-choreographer. Kurt Jooss and the Jooss Ballet are dealt with under his own separate biographical sketch.

Leslie Edwards

THE SADLER'S WELLS BALLET IS PROBABLY REGARDED BY Leslie Edwards as his "home from home", for he has spent quite half his life to date as a member of that famous Company's happy family of dancers.

A Londoner, born at Teddington in 1916, this now really fine character dancer never thought of any other career than that of dancing. On leaving school in 1932, he began to study at once with Madame Marie Rambert—that wonderful creator of so many successful British dancers—subsequently appearing in small and afterwards more important roles with her students at the Ballet Club.

The following year, in December 1933, he was engaged by Ninette de Valois as an extra dancer for a ballet entitled *The Enchanted Grove*, which she was producing at Sadler's Wells Theatre and the Old Vic; and very soon after this, he became a full-time member of the Sadler's Wells Ballet. He danced in the first revivals of the great classics, *Le Lac des Cygnes*, *Coppélia*, *Casse Noisette* and *The Sleeping Beauty*. In the latter he danced Catalbutte, and, later, Carabosse; in *Lac des Cygnes*, he danced Benno; in *Giselle*, he was cast first as Wilfred, and later made an excellent Hilarion; in *Casse Noisette*, he danced l'Arabe Danse and other parts; and in *Coppélia*, he danced first the Duke, and later, Dr. Coppélius. He also danced Florestan in the revival of Fokine's *Le Carnaval*. He travelled with the Company on its first provincial tour; also on its first trip abroad to dance at the Paris Exhibition in 1937.

During this period with Sadler's Wells, he also continued to dance on Sunday nights at the Ballet Club, and thus gained much additional practice and experience. For the Ballet Club he danced the roles of the Trapezist in *Circus Wings*, the Trainer in *Le Boxing*, Bowler in *Le Cricket*, the Lover in *Jardin aux Lilas*, Personage in *Les Masques*, Mephisto in *Mephisto Valse*; and he danced also in *Pavane pour une Infante Défunte*, and in other ballets.

His main work, however, was now with the Sadler's Wells Ballet, with whom he danced in most of their new modern productions. For this Company he created the following roles: in Frederick Ashton's ballets, Arthur in *The Wedding Bouquet*, Archimago in *The Quest*, Allegro in *The Wanderer, Dante Sonata, pas de six* in *Les Patineurs,* and, more recently, the Barber in *Cinderella* and the Chauffeur in *Les Sirènes*, etc.; in Ninette de Valois' ballets he has danced first the Musician and then the Rake in *The Rake's Progress*, a Red Castle and the Red King in *Checkmate,* Mr. Taylor's Lawyer in *The Prospect Before Us,* a Merveilleuse in *Promenade*, a Nobleman in *The Gods Go a-Begging*, etc.; in Robert Helpmann ballets, he created the Beggar in *Miracle in the Gorbals,* and Archbishop in *Adam Zero.* In 1949, he created the role of the Insect King in Leonide Massine's *The Clock Symphony*. Besides these creations, he has danced various other roles in most of the Company's ballets.

Leslie Edwards spent the beginning of the Second World War touring with the Sadler's Wells Company, while rehearsing Ashton's *Dante Sonata,* the first war-time ballet to be produced by the Company. The second war-time Christmas was spent at Dartington Hall with the Company; and during this three weeks' visit, Ashton's *The Wanderer* was rehearsed for later production at the New Theatre—where most of the Company's performances were given after the Old Vic had been bombed and before they took up their permanent quarters at Covent Garden at the conclusion of the war.

Leslie Edwards went with the Company to Holland to perform there under the auspices of the British Council; and when this tour was cut short by the German invasion of that country, with his colleagues he had an adventurous escape from the invading forces. On returning to England, he toured Garrison Theatres for ENSA. Then came his two years with H.M. Forces; after which he returned to the Company, then at the New Theatre, and created the part of Archimago in Ashton's *The Quest*—one of his outstanding roles. This was followed by two further tours abroad with ENSA, to Belgium, France and Germany. In 1946, he moved with the Company to the Royal Opera House, Covent Garden; and in their first performance there on February 23rd, in the presence of Their Majesties the King and Queen, he danced the part of Catalbutte in *The Sleeping Beauty*. Later, he toured Austria, Czechoslovakia, Poland, Sweden, Norway, Holland and Italy. In the late autumn of 1949, he was with the

Company on its historic first visit to U.S.A. and Canada and shared in the truly marvellous welcome and appreciation there accorded to these fine British dancers.

Leslie Edwards is an excellent all-round dancer and has received wide praise for his portrayal of many difficult character roles; in particular, his clever miming of the Beggar in *Miracle in the Gorbals* is a sympathetic and perfect performance—the exact opposite of his equally effective study of the self-important posturings and pomposity of Catalbutte, the Master of Ceremonies in *The Sleeping Beauty*. His creation of the evil magician Archimago in *The Quest* was a remarkably fine piece of work; and he made of the Insect King in *The Clock Symphony* a delightful study. His characterization of the Hoffmann recreated figure of Dr. Coppélius in *Coppélia* is a pleasant relief from the often too comic interpretation given to this role.

On March 9th, 1950, Leslie Edwards took part in the Grand Gala Performance at Covent Garden in honour of the State Visit of the French President and Madame Auriol, at which Their Majesties the King and Queen were present.

In the latter part of 1950, he had an excellent part in the fine revival at Covent Garden of the de Valois ballet, *Checkmate*—that of the ill-fated Red King. In that same programme he took part in the equally successful revival of Ashton's delightful *Façade*. In Ashton's *Cinderella*, he performed the part of the Hairdresser with much humour; he also had two good parts in the same choreographer's version of *The Fairy Queen*, and danced remarkably well in the revival of the latter's *Apparitions*; and in the amusing role of The American in the Company's revival of *La Boutique Fantasque* he was excellent. He also danced in Ninette de Valois' clever ballet, *Don Quixote*, produced at Covent Garden on February 20th, 1950, and took part in Ashton's new presentation of *Daphnis and Chloe* in the spring of 1951. He was the King in Massine's specially created ballet for the Company, *Donald of the Burthens*, produced December 1951. In 1952, he danced the title-role in the revival of de Valois' *Don Quixote*—a character part that suited him well and which he presented with much sympathy and understanding. That year, too, he was excellent as Bilby in Andrée Howard's *A Mirror for Witches*.

André Églevsky

⊙⊙

ANDRÉ ÉGLEVSKY IS ONE OF THE LEADING MALE DANCERS OF TO-day. He is built on generous classical lines, with a magnificent figure, possessing great muscular strength yet graceful in every movement; and his amazing technique surprises all beholders. He is especially remarkable for his slow-turning, but always perfectly timed steady pirouettes—likewise for the incredible speed at which, on occasion, he can likewise spin round in as many as a dozen of the latter at a throw. Technically, he is a superb classical *danseur noble* and a perfect partner to the ballerina; and he is an excellent character dancer. He has danced practically every male role, not only in the classical repertoire, but also in many of the best-known works of modern choreographers—Fokine, Massine, Balanchine, Tudor, Lichine, Nijinska, etc. Though some critics find him somewhat lacking in facial mobility and in his interpretation of a role requiring a delicate subtlety of treatment, others consider that he reveals a perfectly sympathetic understanding of, say, such a strangely complicated character as that of Albrecht in *Giselle*. He certainly takes an enormous personal pleasure in his own actual virile dancing movements; and there is no doubt that, from the physical point of view, he is a very great ballet artist.

André Églevsky is a Russian, born in Moscow on December 17th, 1917; and, owing to the privations of that revolutionary period, he began life as a delicate child, giving no signs of the future Greek god-like physique he displays to-day. When he was four years old, his mother managed to take him away from Russia; and after living for a time in Bulgaria and Turkey, she finally settled at Nice in the South of France, where her child soon grew strong and well.

For his health's sake at first, at the age of eight years, the young boy was sent to the ballet classes of Madame Nevelskaya; but he rapidly developed such an unusual aptitude for dancing and became so proficient that, about three years later, he was taken to see Michael Fokine, Diaghileff's famous choreographer and *maître de ballet*. The latter was greatly impressed by the boy's obvious talent and future potentialities; and as he was at

72

that time on the point of carrying out contracts in U.S.A., he wished to take young André with him. However, his offer was not accepted, owing to the boy's extreme youth; but Madame Églevsky now settled in Paris for the time being, where her son's training was continued. His first teacher there was Alexander Volonine; and later he also studied with Kschesinskaya and with Egorova.

When the young Églevsky was still but fourteen years of age, he was seen by Leonide Massine, who immediately invited him to join the de Basil Ballet Russe, of which the latter was then artistic director and *maître de ballet*. Here he remained in the *corps de ballet* for two years, and then began to dance solo parts. In 1933, he created the role of Count Anselmo in Massine's *Scuola di Ballo*, and danced increasingly important parts in other Massine ballets—*Jeux d'Enfants*, *Les Présages* and *Choreartium*.

In 1935, he travelled with the Ballets Epstein, playing leading roles therein; after which he returned to Paris to continue his studies with Kschesinskaya. Soon, however, he was engaged to dance with the Woizikovsky Ballet in London, where he appeared in leading roles in *Carnaval*, *Petrouchka* and the *Blue-Bird pas de deux* . . . his performance in the latter has always been a joy to behold. On this occasion, his exuberant performance as the Blackamoor in *Petrouchka* brought him forward literally by leaps and bounds; and in 1936, at the age of nineteen, Fokine invited him to join the René Blum Ballet, where he danced leading roles in *Prince Igor*, *Les Sylphides*, *Le Spectre de la Rose*, *Petrouchka*, *Casse Noisette* and *L'Épreuve d'Amour*. In the latter, the part of the young Chinese Lover was devised especially by Fokine for Églevsky, who thus created the role at this delightful ballet's premier performance, Monte Carlo, April 4th, 1936—which proved an equal success during the following London season at the Alhambra. On the latter occasion, Églevsky also created the role of the Chief Jester in Fokine's other new ballet, *Don Juan*. The latter was devised mainly to display the young dancer's already famous *ballon* and astounding pirouettes.

While in London, Églevsky took the opportunity of studying under Nicholas Legat, at Hammersmith; and in 1937, he went to the U.S.A. to study further under Fokine's guidance, and to travel in the latter's productions. Later on, in 1939, he joined Massine in the Ballet Russe de Monte Carlo at the Metropolitan in New York, where he danced with Markova in *Swan Lake*, and also played leading roles in *Prince Igor, Spectre of the Rose*, and in Massine's *Seventh Symphony, Rouge et Noir, Capriccio Espagnol* and *Bacchanale*. In 1940, he danced in Balanchine's version of *Le Baiser de la Fée* and *Poker Game*, in *Casse Noisette* and in *The New Yorker*. After a summer visit to Hollywood to make a film—where Églevsky appeared in *Capriccio Espagnol*—the Company returned to the Metropolitan in the autumn of 1941; and in this season, Églevsky danced in *The Magic Swan* (from *Swan Lake*), and Massine's *Labyrinth and Vienna 1814*. The famous ballerinas with whom he danced while with this Company were Markova, Danilova, Toumanova and Slavenska.

Late in 1942, Églevsky joined Ballet Theatre and played leading parts in *Helen of Troy* (Fokine's last ballet), Fokine's *Bluebeard, Petrouchka* and *Les Sylphides*; Balanchine's *Apollo*; Lichine's *Graduation Ball* and *Fair at Sorochinsk*; Massine's *Mademoiselle Angot* and *Aleko*; also in *Giselle* and *Casse Noisette (pas de deux* with Rosella Hightower). Among the ballerinas he danced with at this time were Rosella Hightower, Zorina, Nora Kaye, Lucia Chase and Riabouchinska.

When the Ballet International (under the direction of the Marquis de Cuevas) visited New York in the latter part of 1944, Églevsky's first choreographic work was performed under its auspices. This was entitled *Sentimental Colloquy,* based upon Verlaine's beautiful poem *Colloque Sentimentale*, with music by Paul Bowles, and *décor* by Salvador Dali. Unfortunately, the ultra-surrealist *décor* and extraordinary stage effects of Dali—bicycles and a giant tortoise surmounted by a dressmaker's dummy crossed the stage at one point for no apparent reason—proved too fantastically confusing, and the music hardly helped to improve matters. Églevsky's choreography did its best to struggle against such abnormalities; and his own splendid dancing, in which he was bravely partnered by Rosella Hightower, managed to work wonders under great difficulties. Nevertheless, the ballet could hardly be called a success. Another new ballet, however, produced under the same auspices, *Brahms Variation*, choreography by Nijinska, music to Brahms variations on themes by Handel and Paganini, and *décor* by Marcel

Vertès provided Églevsky with a fine opportunity for a brilliant display of his top-speed virtuosity.

In 1945, after returning to Ballet Theatre for a season, Églevsky joined Massine's new Ballet Russe Highlights at the Lewisohn Stadium, where he danced in a number of new ballets by Massine with Baronova and Anna Istomina. Then, after another successful season in the autumn of that year at the Metropolitan with Ballet Theatre, he came with that fine American Company to London in 1946. Here he danced classical and leading modern roles to delighted audiences, who had not seen him since 1936 as a newly launched dancer and who now gladly welcomed him back with sincere appreciation as a very considerable *danseur noble* with an astonishing technique.

In 1947, Églevsky was again dancing with the Original Ballets Russes in New York; but in the summer of that year, he joined the Marquis de Cuevas' Grand Ballet de Monte Carlo (the reformed Ballet International) with headquarters at the Principality of Monaco, with which Company he continued to dance as principal male star performer.

This Company visited London in 1948 and 1949; and in all the ballets in which he has appeared, André Églevsky has been seen to greater advantage than ever. His technique is so sure that he appears to perform the most astonishing feats of virtuosity with the utmost ease and in an almost nonchalant manner, yet always landing lightly and with perfect timing.

Among the more recent new ballets in which this fine artist has danced the leading roles may be mentioned Massine's *Mad Tristan*, Nijinska's *In Memoriam*, David Lichine's *The Enchanted Mill*, William Dollar's *The Five Boons*,[1] Balanchine's *Symphony in C* and Serge Lifar's *Noir et Blanc*. In the early months of 1951, Églevsky danced as guest artist with the New York City Ballet in New York, returning to Europe in the spring. He has also appeared very successfully in television programmes in excerpts from *Swan Lake, Casse Noisette*, etc.

During their 1952-53 seasons, Églevsky was again with the New York City Ballet, dancing classical roles in the repertoire and also creating principal roles in their new ballets—*A La Françaix, Caracole, Harlequinade, Scotch Symphony*, and others.

[1] This ballet was billed at Covent Garden as *The Five Gifts*, and it was given as *The Five Boons of Life* by American Concert Ballet in 1943.

Violetta Elvin (Violetta Prokhorova)

A CHARMINGLY PRETTY YOUNG BALLERINA ARRIVED IN LONDON almost direct from the Soviet Bolshoi Theatre early in 1946, just in time to join the Sadler's Wells Ballet as it took up residence at the Royal Opera House, Covent Garden, as its permanent home. She took part during February in the magnificent new production of *The Sleeping Beauty*, several times dancing brilliantly in the Blue-Bird *pas de deux* with Alexis Rassine, and also with Harold Turner.

This fortunate young dancer was billed as Violetta Prokhorova. Just before leaving Russia, however, she had been married to Harold Elvin, a British architect, and on coming to England with him, she decided later to continue her dancing career under his name—by which she has been known ever since.

Violetta Elvin (Prokhorova), was born in Moscow during the Revolution, and received her education and dancing training under Soviet rule. At the age of eight and a half years, she applied, with about five hundred other candidates, for admission to the Bolshoi State Ballet School for training, and was among the fifty selected. She lived as a student at the Ballet School until her seventeenth year, when she duly graduated as a solo dancer. By this time she was one of the three girls and five boys left out of the fifty originally selected.

Just as she finished her training, the evacuation of Moscow took place; and she was forthwith evacuated to Tashkent in Asia, where she very quickly became the leading ballerina of the theatre there. Here she danced the exacting role of Odette-Odile in *Lac des Cygnes* at the age of eighteen. Here also she danced Maria in *The Fountain of Bakhchisaray* and, still during the evacuation period, she danced with the Bolshoi Theatre in *Crimson Sails* and *Don Quixote*. On returning to Moscow she danced in *The Sleeping Beauty*, *Lac des Cygnes* and *Don Quixote*; and at the Slavensky Theatre she danced in *Lola* and in *Straussiana*.

Since joining the Sadler's Wells Ballet, Violetta Elvin has danced many leading roles, as well as minor parts requiring the

76

classical approach. Among these have been the following: the Black Queen in *Checkmate*, the Young Girl in *The Rake's Progress*, Dawn in *Coppélia*, Columbine in *Le Carnaval*, Pas de Deux in *Les Patineurs*, La Bolero in *Les Sirènes*, Cossack Girl in *La Boutique Fantasque*, the Miller's Wife in *Le Tricorne*, La Morte Amoureuse in *Don Juan*, Aurora and the Enchanted Princess in *The Sleeping Beauty*, Odette-Odile in *Le Lac des Cygnes* and the title-role in *Cinderella*, etc. She gave a remarkably sympathetic and also witty rendering of one of the lovers in Roland Petit's *Ballabile*.

In the late autumn of 1949, she went with the Sadler's Wells Ballet to U.S.A. and Canada on their historic first visit out West; and here her charm and the excellence of her work received high praise—in particular for her dazzling performance in the Blue-Bird *pas de deux* in *Sleeping Beauty*, in which her really fairy-like *pointe* work and the graceful use of her lovely arms were greatly admired. This, however, may be said of all the roles she danced.

Violetta Elvin has certainly proved herself a very useful and attractive ballerina to the Company. She is versatile, and is particularly good in lively roles. As the flirtatious La Bolero in Frederick Ashton's amusing Edwardian ballet, *Les Sirènes*, she is excellent; and her performance of the Spanish dancing in this was brilliant indeed, with first Leslie Edwards and later Robert Helpmann as her partners. As the Miller's vivacious Wife in *Le Tricorne*, again her Spanish dancing—with Leonide Massine himself as her partner—was quite remarkable, while her vivacious gaiety was most infectious. In the more dramatic role of La Morte Amoureuse in Ashton's *Don Juan*, produced in 1948, she showed her versatility by giving a really outstanding rendering of the glamorous, but sinister, lady-love who brings death to the much-too-amorous hero. Later that same year she gave a delightfully warm and sympathetic performance of the title-role in Ashton's *Cinderella*, in which the finely devised dances for the heroine reveal constantly the excellence of her splendid Russian Ballet School training. This delightful young dancer is always interesting to watch. She has frequently appeared in television, first taking part in the series *Ballet for Beginners* given early in 1950 at Alexandra Palace, when she danced Odette in Act II of *Le Lac des Cygnes*, with John Hart

77

and David Poole as her partners, and gave fine performances.

On March 9th, 1950, Violetta Elvin took part in the Grand Gala Performance at Covent Garden in honour of the State Visit of the French President and Madame Auriol, at which Their Majesties the King and Queen were present.

In the magnificent ballet which George Balanchine revived for the Covent Garden Company, produced in April 1950, entitled *Ballet Imperial,* Elvin was one of the principal ballerinas taking part. Throughout the Covent Garden Company's 1951 Festival of Britain Season, Elvin shared all principal roles with the other leading ballerinas; and she also appeared in Frederick Ashton's new version of *Daphnis and Chloe* produced during the season. She was lovely in Ashton's *Sylvia* in 1952, and truly glamorous as La Morte Amoureuse in his revived *Don Juan.* Early in 1953, she danced as guest artist in classical roles at La Scala, Milan, and later created La Favorita in Howard's *Veneziana*; and in Ashton's grand Coronation ballet *Homage to the Queen,* she was brilliant as Queen of the Waters.

Michael Fokine

M ICHAEL FOKINE IS JUSTLY REGARDED AS THE FATHER OF OUR modern ballet. This great choreographer was born in St. Petersburg on April 26th, 1880. At the age of nine he entered the famous Imperial School of Dancing and Drama at St. Petersburg where he studied with Volkov, Shirayev, Gerdt and N. Legat; and after his years of training were completed, he became one of the leading male dancers of the Maryinsky Theatre, where he danced principal roles and gained a great variety of experience, studying in his spare time with Johannsen. Eventually he became *maître de ballet.*

Besides being an excellent dancer, however, the young Fokine was a thinker and a critic; and greatly though he loved the old classical ballets in which he danced, he very soon began to realize that the beautiful art of ballet had become more or less static, and that it needed new life and new ideas infused into it if it were to maintain the great heights it had attained. He saw that the action of a ballet was constantly held up in order to show off the ballerina in some intricate solo dance; that the male dancer was quickly becoming merely an obliging partner, with little of importance to do; that the music and scenery of a ballet were often second-rate and even alien to the subject; and that little thought was given to the welding of the various components of the ballet into a harmonious work of art.

Greatly though he admired the perfect execution of the ballerinas and their partners, he felt that very drastic reformations were needed for the majority of the works still being presented at the Maryinsky Theatre and that future ballets should now be produced in a different form. He himself had many original and revolutionary ideas for such reformations; and, young though he was, he determined to set these down on paper and to invite the Directors and other Authorities of the Imperial Ballet Schools to consider them.

This he did; but no notice was taken of his daring suggestions. Nevertheless, undaunted by his rebuff, the young dancer began to turn his thoughts to choreographical works of his own and to create ballets into which he could gradually incorporate his new ideas. These he was allowed to produce at students' shows, though still looked upon by the ultra-conservative authorities as being somewhat too revolutionary to be encouraged unduly.

His first ballet, *Acis and Galatea*, was produced on April 23rd, 1905, at the usual students' Graduation Display; and, strange to say, the then very youthful Vaslav Nijinsky took part in it— neither creator nor boy dancer dreaming at that time that they were both destined to become famous personalities in the ballet world. In this ballet the young choreographer used ancient Greek movements—an innovation regarded with disfavour by the more static academic-minded teachers and ballet supporters present.

But Fokine still persisted with his new ideas; and later that same year he devised for Anna Pavlova—then *première danseuse* at the Maryinsky—that dramatically expressive solo dance, *The Dying Swan*, to the lovely music of Saint-Saens, which she danced for the first time at a charity performance in St. Petersburg and which afterwards became for ever associated with her name. This little masterpiece was composed in a few hours only; and yet it embodied his own original ideas, while containing also the perfect technique and classical steps of the old school.

Two years later, Fokine created another ballet on a Greek subject, *Eunice*, in which the female dancers wore the Greek dance dresses known as *chitons*, instead of the customary academic *tutu*, and performed processional dances in the ancient Greek classical manner. This ballet (which had as its subject an episode from Sienkiewicz's *Quo Vadis*, afterwards made into a famous silent film) was given at another charity performance on February 23rd, 1907; and it aroused considerable interest.

By this time, Fokine was already well known to the group of intellectuals—University students, artists and musicians—among whom Serge Diaghileff, Alexandre Benois, Walter Nouvel, D. F. Filosofov, Tcherepnine, Serov, etc., were the leading spirits; and they were watching his work with considerable interest, since his original ideas on art coincided with their own.

In 1907, Benois arranged with Fokine to prepare the choreography for a score by Tcherepnine which he, Fokine, had already given at a students' display under the title of *The Animated Gobelins*. The latter was now arranged into a one-act ballet with three scenes; and, with the fine music of Tcherepnine and the magnificent scenic decorations and dazzling costumes designed by Benois—who wrote the "book", based on Gautier's short story *Omphale*—this ballet was produced at the Maryinsky Theatre on November 25th, 1907, under the new title of *Le Pavillon d'Armide*, with Pavlova as principal *danseuse*. Despite many difficulties encountered during the rehearsals and obvious discouragement from the Directorate, the new ballet was very successful.

Fokine and his friends were keenly interested in the naturalistic balletic form introduced to the civilized world by Isadora Duncan, danced in Greek draperies and with bare feet. Fokine was undoubtedly impressed by the dancing of this newcomer; and it has even been suggested that this meeting of the classical and the classic-academic schools may have resulted in a combination of the best points of both, with the resultant emergence of the modern Russian School as exemplified by Fokine. Be that as it may, however, the fact remains that Fokine had already formulated his own major reforms in the Russian ballet, had even introduced Greek movements and Greek draperies, and was eager to include the work of great composers and painters on equal terms with his own creations long before Isadora Duncan appeared upon the scene.

Notwithstanding the undoubted success of *Pavillon d'Armide*, the brilliant choreographer-dancer was still regarded by the powers behind the scenes with distrust because of his original views and disregard for the old cut-and-dried and, in many cases, out-worn formulae for ballets; and Fokine felt that it might be many years yet before he could develop in his own country the new plans he had devised.

Consequently, when in 1909 Diaghileff recognized the young ballet master's unique gifts, seeing in him the very man to develop and carry out his own views on ballet, he invited him to become choreographer of the Company of Russian operatic singers and ballet dancers he was about to take to Paris. Fokine gladly accepted, realizing that in this adventurous step lay a chance for the artistic recognition and encouragement he was seeking; and he was engaged as one of the principal dancers in the Company.

For the Diaghileff Company from 1909 to 1914, Fokine was the sole choreographer of all ballets other than the classical works which were also included from time to time; and he was now at liberty to incorporate into his creations his own original reforms and thus to sweep away the accumulated cobwebs of the past century. His ballets could now express themselves freely in accordance with any chosen subject, and their dance movements, music, stories, decorations, costumes and lighting, were always presented as one complete, harmonious whole— each ingredient being the complement of the others, with no undue stress being laid on showing off the virtuosity of the leading dancers beyond the necessary revelation of their importance in regard to the dramatic subject in hand.

These first five years, with Fokine as choreographer, are universally acknowledged to be quite the most brilliant periods of the Diaghileff Ballet. The following are the perfectly constructed and famous ballets Fokine created for the Company:

C

1. *Le Pavillon d'Armide*. Music by Tcherepnine; book by Benois—based on Gautier's *Omphale*; costumes and *décor* by Benois; produced Chatélet, Paris, May 18th, 1909.

2. *Polovtsian Dances from Prince Igor*. Music by Borodin; designs by Roerich; produced Chatélet, Paris, May 18th, 1909.

3. *Le Festin*. Music by Tchaikovsky; designs by Benois, Korovin, etc.; produced Chatélet, Paris, May 18th, 1909.

4. *Les Sylphides* (First entitled *Chopiniana*). Music by Chopin; book by Fokine; designs by Benois; produced Chatélet, Paris, June 2nd, 1909.

5. *Cléopâtre*. Music by Arensky; book by Bakst and Fokine; designs by Bakst; produced Chatélet, Paris, June 2nd, 1909.

6. *Schéhérazade*. Music by Rimsky-Korsakov; book by Benois; designs by Bakst; produced Opéra, Paris, June 4th, 1910.

7. *Le Carnaval*. Music by Schumann; designs by Bakst; produced Opéra, Paris. June 4th, 1910.

8. *L'Oiseau de Feu*. Music by Stravinsky; book by Fokine; designs by Golovin and Bakst, later by Gontcharova; produced Opéra, Paris, June 25th, 1910.

9. *Le Spectre de la Rose*. Music by Weber; book by J. L. Vaudoyer—from poem by Gautier; designs by Bakst; produced Monte Carlo, April 1911.

10. *Narcisse*. Music by Tcherepnine; designs by Bakst; produced Monte Carlo, April 1911.

11. *Sadko*. Music by Rimsky-Korsakov; designs by Anisfeld; produced Constanza, Rome, May 1911.

12. *Petrouchka*. Music by Stravinsky; book by Benois and Stravinsky; designs by Benois; produced Chatélet, Paris, June 13th, 1911.

13. *Le Dieu Bleu*. Music by R. Hahn; designs by Bakst; produced Chatélet, Paris, May 13th, 1912.

14. *Thamar*. Music by Balakirev; book by Bakst; designs by Bakst; produced Chatélet, Paris, May 20th, 1912.

15. *Daphnis et Chloe*. Music by Ravel; book by Fokine; designs by Bakst; produced Chatélet, Paris, June 8th, 1912.

16. *Papillons*. Music by Schumann; designs by Dobujinsky and Bakst; produced Opéra, Paris, May 14th, 1913.

17. *La Légende de Joseph*. Music by Richard Strauss; designs by Sert and Bakst; produced Opéra, Paris, May 15th, 1914.

18. *Le Coq d'Or.* Music by Rimsky-Korsakov; book by Bielsky, revised by Benois; designs by Gontcharova; produced Opéra, Paris, May 21st, 1914.
19. *Midas (Les Métamorphoses).* Music by Steinberg; designs by Dobujinsky; produced Opéra, Paris, June 2nd, 1914.

Pavlova appeared in the first opening season only, and her immediate place in the Diaghileff Company was taken by Tamara Karsavina—always regarded as the Star Ballerina of the Fokine Romantic Period—and later by a whole succession of other exquisite, Russian-trained ballerinas.

It was as early as 1912 that differences began to arise between Fokine and Diaghileff. The latter, ever seeking for novelty and fearing to become in any way static, was then possessed by the desire to present Vaslav Nijinsky—to whom he was greatly attached—as a choreographer as well as the most famous dancer of the day; and the vastly experienced Fokine felt that the immature ideas and principles which would thus be introduced might not accord with the principles of the new ballet now at last firmly established by himself with Diaghileff and his "group". Therefore he resigned from the Company; and though he returned for short periods in order to produce certain new ballets of his own, his relations with Diaghileff were finally severed in 1914.

During the following war years, Fokine was again in Russia at the Maryinsky Theatre, St. Petersburg, where he produced several new works, among these being *Eros, Stenka Razin, Jota Aragonesa* and *Francesca da Rimini*, in addition to revivals of many of the older ballets.

In 1934, he created for the Ida Rubinstein Company *Diane de Poitiers, Semiramis* and *La Valse.*

In 1936, for René Blum's Ballets Russes de Monte Carlo, he created that most interesting and well-constructed romantic ballet, *L'Épreuve d'Amour,* a delightful work always greatly admired. The music for this charming ballet was by Mozart, the book was by Fokine himself and André Derain, the designs also by Derain, and the first production was at Le Théâtre de Monte Carlo on April 4th, 1936. It was also given in London at the Alhambra Theatre by the Company that same year. That year, for the same Company, he created his *Don Juan* (music by Gluck, designs by M. Andreu, and presented at the

Alhambra, London, on June 25th). During the following year, at the Coliseum, London, on June 24th, he produced *Les Éléments* (music by Bach, and designs by Bouchène). In 1939, for Educational Ballets Ltd., he created and produced another interesting ballet on the subject of Paganini (with music by Rachmaninov and designs by Soudéikine), this being produced at Covent Garden on June 30th, For this Company he also produced *Cendrillon* (music by Baron d'Erlanger, *décor* by Gontcharova).

In 1919, long before the creation of these last-named ballets, Fokine, on the conclusion of the 1914-18 war, had opened his School of Dancing in New York, and his interest and influence in developing ballet in America was very considerable. In 1941, he created for Ballet Theatre a new ballet on the subject of *Bluebeard* (after the well-known opera-bouffe of Meilhac and Halèvy, with music by Offenbach, arranged by Anatal Dorati, designs by Marcel Vertès, produced October 27th at Bel Artes, Mexico). In October 1942, for the same Company, he created another ballet, *Russian Soldier* (with music by Prokofiev, designs by Dobujinsky), which was produced in Chicago.

It was while he was working upon a third ballet for Ballet Theatre on the subject of *Helen of Troy* (to the music of Offenbach's *La Belle Hélène*, with designs by M. Vertès), that Fokine was taken ill and died in New York on August 22nd, 1942. This ballet was revised later with new choreography by David Lichine, and produced in 1943. Fokine created many other ballets for various companies. Altogether, his works number over seventy.

Michael Fokine is still regarded by many critics as the finest choreographer of modern times; and his creative brain was undoubtedly the pivot upon which the stupendous success of Diaghileff's early period of ballet production turned. Always a brilliant dancer himself, his work as ballet-master, combined with his remarkable creative gifts, brought to the modern ballet the far-reaching influences of an artistic integrity that seem likely to continue for many years to come. Despite the growth of the psychological ballet during recent years, of the symphonic and other new types of choreographic works, the perfection of the well-constructed Fokine ballets, with their completely harmonious blending of exquisite dancing fitted to beautiful music, dramatic content and artistic, colourful settings, will be difficult to excel.

Margot Fonteyn

M ARGOT FONTEYN PROVIDES A PERFECT EXAMPLE OF THE VERY gradual but never-for-the-moment-doubted emergence of a world-recognized *prima ballerina assoluta* from the lowest rungs of the ballet ladder into the dazzling realms of stardom. From the beginning of her early connection with the Sadler's Wells Ballet, at the age of fourteen years, there was recognized in her work—and she was always the hardest of hard workers—that subtle, indefinable "something different" that set her apart from the mere learner of steps and technique.

English born—at Reigate, in Surrey—in 1918, Margot Fonteyn has some Brazilian blood in her veins on her mother's side— hence, doubtless, her almost "out-size", well-deep, dark eyes, the pale olive clearness of her complexion, the midnight density of the cloud of dark hair that outlines her well-sculptured face, and her moonbeam beauty generally. Soon after her fourth birthday, the little girl, having already shown a decided tendency to amuse herself by dancing, became a pupil at the Bosustow School of Dancing at Ealing, where the family (her parents, herself and her brother Felix) were then living. Later, when she was eight, her father (Mr. Hookham), an English engineer, found it necessary, owing to the exigencies of his profession, to remove his wife and children first to America and, afterwards, as far afield as China.

However, the young Margot was determined that nothing should prevent her carrying on with tuition in the lovely art of dancing, in which she took such great joy and in which she was encouraged from the first by her sympathetic and far-seeing parents. Even in China such tuition was possible; and in Shanghai, when about twelve years old, she was able to study with George Gontcharoff, an excellent teacher from the Leningrad State Ballet; and she remained under his tuition for two years.

Just before these important lessons began, however, on a holiday visit to England with her mother, she had attended in London some classes with the famous Nicholas Legat. Here, too, she had been taken to see some of the ballets then being given at the "Old Vic" by the Sadler's Wells Ballet, in which

Markova, Dolin and Lopokova were then appearing. This fired her with still further enthusiasm; and on returning to Shanghai, she worked harder than ever with Gontcharoff.

When, at the age of fourteen, she finally left China and returned to London with her parents and brother, the youthful Fonteyn studied for a time with another famous teacher, the Princess Seraphine Astafieva; and finally she became a student at the Sadler's Wells Ballet School—the latter Company being now firmly established and giving regular performances both at Sadler's Wells and the "Old Vic". Consequently, there were many opportunities for the "trying-out" of the more talented students of the School; and as Margot Fonteyn was recognized from the first as being one of the most promising of these, many such chances came her way. After appearing as one of the Snowflakes in *Casse Noisette*, she was given her first real solo part as Young Tregennis in Ninette de Valois' ballet *The Haunted Ballroom*.

When Alicia Markova, the Company's ballerina, left in 1935, the Director, Ninette de Valois made no attempt to secure an outside ballerina to take her place, but permitted her own best dancers, trained in the Ballet School, to take in turns principal parts in the classics, as well as in the modern ballets devised by herself and Frederick Ashton, trying out each one with the utmost impartiality.

Then it was that Margot Fonteyn gradually emerged as something more than a well-trained dancer, revealing herself as a performer with a high ballet sense and a musical and poetical awareness quite unusual in one so young; and she was thus given more and more important roles to dance, in most of which she fully justified her choice and trial. In 1935, she created, with understanding and sympathy, the charming part—first gay, and then tragic—of the Fiancée in Frederick Ashton's ballet *Le Baiser de la Fée*; and in that same year, she also appeared as Odette in *Le Lac des Cygnes*.

The following year she danced with equal success the entirely different part of The Woman in the Ball-Dress in another new ballet by Frederick Ashton, *Apparitions*. In this she had to portray a mature woman of the world of the temptress type, her miming being surprisingly assured; and that same year she gave a wonderfully poetic performance of a Paris work-girl in Ashton's *Nocturne*.

Thus, in 1936, when only seventeen years of age, Margot Fonteyn had already become the leading *danseuse* of the Sadler's Wells Ballet; and since that period to the present day, she has continued steadily to improve her technique and to develop the outstanding individuality with which she invests each role she dances.

In the years immediately before the Second World War, the coming ballerina danced leading roles in the great classics, *Giselle*, *Lac des Cygnes* and *The Sleeping Princess*; Columbine in Fokine's *Le Carnaval*; and she created the principal part in Ashton's *Horoscope*. During the war, she created, in 1940, the charming part of the Bride in Ashton's *The Wise Virgins*—still one of her most beautifully conceived and presented roles; and she danced one of The Children of Light in the same choreographer's *Dante Sonata*. Other roles she danced in 1941 were the principal parts in de Valois' *Orpheus and Eurydice*, Helpmann's *Comus* and Ashton's *The Quest*. Two completely contrasting roles were provided for her later; in 1942 as the sprightly Swanilda in *Coppélia* and in 1943 as the romantic Young Girl in Fokine's lovely ballet *Le Spectre de la Rose*.

The blitzkrieg on London interfered to a certain extent with some of the Company's programmes during the war years; but even after the famous "Old Vic" had been put out of action by bombing, the members, with amazing courage, still continued to give more or less regular performances at Sadler's Wells Theatre, at the New Theatre, and also on provincial and Continental tours. They were in Holland when the Germans entered that country, but made a very exciting escape, after losing most of their baggage and scenery.

Then, at last, when the war was over, the Royal Opera House, Covent Garden, became the official home of this first British National Ballet Company. As a suitable opening event, a grand revival of *The Sleeping Beauty* was given on February 20th, 1946, in the presence of Their Majesties the King and Queen. Again Margot Fonteyn danced as the Princess Aurora, giving a really dazzling performance which served to confirm afresh her already well-established title of ballerina—the first British-trained ballerina, of whom the Sadler's Wells Ballet had every good reason to be justly proud.

Amongst the new works presented at Covent Garden during

more recent years was Frederick Ashton's first abstract symphony ballet, *Symphonic Variations*, produced in 1946, in which Margot Fonteyn has no special "star" part, being simply one of three female dancers performing equal parts with three equal-role male partners.

In 1946, too, there came another revelation, when she created the sparkling role of La Bolero in Ashton's amusing Edwardian ballet, *Les Sirènes*. In this light-hearted frolic, the young ballerina revealed entirely new facets of her diamond-bright versatility, presenting a gay, siren-esque, actress-dancer of Spanish-French type, a very Sprite of Mischief, captivating and irresistible. Nobody having seen her only in her more serious roles could have believed it possible for her thus to lose her true identity in such a frivolous trifle as *Les Sirènes*. In this ballet, too, she revealed an astounding capability for Spanish dancing.

At the end of 1946, when Ashton's Masque-Ballet *The Fairy Queen* was produced, Fonteyn performed a marvellous dance with Michael Somes as her partner, in which the brilliant pair had to skim, almost to fly, down a fairy glade from one end of Covent Garden's enormous stage to the other. Both these splendid dancers seemed like blue-winged swallows floating and skimming hither and thither as they represented the Spirits of the Air in a dance that was truly the "poetry of motion".

When Ashton's first full-evening-length fairy ballet, *Cinderella*, was produced at Christmas, 1948, Fonteyn was, unhappily, unable to appear in the title-role at the beginning of the season, owing to an accident she experienced a short time before when performing in the same choreographer's new ballet *Don Juan*—an accident which incapacitated her for several weeks. It had been arranged that the important role of Cinderella should be danced alternately by Fonteyn and Moira Shearer. During the former's temporary compulsory absence, therefore, the role was now danced alternately by Shearer and Violetta Elvin. When, however, Fonteyn was at last able to appear as Cinderella, her individual success was remarkably brilliant. Later on, the three dancers shared this charming role.

Later in 1948, when Leonide Massine came to Covent Garden as guest artist, Fonteyn danced with him in the welcome revival of his famous ballet, *Le Tricorne*, revealing the Miller's Wife in an entirely new and charming characterization; and in this work again her Spanish dancing was remarkable. During this season, also, she danced the lively *soubrette* role in Massine's new ballet, *Mam'zelle Angot*, a fine choreographic arrangement of Lecocq's charmingly gay comic opera, *La Fille de Madame Angot*.[1]

Another great success was experienced by this brilliant dancer when, early in 1949, she went to Paris as guest artist with the Roland Petit Ballets de Paris at the Marigny Theatre, where she created the extraordinary and most original character-role of Agathe, the White Cat-Girl in Roland Petit's own new ballet, *Les Demoiselles de la Nuit*. In this she gave a most amazing impersonation of a pretty White Cat who is transformed into an equally pretty young woman, falls in love with a handsome young poet, but still returns at night to her cat form in order to meet her former feline friends " on the tiles ", and when her human lover commits suicide in despair at her conduct, elects to die also with him. Her almost feline grace and uncannily intelligent movements in this role are astonishing; and her skilful technique in her most original and intricate dances (with Roland Petit as the Poet and Gordon Hamilton, likewise a member of this new French Company, as the Yellow Cat Baron), brought great ovations from her delighted French audiences.

During 1949, Margot Fonteyn made her first appearance in a television programme at Alexandra Palace, London, in which she danced several times with Harold Turner and Michael Somes in items from *The Lord of Burleigh*, *Horoscope* and *Rendezvous*, also dancing her own exquisite Bride's solo from *The Wise Virgins*. In 1954 she was televised in *Swan Lake*.

One very helpful factor in Margot Fonteyn's successful career has always been her strict self-discipline. While she loves a gay social life in her few spare hours and does not refuse for herself such youthful joys as may come her way, she seems to know exactly when and where to stop; and she permits nothing to interfere with the time she allocates for her daily practice and attendance at class.

When able to, she is a regular attendant at the classes of the famous Russian teacher, Madame Volkova, and she frequently takes an extra private lesson in addition. Even when on holiday, she prefers to stay in some place where a good

[1] In 1948, Fonteyn created the role of The Ballerina in Ashton's *Scènes de Ballet*.

teacher is available. She is never satisfied with her own achievements, but always feels that she must continue to learn. These everyday exercises, of course, are in addition to the almost daily rehearsals unavoidable to the principal ballerina of a successful and important Company, where new ballets are always more or less "in the offing", together with frequent revivals of older works. Her versatility is one of her greatest assets; and her real sense of humour is remarkable in one so pre-eminent in classical and more serious roles.

Margot Fonteyn is very fortunate in having a happy home life, where every consideration and help is given to her willingly by all members of the household; and she also has been fortunate in the possession of a most understanding and encouraging mother.

This charming ballerina has many outside interests; for her tastes are catholic. Above all, she loves music passionately. In addition, she has many friends; for, despite a certain surface reserve and the fact that she occasionally seems slightly enigmatic to some of her most devoted admirers, she has a real gift for friendship. Among her colleagues and co-stars, too, she has always been generously ungrudging in her genuine admiration for the dancing achievements of others.

When in the late autumn of 1949, the Sadler's Wells Ballet Company visited the United States of America and Canada, Margot Fonteyn gained many fresh laurels; and she was hailed by the enthusiastic critics in New York and elsewhere as the greatest of present-day ballerinas, indeed—to quote one of them —as "a dancer fit to be ranked with the all-time greats". Her effortless grace and flawless technique, the beauty and fluidity of her every movement, were a revelation to all her American and Canadian audiences, who could not praise her enough.

On February 20th, 1950, when Ninette de Valois' new ballet, *Don Quixote*, was produced at Covent Garden, Margot Fonteyn created the highly contrasted double-role of Aldonza and the Lady Dulcinea with brilliant skill, her co-stars being Robert Helpmann as The Don and Alexander Grant as Sancho Panza.

On March 9th, 1950, she danced in the Grand Gala Performance at Covent Garden in honour of the State Visit of the French President and Madame Auriol, at which Their Majesties the King and Queen were present.

On April 5th, 1950, Margot Fonteyn created one of the leading roles in Balanchine's splendid personal production of his *Ballet Imperial* at Covent Garden.

Later in 1950, she was invited to take part in a special grand season of ballet, opera and music at the Scala Theatre, Milan, where she secured a further triumph. She was accompanied by Robert Helpmann and Pamela May, and performed in *The Sleeping Beauty*. She also undertook that same year an English tour with Robert Helpmann on recital lines. During this tour she appeared with her partner in a new short ballet by Alfred Rodrigues, *L'Ile des Sirènes* (music by Debussy, costumes by Loudon Sainthill).

When the Sadler's Wells Company paid their second visit to U.S.A. and Canada, in the late autumn of 1950, Fonteyn met with even greater acclaim than in the previous year. On the Company's return in February 1951, she danced more brilliantly still throughout the Covent Garden "Festival of Britain" spring and summer seasons. The highlight of this was the production of Frederick Ashton's new choreographic version of *Daphnis and Chloe*, and of his *Tiresias*, in which she created the leading roles. In 1952, in Ashton's *Sylvia*, she created the title-role; and in his gorgeous Coronation ballet, *Homage to the Queen*, she was truly magnificent as Queen of the Air.

Margot Fonteyn is now at the height of her powers as a *ballerina assoluta*. It was with great pride that her world-wide admirers and friends learned that in the Birthday Honours of June 1951 she had received the award of C.B.E. for her services to the lovely Art of Ballet.

Celia Franca

CELIA FRANCA IS ONE OF THE FEW BRITISH WOMEN DANCERS to show also a gift for the difficult art of choreography, in which she has met with considerable success.

Born in London in 1921, she soon made up her mind to be a dancer. Having also a definite musical gift, she studied first of all at the Guildhall School of Music to which she had won scholarships both for music and for dancing. From here she now won a scholarship to the Royal Academy of Dancing. Among her famous teachers were the late Judith Espinosa, Marie Rambert and Stanislas Idzikovski. In 1936, she joined the Ballet Rambert, where she continued her training and soon began to dance in the Rambert Ballets at the Mercury Theatre. She made her début there at the age of fifteen in *The Planets*; and that same year she also danced the quite mature role of the Woman in His Past in Antony Tudor's *Le Jardin aux Lilas* —a surprising part for one so young. Her striking beauty was already of the dark-eyed, dark-haired exotic type; and she has since found her vivid good looks a great asset in the many dramatic and glamorous roles she has danced from time to time.

Celia Franca made remarkably quick progress with the Ballet Rambert, for which Company she created various roles in their ballets. Among these were the Bird in Frank Staff's *Peter and the Wolf*, the Dope Fiend in Walter Gore's *Paris-Soir*, and the *pas de deux* in Antony Tudor's *Suite of Airs*. She also danced in the Blue-Bird *pas de deux* in *Aurora's Wedding*, the Nymph in *L'Après-midi d'un Faune*, Goulue in *Bar aux Folies-Bergère*, Sports Girl in *Boxing*, Night in *The Descent of Hebe*, Polka in *Façade*, Marguerite in *Mephisto Valse*, Bride in *The Mermaid*, Mazurka and Prelude in *Les Sylphides*, pas de trois in *Lac des Cygnes*, Pavane in *Capriol Suite*, etc.

In 1939, she danced for a short time with the Ballets des Trois Arts, for which Company she created her first choreographic work, the ballet *Midas*, to music by Elizabeth Lutyens. She next danced with Mona Inglesby's International Ballet; and finally she joined the Sadler's Wells Ballet—with which (and its Junior Company, the Sadler's Wells Theatre Ballet) she remained until 1947. For the Sadler's Wells Ballet she created a number of interesting roles. Among these were the Queen in Robert Helpmann's *Hamlet*, and the Prostitute in his *Miracle in the Gorbals*; The Spider in Andrée Howard's *The Spider's Banquet* (*Le Festin d'Araignée*); and she also danced a very dramatic and ruthless Queen of the Wilis in *Giselle*, Street Dancer in Ninette de Valois' *The Prospect Before Us*, Ursula in *The Haunted Ballroom*, and a daughter in *Job*, etc.

When the Sadler's Wells Ballet moved into the Opera House.

Covent Garden, as their permanent headquarters, and the Company's Junior or Second Company was then formed in 1946 under the title of the Sadler's Wells Theatre Ballet (with their own separate premises at Sadler's Wells Theatre), Celia Franca went to the latter as guest artist, and danced leading roles in many of the works being presented there. She also created for the Junior Company a new ballet entitled *Khadra*—an Oriental Fantasy—(to the music of Sibelius' *Belshazzar's Feast*, and with *décor* and costumes by Honor Frost); and this choreographic work, though slight in subject, was most skilfully handled and suited beautifully to the music. It proved a great success, and has continued in the repertory of the Company ever since its production in 1946.

Khadra was Celia Franca's third ballet, her second one, *Cancion* (music by Turina), having been created for the Ballet Guild in 1942. Her fourth ballet, created for the Sadler's Wells Theatre Ballet in 1947, was *Bailemos*, again with *décor* and costumes by Honor Frost and to music from a suite of dances based on Massenet's opera *Le Cid*. This ballet, however, was not so well constructed as *Khadra*, and proved somewhat disappointing, although the choreographer herself danced well in the principal role. Nevertheless, this young dancer showed definite choreographic gifts, and was expected to produce later really interesting ballets—of which *Khadra* gave very likely promise.

The Metropolitan Ballet Company was formed in London in 1947, and Celia Franca joined it a couple of years later as a principal dancer and also as ballet-mistress. Her glamorous appearance and dramatic force were soon seen in several of the ballets presented by this most interesting Company, notably in Gsovsky's *The Dances of Galanta*, in which she danced the role of a seductive gipsy-girl with the utmost grace. She gave an excellent performance as the kindly street-girl in Rosella Hightower's *Pleasuredrome*, when the Company produced it at Harrow in 1949.

On December 9th and 14th, 1949, the Company gave an excellent television performance of *The Dance of Salome*, with choreography by Celia Franca, music by James Hartley, and *décor* and costumes by Stephen Bundy. In this ballet—specially created for television—the young choreographer, as Salome, gave what many critics have declared to be the best performance of her career, so far. Her dance of the Seven Veils was a lovely composition, and her vividly dramatic miming throughout reached a very high level. Her direction of the entire ballet—in which the Company gave an excellent account of themselves—was nothing short of first-rate in every respect; and it proved that ballet, intelligently handled, was an entirely satisfactory medium for television.

When Metropolitan Ballet collapsed, Celia Franca continued in television work for a time; and she also became one of the leading lights of the newly established Ballet Workshop, a Sunday night group giving performances of new ballets at the Mercury Theatre. For this experimental company she created a ballet entitled *Colloque Sentimentale*, to Debussy's setting of poems by Verlaine, which was produced in March 1951.

Later on in the spring of 1951, Celia Franca was invited by a group of Canadian business folk in Toronto to visit Canada, in order to establish there a Canadian National Ballet Company; and, soon after, she set off, visiting all the important cities and towns in the Dominion, where she gave lectures and saw performances by already existing Ballet Companies, Clubs and Dance Teachers. From this excellent and most enthusiastic material, she hoped to establish a really first-rate National Resident Ballet Company. She is a very good organizer; and as an accomplished dancer, choreographer, ballet-mistress and television expert, she was without doubt the right person for this most important task. She was to spend eight months in Canada, at the end of which time the Canadian National Ballet Company hoped to be established and successful.

Frederic Franklin

FREDERIC FRANKLIN IS ONE OF THE MOST VERSATILE BRITISH male dancers of to-day; and his wide range of ability extends from dancing leading roles in the great classics, the works of Fokine, Massine and other moderns, to the highly typical and often syncopated ballets of the American choreographers. His experience has been, and continues to be, immensely varied.

Born in Liverpool in 1914, he was fortunate in having parents who, though not actively connected with the stage in any way, were both very musical. So their son grew up in an atmosphere of music; and a natural sense of rhythm soon set him dancing to every tune or even to any elaborate musical composition he heard. He first danced for an audience at the age of six, before he had been given any serious lessons; but this preliminary event was so successful that it was then decided that he should become a dancer. He began to study dancing forthwith with a Mrs. Kelly and afterwards with Miss Shelagh Elliott-Clarke, both of Liverpool. From the latter he also received dramatic as well as ballet training; and in due course he passed the examinations of the Royal Academy of Dancing, in addition to gaining medals and diplomas in various competitions and appearing at local entertainments.

At the age of seventeen, he went first to London, and then to Paris, with a troupe of dancers known as The Lancashire Lads, appearing at the Casino de Paris—where he was chosen to dance one night with the famous Mistinguet during the temporary absence of her regular partner, to whom he then became understudy.

On returning to London, the young Franklin danced in various musical comedies, and partnered Wendy Toye in her popular dance shows at the Grosvenor House, while continuing his ballet training now with Nicholas Legat, Anna Pruzina and Lydia Kyasht. In 1933, he appeared in *Ballerina* (adapted from Lady Eleanor Smith's novel of that name), in which Anton Dolin was the star dancer. A couple of years later, he joined the Markova-Dolin Company as soloist, with whom he remained for two years, dancing such roles as the Athlete in *Les Biches,* Harlequin in *Carnaval,* Buffoon in *Casse Noisette* and the Blue-Bird in *Aurora's Wedding*.

In 1937, Franklin was seen by Leonide Massine, who invited him to join his newly formed Ballet Russe de Monte Carlo as principal male dancer; and he remained attached to this Company many years. He made his début with the Company at Monte Carlo by creating the Baron in Massine's *Gaieté*

Parisienne; and in London in 1938, he created the Spirit of
Creation in Massine's *Seventh Symphony*. Other roles he
created during the first season were the Knight in *Nobilissima
Visione*, and the Hero in *Bogatyri*; and other roles he danced
were the Blackamoor in *Petrouchka*, the Golden Slave in
Schéhérazade, the Lover in *L'Épreuve d'Amour*, the King of
the Dandies and, later, the Hussar in *Le Beau Danube*, and the
Warrior in *Prince Igor*.

The young dancer's first appearance in America was in 1938,
as the Baron in *Gaieté Parisienne*; and after returning to Paris
for a short time, the outbreak of war in 1939 sent the Company
back to New York. Here Franklin made a great hit as the
Beggar in Frederick Ashton's *Devil's Holiday* and as Franz in
Coppélia; and he now became understudy to Massine himself.

In 1940, the Company toured South America; and on returning to New York in the autumn of that year, Franklin had an
excellent part in Massine's American ballet *The New Yorker* (to
music by Gershwin), in which he excelled as a Fred-Astaire-like
ballet tap-dancer. In 1941, the Company went to Hollywood to
make pictures, and Franklin was found to screen well in *Gaieté
Parisienne* and *Capriccio Espagnol*. During the following New
York season, Franklin had to deputize for André Églevsky—
who had met with an accident—in *Baiser de la Fée*; and after
this he shared several other Églevsky roles for the remainder of
the season. He also took over Massine's part in *St. Francis*, after
two rehearsals only, when the great *premier danseur* left the
Company. From then onwards he has danced leading roles in
the classics, *Lac des Cygnes*, *Casse Noisette* and *Giselle*; and he
has proved his versatility by dancing such ultra modern roles
as the Gossip Columnist in *The New Yorker*, Jockey in *Saratoga*,
Johnny in Ruth Page's *Frankie and Johnny* and Billy in *Billy
Sunday* (Ruth Page). Other famous parts he has danced in
America are The Minotaur in *Labyrinth*, Russian Sailor in *The
Red Poppy*, Chivato in *Cuckold's Fair*, Mazurka in *Vienna 1814*,
Red and Black in *Rouge et Noir*, the Bridegroom in *The Bells*,
Farucca in *Madronos*, Principal in *Virginia Sampler*, Principal
in *Danses Concertantes*, Principal in *Mozartiana*, Principal in
Étude, the Poet in *Night Shadow*, Tarantella in *Cimarosiana*,
Principal in *Ghost Town*, Sacher Masoch and Faun in *Bacchan-
ale*, Day in *Nuages*, Joker in *Jeu de Cartes*, Waltz in *Serenade*,

Jean de Brienne in *Raymonda*, the Hero in *Lola Montez*, etc. In many of these ballets he created the parts named. His performance in *Danses Concertantes* (Balanchine—Stravinsky—Berman) was so excellent that it delighted Stravinsky himself. He was equally excellent in Balanchine's *Mozartiana*.

During the summer of 1944, the Ballet Russe de Monte Carlo was engaged to travel with the West Coast production of the very charming operetta *The Song of Norway* (arranged to the music of Grieg and dealing with incidents in that composer's life), for which its members provided the ballet. In this Franklin had a speaking part, in addition to appearing in some of the dances and in the final ballet.

In 1944, Frederic Franklin was appointed *maître de ballet* to the Company, this being a great honour for a non-Russian; and during the next four years, while exercising this exacting office, he continued to dance many leading roles.

In 1948, he came to England for a short visit—his first since the war; and in 1949, he returned at the invitation of Ninette de Valois and the Covent Garden Authorities, to dance as guest artist for a month with the Sadler's Wells Ballet at Covent Garden. Here he appeared with Alexandra Danilova as Franz in *Coppélia*, Siegfried in *Lac des Cygnes*, and as Albrecht in *Giselle*; and in these *danseur noble roles*, he danced brilliantly, proving himself to be a classical partner of great ability, with perfect stage manners as a ballerina's cavalier. He also danced with Moira Shearer in the *La Boutique Fantasque Can-Can*, and with other ballerinas of the Company in various ballets. Before returning to continue his work with the Ballet Russe de Monte Carlo, he also fulfilled an engagement to dance with the Metropolitan Ballet Company at the Empress Hall, Earl's Court, where Massine and Danilova were also guest artists. During this engagement, *Le Beau Danube* was given; and it was a joy to many in the vast audience to have the opportunity of seeing these three dancers appearing in the roles they had danced when this delightful ballet was produced for the Ballet Russe de Monte Carlo in 1938. On this occasion, too, Franklin also partnered Danilova in *The Black Swan* (Act 3 of *Lac des Cygnes*).

Frederic Franklin has worked successfully with most of the famous choreographers of the present day—Fokine, Massine, Nijinska, Balanchine, Ashton, etc.; and he has partnered many of the equally famous ballerinas of recent years: Danilova, Markova, Toumanova, Baronova, Slavenska, Krassovska, etc.

Franklin has developed his technique and his dramatic sense to the pitch where he can be relied upon always to give a really finely styled, sensitive performance of any of the roles he has already created or included in his repertoire.

In 1952, Frederic Franklin joined with Mia Slavenska in establishing The Slavenska-Franklin Ballet. One of their successes was in *A Streetcar named Desire* (chor. Valerie Bettis, music Alex North, *décor* Peter Larkin).

Moyra Fraser

I T IS NOT OFTEN THAT A BRITISH DANCER ATTAINS TO A BRILLIANT success and an assured position in the ballet world while still in the early twenties. Such, however, has been the good fortune of Moyra Fraser, one of the most beautiful and charming of our younger ballet dancers. Nor is "good fortune", perhaps, quite the correct expression to use in this connection—for solid hard work, excellent training and an intelligent personal development of her many natural gifts have been the main factors in producing this happy result.

Though born in Sydney, Australia, Moyra Fraser is not an Australian, her father being a Scotsman from Inverness and her mother a Yorkshirewoman, while England is her homeland. She began to learn dancing at the age of four, with a Russian teacher, Madame Lindouska; and later, when ten years old, she became a pupil at the Ripman School of Dancing.

Here she was taught mainly by one teacher, Lillian Thomas, who gave wonderful classes and who soon recognized that the young Moyra was specially gifted—not only as regard her actual dancing, but also because she showed definite dramatic talent, being an excellent mime even in these early days and revealing in particular a quite astonishing sense of humour in comedy parts.

Two years later, at the age of twelve, this most enthusiastic and talented child won a scholarship to the Sadler's Wells Ballet School, where she took her training very conscientiously and remained until admitted into full membership of that famous Company in 1938. Even in these early days, she was often singled out for the performance of small parts, her first character and dancing role being one of the little boy guests in the jolly children's Christmas Party scene in Act 1 of *Casse Noisette* at the Sadler's Wells Theatre.

Later on, she was given many other small parts. Among these, at the age of thirteen, she danced the Dawn Fairy in *Coppélia*, Act III. When still only fifteen years old, during the second World War, she went with the Company to Holland in 1940; and here, with her companions, she passed through a terribly anxious time when, on the actual day that the German Army invaded that country, a hurried and most exciting escape was made just in the nick of time—an alarming experience for one so young. However, the Company returned safely to the Wells; and this young dancer continued to dance with them throughout the war years, despite the many dangers and harassing events of those dark and dangerous days and nights. Later on, too, she went with the Company on an ENSA tour to France, Belgium and Holland.

She continued to be given more and more important parts to perform, dancing Prelude in *Les Sylphides*, Prayer in *Coppélia*, one of the Chief Swans in *Lac des Cygnes* (she also performed in the Spanish Dance in the ballroom scene of that ballet), Sabrina in *Comus*, various parts in the orgy scene of *The Rake's Progress*, one of the lovers in *The Wanderer*, the Street Dancer in *The Prospect Before Us*, one of the Children of Light in *Dante Sonata*, etc. Her more important parts were Myrtha, Queen of the Wilis, in *Giselle*, Duessa and Pride in *The Quest*, Josephine in *A Wedding Bouquet* (she first danced this role, by the way, at the age of sixteen) and The Hen in *The Birds*.

It will be noted that most of these roles entail outstanding acting ability on the part of the dancer. Moyra Fraser has always stood up well to such tests and has constantly revealed the gradual development of her natural dramatic qualities. In particular, her gift for comedy and her undoubted sense of humour were shown in her portrayal of The Hen in *The Birds*. In this most charming and amusing little ballet (devised by

99

Robert Helpmann more particularly for the younger members of the Company in 1942) the Hen is the main character; and it revealed Moyra Fraser as a real humorist. Her dancing picture of this vain barndoor fowl, perfectly mimed, won the whole-hearted applause and laughter of every audience who beheld it. Not many beautiful young dancers would have cared to perform a part so comical and even absurd, in which grace and beauty of dancing steps are exchanged for almost farcical clowning.

In *The Sleeping Beauty* she proved her ability for classical dancing; and in this lovely ballet, she first danced the charming and important part of the Lilac Fairy when eighteen years old. It was, by the way, when dancing the part of the Lilac Fairy one time that a very awkward moment occurred for her and her partner. Just as she and the Prince (Robert Helpmann) had stepped into the butterfly-drawn pearly boat that was to convey them both down the stream to the Enchanted Palace of the Sleeping Beauty, the magic skiff refused to move! So, instead of gliding away in a fairy-like manner, they had to arrange themselves in a set-piece tableau until the curtain was lowered.

Her own favourite roles are the Lilac Fairy in *Sleeping Beauty*, Prelude in *Les Sylphides*, Queen of the Wilis in *Giselle*, the Vain Hen in *The Birds* and Josephine in *Wedding Bouquet*—but she declares that she has liked all the parts she has danced, which can easily be believed of such an enthusiast. She always enjoys getting ready for a performance and its general excitement—especially where new ballets and acting roles are involved. Nevertheless, she is always nervous before dancing; and she has a great dislike for new shoes and slippery floors.

In 1946, Moyra Fraser left the Sadler's Wells Company, after seven years' continuous training and work with them, in order to take up an interesting and important engagement in the cast of *The Song of Norway*, an operetta based on the life and music of Edward Grieg. In this popular musical piece, she had two strongly contrasted parts—that of Adelina, a highly tempera-mental ballerina, and the principal dancing part in a beautiful ballet depicting the Spirit of Norway. The latter was arranged for her by Pauline Grant, who also designed four additional dances and the Peer Gynt Ballet. For the other dances and ballets in the operetta, the choreographer was Robert Helpmann, the whole of the dancing being set to the lovely music of Grieg.

As Adelina, the temperamental and hysterical ballerina of the Italian Opera, she again had the opportunity to reveal her astonishing versatility and flair for acting; while in the final ballet, when she appeared as the Spirit of Norway—a ravishing apparition arrayed in wispy, cloud-like draperies, her dancing technique was excellent and plainly revealed her sound classical training.

Since her successful appearance in *The Song of Norway*, Moyra Fraser has acted and danced as the Good Fairy in the pantomime, *Goody-Two-Shoes*, at the Theatre Royal, Glasgow, in 1948-49, in addition to carrying out the arduous duties of ballet-mistress therein—surely one of the youngest and most charming ballet-mistresses on record. She has also danced frequently in the various opera-ballets at Covent Garden and Sadler's Wells Theatre.

For the time being, at least, she has found it convenient to remain a "free-lance" dancer, since this gives her more time to devote to her home-life and to her husband and small daughter, Carol. She was married in 1944 to Mr. Douglas Sutherland. However, she never neglects her daily dance practice, and attends regularly at class. Her main ambition for the future is to find a really good full-length acting (speaking) and dancing role combined—comedy for preference, though she retains an open mind on this latter point. She has already danced in films—one of these was in *The Dancing Years* (Ivor Novello) produced by Frank Stafford; and in television programmes. She is not the only member of her family to reveal a strong histrionic bent, for her sister, Shelagh Fraser, is a "straight" actress and is, in addition, a playwright who has had several of her plays performed.

Moyra Fraser created the exacting role of Venus in *The Olympians*, an opera with music by Arthur Bliss to an amusing libretto by J. B. Priestley, which was produced at Covent Garden on Thursday, September 29th, 1949. For this part she was selected from among two hundred youthful and beautiful aspirants; and, in addition to her fresh beauty and excellent classical dancing training, her success in obtaining so coveted a role was also due to her versatility in mime and to her natural charm. This was an extremely difficult characterization, as it was a silent and non-dancing role. Nevertheless, her miming as a wandering player among her down-and-out fellow Olympians was vivid and amazingly clever; while, upon her transformation into the glorious Goddess of Beauty, her every movement was full of balletic grace and feeling, her statuesque poses being always reminiscent of the lovely art of Ancient Greece. Her Venus was a really remarkable and most beautiful character-study. In June 1950, she appeared with brilliant success in the new musical show produced and choreographed by Robert Helpmann, entitled *Golden City*, in which she had a good acting part as a nonchalantly amusing *café* waitress, with some charming dances besides.

At the end of 1950, Moyra Fraser again appeared as a Fairy Queen in pantomime—this time in *The Babes in the Wood* at Birmingham, where she met with great favour for her delightful dancing. After this, in the spring of 1951, she took part in the popular revue, *Penny Plain*, in which she secured an undoubted personal success on the first London presentation. In 1953, she was a star performer in another popular revue, *Airs on a Shoe-string*, appearing also in the latter in a television programme. In the Casino pantomime 1952-53, she was the Witch. She also took part in the film *The Man Who Loved Redheads* (from Terence Rattigan's play *Who is Sylvia*) in which Moira Shearer starred.

This charming and most versatile young artist is certainly making good in various directions. Above all, she remains always a lovely dancer whose excellent training in the Sadler's Wells Ballet is manifest in every role she undertakes.

Adeline Genée

I T WAS IN 1897 THAT ADELINE GENÉE, THE MOST FAMOUS ballerina of her day, first appeared in this country and shone upon the London entertainment world as a new and bright star. Ever since the dazzling days of Marie Taglioni—with her co-stars Fanny Elssler, Carlotta Grisi, Fanny Cerrito and Lucile

Grahn—had departed, the ballet in England had gradually dwindled until it had become little more than an exhibition of high-kicking, petticoat-tossing, music-hall "turns".

But a charming young dancer from Denmark now appeared upon the scene in time to revive the glories of the Taglioni tradition. The management of the Empire Theatre invited the famous ballerina, Adeline Genée, to come to London in 1897 to perform in a grand revival of the "Treasure Island" scena from *Monte Cristo*. This ambitious engagement was at first intended to be for six weeks only; but the exquisite dancing of the new-comer created such a furore that the contract was renewed again and again—with the happy result that Genée remained in London at the Empire for ten unbroken years, and then, after a short sojourn in America, returned to this country to dance here again and to make it her professional home.

Adeline Genée was born in 1878 at Copenhagen; and at a very early age she showed such great aptitude for dancing that there was never any doubt about her making ballet her life-work. Although Denmark, like Russia, had its own State Ballet School, where students were not only trained as dancers, but likewise received an excellent general education, Adeline Genée had no need to take advantage of this fact. She came of a dancing family, and her uncle and aunt—Alexander Genée and his wife, Antonie—were both among the most brilliant dancers of their day in Denmark; and they took over the training of their little niece. They were her sole teachers; and so excellent was their tuition that the young Adeline, in due course, became recognized as a perfect executant and as one not only possessing a real genius for dancing, but as also revealing a highly intelligent, original mind and a deep understanding of music. She worked very hard indeed, practising many hours daily not only her dancing exercises but also studying mime and acting, and music, all in addition to her general educational subjects.

At the early age of nine years, she appeared on the stage at Oslo; but her first real début as a finished and highly trained ballet dancer was made at the Imperial Opera House, Berlin, in 1896, when she appeared as Hélène in *Robert le Diable*, and as Centifolie in *Rose von Schiras*. So remarkable was her success that she remained as *première danseuse* at that theatre, leaving during the following year to become *première danseuse* at the

Munich Opera House. After this she appeared in Copenhagen (where she danced with the famous ballet-master, Hans Beck) and in Paris and elsewhere. She was hailed as an exquisite ballerina with a wonderful future before her. Alexander Genée was often her partner.

It was, however, not on the Continent that her greatest fame was to be achieved, but in England, so long starved of classical ballerinas of a high order. Although some excellent spectacular dancing shows were already being staged at the Empire and Alhambra music halls, it was not until the arrival of Adeline Genée at the Empire in 1897 that these ballets began to take on a more special character and to improve in general taste, in technical quality and in revived artistic appeal.

The new ballerina immediately became immensely popular; and her charming personality pervaded all her work. Some of the ballets in which she danced were created by her uncle, Alexander Genée; and her other principal choreographers were Emil Graeb (ballet-master at the Berlin Opera House), Madame Katti Lanner and others. At that time, the Empire's *décor* and costumes were in the capable and most artistic hands of C. Wilhelm. Genée's own favourite ballet composer was Dora Bright, who wrote very charming music for several of her ballets. Another composer of her ballet music was Leopold Wenzel; and he, Katti Lanner and Wilhelm were the creators of many of her most popular ballets.

The second ballet in which Genée performed at the Empire in 1897 was *The Press* (Lanner, Wenzel, Wilhelm), in which she appeared as the Spirit of the Liberty of the Press—a truly wonderful and most elaborate ballet, in which the dancers represented the various London newspapers and their most famous features. This remarkable ballet provided Genée with many dazzling dances; and from then onwards she became easily the most popular and universally admired ballerina of her day.

In the following year, 1898, there came another and even more lavish ballet, *Klondyke* (the Klondyke Gold-Rush fever was just then at its height), and Genée won further laurels for her delightful portrayal of the Fairy Good Fortune. After this, there followed for several years a whole succession of most elaborately conceived and gorgeously produced ballets. Among these were: *Seaside, Les Papillons* (in which Genée was the exquisite

Butterfly Queen, Vanessa Imperialis); *Old China* (as a Dresden Shepherdess in this, Genée revealed the truly *porcelaine* quality of her beauty), *Our Crown* (an Edward VII Coronation piece), *The Milliner Duchess, Vineland* (in which Genée won all hearts by her literally sparkling performance in the Champagne Dance), *The Dancing Doll, The Bugle Call, Cinderella* (a grand panto-mime ballet), etc.

In 1906, the classic ballet *Coppélia* (complete with the Delibes music, Mérante choreography, book by Nuittier and Saint-Léon) with Genée as Swanilda (a part she had already danced some years previously in Copenhagen before the King of Denmark), supported by Fred Farren as Dr. Coppélius, and Dorothy Craske as Franz—for in England, girls still danced the lover or "Prin-cipal Boy" in ballet as in pantomime. In this Genée again revealed more vividly than ever her great natural powers as a mime; and the whole production was a brilliant success. This was certainly a ballet event of the utmost importance at that time. The fact that it was received with such popular enthusi-asm proves how great was the advance of true ballet in London since Adeline Genée's magic touch had been laid upon it.

After this came another magnificently produced ballet, entitled *Fête Galante*, in which the lovely art of the famous French painters Fragonard, Lancret and Watteau was revealed in ballet form, the dancers being dressed in the exquisite garb of the period and seeming to have stepped from the frames of the actual pictures as they performed the stately measures of the period.

In 1906, Genée danced one of her most famous roles in *The Débutante*, in which she represented a young girl of inexperience but of amazing talent who takes, at the last moment, the part of an established ballerina. This year marked the tenth of Genée's sojourn in London; and after scoring another triumph in the production of *The Belle of the Ball* (in which Phyllis Bedells made a successful début), she left the Empire for a while in order to rest, intending, later on, to visit America. Her place in the last-named ballet was taken over by Miss Topsy Sinden.

Coppélia was revived in 1908; and Genée was induced to return and to take up again her famous creation of the part of Swanilda. Never had she received such an ovation of admiration and affec-tion as on the first night of this revival.

It was later that same year that Genée's own delightful ballet, *The Dryad* (book and music by Dora Bright, *décor* and costumes by C. Wilhelm), was produced at the Playhouse Theatre. This was a perfect little *pastorale* in which the dancer-choreographer's fine dramatic gifts had full play. It was received with great enthusiasm; but as it was appearing concurrently with *Coppélia*, she found it necessary—in order to conserve her strength for the final performances of *The Dryad*—to relinquish the part of Swanilda. The latter role was therefore taken over by the charming Russian dancer, Lydia Kyasht, who had already made a name for herself over here, being the first of the famous Russian ballerinas to appear in London.

Genée now departed to fulfil her long-promised engagements in America, where she met with equally popular success and where she was instantly taken to the hearts of all her Western audiences. It was while she was in America that another of her own choreographic works, *La Danse*, was produced at the Metropolitan Theatre in New York. This ballet was given elsewhere overseas; and, later on, it was produced at the Coliseum in London.

1909 saw Genée, returned from her American tour, appearing again at the Empire in the ever-popular ballet scenes from *Robert le Diable*; these being arranged and produced by her uncle, Alexander Genée, and proving again a brilliant success. In 1909, too, Genée was married on June 6th to Mr. Frank Isitt. The following two years each saw the production of a new ballet with Genée's own choreography at the Coliseum: in 1911, her *Butterflies and Roses* was produced, in which she danced as charmingly as ever; and in 1912 her own version of *La Camargo* (designed by Wilhelm and with music by Dora Bright) was given, with Genée dancing as the sparkling Camargo in an interesting and dramatic story giving an enthralling picture of the gorgeous Court of Louis XV.

In 1914, Genée was again at the Coliseum in another revival of *Robert le Diable* produced by Alexander Genée. Her partner on this occasion was the Russian dancer, Volonine; and this was the first time the famous ballerina had appeared on an English stage with a dancing partner of the opposite sex—a unique departure from the old Empire tradition. In 1915 she danced in a revival of *La Danse* at the Coliseum. A year later, in 1916, she danced again at the Coliseum in *The Pretty Prentice*; and this year, also, she danced at the Alhambra in *Spring*.

In between her London appearances during these last few years, she had visited the large provincial cities and towns; and everywhere she was received with great acclaim as a popular favourite.

Genée decided to retire from active professional dancing in early middle life; and her farewell season took place at the Coliseum in 1917. At her final performance the display of real affection and deep regret for her retirement was quite overwhelming.

But, although no longer a professional dancer herself, Madame Genée has continued to show always the keenest interest in the welfare of British ballet and dancing; and she has supported it generously to the utmost of her ability. With Mr. P. J. S. Richardson, editor of *The Dancing Times*, she was the leading spirit in the formation of the Association of Operatic Dancing in 1920, and was its first President; and when, on receiving its charter from King George V in 1935, the association became known as the Royal Academy of Dancing, she continued to be President and has retained this position ever since. The headquarters of the Academy are at Holland Park Avenue, the treasurer is Mr. P. J. S. Richardson, and Madame Karsavina is a member of the committee. In addition to upholding the great ballet traditions of the past and the continued raising and establishment of dancing as a beautiful art, the chief aim of the Academy has been to ensure that all Teachers of Dancing (both Ballet and Ballroom Dancing) shall be of a highly qualified order—to which end it has initiated Examinations and Teachers' Certificates. It also holds classes for the training of students of Operatic and Ballet Dancing, with regular examinations of all such students.

Madame Genée has also strongly supported all the efforts that have been made during the past difficult years to bring British Ballet to its present high level, and has shown the greatest interest in the various Ballet Clubs and Societies that have gradually brought this happy state of things into being. She was Chairman of the Camargo Society, established in 1930. She still takes a very large share in the organization and welfare of the Royal Academy of Dancing, attends its examinations as an examiner, and has established the Adeline Genée Gold Medal Award for competition.

Although so greatly interested in everything to do with the development and beauty of dancing, Genée admits to a dislike of the Central European School's style in ballet. She naturally prefers the classical dancing traditions in which she was herself brought up. She loves the Romantic Period in Ballet.

Like most great ballerinas, Genée has had to endure several awkward moments during her stage career. On one of these occasions, as a young *danseuse* of fourteen, the contraption carrying her across the stage, which represented the sea or river in the ballet *Undine*, suddenly refused to move from the centre of the stage. Young though she was, however, she did not lose her presence of mind. She plunged into the "water", but reappeared, perfectly dry, a few seconds later and danced the remainder of her part as arranged with complete aplomb! Needless to say, this emergence from "dry" water amused the audience considerably more than it did the youthful but resourceful dancer.

Genée's own favourite ballet roles have been Swanilda in *Coppélia*, the Wood Nymph in her own charming ballet *The Dryad*, and the title-roles in *The Débutante* and *La Camargo*. Apart from her dancing, her personal interests have always been in music, in the working of beautiful embroideries, and in travelling.

Her exquisite dancing has played an immensely important part in the history of ballet in this country; and she has always been recognized as a great artist in every sense of the word.

In the New Year's Honours of 1950, Adeline Genée was created a Dame of the British Empire, in recognition of all the valuable work she has done for the Art of Ballet. This is the highest title that can be bestowed upon a woman in this country.

Sally Gilmour

DESPITE THE MANY INTERESTING CHARACTERS IN BALLET depicted so successfully by Sally Gilmour, one immediately thinks of her first as that charming lady, Mrs. Sylvia Tebrick, who changed into so equally charming a fox one day. Incredible as the whole idea of this curious episode seemed to be, it most amazingly became entirely credible long before the curtain fell upon the final vanishing into the night of this transformed dancer from Wonderland, with a last flick of her long, bushy, chiffon tail. She really *was* a Lady who had turned into an undoubted Fox!

Sally Gilmour was born at Sungei Lembing, near Singapore, in 1921, the daughter of a Scots doctor practising in Malaya. Though having no ballet or theatre family connections, the little Sally—always small, fair and of dainty, elf-like build—was believed by her parents to have the makings of a ballet performer and they had her taught at a good dancing school at an early age.

On the family's return to London in 1929, the little girl—a great enthusiast herself by this time, after having been taken to see the great Pavlova in Singapore—was sent to the Dance School then being conducted by Madame Tamara Karsavina in York Street. After spending some years with this famous dancer, Sally Gilmour entered the Ballet School of Madame Rambert at Notting Hill Gate, connected with the little Mercury Theatre there; and she remained with the Ballet Rambert Company for many years.

While still little more than a child, Sally Gilmour revealed such a remarkable dramatic gift and such a real psychological understanding of character, that she was given many important, and even mature, roles to dance, despite her extreme youth. When only fifteen years old she danced the gay part of Maria in Antony Tudor's *Cross-Gartered*; and two years later, she most amazingly created the wonderful and famous title-role in *Lady Into Fox* (choreography by Andrée Howard from David Garnett's novel of the same name, to music by Honegger and *décor* and costumes by Nadia Benois), which

109

brought her instantly into the forefront of British character-dancers.

That same year she appeared in Walter Gore's *Paris-Soir* and Frank Staff's *Czernyana*. In 1940, she danced the Grand-daughter in Gore's *Cap Over Mill*, and the ever-delightful Duck in Staff's *Peter and the Wolf*. In 1941, she created another of her most famous parts, that of the Young Girl in Gore's *Confessional*; and in 1944, the Younger Sister in Andrée Howard's dramatic ballet, *The Fugitive*. Besides these more outstanding creations, Sally Gilmour has also danced leading roles in *The Descent of Hebe*, *Gala Performance*, *Fête Étrange*, *Façade*, *Dark Elegies*, *Bar aux Folies-Bergère*, *Le Jardin aux Lilas*, *Mr. Punch*, *Spectre de la Rose*, *Lac des Cygnes*, *Giselle*, etc.

Sally Gilmour's Giselle is often regarded as one of the most sensitive, poetical and sympathetic performances of this famous role ever given by a British dancer. Her natural, almost "fey" realization of herself as the spirit of the dead, betrayed village maiden has a quite uncanny quality, and one that stands out clearly and irresistibly.

A later performance of hers—that of Tulip, the Negress, in *The Sailor's Return* (based on another of David Garnett's novels, with choreography, *décor* and costumes by Andrée Howard, to music by Arthur Oldham), created in 1947 and produced at the Sadler's Wells Theatre, was an equally wonderful, though entirely different, conception. She seemed to get herself completely inside the skin and understanding of the charming but unfortuante young negress, who loves her English sailor husband so dearly but realizes the distaste for herself felt by his people when he brings her into their midst.

Sally Gilmour, though a dainty and delightful dancer, did not easily attain the strong and perfect technique of the classical ballerina; and, at first, she even appeared to be almost too slender and lightly built ever to do so. Nevertheless, she later very definitely proved that her seemingly frail delicacy of build was of the deceptive kind that eventually develops a latent strength. In her particular case, however, a strong technical virtuosity would certainly always prove to be a secondary matter. Her fame has rested upon her never-failing true portrayal of real character in ballet—whether of the highly dramatic kind, of comedy or fantasy, simple or complicated, matters not, for her versatility is amazing; and in this great gift, she has been out-standing among our British dancers.

When the Ballet Rambert made its most successful tour in Australasia during 1947-48, Sally Gilmour was married to Dr. Alan Wynne, of Australia; and the Company returned to London without their bright particular star. She returned to the Ballet Rambert in May 1950, to dance in their late Spring Season at the Lyric Theatre, Hammersmith. She danced in most of the programmes of the Company during that year. Then, early in 1951, she danced in the musical show, *Carousel*, at Drury Lane Theatre. She was released from the latter show to dance the part of Grace, the charming cat partner to Harold Turner's Orlando, the Marmalade Cat, during the Festival of Britain's ballet given daily in the Pleasure Gardens Amphitheatre. This ballet, *Orlando's Silver Wedding* (choreography by Andrée Howard, book and *décor* by Kathleen Hale, music by Arthur Benjamin), turned out to be a most delightful work; and Sally Gilmour was as happily perfect in the role of a coquettish cat as she had been in the more famous and dramatic Fox. This little ballet was a joy to children and adults alike.

Sally Gilmour has now retired to her new home in Australia.

John Gilpin

BEFORE HE WAS TWENTY-ONE YEARS OLD, JOHN GILPIN WAS already winning for himself a name as a virtuoso dancer with an excellent technique and a surprising elevation. An Englishman, born in Southsea on February 10th, 1930, he began dancing at an early age, his first training taking place at the Cone-Ripman School, while his later work was with Madame Rambert. For a few years he performed in several plays as a child, one of his roles being in *The Years Between*.

On taking up his dance training with Madame Rambert, he finally decided to make ballet his career. His début with the Ballet Rambert was made in Antony Tudor's *Soirée Musicale* at the age of fifteen; and he remained a member of this famous Company until 1948. He has danced in most of their ballets; and, owing to his excellent jumping power, he was given the role of the Spectre in *Le Spectre de la Rose*, in which he made an amazing and almost Nijinsky-like entrance. He also danced a Cavalier in *Gala Performance*, Mercury in *The Planets*, Harlequin in *Le Carnaval*, *pas de deux in Giselle*, *pas de trois* in *Lac des Cygnes*; and he has danced leading roles in *Czernyana*, *Façade*, etc. He created several roles for the Company, among these being Jack Ketch in Walter Gore's *Mr. Punch*, and Charlie in Andrée Howard's *The Sailor's Return*; and he also danced in Gore's *Plaisance*.

His fresh youthfulness at first marked out John Gilpin as an always popular junior member of the Rambert Company; but soon his ever-increasing virtuosity caused him to be more closely noted as a coming important male dancer, with considerable potentialities.

When the Ballet Rambert went on tour to Australia in 1947-48, the youthful John Gilpin went with them and attracted much favourable attention. On his return in 1948, he joined Roland Petit's newly formed Ballets de Paris, in which two other British dancers, Gordon Hamilton and Joan Sheldon, were already dancing. With this fine French Company, he has gained much new and valuable experience. Among his roles have been the Dandy in *Le Beau Danube*, which, though somewhat young for the part, he danced with the greatest spirit and with really splendidly proficient technique. Another of his successes with this Company has been his appearance in the several wonderful dances contained in Frederick Ashton's *Rêve de Léonor*—an extremely fantastic and somewhat obscure ballet—in which he performed brilliantly the many complications in his solos, despite the fact that he had to wear a heavy curled wig surmounted by a leaf-like crown. He also danced very cleverly in *Que le Diable L'Emporte*, again in a most fantastic and somewhat hampering garb. He left the French Company to join the Marquis de Cuevas' Grand Ballet de Monte Carlo, where he had many further opportunities for gaining excellent experience as a principal dancer—his dazzling *Blue-Bird* being already regarded as one of his "star turns". Early in 1951, he joined Anton Dolin's Festival Ballet and danced at the Stoll Theatre as one of that Company's principals. Here he danced most of the roles requiring unusual elevation and spectacular leaps; and his performance as the Spirit in *The Spectre of the Rose* was outstanding. He was also excellent in Lichine's new ballet, *Harlequinade*, where his dancing with the ever-delightful Riabouchinska was very fine indeed.

During the past few years, John Gilpin has developed in a remarkable manner; and with his tremendous enthusiasm for his chosen career and his already excellent technique, there is every likelihood of his becoming a first-rate *virtuoso* and dramatic dancer in the near future.

Nana Gollner

THAT BEAUTIFUL DANCER, NANA GOLLNER, IS AN AMERICAN artist and was born at El Paso, Texas, in 1920. She trained first of all with Theodore Kosloff, and later with those famous Russian teachers, Olga Preobrajenska, Lubov Egorova, Mathilde Kschesinskaya and others. Her training, therefore, was entirely of the Russian School. She became an excellent classical dancer, and her natural beauty and grace rendered her outstanding in the famous classic roles. She is married to Paul Petroff, also a good classical dancer.

Unfortunately, Nana Gollner seems to prefer being a guest artist, moving in and out of various Companies, rather than remaining—for at least a reasonable length of time—in one special *venue*, where she would have more chance of coming under regular and steady guidance. She is a ballerina of real talent, but touring with various Companies as a " Star " performer in a few special ballets only, tends to be somewhat too cramping for a first-rate dancer who might tackle many further interesting roles.

Nana Gollner made her début in 1935, at the early age of fifteen years, in the Max Reinhardt film of *A Midsummer Night's Dream*; and after this, she danced with several different ballet companies, among them the de Basil Ballet and René Blum's Ballet Russe de Monte Carlo. With the latter Company she danced Odette-Odile in *Lac des Cygnes*, Swanilda in *Coppélia*, and other leading classical roles.

In 1938, she joined the American Ballet; and when Ballet Theatre opened in 1940 she became one of its original members and danced leading classical roles. She soon left, however, to become a principal ballerina with the Original Ballet Russe, rejoining Ballet Theatre in 1944. Two years later, she joined a new Company known as Ballet for America; and the following year she came to England with her husband, Paul Petroff, as guest artist to International Ballet. For the latter Company it was intended that she should dance in scenes from Petipa's *La Bayadère*, which had been arranged for them under the direction of Nicolai Sergueeff, formerly *régisseur* of the Imperial Maryinsky Theatre, St. Petersburg, and which had never been given in this country before. Unfortunately, however, Nana Gollner was taken ill on arrival in London, and the project had to be abandoned. In consequence of her illness, Mona Inglesby, Director and chief ballerina of International Ballet, herself danced the leading roles in the Company's *premières* of their full-length productions of *Lac des Cygnes* and *Coppélia*; but on recovery the guest artist was able to take over these parts, as arranged in her contract, but was not strong enough to undertake the much more strenuous *La Bayadère*. The Company hope to produce the latter at some future date.

In 1948-49-50, Nana Gollner has been dancing again with Ballet Theatre, for whom she performed several new and difficult roles. Among these were Lisette in *La Fille Mal Gardée*. She also danced Princess Aurora in *The Sleeping Beauty* alternately with Nora Kaye and Maria Tallchief; and she gave a beautiful performance of *Giselle*; also appearing very successfully in Antony Tudor's *Shadow of the Wind*. During this period she also danced as guest artist with Serge Denham's Ballet Russe de Monte Carlo; and she had the unique and exciting experience while with that Company of having to dance the leading role in Tatiana Chamie's new ballet, *The Birthday*, at a moment's notice, owing to the sudden indisposition of Mia Slavenska—acquitting herself surprisingly well.

Nana Gollner is one of the most beautiful and gifted ballerinas of to-day, with the regal bearing so seldom seen since the Russian dancers of the Diaghileff period delighted us; and as she is now at the height of her classical career, it is greatly to be hoped that she will be visiting this country with greater regularity than of recent years. Perhaps we may even see her yet in *La Bayadère*.

Walter Gore

ONE OF THOSE FORTUNATE THREE-DIMENSIONAL ARTISTS, HAVing made an equally good success as a dancer, a choreographer, and a "straight" actor, Walter Gore has managed to combine this trinity of good gifts into one completely satisfactory whole. He could have made his way as a "straight" actor with ease, his natural versatility standing him in good stead; he has proved himself to be a fine all-round dancer, though not quite of the classical *danseur noble* variety; and as a choreographer he is original and vigorous. It is as the latter that he is, perhaps, becoming best known.

British born, Walter Gore began his ballet training with Madame Marie Rambert; and he has remained with her Company for many useful experimental years, first as a beginner and then as a leading male dancer and choreographer. He made his début at the little Mercury Theatre in Notting Hill Gate, where Madame Rambert has her Ballet School; he has travelled with the Company wherever they have been; and he constantly returns, to add his quota to the ever-increasing brilliance of the Company that saw the birth of his talent, and to continue to grace its name with his own new and matured work.

True, for a short time he danced with the Vic-Wells Ballet and with the Camargo Society and during this period danced in the de Valois ballets *The Rake's Progress* and *Job*; and when the Ballet Rambert was temporarily out of action from time to time, he took short engagements in various revues. During the Second World War, he served with the Royal Navy. But after each interruption, he always returned to his old Company with renewed zest.

While training, he danced many good roles; and he afterwards created the Lover in Tudor's *Les Masques*; Faust in Ashton's *Mephisto Valse*, the Lover in his *Lady of Shalott* and the Cat in Staff's *Peter and the Wolf*. In 1937 he danced Malvolio in Tudor's *Cross-Gartered*, in Wendy Toye's version of that ballet.

It was in 1938 that Walter Gore produced his first ballet for the Rambert Company. This was *Valse Finale* (with music by Rossini arranged Britten, and *décor* and costumes by Sophie Fedorovich); and he was greatly encouraged by Madame Rambert to continue his creative work since, by this time, Antony Tudor had already left her ranks. The following year he created his *Paris-Soir* (music by Poulenc, *décor* and costumes by Swinstead-Smith), which met with considerable success. In 1940, he produced *Cap Over the Mill* (music by Bate, *décor* and costumes by N. Benois), following this in 1941 with *Confessional* (music by Sibelius, *décor* and costumes by Andrée Howard), by many considered his best and most dramatic work. That same year he also created *Bartlemas Dances* (to music by Holst and *décor* and costumes by William Chappell); and these two latter ballets were first written specially for the Oxford University Ballet Club productions. In 1944, he produced his *Simple Symphony* (music by Benjamin Britten, *décor* and costumes by Ronald Wilson).

In all his own ballets, Walter Gore danced the leading roles himself with great brilliance; and he was also the leading dancer in the following Rambert productions by other choreographers: de Valois' *Bar aux Folies-Bergère*; Susan Salaman's *Le Boxing* and *Le Cricket*; Ashton's *Capriol Suite*, *Façade*, *Foyer de Danse*, *Mars and Venus*, *La Péri*, *The Planets*, *Passionate Pavane* and *The Tartans*; Andrée Howard's *Alcina Suite* and her *Lady Into Fox* (Mr. Tebrick); Howard and Salaman's *Mermaid*; Frank Staff's *Czernyana*; Antony Tudor's *Dark Elegies*, *Le Jardin aux Lilas*, *Soirée Musicale*; Fokine's *Le Carnaval* and *Les Sylphides*, etc. He also danced in the classics, *Giselle* (Albrecht), *Lac des Cygnes* (Prince Siegfried), *Aurora's Wedding* (the Blue-Bird).

Walter Gore's rendering of Albrecht in *Giselle* (with Sally Gilmour as his partner) is an excellently restrained and well-danced performance. He never over-acts, yet always manages to present his noble youth with real grace and definite authority. In the production of Andrée Howard's *The Sailor's Return*, given during the Ballet Rambert's Summer Season at Covent Garden in 1947, Walter Gore had a splendid role as the returned sailor who brings home with him a young negress as his bride—the part of Tulip being danced by Sally Gilmour with her usual outstanding sensitive intuition. In this ballet he once more proved his high dramatic powers and his great versatility.

In 1946, Walter Gore created his excellent comic, fantastic ballet *Mr. Punch* (music by Harold Oldham, *décor* and costumes by Ronald Wilson), which received a flattering reception. This ballet—which deals with our own popular fairground character and the favourite of our childhood days—is regarded by many critics as the British equivalent of Fokine's *Petrouchka*; and it brought him into great prominence. It also provided him with an excellent role particularly well suited to his humorous qualities, that of the rascally Punch himself, of which he made the best possible use. It should always provide a good holiday attraction. In that same year, also, he created his extremely amusing *Concerto Burlesco* (music by Bartok, arranged Arthur Oldham, *décor* and costumes by Eve Swinstead-Smith), which has proved very successful. He created another important ballet, *Plaisance* (music by Rossini, *décor* and costumes by Harry Cordwell), in 1947; but this is more of the dance suite variety of ballet.

When the Ballet Rambert made their important and most successful tour in Australasia in 1947-48, Walter Gore went with them as principal character dancer, playing the leading roles in several of his own ballets, and supporting the Company's principal *danseuse*, Sally Gilmour; and he met with an excellent reception. He also worked on several new ballets, one of which, *Winter Night*, was produced during the tour with great success. Later, this ballet had its English *première* at Bath in April 1949; and its London production was with the Rambert Company at the Lyric, Hammersmith, on May 2nd, 1950. It is set to the music of Rachmaninov's Second Piano Concerto, and has costumes and *décor* by the Australian artist, Kenneth Rowell.

On the Company's return, their brilliant choreographer created *Kaleidoscope* (music by Brahms-Paganini, *décor* and costumes by Ronald Wilson), which was produced in May, meeting with an enthusiastic reception. It is a gay, light-hearted piece, very wittily conceived, providing some clever dances for performers arrayed as insects; and it was a feast of dazzling colour and distracting but delightful movements. It makes a very happy interlude, and is a work that could be expanded into something more important.

That same year came a complete contrast in *Antonia* (music by Sibelius, *décor* and costumes by Harry Cordwell), for this proved to be a highly dramatic and passionately sensual work totally different from any other Walter Gore ballet. Its tragic theme deals with love and jealousy, leading on to murder; and it is emotional and exciting in the extreme, providing Walter Gore himself and the other leading dancers with some very realistically vivid and passionate pictures to depict—in some respects almost too realistic. It was produced at the King's Theatre, Hammersmith, on October 17th.

Another new ballet by Walter Gore, entitled *Largo* (with music by Sibelius and *décor* and costumes by Harry Cordwell), was to have been produced in the late autumn of 1949; but it had to be held over for later production, and *Antonia* was given instead.

Since the advent of television in its now quickly improving form, Walter Gore has taken considerable interest in this new art form as a medium for the presentation of Ballet in the home; and he has worked as choreographer in certain dance drama and ballet programmes being produced at the B.B.C. Studios. Included in his more recent work in this connection was a very successful performance of his ballet *Bartlemas Dances*, produced by him with Continental Ballet, in which he and Paula Hinton danced extremely well. With Paula Hinton, he danced a delightful little sketch-ballet he created for Ballet Workshop— a new Ballet Group formed in 1951—entitled *Pastorale for To-day* and described as "a Sketch for a Ballet", with music by Poulenc; it proved to be an enchanting, convincing work. Paula Hinton, by the way, is Walter Gore's wife, and is now regarded as one of the coming stars in modern ballet. Another charmingly fascinating little sketch-ballet produced by Gore for Ballet Workshop was set to a gay polka by Shoshtakovitch, and was entitled *Mathilda* and danced by Paula Hinton.

During the spring of 1951, Walter Gore was invited to choreograph some mime and dancing interludes introduced into a play produced at the Garrick Theatre, in which Elisabeth Bergner was the star actress. This dealt with a somewhat light and free translation of Molière's *Le Malade Imaginaire*, with the title *The Gay Invalid*. For Ballet Workshop he has also created *Hoops, Street Games, Peepshow, Tancredi* and *Clorinda*.

In May 1952, his very dramatic ballet *Crucifix* (Barber and Hobson—Rowell) was given in Melbourne, with Paula Hinton leading magnificently. In 1953, he established his own Company, entitled The Walter Gore Ballet. For this he created that year *Light Fantastic* (Chabrier—Rowell) and *The Gentle Poltegeist* (Fauré—Cordwell). Among Gore's other important ballets are *La Damnée* (Barber—Bonnat), and *Carte Blanche* (Addison—Rowell).

Alexander Grant

ⓥⓥⓥ

THOUGH HE HAS BEEN DANCING IN THIS COUNTRY ONLY SINCE 1945, that clever young dancer from New Zealand, Alexander Grant, has already made a name for himself as an excellent character dancer.

Born in Wellington, New Zealand, February 22nd, 1925, he was always keen on dancing, and at the age of seven years he began to study with Jeane Horne and Kathleen O'Brien. Throughout his school life he continued to keep up his dancing lessons, with the hope of making ballet his career. With this idea firmly fixed in his mind, he went in seriously for examination work; and in 1945, at the age of twenty, he won a Royal Academy of Dancing Scholarship, which entitled him to a full training course in London. To London, therefore, he gladly came and entered himself as a student at the Sadler's Wells Ballet School.

The following year he was sufficiently advanced to take part in the grand opening night at the Royal Opera House, Covent Garden, when Sadler's Wells Ballet gave their first performance there on its becoming their permanent home. It was a Gala Performance, honoured by the presence of Their Majesties the King and Queen; and the ballet given was *The Sleeping Beauty*, in which the young New Zealand dancer had a small part among the other students from the School. Later on, already showing a decided gift for mime, he was loaned to Sadler's Wells Theatre Ballet, where he created the role of the Old Man in Celia Franca's new ballet *Khadra*. With the Junior Company, also, he danced the Popular Song in *Façade*, and took solo parts in other ballets.

On returning to the Covent Garden Company, he was found to be ready for many good and increasingly important roles. Among these were the youthful Lover in *Miracle in the Gorbals*, a Masker in *Nocturne*, Mazurka in *Coppélia*, Grave-digger in *Hamlet*, a Child and Oriental in *Les Sirènes*, the Dandy in *Le Tricorne*, a Poodle in *La Boutique Fantasque*, a Child of Darkness in *Dante Sonata*, a Follower of Night and a Savage in *The Fairy Queen*, Gentleman with the Rope in *The Rake's Progress*, and War, Pestilence and Famine in *Job*.

In November 1947, when Leonide Massine's *Mam'zelle Angot* (music Lecocq, *décor* and costumes, Derain) was presented at Covent Garden, Alexander Grant took the amusing character role of The Barber, and danced with Margot Fonteyn, Moira Shearer and Michael Somes; and he was declared by one critic to have thus established a reputation for the same kind of clever drollery for which the great choreographer himself is so famous. His dancing and miming were certainly admirable in every way; and the excellence of his early dance training in New Zealand, plus the intensive hard work put in at the Sadler's Wells Ballet School, were now evident.

In June 1948, Grant had a part in another new Massine ballet composed especially for the Sadler's Wells Ballet Company and presented at Covent Garden. This was *The Clock Symphony* (music Haydn Symphony, *décor* and costumes Bérard), a fantastic ballet—by no means a symphonic one—dealing with a fairy-tale adventure in the Insect Kingdom, in which a poor young clockmaker, as one of the suitors for a lovely Princess's hand, circumvents all his highborn Insect rivals and wins his lady-love. Alexander Grant created the role of the Clockmaker and proved himself to be a really splendid dancer; and again he showed himself capable of dealing successfully with another somewhat Massine-like type of character.

Just before this production, he had taken part in the documentary film *Steps of the Ballet*, in which he led very spiritedly the exhibition dancing with Gerd Larsen as his partner. He has already taken part in ballet work in connection with television, and, in common with other young dancers, considers it of ever-increasing importance.

When Frederick Ashton's first full evening-length fairy ballet, *Cinderella*, was produced at Christmas, 1948-49, Alexander Grant had another "droll" to dance—that of the Court Jester, who attends wittily upon the Prince; and in this role he had some wonderful dances to perform, which revealed his remarkable elevation to great effect.

When the Sadler's Wells Ballet paid their now famous first visit to the United States and Canada in the late autumn of 1949, Alexander Grant went with them and was remarked upon as being one of the Company's most brilliant younger dancers— his excellent technique and witty miming as the Jester in *Cinderella* being particularly outstanding.

On his return, when Ninette de Valois' new ballet, *Don Quixote*, was produced at Covent Garden in February 1950, he created the comical, but somewhat pathetically Chaplin-esque role of Sancho Panza with real genius, being full of amusing vitality at the beginning and gradually dwindling into disillusionment at the end, in sympathy with his beloved lord, to whom he showed the utmost devotion. It was a powerful piece of miming.

On March 9th, 1950, Alexander Grant took part in the Grand Gala Performance at Covent Garden in honour of the French President and Madame Auriol, at which Their Majesties the King and Queen were present. He also danced with great wit and brilliance in Roland Petit's specially composed ballet, *Ballabile*, for the Sadler's Wells Ballet, presented at Covent Garden in May 1950.

During the Company's second visit to U.S.A. and Canada, Grant again was greatly admired. During the tour he performed the role of the Rake in *The Rake's Progress* for the first time and gave a really fine rendering. He also danced the Bridegroom in *Wedding Bouquet* and was a leading dancer in *Dante Sonata*, while his Sancho Panza in *Don Quixote* was a highlight.

In Ashton's revised version of Fokine's *Daphnis and Chloe*, Grant had another excellent character part as Chief of the pirate gang. In 1951, he was fine in Massine's Scotch ballet, *Donald of the Burthens*; and his humorous gifts had full play in John Cranko's amusing *Bonne Bouche* in 1952. As the Spirit of Fire in Ashton's splendid Coronation ballet in 1953, *Homage to the Queen*, he was outstanding.

It should be remembered that although Alexander Grant is undoubtedly a first-rate character dancer, he is also an executant of remarkable agility, with the real rhythmic strength necessary for the *danseur noble*; and it is to be hoped that this fine young dancer from New Zealand will soon be seen in the hero roles of the great classics.

Beryl Grey

N ALREADY FIRMLY ESTABLISHED CLASSICAL DANCER WITH A beautiful line and a brilliant technique, Beryl Grey, still in her early twenties, is regarded with much pride by the Sadler's Wells Ballet authorities as a vivid example of their School's own excellent and thorough training.

Born at Muswell Hill, London, in 1927, Beryl Grey, after joining a children's class at the Royal Academy of Dancing, won a Scholarship to the Sadler's Wells Ballet School, which she entered at the age of nine. Here she thus received her only and entire training in ballet work; and under the careful guidance of Ninette de Valois and her various instructors, she steadily advanced.

She entered the *corps de ballet* of the Sadler's Wells Ballet at the age of fourteen; and being already tall for her years, she was tried out in small roles, making her début in Robert Helpmann's *Comus* in 1942, in the part of Sabrina. When only fifteen, in the temporary absence of Margot Fonteyn, she danced Odette-Odille in the Company's full presentation of *Le Lac des Cygnes* at the New Theatre. In 1942, she created the role of The Night-ingale in Robert Helpmann's charming Chinese ballet *The Birds*. After this she danced in most of the Company's produc-tions. These included the Lilac Fairy in *The Sleeping Beauty*, the Serving-maid in *The Gods Go a-Begging*, Ophelia in *Hamlet*, the Valse in *Les Sylphides*, and various roles in *Le Carnaval, The Quest* (Duessa), *Dante Sonata, Les Rendezvous* and *Orpheus and Eurydice*.

In later productions of the Company, this young dancer has appeared in *The Fairy Queen* (Echo Dance), *Coppélia* (Prayer), *Dante Sonata* (A Child of Light), *The Three-Cornered Hat* (Jota), *Giselle* (The Queen of the Wilis), *Checkmate* (The Black Queen), *Les Sirènes* (Countess Kitty).

When Beryl Grey first began to appear in important roles, it was feared that her unusual height might prove to be a some-what serious handicap to her final success as a classical ballerina. Fortunately, however, this fear has now been swept away, and the clever young dancer by means of her remarkable technique and natural grace has overcome all doubts on this matter. She now even uses to advantage the greater sweep and range in arabesques, attitudes and similar movements made possible by her additional extent of limb. Given a suitable partner, she never appears awkward in any position, her flexibility, graceful head carriage, poise and balance being always equal to any occasion.

Though she has already emerged as one of the Company's most brilliant classical dancers—her recent performances as Giselle, Princess Aurora and Odette-Odile have proved this statement—she excels in dramatic roles in certain present-day ballets, and also in lighter character roles. Her Countess Kitty in Ashton's *Les Sirènes* is a perfect example of the latter. Another is provided by her dainty, teasing movements as the Lilac Fairy in *The Sleeping Beauty*—though her sweeping and gracious lines in the latter part are equally notable. Her light, fairy-like grace, too, is charmingly exhibited in her intricate dance as the Winter Fairy in Ashton's *Cinderella*, and in the various lovely movements in *Les Sylphides*. Two of her most dramatic roles are: (1) the Queen of the Wilis in *Giselle*, in which the ruthlessness of the avenging spirit is clearly shown despite the majestic grandeur of her carriage—her additional inches here being a decided asset; (2) the Black Queen in *Check-*

mate, where her commanding presence is again an advantage.

During the 1949 late autumn visit of the Company to the U.S.A. and Canada, Beryl Grey's performances were hailed by the critics there as "nothing short of entrancing", and she scored a great personal success. She has since danced Odette-Odile in *Lac des Cygnes* and Aurora in *The Sleeping Beauty* frequently at Covent Garden with brilliant success, in addition to dancing the title-role in Ashton's *Cinderella*.

In July 1950, Beryl Grey gave an excellent performance as principal dancer in a television programme, with Alexis Rassine, John Field, Margaret Dale and others. On July 14th, 1950, she was married to the well-known Swedish osteopath, Sven G. Svensen.

On April 5th, 1950, Beryl Grey created one of the leading roles in Balanchine's splendid personal production of his *Ballet Imperial* at Covent Garden, not previously seen in this country. Her performance in this magnificent ballet was remarkably fresh and sparkling. In 1951, she was outstanding as Death in Massine's new ballet *Donald of the Burthens*; and in 1952, she was seen to advantage in a stereoscopic film, *The Black Swan*, with John Field. In 1953, in Ashton's Coronation ballet *Homage to the Queen*, she was dazzling as the Queen of Fire.

Gordon Hamilton

ANOTHER FINE YOUNG DANCER FROM AUSTRALIA WHO HAS MADE good with British and French Companies is Gordon Hamilton. He was born in Sydney on November 5th, 1918, where he received his first ballet training, his teachers being Jan Kowsky and Mischa Birlakov. After appearing for a short time with the Australian Ballet Company, he went to Paris to continue his training with Madame Egorova; and in 1939, he visited Copenhagen to dance with the Lydia Kyasht Ballet de la Jeunesse Anglaise there.

Later in 1939, Gordon Hamilton came to England and joined

the Ballet Rambert for a few months only, during which time he danced the Lover in *Paris-Soir*. Then, after a short season with Les Ballets des Trois Arts, he joined the Anglo-Polish Ballet in 1940, with which Company he remained a year, dancing in their popular ballets *Cracow Wedding, Matthew is Dead*, etc.

In 1941, he joined the Sadler's Wells Ballet, where he danced for five years, first lesser roles, and, later on, more important ones. Among these were *Czardas* and *pas de trois* in *Lac des Cygnes*, one of the Three Ivans and Carabosse in *The Sleeping Beauty*, Pantalon in *Le Carnaval*, The Man with a Rope and the Dancing Master in *The Rake's Progress*, Dr. Coppélius in *Coppélia*, Blue Boy in *Les Patineurs*, Polonius in *Hamlet*, Street Boy in *Miracle in the Gorbals*, Lepidopterist in *Promenade*, Cuckoo in *The Birds*, Avarice in *The Quest*, also principal roles in *Comus, Adam Zero, Façade*, etc.

Having already established himself as a good character dancer, Gordon Hamilton again went to Paris in 1946, to join the Ballets des Champs-Élysées to dance in that capacity and to act as assistant *maître de ballet*. Here he danced some excellent roles, among them being Madge, the Witch Hag in *La Sylphide*, the Clown in *Les Forains*—in which role he gives a remarkable performance—the Stranger in *Los Caprichos*, the Bat in *La Fiancée du Diable*, the Hunchback in *Le Rendezvous*, etc. After a short return to Sadler's Wells to dance in Massine's revivals at Covent Garden in 1947 of *La Boutique Fantasque, Le Tricorne*, etc., he danced again with the Ballets des Champs-Élysées in 1948.

Then, when Roland Petit left the latter Company and in 1949 formed his own separate Company, Les Ballets de Paris, he invited Gordon Hamilton to join him. With the latter successful French Company, he has danced some very interesting character roles. Among the more outstanding are the Ginger Cat Baron in *Les Demoiselles de la Nuit*, the Dancing Master in *Que le Diable l'Emporte*, the Bandit with Red Hair in *Carmen*, the Manager in *Le Beau Danube*, etc.

Gordon Hamilton is a very virile and, at times, even exotic dancer, and his characterization in eccentric roles is remarkable. He has good elevation and a clean-cut technique. Since his sojourn with the French Companies, his work has gained much in style and polish. When Margot Fonteyn visited the Ballets des Champs-Élysées in 1949 to create Agathe the White Cat in Roland Petit's fantastic ballet *Les Demoiselles de la Nuit*, one of her most successful items was her wonderful bedside *pas de deux* with Gordon Hamilton as the Ginger Cat Baron; and the latter depicted surprisingly well the constant struggle required to be expressed in dance movements between his mimed feline and human characteristics. He gave a really remarkable performance which created a sensation both in Paris and, later, in London. He has a wonderful solo as the Cat Baron. A complete contrast was afforded by his highly entertaining portrayal of the finicky dancing-master in *Que le Diable l'Emporte*. Again in *Carmen*—the most breathtakingly intense dance drama seen in London for many a long year—as a ferocious-looking, red-haired bandit ruffian, he might have passed all his young life as this truly terrifying Latin mountain gangster who is, nevertheless, as neat a " snatcher-up of unconsidered trifles " as any of the light-fingered gentry of Paris or London streets. In the lighter role of the Manager in *Le Beau Danube* he is equally at home with his exaggerated elegance.

He has been to America several times with Petit's Ballets des Paris, and has always met with high praises there. During their U.S.A. tour early in 1951, the Company was invited by RKO to make a Technicolor film, and he was one of the stars signed on with Renée Jeanmaire, Colette Marchand and Roland Petit. In 1952, he appeared in the revue *Love in Paris*.

Gordon Hamilton is an extremely versatile, artistic and witty performer, with a fine technique that is quickly bringing him into the front line of present-day character dancers.

John Hart

O NE OF THE SADLER'S WELLS BALLET'S REALLY GOOD ALL-round younger male dancers is John Hart.

Born in London, 1921, he trained mainly with the late Madame Judith Espinosa. He won a five-years' student's

Scholarship, plus a Choreographic Scholarship, at the Royal Academy of Dancing; and here he did so remarkably well that in 1939 he earned the much-coveted Adeline Genée Gold Medal for Male Dancers.

He joined the Sadler's Wells Ballet in 1938, and made his début with the Company that same year by dancing the trepak in *Casse Noisette* (Act III). Two years later he danced the principal part (the young Shepherd-God) in Ninette de Valois' charming ballet *The Gods Go a-Begging*.

After this, from 1938-42, he danced principal roles in all the classical ballets: *Lac des Cygnes, Giselle, The Sleeping Beauty, Casse Noisette* and *Coppélia*. He also danced principal roles in the de Valois ballets *The Gods Go a-Begging* and *Orpheus and Eurydice*; in the Frederick Ashton ballets *Les Rendezvous, Dante Sonata, The Wise Virgins*; and the sole male character in Fokine's *Les Sylphides*. He also danced Laertes in Robert Helpmann's *Hamlet* and the Elder Brother in *Comus*; the Dancing-Master in de Valois' *The Rake's Progress*; the Bread Boy in Ashton's *Harlequin in the Street*, and several solos in the latter's *Wedding Bouquet*; and he danced in the famous Blue-Bird *pas de deux* in *The Sleeping Beauty*.

Then came four years' war service with H.M. Forces—a big gap in his career.

Upon his return, however, to Sadler's Wells Ballet in 1946, he again performed many interesting roles in the current and succeeding repertoires; and he has continually advanced with this Company ever since. Among these main roles have been the title-role in the de Valois ballet *Job*; the King in Helpmann's *Hamlet*, and the Official in his *Miracle in the Gorbals*; a Principal in Ashton's *Dante Sonata*, one of the three equal male dancers in his *Symphonic Variations*, a Principal in *Scènes de Ballet*, Don Juan in the ballet of that name, and the Prince in *Cinderella*. In Leonide Massine's 1947 revivals for the Company at Covent Garden of his two famous ballets *La Boutique Fantasque* and *Le Tricorne*, John Hart danced the Shopkeeper in the former and the Corregidor, or Governor, in the latter: and he has danced all principal roles in the classics revived from time to time. He gave exactly the right rendering of the suave and fussy Shopkeeper in *La Boutique Fantasque*; and on other occasions he also danced the famous *Can-Can* in this ballet. He gave an excellent picture of the amorous old Corregidor in *Le Tricorne*, when his quavering attempts to match the deliberately high-speed dancing of the Miller's charmingly saucy wife were most ludicrous to watch. His whole performance, indeed, was a really clever character study.

John Hart accompanied the Company on its first visit to U.S.A. and Canada in the late autumn of 1949; and he gained high praise for his participation in that beautiful but most exacting ballet, *Symphonic Variations*—also for his remarkably fine performance as the self-righteous, jealous Official in *Miracle in the Gorbals*. He gets through the extremely intricate dancing of Don Juan in de Valois' ballet of that name extremely well, and makes a really dependable and courteous cavalier partner to the ballerina in *Cinderella*—his bearing here is sedately dignified. He makes the ideal romantic poet-youth in *Les Sylphides*.

On March 9th, 1950, John Hart took part in the Grand Gala Performance at Covent Garden in honour of the State Visit of the French President and Madame Auriol, at which Their Majesties the King and Queen were present. In 1953, he was one of the principal cavaliers in Frederick Ashton's splendid Coronation ballet *Homage to the Queen*, in which he danced remarkably well.

John Hart has taken part in several television programmes, having performed, early in 1950, in the educational series *Ballet for Beginners*, when he danced Prince Siegfried in Act II of *Le Lac des Cygnes*, with Violetta Elvin as Odette and David Poole as Benno.

Robert Helpmann

H AD ROBERT HELPMANN BEGUN HIS REAL BALLET TRAINING at an earlier age and had he shown less ability as a "straight" actor, he might, possibly, have become the greatest male dancer of this century and have even put in the shade the marvellous Nijinsky himself. But his undoubted genius is a split one—and he is "fifty-fifty" a fine dancer and a fine actor. True, each of his widely acclaimed gifts is the complement of the other and he has developed both to the highest degree compatible with twin gifts each equally eager to assert itself.

An excessively spectacular technique is by no means the highest essential in ballet—indeed, extreme virtuosity is often decried. So much depends, in addition to excellence in dancing, upon the artist possessing also a real acting gift, high intelligence, good theatre sense, and a quick grasp of, and close attention to, detail. All these qualities are possessed in abundance by Helpmann, plus a keenly witty sense of humour, a sympathetic understanding of the tragic and human aspects of life, and an exquisite natural grace of movement.

Robert Helpmann is an Australian, and was born at Mount Gambier in South Australia in 1909; and from his earliest days he showed real acting ability and a strong inclination for the stage—being encouraged therein by his lively mother who, herself a good natural actress, loved to take part in family "dressings-up" and in the amateur acting of which she made a great feature in the happy family life she provided. The young Robert began his stage career in musical comedy and pantomime work; and he was fond of inventing and taking part in amusing dances. The first musical comedy he appeared in was *Frasquita*, in which Marie Burke was the star.

It was not until the early twenties, when Anna Pavlova visited Australia with her Company that this then very youthful actor began to be really interested in ballet. He was intensely thrilled by the lovely dancing of the incomparable Russian ballerina; and he joined her classes and attended her performances on every possible occasion. He even travelled around with her Company throughout her whole tour of Australia—during which period he took lessons from Laurent Novikoff, then the famous ballerina's partner.

However, when Pavlova left Australia to continue her world tour, the young male enthusiast she left behind was unable to continue the exquisite ballet work to which she had introduced him for lack of good teachers; and consequently, for a time, since ballet seemed to lie out of his reach temporarily—though the desire to be a good dancer never left him—he went touring once more with various dramatic and musical comedy companies throughout Australia. With these he greatly developed his natural dramatic gifts and revealed an ever-increasing true theatre sense, which is still one of his most important assets.

But the influence of Pavlova and the absorbing impression she had made upon him remained uppermost; and in 1930, after making the acquaintance of Margaret Rawlings and her Company, he determined to go to England with them on their return and to study ballet there.

Robert Helpmann entered the Sadler's Wells Ballet School in 1932; and in him the Director, Ninette de Valois, instantly recognized the excellent male material for which she was then looking. She saw that he had a distinctive personality, a strong belief in himself, and the keenness of the born stage enthusiast; and she felt she could make of him a principal dancer, despite his somewhat late start in regular classical work at twenty-three years of age. The new student lived up to her expectations, putting in an immense amount of intensive technical training, and quickly revealing his strong dramatic gifts in everything he undertook—plus the quick grasping ability of a high intelligence and an enviable artistic gift.

Within a far shorter time than usual, Robert Helpmann began to dance leading roles in the many new ballets by Frederick Ashton and Ninette de Valois herself then being produced by the Sadler's Wells Company; and this being a period of shortage of good male dancers, many splendid opportunities for proving his undoubted worth came his way—opportunities of which the fortunate young man only too gladly and conscientiously availed himself.

A few years later, he was universally acclaimed as a leading British male dancer—a dancer, too, of the utmost versatility, a brilliant mime, and one capable of undertaking even the most difficult and complex impersonations in any modern ballet. In the classical ballets, too, he could likewise hold his own, proving himself always to be a perfect partner to the ballerina. He partnered Alicia Markova until she left Sadler's Wells to form her own Company with Anton Dolin; and with the following emergence of Margot Fonteyn, he continued as partner to that now scintillating star.

After dancing a few smaller roles in various ballets, he created in 1934 the part of The Master of Tregennis in Ninette de Valois' *The Haunted Ballroom*—an excellent dancing and character role in which his great dramatic gifts had full play and for which he received high praise from the critics. Soon afterwards, the opportunity came for him to dance the exacting part of Satan in de Valois' *Job*—which part had just been relinquished by Anton Dolin on retiring from the Wells to take up other engagements; and in this he likewise met with a brilliant success.

From now onwards, Helpmann became leading male dancer with the Sadler's Wells Company, with each performance standing out with more and more importance and giving ever further evidence of his truly amazing versatility. In succeeding de Valois' ballets, *Checkmate* (1937), *The Prospect Before Us* (1940), and *Orpheus and Eurydice* (1941), he created the leading roles, in addition to dancing lesser but yet important roles in some of her other ballets. He danced The Rake in *The Rake's Progress* after the departure of Dolin; and in this ballet he is considered by many to have entered even more fully into the true spirit of the Hogarth pictures upon which this remarkable choreographical work is founded. In Frederick Ashton's ballets he created the leading roles in *Apparitions* (1936), *Nocturne* (1936), *Les Patineurs* (1937), *A Wedding Bouquet* (1937), *Dante Sonata* (1940), *The Wanderer* (1941), *The Quest* (1943). As leading dancer in the classics, he danced Albrecht in *Giselle*—this dramatic part, by the way, is still one of his favourite roles—Prince Florimund in *The Sleeping Beauty*, Prince Siegfried in *Lac des Cygnes*, the Nutcracker Prince in *Casse Noisette*, Dr. Coppélius in *Coppélia*: and the principal parts in the two Fokine ballets first produced by the Company, *Les Sylphides* and *Le Carnaval*.

It was not until 1942 that Robert Helpmann began seriously to turn his attention to choreography, his first important ballet being *Comus*,[1] produced in January of that year by the Sadler's Wells Company at the New Theatre, London. The music for this ballet was by Purcell, arranged by Constant Lambert, and

---

[1] Before *Comus*, Helpmann had already created, with Wendy Toye, a small ballet-divertissement, *La Valse*, for the R.A.D. Production Club in 1939. It had music by Ravel. This was later taken into the repertoire of The Ballet de la Jeunesse Anglaise.

the *décor* and costumes were by Oliver Messel. The subject is, of course, the famous Masque by Milton; and the two fine speeches allotted by the poet to Comus were declaimed very dramatically by the choreographer himself taking the difficult part of the evil Magician. Though there was not overmuch originality in the dances, the whole masque-ballet revealed much promise for the future.

This promise was certainly more than fulfilled when Helpmann's second ballet, *Hamlet*, was produced by the Company at the New Theatre later that same year, May 19th, 1942, with the choreographer again in the title-role. This most remarkable and thoroughly well-constructed ballet deals with the last confused thoughts of the dying Hamlet as he is borne by retainers across the hall of the Castle of Elsinore, his head with its ghastly chalk-white face drooping limply over the shoulders of the sable-clad bearers; and the succeeding scenes depict the kaleidoscopic, distracted and fantastic memories of the almost dead royal youth. Though by some regarded more as a mime-spectacle—at times gruesome, at others brilliant and even sparkling—rather than a ballet, the work is impressive and dramatic in the extreme, is cleverly devised and well constructed, and gives immense scope for good miming. There is not very much actual dancing in it, but the groupings are particularly well contrived and the many tableaux are full of colour and life. The scenery, by Leslie Hurry, is somewhat confusing and distracting, because of the exaggerated size and vividness of the wall and roof designs, consisting as they do of long, sinister-looking arms clutching swords and daggers—this, however, being obviously intended to convey an impression of the distorted vision of the dying prince.

The ballet is a most remarkable piece of work, constructed with great skill, and its original treatment as a psychological study presented in terms of the dance, while causing controversy from the conventional ballet point of view, immediately placed its constructor among front-ranking modern choreographers. The music for *Hamlet* is by Tchaikovsky.

Later still in 1942, Helpmann's third ballet, *The Birds*, was produced at the New Theatre. This is a charming little comedy piece, dealing mainly with the amusing antics of a Hen—excellently mimed by Moyra Fraser—a Cuckoo, a Dove, a Nightingale and a couple of cheeky Sparrows. The delightful setting and costumes are by the Chinese artist, Chiang Yee, and look as though they had come straight from the pages of a Chinese fairy-tale. The music is taken from Old Masters arranged by Respighi, and has an overture, "The Bird Actors", by Constant Lambert.

On October 26th, 1944, Helpmann's fourth ballet, *Miracle in the Gorbals* (with book by Michael Benthall, *décor* and costumes by Edward Burra, music by Arthur Bliss), was produced by the Sadler's Wells Company at the Prince's Theatre, London; and this is regarded by many critics as his masterpiece to date—though here again other ballet-lovers deprecate its lack of actual dancing features. It is, however, a real dance-drama; and it deals with the appearance of a Holy Stranger upon a dockyard scene in the sordid Gorbals district of Glasgow, the Stranger's restoration to life of a girl suicide and the consequent jealousy of a Social Worker, and the murder of the Christ character. The stark realism and almost uncanny character-drawing in this ballet are truly remarkable. Though its subject matter is by no means of the popular kind, its highly dramatic quality, skilful presentation, tragic intensity and underlying moral thought make it an extremely impressive piece of choreographic work which grips the audience throughout.

Adam Zero, Helpmann's fifth ballet, and his last to date, was produced at Covent Garden on April 10th, 1946 (book by Michael Benthall, music by Arthur Bliss, and *décor* and costumes by Roger Furse). The theme, however, is not a particularly original one, since it deals with the life-cycle of a man—the story of the main features and landmarks of his life being retold or reviewed by the latter in his old age as he looks back upon these. Though somewhat over-long, this ballet is, nevertheless, amazingly well constructed and provided Helpmann, as the hero, with an excellent medium for revealing the many facets of his miming and dancing gifts. It was revived with some important improvements in December 1947.

During his seventeen years' highly successful connection as premier dancer with the Sadler's Wells Ballet, Robert Helpmann has several times left the Company temporarily for "straight" stage work, his brilliant acting gift and strong theatre sense having asserted themselves at regular intervals and caused him to accept various attractive dramatic offers. He always intended to develop his talent as a "straight" actor, and has certainly succeeded in doing so and in gaining excellent experience. His love of the drama, and even of light-comedy acting, seems to be as great as his real love of dancing.

His first departure from the Sadler's Wells Company was in 1938, when he appeared at the Old Vic in *The Taming of the Shrew*, *A Midsummer Night's Dream* and later in 1944, in *Hamlet*, his performances in all his Shakespearian roles receiving high praise and adding greatly to his popularity. He arranged the ballets and dances in other theatres in Revues and other musical shows, among these being *Stop Press*, *Swinging the Gate*, *Fine and Dandy*, *Wild Rose*, *The Merry Widow* and *The Song of Norway*, his choreographic work for these being all of a high order. He also acted in *Precipice* and in *The Insect Play*.

When the Sadler's Wells Ballet took up its permanent home at Covent Garden in 1946, Helpmann returned to take part in the grand opening production of Tchaikovsky's lovely ballet, *The Sleeping Beauty*, on February 23rd that year, performing the dual roles of the Wicked Fairy, Carabosse, and Prince Florimund—two very strongly contrasted parts, in both of which his lively versatility enabled him to cope with great success.

Later that same year, when Frederick Ashton's *The Fairy Queen* Masque-Ballet was given by the Company at Covent Garden, Helpmann played the non-dancing part of Oberon; but despite the fact that he had no set dance to perform, his exquisitely graceful movements and his static poses were beautiful in the extreme—in particular, the unforgettably regal sweep of his magnificent cloak as he moved across the stage. His poetic impersonation of the Fairy King was certainly one of the real high-lights in this ballet.

In 1947, Helpmann formed a Company with Margaret Rawlings and produced at the Duchess Theatre the plays *The White Devil* and *He Who Gets Slapped*, in which he himself acted with deep understanding. He has also acted important parts in films. He played the traitor, De Jong, in *One of our Aircraft is Missing*; the Bishop of Ely in Laurence Olivier's *Henry V*; Wycroft in *Caravan* and Ivan Boleslawsky in *The Red Shoes*. In this latter he was choreographer for the dances, and acted and danced with excellent effect.

In 1948, he was invited to take part in the Stratford-on-Avon

Shakespearian Festival at the Memorial Theatre; and he played *Hamlet* in turn with Paul Scofield. This was a particularly interesting performance, which compared very favourably with his own ballet creation of *Hamlet*. His performance as Shylock, in *The Merchant of Venice*, too, was very vivid and character-istic. He played King John during that memorable season with an entirely new rendering of this cunning and unpopular monarch, making him so interesting, if despicable, as to domi-nate the play completely. Helpmann's King John was a truly brilliant creation.

At the end of 1948, he returned to the Sadler's Wells Ballet to dance at Covent Garden in Frederick Ashton's first full even-ing-length ballet, *Cinderella*, in which he played one of the Ugly Sisters to the choreographer's other Ugly Sister—truly a piece of amazingly humorous buffoonery.

In the late autumn of 1949, Helpmann went with the Sadler's Wells Ballet on their now world-famed first visit to the United States and Canada, where he won a real personal success—though his ballet, *Miracle in the Gorbals*, did not appeal greatly to the audiences out West. Nor did his own performance as Satan in de Valois' *Job* prove particularly popular there. Curi-ously enough, he was preferred in his more lively roles in such ballets as *Façade*, etc., and he was genuinely admired as the dignified, yet debonair, Prince in *The Sleeping Beauty*. On the Company's second visit to America the following year, Help-mann was again one of the stars of the party and once more delighted all his audiences.

At the first performance of the Sir Arthur Bliss—J. B. Priestley grand opera, *The Olympians*, at Covent Garden on September 29th, 1949, Robert Helpmann took the miming and dancing role of Mercury with grace and humour.

On February 20th, 1950, he created the difficult role of the romantic Don in Ninette de Valois' new ballet *Don Quixote* with the utmost sympathy and most perfect miming; and this really fine achievement is now regarded as one of his greatest ballet successes. In May 1950, he went for a few weeks to La Scala, Milan, with Margot Fonteyn and Pamela May, as guest artists to perform in *The Sleeping Beauty* in connection with the Holy Year celebrations. The English dancers were enthusiastic-ally received.

A few weeks earlier, he had made his début in yet another branch of dramatic art, by producing an excellent performance of Puccini's famous and ever-popular opera, *Madam Butterfly*, at Covent Garden. In June 1950, he produced and was chore-ographer for a new musical show, *Golden City*, at the Adelphi Theatre, London. Among well-known dancers in this were Moyra Fraser, Anita Phillips and others.

It is, indeed, his amazing versatility and strongly developed theatre sense that makes Robert Helpmann the first-rate all-round actor and useful leading dancer he undoubtedly is. In addition to being a fine tragic and serious actor and a most reliable classical ballet partner and general modern dancer, he is also a born comic—indeed Dame de Valois has declared her belief that his presence in the ballet and on the legitimate stage has robbed the circus and music-hall world of another Grock. He is often described as " the Chameleon of the Theatre ".

Curiously enough, Helpmann's own choreographic works tend to reveal the more serious and sombre side of his genius. With the sole exception of *The Birds*, the ballets he has so far created are of a tragic or serious kind. He is an extremely interesting choreographer. The same can be said of his dancing and acting. As soon as he appears upon the stage, he dominates it by his personality and all eyes remain, perhaps unconsciously, upon him. Even when, in a ballet, or a play, he has ceased for the moment to dance or to speak and has taken up a static position, he still continues to hold his audience. His graceful immobility, or his silence, are yet always eloquent and full of meaning—one of the acknowledged gifts of the true artist.

To sum up, Robert Helpmann is a real man of the theatre and loves everything connected with it. Although swimming and riding are among his outside interests, nothing pleases him more than to indulge in a real " busman's holiday " and go to the theatre to watch other people act or dance.

On March 9th, 1950, Robert Helpmann took part in the Grand Gala Performance at Covent Garden in honour of the State Visit of the French President and Madame Auriol, at which Their Majesties the King and Queen were present.

In the spring of 1951, the Michael Power-Emeric Pressburger Technicolor film, *The Tales of Hoffman*, was produced (*première*, Carlton Cinema, London, April 18th), with the tuneful music of Offenbach played by the Royal Philharmonic Orchestra conducted by Sir Thomas Beecham. Moira Shearer danced as Olympia the Doll, Ludmila Tcherina was the Venetian charmer, Giulietta, Leonide Massine was Schlemil. Frederick Ashton was the choreographer, and Hein Heckroth the designer. In this amazing film, Robert Helpmann created the role of the Evil Genius of the unfortunate Hoffmann. Mixed opinions greeted this most elaborate film; but one and all expressed admiration for the wonderful miming of Helpmann, who certainly " ran away with the show " whenever he appeared in his three characters—Dr. Coppélius, Dapurtutto and Dr. Mirakel. In particular he gave a really fine performance as Dr. Coppélius, the doll-maker. His make-up and sinister movements were quite thrilling; and he managed—better than most of the other members of the cast—to give the impression that he was actually singing, though this was done " off " by Bruce Dargavel, whose real voice was inspiring and of the rich quality required. Helpmann's work in this film was a real triumph.

In June 1951, Robert Helpmann went on a provincial tour in a concert group with Margot Fonteyn and a few other performers—among them June Brae and Harold Turner—giving excerpts from famous ballets which served to give some idea of the skill and scope of these famous dancers. In a little dramatic ballet-sketch entitled *L'Ile des Sirènes* (music by Debussy and costumes by Loudon Sainthill), specially created for this tour by Alfred Rodrigues, Helpmann as a shipwrecked mariner and Fonteyn as the Siren had fine roles which suited the genius of both and provided an excellent foil to the classic excerpts.

During recent years, Robert Helpmann has devoted himself mainly to production work—plays, operas, musicals—also to " straight " acting. Nevertheless, he made a welcome reappearance as Prince Siegfried in *Swan Lake*, Act II, at the Coronation Gala Ballet performance in 1953.

Several books have been written about this gifted dancer-actor, among which may be mentioned those by Caryl Brahms, and (mainly photographs) Gordon Anthony. The Robert Helpmann Album, also mainly photographs, but containing short appreciations by Alan Dent and Arnold Haskell, is published by Stage and Screen Publications.

Ernest Hewitt

AS ONE OF THE LEADING MALE DANCERS OF INTERNATIONAL Ballet, Ernest Hewitt has made rapid strides recently as a highly satisfactory partner to the ballerina. He has good stage manners and looks the part of the highly born youth, being slender and graceful, with a dignified carriage.

Ernest Hewitt was born in Manchester in 1917, where, at an early age, he revealed highly artistic tendencies. He was extremely musical, and showed a decided gift for design.

Wishing to put his artistic gifts to a further test, he joined the Manchester Ballet Club; and here he soon found himself in his right element and able to develop his natural love of dancing and to make it the complement of his musical gift. He decided to devote himself to the career of a dancer; and he studied with several famous teachers, among the latter being Judith Espinosa, Idzikovsky, Elsa Brunelleschi, Algeranoff and Amina Severskaya. He soon joined the International Ballet School; and there he was able to continue his studies with Judith Espinosa (one of the leading teachers in the School) and with Algeranoff, their chief character dancer; and he now came under the classical guidance of Nicholas Sergueeff (formerly *régisseur-general* of the Imperial Maryinsky Ballet School in St. Petersburg), Supervisor of the School.

Ernest Hewitt now made such rapid progress and was so enthusiastic a worker that in a remarkably short time he was taking leading classical and other parts much sooner than is usually the case. He was soon dancing as *danseur noble* in the classics, and partnering the ballerina in *Lac des Cygnes, The Sleeping Beauty* and *Coppélia*. He also took the role of Orsino in *Twelfth Night*, the Mazurka in *Coppélia*, the Spirit of Wine in the *Masque of Comus*, the Kinsman in *Everyman*, Florestan in *Le Carnaval* and Benno in *Lac des Cygnes*.

Ernest Hewitt is particularly interested in Spanish dancing, and is now making a special study of this branch of his art. He still continues his studies in painting and design, of which more may be heard in the near future.

When Leonide Massine's gay but masterly ballet, *Gaieté*

Parisienne, was revived and produced by that choreographer for International Ballet during their very successful season at the Coliseum, London, in May 1950, Ernest Hewitt danced the role of the Baron remarkably well. When the same choreographer also revived for the Company his Spanish ballet, *Capriccio Espagnol*, in the spring of 1951, Hewitt danced the role of the principal Majo with great spirit and ease.

During International Ballet's six-weeks engagement in the Royal Festival Hall, as part of the Festival of Britain Programme in August and September 1951, Ernest Hewitt performed as leading male dancer in most of the ballets presented. He also danced as principal during the Company's visit to Barcelona in 1953, and made a three-dimensional film there, based on *Swan Lake*, Act II, with Mona Inglesby.

Rosella Hightower

ALTHOUGH ROSELLA HIGHTOWER IS A HIGH-RANKING AMERICAN ballerina with a technique as amazing as that of any Russian-trained dancer of the old Imperial Maryinsky days, she is surprisingly modest in her demeanour. There is nothing showy about her appearance when she is not dancing —but set her in motion upon her *pointes*, and what a magical change is there! Then she is like some enchanted being from Fairyland, the very embodiment of perfect grace in movement. She is truly a dazzling and radiant dancer—at least so far as her technique is concerned. She is not yet quite the perfect dramatic mime, and her style-atmosphere leaves at times a slight something to be desired. Nevertheless, despite her remarkable virtuosity, she has none of the scintillating hardness to be observed in certain other ballerinas from the Western World; and her sensitivity, deep feeling, and dramatic understanding are rapidly developing and will eventually enrich her personality as the truly thrilling classical dancer she already is.

Rosella Hightower was born at Ardmore, Oklahoma, in Missouri; and she is of Indian extraction. She passed most of her early life in Kansas City, where she studied dancing from Dorothy Perkins, a former pupil of the great Cecchetti. She was, consequently, thoroughly well grounded in the Russian system of ballet work; and she studied the Dalcroze system of Eurythmics, together with *demi-caractère* work, and musical comedy— so her training was of a generous all-round character. A final year of additional study in New York then paved the way for her early professional début.

She started her career in 1938 with the Ballets Russe de Monte Carlo, with Leonide Massine as chief choreographer and *maître de ballet*. Here she had the great advantage of working with and watching the performances of such world-renowned ballerinas as Alexandra Danilova, Alicia Markova, Mia Slavenska, Tamara Toumanova, Nathalie Krassovska, etc. Although, to begin with, she was but a very quiet and unimportant member of the *corps de ballet*, her work was good, and she was presently given small solo parts to dance. These gradually extended to more important roles; and when she left the Company at the end of four years, it was as an established soloist.

She then joined Ballet Theatre in New York; and with this Company she worked under the famous choreographers, Michael Fokine, Antony Tudor, Anton Dolin, Agnes de Mille, Jerome Robbins. Here, too, it was not long before she changed her status from soloist to that of an established ballerina of high technical ability. Her first chance came when Markova, the leading ballerina, became ill and had to spend some time in hospital; and Rosella Hightower was invited to dance *Giselle* during her absence. Other members of the Company at that time—or occasional guest artists—were Irina Baronova, Argentinita, Nora Kaye, Alicia Alonso and Nana Gollner; and again the young newcomer was fortunate in seeing great artists at work during her three years' sojourn among them. She then left to undertake a year of concert work with Leonide Massine and André Églevsky, and danced as a guest artist with the De Basil Company. When this engagement ended, she came to Europe at the end of the war and joined the Marquis de Cuevas' Grand Ballet de Monte Carlo, with which Company she has since remained as a leading ballerina.

Included in the repertoire of this charming ballerina are the leading roles in the classics: *Giselle*, *Lac des Cygnes*, *Casse*

Noisette, The Black Swan; Fokine's *Les Sylphides*; and modern ballets such as *Constantia, Sebastian, The Enchanted Mill, Brahms Variations*, etc.; *demi-caractère* roles such as those in *Le Beau Danube, Les Femmes de Bonne Humeur, Mam'zelle Angot, Capriccio Espagnol, Gaieté Parisienne*, etc.

Rosella Hightower has already made her début as a choreographer. Her first ballet was on the subject of *Henry VIII* (with music by Rossini, *décor* and costumes by Russell Hartley), presented at the Metropolitan Theatre, New York, October 1949, with Markova and Dolin dancing the principal roles as the King and Anne Boleyn; but it was somewhat crude and did not meet with much success. Her second ballet, *Pleasuredrome* (book by Peter Williams, music by John Lanchberry and *décor* by Leonard Rosoman), was produced at the Harrow Coliseum by the Metropolitan Ballet Company, October 20th, 1949. It deals with the adventures and disenchantment of a country youth in a London "fun fair", complete with pin-tables, "canned" music, and undesirable frequenters. The latter are almost larger than "life-size" in their realism and viciousness, but very cleverly treated; while the music mainly consists of the popular song ultra-modern dance rhythms. The ballet did not have much general appeal on this first presentation, despite Michel de Lutry's fine portrayal of the innocent country youth who comes to a rude awakening within these, to him, unusual and alarming surroundings, and Celia Franca's equally clever rendering of the kindly street-girl who befriends him. The ballet is, undoubtedly, a remarkable and sincere work. Her third ballet was produced by the Marquis de Cuevas' Grand Ballet de Monte Carlo at the Théâtre des Champs-Élysées in Paris in October 1950. It deals with the subject of *Salomé*, to Richard Strauss's music, and has *décor* and costumes by Celia Hubbard. Miss Hightower herself took the difficult role of the passionate Salomé and performed the famous Dance of the Seven Veils with great intensity and abandon, revealing her increasing dramatic sense. Her future choreographic work is awaited with much interest.

Among Rosella Hightower's most outstanding performances as a ballerina is her Black Swan *pas de deux* (*Lac des Cygnes*, Act 3) in which she has danced with André Églevsky and in which she gives an astounding fireworks display of easily turned *fouettés* at top-speed, her *pointes* being remarkably strong. Her Street-Dancer in *Le Beau Danube* also shows off her dazzling technique. It is still in the realms of her really thrilling virtuosity that this highly gifted young dancer dazzles her audience; but she is constantly adding to her powers of characterization and to her understanding of the psychological side of a role that is so necessary for true greatness in the ballerina's art. Meanwhile, her almost incredible technique won for her in 1949 the *Grand Prix* of *Le Cercle de Journalistes Critiques de la Danse* in Paris for the best technical performance of the year.

In 1952, Rosella Hightower danced the title-role in Ricarda's *Inez de Castro*, and was principal also in Milloss' *Coup de Feu*. That same year, her own new ballet, *Scaramouche* (Sibelius—Wakhevitch) was produced by the Company. In 1953 she danced La Grande Morphide in Taras' *Piege de Lumiere* and was brilliant in Bartholin's *L'Aigrette*.

Andrée Howard

⊚⊚⊚

ALTHOUGH AN EXCELLENT ALL-ROUND DANCER, ANDRÉE HOWARD has made her name more particularly as a choreographer; and by many she is now regarded as the leading British woman ballet creator of the present day—indeed, Nadia Benois has described her as "one of the most original and highly sensitive choreographers of our time". She is also a good artist-designer and has done the *décor* and costumes for a number of her own ballets. She was born in 1910; and she has worked with Madame Rambert and her Company practically throughout the whole of her dancing and choreographic career.

Andrée Howard first began to study ballet-dancing with Madame Rambert in 1924; and three years later, at the age of seventeen, she made her début with the Company, creating the roles of Entrée de Cupidon in *Dances from Les Petits Riens*, the Girl Lover in *Lady of Shalott*, Lampito in *Lysistrata*, Tordion in *Capriol Suite*, Ariel in *Rape of the Lock*, an Ugly Sister in

Cinderella, Maiden in *Death and the Maiden,* etc. Later, she also danced principal roles in several of her own ballets; also Goulue in *Bar aux Folies-Bergère,* Papillon in *Le Carnaval,* Vamp-de-Luxe in *Le Boxing,* Young Girl in *Le Spectre de la Rose,* the Mazurka in *Les Sylphides,* and danced in *The Tartans, Façade, Croquis de Mercure* and *Valentine's Eve,* etc.

Her first two ballets for the Ballet Rambert she created in partnership with Susan Salaman. The first of these was *Our Lady's Juggler,* in 1933, with music by Respighi and *décor* and costumes by the two choreographers themselves; the next was *The Mermaid* (music by Ravel, *décor* and costumes by herself). Her first unaided ballet, produced in 1934, was *Alcina Suite,* with music by Handel and her own *décor* and costumes. This proved a successful work; as did her next two ballets, produced the following year, *Cinderella* (music by Weber, *décor* by herself) and *The Rape of the Lock* (music by Haydn, *décor* by herself). In 1936, she composed *La Muse s'Amuse* (music by de Severac, and her own *décor* and costumes); and in 1937 came *Death and the Maiden* (music by Schubert, and again her own *décor* and costumes). This latter was a clever and compact little work, which has remained almost continuously in the Company's repertoire. In 1938, she created *Croquis de Mercure* (music by Satie, *décor* and costumes to her own designs). In all these ballets, she herself danced the leading parts.

Then, in 1939, came her quite brilliant *Lady Into Fox* (adapted from David Garnett's novel of the same name, with music by Honegger and *décor* and costumes by Nadia Benois); and this ballet immediately placed her among the front-ranking British choreographers and caused not only an immense sensation in the ballet world but likewise established Sally Gilmour, the sensitively clever young creator of Mrs. Tebrick, the delightful Fox Lady herself, as the leading girl character-dancer of the day.

The following year, Andrée Howard created her charming period ballet of a somewhat psychological kind, *Fête Étrange* (music by Fauré, *décor* and costumes by Sophie Fedorovich), which met with considerable success, though entirely different from her brilliant *Lady Into Fox.* This ballet was first produced for the London Ballet, but afterwards came into the regular repertoire of the Ballet Rambert. In 1944 she composed a delightful ballet, *Carnival of Animals*, to the Saint-Saens music of the same title and with *décor* and costumes by herself. Then, in 1944, she created another interesting and most dramatic ballet, *The Fugitive* (music by Salzédo, *décor* and costumes by Dorothy Stevenson), which again gave Sally Gilmour one of her most effective roles as a young girl who falls in love with a fugitive from justice and sees him die at her feet.

Andrée Howard has also created ballets for other Companies. In 1943, she did the choreography of *Twelfth Night* for International Ballet (music by Grieg, *décor* and costumes by Doris Zinkeisen); and this elaborate work was most successful and has remained in that Company's repertoire. For the Sadler's Wells Ballet she created *Le Festin de l'Araignée* (music by Roussel, *décor* by Michael Ayrton), with its most interesting insect characters; and she was also choreographer of *Elegy* and *Pygmalion* for the Fortune Ballet, and of *The Glass Slipper* at the St. James's Theatre (this with the Rambert Company as the ballet performers). For the Sadler's Wells Theatre Ballet in 1946, she created the charming light ballet *Assembly Ball* (music to Bizet's Symphony, *décor* and costumes by herself), and the dramatic *Mardi Gras* (music by Salzédo, *décor* Hugh Stevenson).

In 1947, this fine choreographer was responsible for another brilliant success of the Rambert Company by creating for them *The Sailor's Return* (music by Arthur Oldham, *décor* by herself), in which Sally Gilmour had yet another wonderful character part, that of the negro girl, Tulip, who becomes the bride of a returning sailor. This gave her opportunities not only for moving and pathetic miming, but also for some lovely solo dances. The subject of this remarkable ballet was adapted from another novel by David Garnett, and it provides excellent balletic material.

In 1948, she created a new ballet, *Selina*, for the Sadler's Wells Theatre Ballet, its subject dealing with the Romantic Period. It was a beautiful and interesting ballet, with a perfect period setting and *décor* by Peter Williams, and for music it had a skilful arrangement of airs from Rossini. It was produced on November 16th, and was particularly well suited to the youthful Company who performed it. The gifted choreographer herself took the role of the Witch in this ballet.

In July 1948, the Metropolitan Company produced Andrée

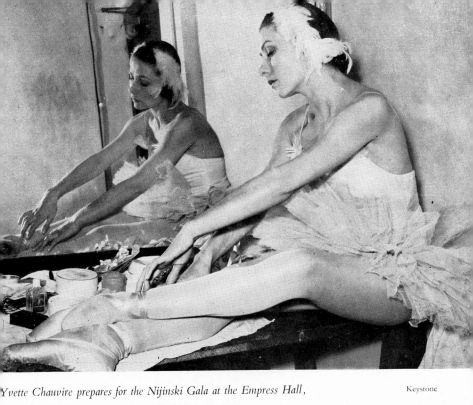

Yvette Chauviré prepares for the Nijinski Gala at the Empress Hall,

while in the wings, waiting for rehearsal, are

Paula Hinton, Natalie Krassovska, Tamara Toumanova and Marjorie Tallchief.

Mona Inglesby and Leslie French in " Everyman ".

Mandinian

Three year old Susan North admires her aunt—Alicia Markova—
dancing with Anton Dolin.

Keystone

Howard's *The Pilgrim's Progress* as a Masque-Ballet at Covent Garden for a fortnight. It had music by Bach, Gluck and Handel, arranged by Sir Malcolm Sargent, *décor* and costumes by Joseph Carl.

Andrée Howard's work has been seen also in films and in television. She created a special ballet for the documentary film, *Steps of the Ballet,* and did other important work in connection with this educational film, which was presented in 1949. On February 6th, 1950, her two ballets, *The Fugitive* and *Death and the Maiden,* were presented very successfully in a television programme with the Rambert Ballet Company.

When the Ballet Rambert toured Australia in 1948-49, Andrée Howard's ballets, *Lady Into Fox* and *The Sailor's Return,* were unanimously praised as among the strongest and most richly coloured works in the repertory. *Death and the Maiden, The Fugitive* and *The Mermaid* also received excellent notices.

In 1951, Andrée Howard was specially commissioned by Festival Gardens Ltd., in connection with the Festival of Britain, to choreograph a delightful ballet adapted from Kathleen Hale's series of children's books about Orlando, the Marmalade Cat. Entitled *Orlando's Silver Wedding,* this charming ballet was performed daily throughout the Festival of Britain Season in the Open-Air Amphitheatre at Battersea Park. The music was specially composed by Arthur Benjamin; and the *décor* was by Kathleen Hale herself. The principal dancers were Harold Turner as Orlando, and Sally Gilmour as his wife, Grace; and the whole performance was a joy to adults and children alike.

Also in 1951, Andrée Howard was commissioned to create a special ballet and some *divertissement* dances for the film *The Secret People,* made by Ealing Studios.

On March 18th, 1952, Andrée Howard's *A Mirror for Witches* (ApIvor—Adams) was produced at Covent Garden; and on April 9th, 1953, again at Covent Garden, came her colourful *Veneziana* (Donizetti—Fedorovich).

This most versatile choreographer is always busy with new projects; and ballet-goers look forward eagerly to further delightful creations from her in the future. With her particular flair for animal characters, how one hopes that, some day, she may tackle *Alice in Wonderland* as a ballet![1]

[1] The subject of *Alice in Wonderland* has now been dealt with in 1953 by Michael Charnley for Festival Ballet.

Mona Inglesby

ⓈⓈⓈ

MONA INGLESBY IS NOT ONLY THE BRILLIANT PRINCIPAL ballerina of International Ballet, but is also the enterprising Founder and Director of that most successful Company, in addition to being one of its original choreographers. She thus reveals a remarkable versatility, combining high artistic and creative gifts with very considerable organizing and directive ability.

She is a Londoner and was born in 1918. At a very early age —she first appeared as a child dancer on the stage of the Scala Theatre when only five years old—she decided to make dancing her life's career; and with this end in view, she made every effort to secure for herself the best training available.

Her first real ballet training was received as a pupil at Madame Rambert's Ballet School, where she studied from the age of twelve to seventeen; and later on she studied with Margaret Craske—the latter being a former pupil of the famous dancer and ballet-master, Enrico Cecchetti, and a one-time member of the Diaghileff Company. She continued her training with Nicholas Legat and Madame Egorova; and then she went to Paris to study with Madame Kschesinskaya. During more recent years, too, she has continued to study untiringly and to perfect further her technique with Judith Espinosa and with Nicolai Sergueeff, when the two latter celebrated trainers and producers became the inspiring directors of her own International Ballet School. Consequently, her training has been excellent—and continues to be so, since the true artist never ceases to learn.

From the beginning, Mona Inglesby showed signs of definite technical skill; and at the early age of fourteen she began to dance good preliminary roles, appearing in 1932 in Frederick Ashton's ballet *Foyer de Danse* under the auspices of Madame Rambert's Ballet Club—a valuable enterprise which proved to be the "jumping-off" platform for many of our present-day dancers and choreographers. From here she joined the Rambert Company, where she had further opportunities for trying out her always undoubted capabilities for dancing worth-while parts. These included Papillon in *Le Carnaval* at the Duke of York's Theatre at the surprisingly early age of fifteen, the Green Lady in *Our Lady's Juggler* (1933), the Spanish Bride in *The Mermaid* (1934), and many others. Later on, she understudied Markova in Ninette de Valois' *Bar aux Folies-Bergère*.

Here, also, she first became interested in developing her latent desire to engage in the creative work of choreography. Among her Rambert colleagues were the then youthful, but soon afterwards famous, choreographer-dancers, Frederick Ashton, Andrée Howard, Antony Tudor, Ninette de Valois, Walter Gore and others, whose original ballet creations then being produced served to inspire and to encourage her own ambitions in that direction. She soon began to devise ballets herself; and in 1939, a wonderful chance came her way. An All-Star Charity Matinée was to take place at the Cambridge Theatre, and Mona Inglesby was invited by Adeline Bourne to create a new short ballet for this function and to dance in it herself. Very joyfully, the young dancer accepted, and chose *Endymion* as her subject (with music by Moskowski, *décor* and costumes by Sophie Fedorovich). The result was most successful; and this first choreographic production of hers, together with her own charming freshness and dancing, brought her much favourable comment and encouragement. She felt herself to be in good company since, at this particular matinée, Lydia Kyasht's *Ballet de la Jeunesse Anglaise* and Robert Helpmann's first ballet *divertissement, La Valse*, were also in the programme.

In 1939, too, came Mona Inglesby's first appearance as a dancer upon the boards of Covent Garden Opera House, where she danced with Dandré's Russian Ballet, with Fokine as *maître de ballet* and among such famous principal dancers as Riabouchinska, Baronova, Griegorieva, Lichine, Algeranoff and Paul Petroff.

Then came the Second World War, and Mona Inglesby joined the Civil Defence Service as a motor ambulance driver in London. Even during those terrible war years, however, she managed to keep up her training; and she gathered around her a group of equally enthusiastic young dancers who met together in her private studio during their few precious hours of leisure, for practice—even optimistically rehearsing for possible productions. Her second ballet, *Amoras* (music by Elgar, *décor* and costumes by William Chappell), was created and actually produced during this dangerous period. Again, the production was at an All-Star Special Performance at the Cambridge Theatre, January 4th, 1940, where, at the same time, her *Endymion* was again given.

All this time, another and most ambitious plan—amazing, indeed, for a war-time effort!—had been maturing in the fertile brain of Mona Inglesby in between her arduous periods of ambulance driving, and was quickly coming to fruition. This was nothing less than the personal formation of an entirely new ballet company—consisting mainly of the dancing enthusiasts who had kept up their training and had rehearsed together under the leadership of this intrepid and ever-optimistic young ballet-lover.

Consequently, in 1941, after a hectic, but thorough, initial period of untiring and most exacting rehearsals and anxious business and commercial preparations—she had the good fortune to have well-to-do and sympathetic parents willing to lend their valuable aid—International Ballet actually came into being and was cheerfully and confidently sent forth upon its first tour with the utmost optimism by all concerned. It opened at the Alhambra, Glasgow, on May 19th that year, the Company consisting of twenty-one dancers, having a repertoire of eight ballets and an orchestra of fifteen players; with Idzikovsky as ballet-master and Mona Inglesby, Harold Turner, and Nina Tarakanova as principal dancers. This brave venture met with a great reception; and the following week a new and most amusing ballet, *Planetomania* (music, Norman Delmuth, *décor* and costumes, Doris Zinkeisen), with choreography by the resourceful young founder, was produced at Birmingham on March 28th. In 1942, at Liverpool, Andrée Howard's *Twelfth Night* (music Grieg, *décor* Doris Zinkeisen) was produced on May 18th.

After a successful year's tour, the new Company came next to His Majesty's Theatre, London, in 1942, where *Aurora's Wedding*, *Giselle*, and other ballets were produced; and then, in 1943, to the Lyric Theatre, where the old Morality Play, *Everyman*, was produced in Masque-Ballet form, with choreography by Mona Inglesby (music Richard Strauss, *décor* and costumes William Chappell and the late Rex Whistler). In 1945 they were at the Piccadilly and His Majesty's Theatres before going again on tour; and everywhere the new Company met with a most encouraging reception. In 1946, they were at the Coliseum for a long season; and in 1947, they were at the Adelphi. By this time, the full-length classics, *Coppélia*, *Giselle*, *Swan Lake* and *The Sleeping Beauty* had been produced, all in their entirety; and the old English masque, *The Masque of Comus* (music Handel, *décor* and costumes Doris Zinkeisen), with choreography by Mona Inglesby, had been produced at the Coliseum on September 3rd, 1946.

In producing the classical ballets in their entirety, Mona Inglesby was well guided by Nicolai Sergueeff, formerly *régisseur* and *maître de ballet* at the Imperial Maryinsky Theatre, St. Petersburg; and his splendid productions have always been in exact accordance with the original productions there. Her now large orchestra was under the main direction of James Walker, with Anthony Baines as associate conductor; as guest conductors she has had Ernest Irving, Wynn Reeves, George Weldon and Gilbert Vinter. Among those who have danced with the Company as principals, or as guest artists, have been, in addition to Mona Inglesby as resident ballerina, Nina Tarakanova, Nina Nikitina, Nana Gollner, Algeranoff, Harold Turner, Paul Petroff, Michel de Lutry, Jack Spurgeon, Yurek Shablevsky, Claudie Algeranova, Domini Callaghan, Hélène Armfelt, Sandra Vane, Errol Addison, Denys Palmer, Ernest Hewitt.

On February 24th, 1948, the Company produced a new ballet, *Sea Legend*, by the Australian choreographer and dancer, Dorothy Stevenson (music by Esther Rofe, *décor* John Bainbridge), which met with considerable success and has proved one of their most interesting productions—mainly because of the very original choreography for the *corps de ballet*, whose movements give the impression of the rise and fall of ocean waves. On December 1st, 1949, another new ballet was presented at the New Theatre, Oxford, *Visions* (choreography and *décor* by Julian Algo, to music by Moussorgsky). The ballet had won the chief award at the International Archives of Paris at Stockholm in 1945; and, though a somewhat complicated work, is considered to be a valuable addition to the repertoire.

International Ballet now has its own flourishing School of Ballet, under the immediate direction of Mona Inglesby herself,

Nicolai Sergueeff, Madame Sergueeff[1] and Madame Lea Espinosa. Madame Judith Espinosa, until her death in 1949, was also in charge of certain sections; and Algeranoff conducts the character-dancing classes. Lectures are given to schools in the various towns visited by the Company.

Through lack of a permanent home-theatre and the difficulties of securing a West-End London Theatre for more than a few weeks at a time, Mona Inglesby has been compelled to take her Company on provincial tours for the greater part of its successful existence. Thus, willy-nilly, she has become a real pioneer and has introduced her well-trained Ballet into most of the great cities and many of the smaller towns of Great Britain. She is doing an excellent educational artistic work and the frequent visits of International Ballet are now looked forward to eagerly in every town in which they appear. Recently, too, the London theatre shortage is being eased; for during the past two or three years, International Ballet has been able to secure accommodation in several of the larger cinemas, such as the Gaumont State Cinema, Kilburn, and others, for seasons of varying lengths. Thus, ballet is being introduced to many different audiences who have never seen it before, but with whom it is now immensely popular. In 1949, too, International Ballet accepted an invitation to visit the various Butlin's Holiday Camps; and here again new and enthusiastic audiences have greeted them.

Yet another welcome invitation came in January 1950, when Mona Inglesby and her Company were asked to give a two-weeks' season of Ballet in the great Hallenstadion Arena at Zurich; and this Swiss engagement proved to be an amazingly successful one. Vast crowds filled the arena every day; and the enthusiasm and delight of these huge audiences were gratifying in the extreme. What was more, despite the heavy expenditure involved—transport of the Company alone accounted for over £2,000, with additional maintenance costs, plus £4,500 for electrical equipment (though the Directors of the Arena bought £2,500 of this when the Company left)—they more than covered their expenses by a considerable amount.

Some critics are inclined to wonder whether Mona Inglesby

---

[1] These two famous teachers have recently died. Madame Maria Zybina has since become a member of the Staff.

may be undertaking too much work as Director of an important Ballet Company, its occasional choreographer, and its leading dancer. The fact remains, however, that this charming and skilful artist, despite her triple undertakings—she is, of course, able to devolve much of the business side of her work on to other shoulders—is still improving year by year, adding to her technical attainments in classical roles, developing her imaginative gifts of interpretation, and ever reaching out towards that seemingly effortless yet scintillating finish in performance which is always the ultimate goal of the true ballerina. She is full of energy; and despite the feather-weight lightness of her quite remarkable elevation, her often sensational speed, and the ethereal quality of her portrayal of such sensitive, fey characters as Odette and Giselle, for example, she also gives the impression of a latent strength. She can be gay as Swanilda or Princess Aurora, sad as Odette, humorous as the maid in her own *Planetomania*, almost sinister as Odile in *Swan Lake* or as Cotytto in *Comus*—her dancing and characterization of the latter role is a quite startling achievement—dignified and full of sweet sympathy as Good Deeds in *Everyman*; all these examples serve to reveal her surprising versatility. In her leisure moments, she is quiet and restful; and she has a great natural charm. She is extremely musical, and was an excellent pianist in her earlier girlhood—indeed, at one time, she engaged in a certain amount of concert work. She was also very fond of riding and, as a child, competed at the Olympia Horse Show in the children's classes. This early pastime probably accounts for her present remarkable balancing powers.

During the Company's London season at the Coliseum in May 1950, a revival of Massine's popular ballet *Gaieté Parisienne* was given, rehearsed by the famous choreographer himself; and in this brilliant performance Mona Inglesby gave a very excellent interpretation of the charming part of the Glove-Seller. Another Massine ballet, *Capriccio Espagnol* (music by Rimsky-Korsakov, *décor* and costumes after Mariano Andreu), was also revived for the Company in 1951, and received its first presentation by them on April 25th at the Coventry Hippodrome. In this, Mona Inglesby was excellent as the gipsy-woman and scored a new triumph.

During the Festival of Britain in 1951, International Ballet undertook a six-weeks' season at the Royal Festival Hall, presenting a repertoire of ten ballets in a manner not previously seen in this country. In the absence of normal stage facilities, a floor 70 feet wide and 34 feet deep was fitted over the orchestra area, and a period setting was devised by Dennis Wreford. Conventional *décor* was replaced by settings incorporating a special system of light-*décor*. The classical ballets *Giselle*, *The Sleeping Princess* and *Lac des Cygnes*, were conducted by George Weldon. A new ballet by Algeranoff, *For Love or Money* (music by Gilbert Vinter, *décor* by Dennis Wreford, and costumes by John Bainbridge), received its London *première* in the Royal Festival Hall on July 31st, with the composer as guest conductor.

In 1953, International Ballet gave a successful season in Barcelona, afterwards making a three-dimensional film based on *Swan Lake*, Act II, with Mona Inglesby and Ernest Hewitt as principals. This was the first time a British Ballet organization had ever visited Spain.

Mona Inglesby was married in 1946 to Mr. E. G. Derrington, then a Major serving in the army. Her husband now acts as Public Relations Officer for the Company.

Renée Jeanmaire

WHEN THIS CHARMINGLY PRETTY YOUNG FRENCH DANCER, with her big dark eyes—now mischievous, now serious, tragic or pathetic—and her dainty figure, so *chic* and stylishly Parisian, suddenly, in 1949, sprang into top ballet news overnight with her amazing performance as the passion-torn, unscrupulous, but ever fascinating Carmen, even her staunchest admirers—and she already had many—could scarcely credit so surprising a fact. That she was a beautiful dancer of excellent technique they were well aware; that she was a good and versatile mime who had already depicted quite a number of interesting characters, they were likewise aware; but that she could portray the sensual, greedy, siren-esque soul of Merimée's sordid heroine in such a breath-taking dramatic dance form without a single hesitant flaw or break in the remorseless continuity of its presentation, was an unexpected revelation indeed. Yet, there it was; and they were just left gasping, like every other spectator since.

What a triumph for this very youthful dancer, still in her early twenties; but a triumph well deserved by one who has worked hard and constantly all her young life to perfect herself in her beloved art. It is a known fact that she never misses her daily practice and never arrives late at the theatre; nor does she ever neglect the most trivial thing likely to bring improvement to a dance or even to its smallest accessory. She is one of those happy artists who takes a real joy in her work.

Born in Paris, a true Parisienne from head to dainty foot, Renée Jeanmaire had no dancing ancestors; yet, having seen performances of ballet at the Opéra, she developed a passion for dancing at a very early age and soon discovered that she had a natural aptitude for this lovely art, which she determined to adopt as her life's career. She began her training at the Opéra at the age of nine years, among her later teachers being Serge Lifar. Making excellent progress, and being still full of enthusiasm on the completion of her main training, she was disappointed on finding but little prospect of advancement from the *corps de ballet* for several years to come.

Boldly leaving the Opéra, therefore, she gave some recitals with a dancing partner, and received several helpful engagements from time to time. She danced leading roles in several of the earlier ballets created jointly by Roland Petit and Boris Kochno at Le Théâtre Sarah Bernhardt in 1945; and in 1946, she joined the New Ballet de Monte Carlo and went on tour with that Company, dancing in *Aubade* and in *La Fille Mal Gardée*; and she also danced in the Blue-Bird *pas de deux* and in other *pas de deux* with Boris Trailine. She made a popular success in *Aubade*; and she was now established as a dancer of considerable talent and charm.

She next joined Colonel de Basil's Original Ballet Russe; and with this Company she danced many attractive roles, among them being: The Siren in Lichine's *The Prodigal Son*; one of the girl *fouetté* competitors in the same choreographer's delightful *Graduation Ball*—a part which suited her excellently well, since she was always a wonderful *pirouette* and *fouetté* executant. She also danced in Kniasev's *Piccole* and in *Les Sylphides*, etc.

Later on, after dancing for a short time with *Les Étoiles de la Danse* in London, she became a leading dancer in Roland Petit's Les Ballets de Paris in 1949; and here she seems to have found her real niche, since this brilliant young choreographer's modern type of ballet treatment undoubtedly suits her excellently.

Already, among other works, she has appeared in Kniasev's *Études Symphoniques*, Massine's *Le Beau Danube* (the Street Dancer), Petit's *L'Oeuf à la Coque*; and, in 1949, the marvellous *Carmen*, which was the ballet sensation of that year all over Europe, and has since enjoyed immense popularity in the United States and elsewhere.

In *L'Oeuf à la Coque*, Renée Jeanmaire had an amusing role as one of three strange feathered glamour-girls who issue forth from a cauldron in which a magic egg has been placed to boil; and by her lithe, snaky undulatory actions in this part, she gives a cleverly exaggerated caricature of the exotic type of revue artiste. Her dances as this hybrid, bird-like creature are likewise very clever, and also extremely strenuous, since she is seized by her various partners and swung from one to another at a dizzy speed. Nobody seeing her in such a light-hearted frolicsome absurdity as this could ever imagine her as the dramatic, ultra-seductive and sex-ridden Carmen she also presents with such sophisticated abandon and inimitable skill. *Carmen*, by the way, had its *première* at the Prince's Theatre, London, on February 21st, 1949, during the first season there of Roland Petit's Ballets de Paris; and it certainly created an immense furore, owing—in addition to the remarkable performance of Jeanmaire in the title-role—to the daring and even violent episodes devised by its choreographer, Roland Petit, who danced the passionate and tragic part of Don José. The music, of course, is from Bizet's opera, the *décor* and costumes are by Clavé, and the book is very freely adapted from Merimée's novel.

Jeanmaire also had the leading role in *Le Rêve de Léonor* (choreography by Frederick Ashton, music by Benjamin Britten and *décor* and costumes by Léonor Fini), produced by Petit during his Company's second season at the Prince's Theatre, London, on April 25th, 1949; but though she danced a very fantastic part with her now established brilliance, the ballet did not turn out to be the success hoped for.

In 1950, Roland Petit created for her a special ballet, *La*

Croqueuse de Diamantes (music by Jean-Michel Damase, *décor* and costumes by Wakhevitch). In this fantastic, but fine and amusing ballet, magnificently presented, Jeanmaire had again a wonderful part as the Woman who bites Diamonds, a mysterious thief who, however, reforms in the end; and her performance was really splendid, so that she scored another triumph.

In the late spring of 1951, Roland Petit's Ballets de Paris went to Hollywood to make a special film for Howard Hughes, and Renée Jeanmaire went with them. She was brilliant in the film *Hans Christian Andersen*, choreographed by Roland Petit and released in 1953.

That Renée Jeanmaire has still further triumphs in store there can be no doubt. Young though she still is, she is a surprisingly matured actress for her short years; and her dancing—though her *forte* is *demi-caractère* rather than classical—is remarkably fine and instinct with artistry. She is charming in appearance, with expressive and vivacious features and a flowing poetic grace of movement; and her versatility is surprising. She revels in contrasts, and is full of abounding energy and ready to tackle any new role that may come her way with the consummate skill that is already hers.

Kurt Jooss

THE KURT JOOSS SCHOOL OF BALLET, WITH ITS REVOLUTIONARY theories, is now regarded with the tolerance and respect it deserves by all interested in the development of modern dancing. When it first became known outside Germany in the nineteen-thirties, however, it created not only a great sensation, but an equally great opposition.

The then surprising facts that the Jooss dancers were not permitted to wear block-shoes or the classical *tutu*, to dance on the tips of their toes, to indulge in sustained *pirouettes* or *fouettés*, *entrechats*, or double or more air-turns, and that star solo performances were discouraged, aroused strong protests and disapproval from most classically and traditionally trained ballet dancers and their admiring supporters; and, at first, wild uproars and outbursts of booing greeted early performances by the New School group. Gradually, however, this undignified opposition gave way to tolerance and consideration of the group's unusual possibilities; and to-day it is firmly established as an interesting Ballet System capable of holding its own and worthy of comparison with the long-accepted traditional systems of France, Italy and Russia.

Kurt Jooss was born in Wasseralfingen, Germany, in 1901. His family was connected with land and farming interests; but though the young Kurt spent his early life in a rural atmosphere, it soon became evident that his main capabilities lay in matters of Art, and of music and dancing in particular. He became a student in the Musical Academy at Würtemberg, and also at the Stuttgart College of Drama, where his special gifts found scope. It was here that he met with Rudolf von Laban, the inventor of Plastic Rhythm and Naturalistic Dance Movements, and soon became one of the latter's most enthusiastic and devoted pupils.

Laban quickly recognized the true disciple in the young Jooss, who early came to share his teacher's ideals and to absorb much of his philosophy. Kurt Jooss, however, went further still and had his own original ideas which he desired to develop in addition; for he differed from Laban inasmuch as the latter believed in an all-out Naturalism, whereas his pupil did not disdain to adopt also certain points from the traditional system which he considered helpful to incorporate with his own.

When, presently, he left Laban, Jooss, after working for a time on his father's farm at Wasseralfingen, accepted an engagement as Director of Theatrical Movement at the Münster Theatre, where he soon gathered around himself a small body of similar enthusiasts. Among the latter were F. A. Cohen (composer), Sigurd Leeder (dancer and teacher), Hein Heckroth (artist and designer), and a charming young woman dancer, Aino Siimola, who later on became his wife and the principal female dancer in his own eventual Ballet Company. Here, also, his first youthful ballet, *A Persian Ballet*, was performed in July 1924 at the International Festival of Modern Music at Donaueschingen. This was given by his own newly formed group of dancers, now known as the *Neue Tanzbuhne*, with music by Egon Welleszz, Hein Heckroth as designer and Aino

Siimola as leading dancer; and from thenceforward his career as a choreographer and dancer was firmly established.

A little later on, with Sigurd Leeder, he took a course of classical dance training, for comparison with his own ever-developing original ballet ideals; and he also worked under various teachers in Paris and Vienna for similar experimental purposes. He also gave exhibitions of his new Dance Form at concerts from time to time.

In 1927, he became Director of the Dancing Section of the Essen Dramatic Academy where, later on, he became Ballet Master, with Sigurd Leeder working under him as assistant teacher, and with Aino Siimola as leading dancer. Here he had every opportunity for developing and perfecting his own original system of ballet training and presentation, plus the gathering together of an enthusiastic band of young dancers, all eager to help in the carrying out of his ideals and forming the nucleus of the coming Ballets Jooss. He also produced operas at Essen.

Then came his first brilliant success. In 1932, he won the first prize of 25,000 francs in the Choreographic Competition organized by Les Archives Internationale de la Danse at Paris, with his truly dynamic and now famous ballet, *The Green Table* (music F. A. Cohen, *décor* Hein Heckroth), which immediately placed him in the forefront of originally-minded modern chore-ographers. This ballet created a great sensation when first presented by the Jooss Company at the Théâtre des Champs-Élysées, not only because of its highly topical subject, but also because of its presentation of an entirely new ballet form, which disregarded the formulae of the traditional dance. Many people see in *The Green Table* a satire on the failure of the League of Nations to establish and sustain peace, though Jooss himself regards it simply as an exposition in dance movement of the evils of war in general and of the uselessness of Peace Confer-ences—composed of politically biassed members—in particular. It aroused much controversy and opposition, not only be-cause of its departure from the accepted classical dance tradition, but because of its subject. Gradually, however, even opposing audiences came to recognize that a starkly realistic modern problem was being shown to them in an undoubtedly well-constructed dramatic style for the first time in the history of ballet; consequently, hostile demonstrations ceased and immense crowds flocked to see it. Kurt Jooss's reputation as an original choreographer and presenter of an entirely new modern system of ballet was now fully recognized; and wherever taken, *The Green Table* has always been received with the greatest interest.

Other vivid and original ballets that followed established more firmly still this successful exponent of the Central European Dance Movement—or, perhaps, one should more correctly say, part-exponent, since, as stated above, Kurt Jooss had blended portions only of the latter with his own even more original ideas. Among the best known of his ballets are: *The Big City* (music A. Tansman, *décor* and costumes Hein Heckroth, produced Cologne 1932), *The Prodigal Son* (music F. A. Cohen, *décor* Hein Heckroth, costumes Dmitri Bouchène), produced Amsterdam 1933), *The Seven Heroes* (music F. A. Cohen, *décor* and costumes Hein Heckroth, produced Holland 1933); *Ballade* (music John Colman, *décor* and costumes Hein Heckroth, produced Manchester 1935), *Johann Strauss To-night* (music Strauss arranged F. A. Cohen, *décor* and costumes George Kirsta, produced London 1935), *The Mirror* (music F. A. Cohen, *décor* and costumes Hein Heckroth, produced Manchester 1938), *A Spring Tale* (music F. A. Cohen, *décor* and costumes Hein Heckroth, produced Oxford 1939), *Chronica* (music Berthold Goldschmidt, *décor* and costumes Dmitri Bouchène, produced Cambridge, 1939), *Company at the Manor* (music Beethoven arr. J. Cook, *décor* and costumes Doris Zinkeisen, produced Cambridge, 1943), *Pandora* (music Gerhard, *décor* and costumes Heckroth, produced Cambridge, 1944), etc. Jooss Company ballets by other choreographers are: *Le Bosquet* (music Rameau, *décor* and costumes Doris Zinkeisen, choreographer Hans Zullig, produced Cambridge, 1945) and *Sailors' Fancy* (music Martin Penny, *décor* and costumes Hein Heckroth, choreographer Sigurd Leeder, produced Cambridge, 1943).

Having found it necessary to leave Germany owing to Nazi persecution, Kurt Jooss was invited by Mr. and Mrs. Elmhirst, in 1934, to establish his Ballet Headquarters and School at Dartington Hall, Totnes, Devon, as the Artistic Section in connection with their Educational and Cultural Scheme of Rural Life. He accepted the offer; and, with Sigurd Leeder as resident teacher, the Jooss-Leeder School of the Dance was opened.

Here, ballet students could live and study amidst beautiful surroundings, under equally ideal conditions of life, while receiving an excellent and thorough training in the Jooss System of Ballet —with the ultimate prospect of being eventually drafted into the Jooss Company, should they so desire and prove acceptable.

Unhappily, the outbreak of the Second World War ended all this for the time being, since Dartington Hall was soon taken over by the British Government for war-time needs. New headquarters were, however, found for a time at Cambridge, where several new ballets were presented.

After the war was over, the Jooss Ballet toured in Belgium, Holland, Germany, Scandinavia and France several times. In 1946-47 the Company visited America, Switzerland, Paris and England again; and then it was disbanded. In 1948, Kurt Jooss himself was in Santiago, Chile, working with an offshoot of his own Company, the Chilean State Ballet, which had been formed nine years previously and was, and is still, conducted by his former pupil, Ernest Uthoff. Here, also, he created and presented at the Municipal Theatre, Santiago, on November 12th, 1948, a new ballet entitled *Juventud (The Song of Youth)* to music by Handel, arranged by Salas and Horst Bitter, *décor* by Juan Venturelli, and costumes by Bouchène and Bunster.

In the autumn of 1949, Kurt Jooss was invited to return to his old School in Essen, which he had founded in 1927; and here he is continuing his own original system of dancing, plus certain improvements and developments gained during his intervening years of experience. Hans Zullig, the Company's chief male dancer, rejoined him as leader of his teaching staff. Here he expects within a year or two to reassemble and rebuild his Company and to send them forth once more on German and International tours under the title of "Ballets Jooss, Folkwang-Tanz Theater der Stadt, Essen".

Many of those in sympathy with the work and ideals of Kurt Jooss, while appreciating his presentation of dance-dramas with the more naturalistic movements he has evolved, now look forward to a possible blending of the old and the new systems. Fokine, Duncan, Nijinsky, Massine, Balanchine, Lifar, Nijinska, together with some of the more recently established choreographers of to-day—Robert Helpmann and Frederick Ashton, to name but two—have more or less paved the way for this.

They, too, broke away to a certain extent from the old traditions, introducing many new ideas into their ballets and gradually realizing the more artistic effect of a complete union of dancing, music, *décor*, costumes and dramatic miming in the story to be danced or the moving picture to be presented. Some may already be inclined to think, therefore, that there remains practically only the vexed question of reconciling the actual traditional ballet steps, figures and former rigid rules for soli, duos, trios, quartettes, and similar "set pieces" by stars, near-stars and other "runners-up" in a Company, with the more naturalistic grouping and *ensemble* presentations of the Jooss School—where emphasis on technique or virtuosity is regarded as unnecessary and even superfluous for the blending of dramatic effects into the whole perfect scheme.

Whether a true blending of the two systems will ever be considered sufficiently desirable to be entirely achieved, or whether the new and the old schools will prefer to retain their own separate entities apart, remains to be seen. Actually Hans Zullig, just before returning to his chief in Essen, danced for several months with the Sadler's Wells Theatre Ballet, in London, for the purpose of studying more closely the academic dance.

Among Jooss's new ballets since his return to Essen may be mentioned *The Night Train, Journey in the Fog,* and *Colombinade*; and he has produced Hans Zullig's *Fantasy*.

Tamara Karsavina

◎◉◉◎

WHEN TAMARA KARSAVINA FIRST SHONE FORTH UPON THE dull boards of the Coliseum Theatre, London, in 1910, she seemed to be the very incarnation of the Spirit of Youth; and this same attribute clung to her and lingered on through the passing years as a special personal joy to be shared with all who have since beheld her—a satisfying joy equalled only by the perfection of her seemingly effortless dancing.

Robert Helpmann as Mercury

in " The Olympians " at Covent Garden.

Left

Rosella Hightower.

Right

*Sixteen year old
Svetlana Beriosova
with David Adams
in the Pas de Deux
in " Design for
Strings."*

Melvin

Tamara Platonova Karsavina was born in St. Petersburg, where she lived mainly until her education and training officially ended, though her family also spent a certain amount of time at Ligova near by. Her father was a dancer, and during Tamara's early years held the position of first dancer and mime at the Imperial Ballet, where the famous choreographer, Marius Petipa, had been his teacher.

At first, the father strongly opposed the idea of his clever and dainty little daughter following in the family dancing tradition, fearing the severity and disappointments of such a life for her; but, finally, he gave way to the inevitable, since the little Tamara early showed a definite trend that way, being passionately interested in everything appertaining to the stage, and to dancing in particular. In this she was supported by her mother, who arranged for her first dancing lessons with a retired ballet friend of the family. The latter started her in the traditional Russian way, which at first seemed very dull to the lively child who, a little later on, was also taught by her father.

In 1894, she was accepted by the Imperial Ballet School. At first she was a daily pupil only; but after about a year and after passing a further examination, she became a full-board student. The State now took complete charge of the young dancer, providing even her food and clothing and completing her general education in addition to the constant gruelling ballet training for which the School was so famous. Special stress was laid on the teaching of music, with which ballet is so closely connected; and for this Tamara had a natural aptitude.

Despite the severity of the training and the formality of the strict régime, the young student thoroughly enjoyed it all; and she made many friends in this new and exclusive little world. Among these was Lydia Kyasht, who remained always her dear friend. Also among her fellow students was the dazzling and already almost worshipped Anna Pavlova who, however, finished school before her and became *prima ballerina* at the Maryinsky Theatre very soon after; another was the gay and beloved-by-all little Lydia Lopokova, who entered the School later. Among her teachers during the long period of training were Johannsen, Gerdt and the famous Cecchetti—with the latter she continued to study regularly long after attaining ballerina status. The students were often sent to perform as "supers" in the various ballets at the Maryinsky and other theatres, and were also given very small parts from time to time; and, owing to her excellent progress and her natural gifts, many of these came the way of the young Karsavina. The students were also taken to plays to encourage their theatre sense, and to operas to help in their excellent musical training.

Some time before the end of her final training year, Karsavina came to be recognized as an unusual star pupil, her keen dramatic sense and naturally good miming being additional to her grace, her dazzling beauty and the ever-growing excellence of her execution. When, at the age of seventeen and a half, she left the School, she was given a principal part in the ballet at the School performance; and soon after, at a gala evening at Tsarkoe Selo in honour of the visit of the then French President, Monsieur Loubert, she was invited to dance with Fokine in *Le Lac des Cygnes*, at which performance the Imperial Family and Court were present. She passed all her general educational examinations with the utmost ease and secured a leaving prize; and at her theatre début she received quite an ovation—plus a charming and encouraging commendation from the already well-established Anna Pavlova.

Karsavina now became a full member of the Maryinsky Theatre, where she gradually rose from a *coryphée* to be a second and a first soloist; and finally, she attained to ballerina rank. Before her latter status arrived, however, she had a breakdown in health, after which her mother took her to Italy to recuperate; and while in Milan, she underwent a special course of Italian training under Signora Beretta, which she found interesting and beneficial. On returning to St. Petersburg, another two years passed with performances only of small or secondary parts; but during this period she made the acquaintance of Vaslav Nijinsky, still a youth, but already remarkable for his outstanding and most unusual elevation. Little did she then dream of the breath-taking triumphs they were to enjoy together in a few short years' time, though already the future creator of the *Spectre of the Rose* was frequently her partner in small roles.

In 1905, the young dancer went on a short summer tour to provincial towns with Lydia Kyasht, this being arranged by the latter's brother; and, though on a small scale, the tour served to give her confidence and helped her to overcome somewhat her natural nervous shyness. Soon afterwards, changes came. The famous Petipa, now nearly ninety years old, retired, and the young Fokine became ballet-master; and though at first his revolutionary ideas as a choreographer somewhat alarmed the traditionally trained young Karsavina, she gradually came to believe in him and to admire his originality. In her, Fokine soon found his dancing ideal for the principal parts in his ballets, her musical interpretations being of a similar high order.

About this time, the rebel, Greek-dancing Isadora Duncan appeared on the scene; and despite the latter's opposition to the traditional ballet, she was nevertheless sincerely admired by the classically trained Tamara.

An engagement in Prague soon brought important outside recognition for the young dancer and this time definitely gave her the self-confidence she had formerly lacked; and on her return to the Maryinsky, she danced the brilliant leading role in *Corsair* with her former teacher Gerdt so successfully that she was now firmly established in her full ballerina status. Consequently, when the great Pavlova presently left to become an independent artist, Karsavina took her place as *prima ballerina* of the Maryinsky.

It was in 1909 that the great impresario, Serge Diaghileff—so soon to become world famous—invited her to join him as principal ballerina in his ambitious and daring scheme for introducing the Russian Ballet into Europe where, until then, it was entirely unknown. With his vivid and charming personality, he quickly fired her with his own unbounded and infectious enthusiasm; and the two eventually became life-long friends.

Having collected into his Company all the best dancers available—including, as well as Karsavina, the amazing Nijinsky, Anna Pavlova, Ida Rubinstein, Vera Karalli, Adolf Bolm, Michael Mordkin—Diaghileff now took his first Russian Ballet to Paris in 1909, to the Théâtre du Chatélet, where it created a tremendous furore. Here he gave Fokine's *Pavillon d'Armide, Prince Igor, Le Festin, Cléopatre*; and Karsavina was given a marvellous *pas de deux* with Vaslav Nijinsky, which instantly brought them both into front-rank notice.

At the end of the Paris season, Karsavina, in 1910, under the auspices of another manager, Marinelli, made her first appear-

ance in London at the Coliseum, with Kosloff and Siebova—
with the result described in the opening paragraphs of this
article; and in 1911, she came again as leading ballerina with
Diaghileff's Russian Ballet in that first famous season of his at
Covent Garden, which literally took London by storm and provided the greatest and most important landmark in the history
of dancing in this country.

In addition to the classics, *Giselle* and *Lac des Cygnes*, the now
famous but then—out of Russia and Paris—entirely new and
original Fokine ballets, *Pavillon d'Armide*, *Les Sylphides*, *Prince
Igor*, *Schéhérazade*, *L'Oiseau de Feu*, *Le Carnaval*, *Cléopatre*,
Le Spectre de la Rose were given. Karsavina, Nijinsky and
Bolm were the principals—Anna Pavlova had by this time left
Diaghileff in order to form her own Company—and the effect
they created was stupendous.

This English triumph finally established Karsavina as the
star ballerina of Diaghileff's Company; and with them she
appeared regularly in London at Covent Garden, or elsewhere,
in 1912, 1913 and 1914, during which period the new ballets
Petrouchka and *Thamar* (Fokine), *L'Après-midi d'un Faune* and
Le Sacre de Printemps (Nijinsky) were added to the repertoire.
She also appeared regularly with the Company in Paris, Monte
Carlo, Vienna, Rome, Berlin, Dresden, etc. These visits had to
be fitted in with her periodic performances at the Maryinsky
Theatre, St. Petersburg, where she was still Principal Ballerina.
Among other ballets of the Diaghileff Company in which Kar-
savina danced were *Narcisse*, *Le Dieu Bleu*, *Thamar*, *Daphnis
et Chloe*, *Coq d'Or*, *Papillons*, *Midas*, *Le Légende de Joseph* (all
by Fokine), *Jeux* (Nijinsky), *Le Tricorne* (Massine), *Roméo et
Juliet* (Nijinska).

With the outbreak of the 1914 World War, there were no
more Diaghileff Seasons in London until 1918; and Karsavina,
in St. Petersburg, passed through some terrible times during the
Russian Revolution. The Maryinsky performances took place
as before, since military and civilians alike needed entertainment to distract their minds from the horrors that might befall
them. Later, when Diaghileff was in Spain, he begged her to
rejoin him there and to go on with his troupe to New York; but
she refused, preferring to use her inimitable gifts for the benefit of her own people at such a time.

Then came the Revolution, the establishment of the Bolshevik régime, the assassination of the Imperial Family; but even amidst all these fearful upheavals, the Maryinsky Theatre still continued to give the distracted people the healing joys of music, beauty and the dance; and Karsavina still remained as their bright particular star. The new rulers wisely upheld the long-established ballet tradition, and treated their artists well.

Nevertheless, Karsavina fell under political suspicion once or twice; and at last the time came when her safety was threatened and it was necessary for her to get away to an atmosphere of unfettered freedom if her Art was to survive. Her husband— for, by this time, she was married to an Englishman, Mr. H. J. Bruce, a diplomat, and had a small son and his devoted nurse to consider—managed, with great difficulty, to secure passports; and they set forth. After passing through incredible set-backs and dangers they at length arrived safely in a collier steamer at Middlesbrough in England.

In 1919, Karsavina rejoined Diaghileff in London, where the Company performed at the Coliseum, Drury Lane and Covent Garden. Leonide Massine was now choreographer; and his delightful *La Boutique Fantasque*, *Good-Humoured Ladies*, *Three-Cornered Hat* and *Children's Tales* (*Contes Russes*) had been added to the repertoire. *Le Tricorne*, in particular, provided Karsavina with another outstanding triumph—as did *Thamar* and *Petrouchka*. She also performed in J. M. Barrie's *The Truth About the Russian Dancers*, and danced with Novikoff in *Nursery Rhymes* in 1920.

In 1921, 1922 and 1925, Karsavina again appeared in London at the Coliseum under other auspices; but she performed with the Diaghileff Company in 1926, when, at His Majesty's Theatre, she danced in *Roméo et Juliette*, with Serge Lifar as her co-star. In 1927, she was at the Coliseum, dancing with Anton Dolin in *The Spectre of the Rose*.

Nineteen twenty-nine saw the last appearance of the famous Diaghileff Company in London (at Covent Garden, most fittingly), when the new ballets produced were *The Prodigal Son*, *Le Bal* (both by Balanchine), and a new version of *Le Renard* (by Lifar); also revivals of *Le Sacre de Printemps* (with Sokolova) and *Le Lac des Cygnes* (with Spessiva); and Karsavina also appeared in *Petrouchka*. It was soon after this season that Diaghileff was taken seriously ill in Venice and died there.

This sad event was a great blow to Karsavina who, though they had of recent years often gone separate ways, had never ceased in her deep regard and admiration for him. Possessive and dominating, he had always resented—or, at least, been impatient of—her acceptance of outside engagements and of her loyalty to the Maryinsky State Theatre, where she had received her training. He, too, was impatient of her love of home life and of her devotion to her husband and young son. When her husband's professional duties as a member of the Diplomatic Service took him to many places abroad—to Tangier, Budapest, Bulgaria, Switzerland, South Africa, etc.—Karsavina would join him whenever possible, in order to make a happy home life for him and their son. To all these places there would come eventually urgent telegraphic messages from Diaghileff, with entreaties for Karsavina to join in some important tour the Company was taking.

As a ballerina, Karsavina was quite stern with herself, and, when fulfilling her dancing engagements, nothing was allowed to interfere with her routine discipline for a perfect performance. In addition to her regular daily practice, she always arrived in her dressing-room at the theatre at least two or three hours before the curtain went up; and she was quite adamant about receiving no visitors of any kind until the performance was over. After dressing for her part, she always liked to spend the intervening time before her first call came in getting into the "skin" of the character she was about to interpret. Though she declares that every role became a favourite one with her, she admits, on looking back, that the following perhaps stand out more particularly in her memory as special joys: The Queen in *Thamar*, the Firebird in *L'Oiseau de Feu*, the Young Girl in *Le Spectre de la Rose* and the Queen of Shemakhan in *Le Coq d'Or*—and certainly, all who were ever privi-ledged to see her in these roles—each so widely diverse in character—would agree to an equal joy in such exquisite per-formances.

It was probably owing to her thoroughly well-assimilated knowledge of every character she portrayed, and to her perfect artistry, that on a certain occasion she was able to cope with an extremely awkward *contretemps*, quite unnoticed by her audience. While dancing in *La Légende de Joseph* one time, she felt, to her dismay, that her costume had become unfastened and was slipping off. Nevertheless, her dismay did not make itself visible; and, with skilful ease, she managed to hold on to her slipping costume with one hand while making all the appropriate gestures with the other. A less practised artist might have been totally unnerved by such an incident; but Karsavina finished her dance and made her exit without turning a hair—or leaving her costume behind!

After the death of Diaghileff, when the dancing world suffered a severe slump, Karsavina chose to remain in London and help to keep the torch of ballet still burning by encouraging the heroic efforts of the newly formed Ballet Clubs and Societies which were now being established for this purpose. In 1930, she danced *Le Spectre de la Rose* with Harold Turner at the Arts Theatre Club, where she also danced in *Les Sylphides*. In 1930, too, she appeared during Marie Rambert's seasons at the Lyric, Hammersmith; and she danced with the Camargo Society —of which she was Vice-President. In 1931, she further encouraged the Rambert Ballet by becoming their guest artist and creating parts in some of their new ballets. Thus she greatly encouraged the early efforts of many young dancers and choreographers who have since "arrived".

It was in 1930 that Madame Karsavina's autobiography, *Theatre Street*, was first published—a truly fascinating literary work, giving vivid sketches of her early life, training and career. Her husband, Mr. H. J. Bruce, also wrote two charming books about his famous dancing-star wife, *Silken Dalliance* and *Thirty Dozen Moons*. He died on September 10th, 1951.

It was about 1930 that Madame Karsavina began to be entreated by many aspirants for a ballet life to give them lessons in dancing, all of them being eager to be taught by so perfect a performer; and thus, gradually, she built up her very success-ful School of Dancing in Baker Street. She also gave a certain amount of teaching at the Royal Academy of Dancing, Holland Park—of which Dame Adeline Genée is President. Karsavina was a member of the Academy's first committee, and is at the present time one of its Vice-Presidents.

One of Karsavina's outstanding characteristics is that her

general cultural knowledge has always been far beyond the average; and this has always proved to be a great asset, together with her sound musical knowledge—assets which Diaghileff certainly appreciated. Hence her quick and thorough grasp of the meaning of a ballet—even in its embryo stage. Her versatility, too, has been nothing short of amazing; she could portray and bring alive an infinite variety of characters—simple, complex, tragic, humorous. What was more, she could slip from one role to an entirely opposite one with remarkable speed. She was a born mime, as well as a superb ballerina, possessing not only great beauty of body and mind, but the elegance and dignity to set off her splendid gifts. There was a certain nobility, even grandeur, about the dancing of Karsavina, seldom seen on the ballet stage of to-day.

Madame Karsavina has always demonstrated a natural gift for home-making wherever she has been. As did Pavlova, she loves beautiful furniture and everything that makes a home artistic and lovely. In addition, she has a true domestic gift, and thoroughly enjoys the cares of her present happy London home.

Madame Karsavina has broadcast several times during the past few years, on her own all-absorbing subject; and she also introduced very delightfully a recent television programme of ballet for the B.B.C. At the Rudolf Steiner Hall in May 1948, she gave a delightful Lecture-Demonstration on Mime—of which she is the greatest exponent within living memory. In the September 1949 number of *Ballet and Opera* she contributed a sympathetically understanding article on Serge Diaghileff on the occasion of the twentieth anniversary of the great impresario's death; and she has also written an essay in one of the Sadler's Wells Ballet Books, *The Sleeping Beauty*—this being a picture of her own early memories of the original St. Petersburg production, in 1890, of this evergreen lovely ballet. As first revealed in her autobiography, *Theatre Street*, this perfect little gem of an essay again demonstrates her really charming literary style.

Nora Kaye

THAT STRONGLY INDIVIDUALISTIC ARTIST, NORA KAYE, HAS been dancing with Ballet Theatre, New York, ever since the latter's opening season in 1940; and her fine dancing and unusually vivid dramatic sense have helped greatly in establishing that Company's reputation for good all-round work. Though born and bred in New York, her parents were Russians and, like all their compatriots, were always keenly interested in dancing.

Nora Kaye studied under the excellent guidance of Michael Fokine—formerly ballet-master and leading dancer of the famous Maryinsky Theatre in St. Petersburg—than whose teaching there could be none better. He had been settled in New York for many years. The young dancer's family name was Koreff; and it was under that name she became an original member of the American Ballet in 1935, where she remained for two years. Later on she changed her name to Kaye. She was afterwards with the Metropolitan Opera Ballet for a short time, until she became a leading dancer with Ballet Theatre.

When, in 1946, Ballet Theatre paid its first visit to London and danced at Covent Garden for a whole month, it was mainly Nora Kaye's splendidly dramatic performance in Antony Tudor's *Pillar of Fire* that made that season such a notable event. This is one of Tudor's most successful ballets and deals with frustrated lives; and Nora Kaye as Hagar, the American small-town girl who loses her lover through her own hasty mistake and finds him again after much mental and physical suffering, presented the most sincerely understanding and dramatic performance seen in ballet for many years. While obviously seething with an intense emotion, she yet reveals an amazing restraint. Her acting was tragically moving; and her dancing was of an extremely high order.

As Caroline in Tudor's evergreen *Jardin aux Lilas*, she had another opportunity for displaying her remarkable dramatic qualities. Again, as Juliet in this same choreographer's *Romeo and Juliet*, she revealed her power in tragedy, while yet emphasizing the soft tenderness of the youthful heroine—a surprising contrast this from the mature intensity of Hagar in *Pillar of Fire*.

But Nora Kaye is extremely versatile, and she delighted her British audiences in Tudor's charmingly gay and highly stylized ballet, *Gala Performance*, picturing temperamental ballerinas of the three main ballet schools, Russian, French and Italian. As the Russian ballerina, Miss Kaye was perfect. She has certainly a good sense of humour.

On the Company's return to New York, Nora Kaye danced in Jerome Robbins' new ballet, *Facsimile*, though this did not prove a very successful medium for her; but in the 1947-48 season, she scored another as tremendous a triumph as in *Pillar of Fire*. This new ballet was Agnes de Mille's *Fall River Legend* (music by Morton Gould, *décor* by Oliver Smith, and costumes by Miles White), in which frustration again plays a big part—this time caused by a young woman longing for affection, being squeezed out of the family love she craves by a somewhat melodramatic stepmother who finally drives her to murder. This is an even more highly dramatic and tragic work than *Pillar of Fire*, and it is based on an actual American murder trial of the 1890's. It afforded exactly the tragic atmosphere which Nora Kaye's expressive movements can convey so well and with such sympathetic poignancy. In Tudor's much lighter work, *Dim Lustre* —for two performers only—she was equally successful as one of two former lovers who meet again, revive their happy memories for a short, inspired spell, and part once more. She was also excellent as the fickle girl, Zemphira, in Massine's gipsy ballet, *Aleko*.

In the 1948-49 season, too, Nora Kaye had her chance to dance Giselle, that famous role so coveted by all true ballerinas as proving their acknowledged right to the title; and she showed herself highly successful in this classic role.

In 1950, Nora Kaye created the dreaming work-girl in Antony Tudor's ballet, *Nimbus* (music by Louis Gruenberg, *décor* by Oliver Smith, and costumes by Saul Bolasni). In this work she has a less strenuous role, but one to which she brought infinite sympathy and understanding—again of a girl frustrated of the romance she should have enjoyed. On April 23rd, 1950, also, she danced the tennis interlude in William Dollar's new choreography for the Nijinsky sports ballet, *Jeux* (to Stravinsky's music, and *décor* and costumes by David Ffolkes).

In 1951, she left Ballet Theatre and joined the New York City Ballet. Here, in the New York City Center of Music and Drama, she danced in Jerome Robbins' *The Cage* (music Stravinsky's Basler Concerto). This ballet was specially created for her. She has also danced in this choreographer's *The Guests*, and in Balanchine's *Symphonie in C*. In 1952, she created the heroine in Tudor's *La Gloire*.

Nora Kaye is not, perhaps, to be regarded at present so much as a great classical ballerina, but as a high-ranking dancer of real dramatic force with a very strong technique and great emotional power—probably the finest of modern times. Though outstanding in tragic roles, her natural versatility nevertheless enables her to dance practically any leading part in any Company's repertoire—most of these with real brilliance.

Lydia Kyasht

THE FIRST OF ALL THE RUSSIAN DANCERS TO THRILL BALLET-lovers in England was Lydia Kyasht, who appeared at the Empire Theatre in 1908, two years before Anna Pavlova came and three years earlier than the advent of the famous Serge Diaghileff's Russian Ballet which electrified us in 1911. Nevertheless, this fine ballerina was "one of Them", the "Great Ones" of those magical days.

Lydia Kyasht—the name was originally "Kyaksht"—was born at St. Petersburg on March 25th, 1886; and she received her general education and her complete ballet training at the Russian Imperial Ballet School there—among her contemporaries of varying ages being Anna Pavlova, Tamara Karsavina, Lydia Lopokova, Vaslav Nijinsky and many others later to become famous as leading members of the Diaghileff Company. One of her greatest friends of these happy training days was Tamara Karsavina—a friendship which continued long after their dancing careers had taken them in different directions.

Among Lydia Kyasht's teachers were her own brother, George Kyasht, Paul Gerdt and Enrico Cecchetti. On graduating, she passed into the Maryinsky Theatre Ballet, where she later became a *première danseuse*. She danced in several of the earlier Fokine ballets produced at the Maryinsky, among these being *Eunice*, *Chopiniana* and *Pavillon d'Armide*. She made her first appearance on the stage of the Opera House in St. Petersburg, on March 22nd, 1902, when she danced a *pas de deux* in *The Magic Flute*; and she made her début at the Maryinsky Theatre in *Casse Noisette*. On becoming a *première danseuse* at the Maryinsky, she continued as such for several years, usually dancing there for about eight months of each year, and appearing in between times at the Casino, Monte Carlo, and in other European cities. She appeared at the Opera House in Berlin, and at the Opera House in Vienna.

In 1908, Lydia Kyasht came to England, where she danced with Adolf Bolm as her partner at the Empire Theatre, London. Here she was greatly admired, not only for her exquisite dancing—of the wonderfully finished Russian style not seen in this country before—but also because of her handsome statuesque appearance, her dark beauty and her natural grace.

Later on in 1908, when Adeline Genée departed on a tour to America, Lydia Kyasht succeeded her for the time being as *première danseuse* at the Empire, where she won many laurels and became extremely popular. She danced principal roles in many of the elaborate ballets for which this theatre was so celebrated, among these being: Swanilda in *Coppélia*, Sylvia in the ballet of that name, the Fairy Queen in *Titania*, the Débutante in *The Dancing Master*, the Flower Girl in *The Faun*, Spirit of the Wheatsheaf in *The Reaper's Dream*; also appearing in *The Water Nymph*, *Round the World*, *A Day in Paris*, etc. Among the dancers she appeared with at the Empire were Fred Farren and Phyllis Bedells.

Lydia Kyasht danced as *prima ballerina* at the Empire until 1913, after which she toured in America, appearing in New York and elsewhere. On her return to London in 1914, she danced at the Coliseum with Morosoff in *The Enchanted Isle*. She also danced at the Winter Garden Theatre in *The Whirl of the World*. In 1915, she danced in *Javotte*; in 1916, in *Somewhere in France*; in 1917, she danced Lisette in *La Fille mal Gardée*, and also in *Cupid's Conspiracy*. In 1917, also, she appeared at the Ivory Cross Dancers' Matinée at the Alhambra with Fred Farren, Phyllis Bedells, Vera Savina, Little June and Lady Constance Richardson. She then for a time became a member of the Diaghileff Russian Ballet at the Alhambra. She danced in several of the Fokine ballets, among these being *L'Oiseau de Feu*, which always remained a favourite role with her.

During 1924, she toured with *The 7.30 Cabaret*; and then she began to undertake her own impresario and Company work. From 1925 to 1926, she travelled first with an entertainment of her own devising, known as *À La Russe*; and in 1926 she formed a Company known as *Cabaret Entertainment Gala Nights*, touring with it for three years. From 1930 to 1931, she toured in *Piccadilly Cabaret*; and in 1933, with *Spring-Time Cabaret*. Later in 1933, she appeared as the Retiring Ballerina in *Ballerina* at the Gaiety Theatre.

In 1935, Lydia Kyasht opened her well-known School, the Lydia Kyasht Dancing Academy. The School flourished well, and several successful Students' Shows were held. Many famous British dancers studied at the School, and returned from time to time for "refresher courses". In 1939, she formed a Company of very youthful dancers known as The Lydia Kyasht Ballet de la Jeunesse Anglaise. This Company performed at the Cambridge Theatre, where Mona Inglesby's first ballet, *Endymion*, and Robert Helpmann's *La Valse* were given, with other ballets. Later, the Ballet de la Jeunesse Anglaise went to Denmark, where the Company appeared at Copenhagen with great success.

In 1940, the Lydia Kyasht Russian Ballet was formed and produced a number of new ballets, including *Ballerina* and *Heraldic*, both with choreography by her daughter, known as Lydia Kyasht Junior. Other ballets produced at this time by the latter were *Derby Day* and *Marie Antoinette*, by Catherine Marks, and *Katyusha* by John Regan.

In 1943, the Lydia Kyasht Russian Ballet gave seasons at the Palace Theatre, Hammersmith, and at the Whitehall Theatre, and afterwards toured the provinces, mostly with the ballets given in 1940. In 1944, the Company likewise gave a successful season at the Winter Garden Theatre.

Lydia Kyasht has written an interesting book of memoirs, entitled *Romantic Recollections*, which was first published in 1929. This book gives some charming pictures of cultured Russian life before the Bolshevik Revolution, and contains many anecdotes of royal folk and of the Imperial Grand Dukes, of cruelties and of super luxurious customs under the old régime. It also tells of the solid hard work, and of the many keen pleasures of the famous ballerinas of the Imperial Russian Ballet —of whom the authoress herself was one of the most popular. It gives glimpses, too, of Edwardian and early Georgian society and famous folk she met during her long sojourn in this country.

During her career, Lydia Kyasht has danced with many of the most famous partners in the Russian Ballet, among these being Bolm, Morosoff, Fokine, Nijinsky, Volonine, Massine, etc. She was married to Colonel Alexis Ragosin.

Her daughter, Lydia Kyasht Junior, is also a well-known dancer, having been trained mainly by her famous mother on the true Russian system. She has worked with the latter's various companies, was choreographer for the ballets *Heraldic* and *Ballerina*, and has arranged dances for many others. She has also danced principal roles in many of the companies' productions; and she has assisted in her mother's Schools.

Lydia Kyasht is still actively teaching and retains her always keen interest in all matters relating to ballet. She is an active member of The Branch Committee of The Classic Ballet (Russian Method), recently established in London in order to preserve the basic principles of the classic ballet training as taught in the great Imperial Schools in St. Petersburg and Moscow before the first World War of 1914-18 and since in the Soviet Union State Schools.

WHEN ANTONY TUDOR LEFT THIS COUNTRY IN 1939 TO become chief choreographer and ballet-master to the Ballet Theatre in New York, he took with him a very promising young male dancer who had been a future "white hope" for the Ballet Rambert.

This was Hugh Laing, a Britisher born in Barbadoes in the British West Indies of English and Irish parents. At a fairly early age, he was sent to England to study Art. Soon deciding to make ballet his life's career, he began to study dancing first with Margaret Craske, and later with Olga Preobrajenska and Marie Rambert. He presently joined the Ballet Rambert and created several leading roles with this Company. Among these were Mercury in *The Descent of Hebe*, the Lover in *Le Jardin aux Lilas*, Mortal under Mars in *The Planets*, etc. He also danced in many other ballets, among these performing leading roles, such as Death in *Death and the Maiden*, Mars in *Mars and Venus*, Prince in *The Mermaid* and in *Cinderella*, the Faun in *L'Après-midi d'un Faune*, etc.

When Antony Tudor established his London Ballet, Hugh Laing joined him as a principal male dancer, and also did some designing of costumes. He created for London Ballet the roles of Waiter in *Judgment of Paris*, Performer in *Gallant Assembly*, Canzonetta in *Soirée Musicale*, etc.

On joining Ballet Theatre in New York, he quickly developed into one of the Company's leading dancers, proving himself capable of highly dramatic parts, as well as those of a more romantic and lyrical kind. He was particularly successful as the Lover in *Jardin aux Lilas*; and when he visited London with the Company in 1946, he was again admired in this role. He was excellently forceful in the less pleasant role of the undesirable lover and seducer of Hagar in *Pillar of Fire*. His dramatic characteristics were seen to considerable advantage, too, in *Romeo and Juliet*. In this ballet, his fine figure and youthful good looks made him an ideally romantic Romeo.

On returning to New York later on, Hugh Laing danced a number of other interesting roles with the Company. His great emotional side was revealed as the Lover in *Dim Lustre*. He also danced in Jerome Robbins' *Facsimile* with great effect.

In the 1947-48 season, he proved himself to be a very gallant and handsome Prince in a one-act version of *The Sleeping Beauty*, in which he partnered Nora Kaye as Aurora with great success. During the tour that followed he had a character part much to his liking, that of Petrouchka; and he made a brilliant success of the frustrated puppet. He also danced another character role in Tudor's ballet, *Shadow of the Wind*, in which he portrayed a philosophic drunkard with surprising insight and the closest attention to detail. The following spring he had another role that suited him particularly well—that of the fierce, fiery gipsy lover in Massine's *Aleko*; and in this ballet, too, he danced at times the entirely opposite and well-contrasted role of the older and more philosophic gipsy chief, proving again his very considerable versatility.

Hugh Laing had been with Ballet Theatre since its opening season, and had always been one of the mainstays of the Company. Early in 1951, however, he left this Company and joined the New York City Ballet. Here he has already established himself in several leading roles. The first of these was as the Prodigal in Balanchine's *The Prodigal Son* (book by Boris Kochno, music by Prokofiev, and *décor* and costumes by Roualt), in which his interpretation was regarded as excellent. During the same season he also took the role of Rimbaud the poet in *Les Illuminations*, the special ballet which Frederick Ashton was invited to create for this Company, and which has music by Benjamin Britten, and *décor* and costumes by Cecil Beaton. He also danced the romantic hero, Armand, in Antony Tudor's *The Lady of the Camellias* (music by Verdi, and *décor* and costumes by Cecil Beaton); and his rendering of this role was as lyrical and impassioned as was to be expected of the experienced lover in so many other ballets. He has since danced Hyppolytus in *Phaedra*, the title-role in *The Miraculous Mandarin*, and leading roles in other new ballets produced by the Company. His Mandarin was particularly fine. Hugh Laing's future work with this fine Company is bound to be of very considerable interest.

David Lichine

ONE OF THE MOST ORIGINAL OF OUR MODERN CHORE-
ographers is David Lichine. He was born in 1910 at
Rostov-on-Don, in South Russia; and he came of a
musical family, his father being a composer and singer. He did
not attend the Imperial Ballet Schools, but was educated in
Paris at the Russian High School there; and at the age of sixteen, he began to study ballet first with Madame Egorova and
later with Bronislava Nijinska.

A naturally graceful youth, he made quick progress and
within a few years became a remarkably good dancer, though
never very amenable to a strict classical routine. Full of
imagination, he liked to put his own original interpretation
upon a role; and he has always been particularly successful with
parts—modern and otherwise—that require a vivid imagination
and a psychological treatment. He had an eager enthusiasm
and a striking decisiveness in the carrying out of his ideas. On
presently joining the Ida Rubinstein Company (about 1928-30),
he came under the helpful and steadying influence of Bronislava
Nijinska, then choreographer to that Company, whose originality appealed to his own creative gifts and from whom he,
unconsciously, learned much regarding the creation of ballets.

His dancing improved, and he joined the Pavlova Ballet for a
short time, though this Company did not provide him with the
scope he required, since he was mainly a character dancer.

Then, in 1932, he joined one of the earlier Companies of
Colonel de Basil, and has since been mainly connected with this
impresario, rising quite early under him to the rank of a
premier danseur. He has, however, joined other companies
from time to time; and he has recently been connected as choreographer and dancer with the Marquis de Cuevas' Grand Ballet
de Monte Carlo, Les Ballets des Champs-Élysées and with Anton
Dolin's Festival Ballet.

David Lichine created his earlier ballets for the de Basil Ballet
Russe de Monte Carlo, and for this impresario's succeeding
Companies, Educational Ballets, etc. The first of these was
Nocturne (music by Rameau, *décor* and costumes by de Beau-

mont), produced in 1933 at Monte Carlo; in 1934, he created *Les Imaginaires* (Auric—de Beaumont); and in 1936, *Le Pavillon* (Borodin—Cecil Beaton). These three ballets, though revealing a definite originality, were naturally somewhat faulty and immature; but in 1937, his *Francesca da Rimini* (Tchaikovsky—Oliver Messel) was a very vivid and dramatic work, which attracted much attention and is still frequently revived. That same year he also created two other ballets, *Les Dieux Mendiants* (Handel arr. Beecham—Bakst and Gris)—a very charming work; and *Le Lion Amoureux* (K. Rathaus—P. Roy).

In 1938, he created new choreography for a subject used first by Balanchine, *Protée* (Debussy—di Chirico); and in that same year came *Le Fils Prodigue* (Prokofiev—Rouault), a very exciting and originally treated ballet with the old Bible parable as a basis. Then, in 1940, he created his very delightful and most attractive ballet, *Graduation Ball* (Johann Strauss arr. Dorati—Benois), a gay and sparkling work which has always remained a popular favourite.

For Ballet Theatre in New York, in 1943, he created another popular work, *Fair at Sorochinsk* (Moussorgsky—N. Remisoff), a real Russian ballet adapted from the famous composer's opera of the same name. For this Company, too, he revived his charming *Graduation Ball*; and he also completed, and added some new choreography to, *Helen of Troy*, the ballet Michael Fokine was working upon for that Company when he died. This most amusing ballet (to the music of Offenbach's *La Belle Hélène*, *décor* Marcel Vertès) has proved likewise to be a very popular ballet in the repertoire.

For the 1946-47 season of the de Basil's Original Ballet Russe, Lichine created another ballet on a biblical theme, *Cain and Abel* (to music from Wagner's *Siegfried* and *Götterdämmerung*, *décor* Prieto); but it was felt by some critics that the grand Wagnerian score was too well known to operatic and concert lovers to prove anything but distracting when used in conjunction with an entirely different ballet subject, interesting though the latter was in its choreographical treatment.

For the Ballets des Champs-Élysées, in their 1948-49 season, Lichine created a very remarkable new ballet, which proved a great sensation. This was *La Rencontre* (book by Boris Kochno, music by Sauguet, *décor* and costumes Bérard), which has as its subject the fabled meeting of Oedipus and the Sphinx; and the story, designs, choreography, and everything connected with it make this ballet outstanding in the extreme. It conveys the right atmosphere of mystery, the movements of the two protagonists are quite acrobatic at times, yet beautiful, and the drama is perfectly well constructed and mimed. Jean Babilée as Oedipus had splendid opportunities for displaying his always amazing virtuosity; and Lichine's most original choreography provided a ballet thrill indeed. Another new Lichine ballet for the same Paris season was *La Création*, a curious work inasmuch as it contains no musical accompaniment at all, and not a great deal of dancing. Nevertheless, the actual movements and the groupings are beautiful, and the miming is so clearly expressive of the meaning to be conveyed, that the ballet proved a real success. The other new works created by Lichine for this Company's Paris ballet season were certainly less spectacular. These were *Orpheus* (Stravinsky—Mayo) which deals with the classical hero; and *Valse Caprice* (Fauré—Bérard), more or less a *divertissement* ballet which, however, gave much pleasure because of the opportunity it provided for the exquisite dancing of Tatiana Riabouchinska. The latter charming dancer, formerly one of the famous de Basil "Baby Ballerinas", is now the wife of this gifted choreographer.

For the 1949 season of the Marquis de Cuevas' Grand Ballet de Monte Carlo, Lichine created two new ballets on the grand scale. The first of these was *Infanta* (Hubeau—Gontcharova), based on the charming story of Oscar Wilde's *The Birthday of the Infanta*; but this did not work out quite so satisfactorily as one might have hoped from the interesting subject. The other work was *The Enchanted Mill* (Schubert arr. Cloez—Benois), which has a simple romantic subject suitable to the charming rustic venue selected. It is a light-hearted comedy, with some amusing peasant scenes and a number of very effective dances.

When Anton Dolin formed his new Festival Ballet Company, mainly for performances at the Stoll Theatre, London, in connection with the Festival of Britain throughout 1951, he invited many brilliant ballerinas and equally world-famous male dancers to join his Company as guest artists from time to time. Among these stars were David Lichine and his wife, Tatiana Riabouchinska, both of whom danced in many ballets, old and new. He commissioned Lichine to create a couple of new ballets for the Company. The first of these was *Harlequinade* (music by Drigo, and *décor* and costumes by Eleanor Watts); and it was presented as a Christmas piece on December 26th, 1950—Dolin's Festival Ballet having begun operations some few weeks earlier. It was quite a gay and amusing little ballet and provided some excellent opportunities for brilliant dancing by Riabouchinska and John Gilpin.

Lichine's second ballet for this Company, *Impressions* (music, Bizet's Symphony in C, and *décor* and costumes by Hugh Stevenson), was certainly more satisfying from the choreographic point of view. An abstract ballet, it embraces an infinite variety of dance patterns in rhythmic classical style, beautifully presented in three distinct movements. Markova, Dolin, Paula Hinton, Riabouchinska and John Gilpin all had leading roles —the last two providing a wonderful final *pas de deux* at a terrific speed, following the more lyrical second movement performed exquisitely by Markova and Dolin. In 1952-53, he and Riabouchinska toured with Ballet Theatre, when he revived his *Graduation Ball*.

As a choreographer, David Lichine has an amazing gift of invention; and he ranks among the leading original creative dance artists of the day.

Serge Lifar

SERGE LIFAR WAS BORN AT KIEV, IN SOUTH RUSSIA, IN 1905; and, totally unlike most of the star dancers of our modern age, he had no idea of becoming a performer in ballet until he had reached his later teens. Nevertheless, he tells us that the psychological side of dancing had been with him since his earliest days and that he had always been a "dancer in spirit". It was not until, as a slender, poetic-looking youth, visiting with a friend quite casually the dance studio of Madame Bronislava Nijinska in Kiev, that he became deeply stirred by the beauty of academic dancing even in the making and was so filled with enthusiasm that he then and there decided to become a dancer himself. He began to work at once with this famous teacher—the sister of the world-renowned male dancer, Vaslav Nijinsky, and an equally renowned dancer and choreographer herself—and quickly proved himself to be one of the most apt students she had ever turned out. Not only was he filled with a passionate desire to excel in dancing, but he also had the bodily grace and beauty of form so essential to complete success —in addition to which he had musical, literary and creative gifts of a high order.

While still but a youth, his virtuosity and outstanding personality were considerable; and he had made such good use of his excellent training that only a couple of years later, early in 1923, he had already been accepted as a member of the *corps de ballet* in the Russian Ballet Company of the great Serge Diaghileff. The latter was quickly attracted by the brilliant youth, putting him to study particularly under the then elderly but still magnificent dancer and teacher, Enrico Cecchetti, whom he had engaged as *maître de ballet* to his Company— with the result that Serge Lifar, young though he was, was named among the leading male dancers in the Diaghileff Company's 1925 visit to the London Coliseum, along with Anton Dolin, Nikitina and others; and in the Company's visits to London the following years, he was the principal dancer to partner Karsavina, Lopokova and Danilova. Before this time, of course, he had danced smaller but ever-increasingly important roles with the Company in Paris and Monte Carlo.

After appearing in a couple of small parts in Nijinska's ballet *Les Fâcheux* and in Massine's *Cimarosiana*, his fine creation of the role of Boreas in *Zéphyr et Flore* (Massine) was, undoubtedly, Lifar's first step towards stardom; and it revealed his remarkable *ballon* and elevation as well as the ease with which he could get into the "skin" of a character. After this, other ballets in which he danced leading roles with the Diaghileff Company were: in 1925, *Barabau, Les Matelots, Les Biches*; in 1926, *Lac des Cygnes, Romeo and Juliet, L'Oiseau de Feu, Pastorale, The Triumph of Neptune*; in 1927, *Le Pas d'Acier, La Chatte*; in 1928, *Apollon Musagète, Ode, Le Bal*; and in 1929, *Le Fils Prodigue.*

Although from the very beginning of his career, Lifar had

studied the art of choreography and had quite early revealed very considerable inventive and creative gifts with most original ideas behind them, it was not until 1929 that his two first ballets were presented. The first of these, *Le Renard* (music Stravinsky, *décor* Larionov)—a second version of this subject which formerly had choreography by Nijinska—was produced by Diaghileff in 1929. In this piece, Lifar experimented with a combination of the movements of classic dancers and acrobats, and it proved to be a decidedly modernistic ballet.

Just before the production of this first choreographic work, Lifar had experienced a brilliant success as the erring son in Balanchine's *Le Fils Prodigue*, after the first performance of which Diaghileff had declared him to be a "great and true artist".

After the untimely death of Diaghileff in 1929, Lifar entered the Dance Academy of Le Théâtre National de l'Opéra in Paris that same year, where he quickly rose to the position of *premier danseur étoile*, dancing the principal male roles in his own ballets, in the academic classics, and in the many modern ballets also produced by that theatre. Later on, he became *maître de ballet* there and chief choreographer—or choréauthor, as he prefers the title to be—a position he still holds, after an absence of two or three years during the Second World War of 1939-45.

It was during his first year at the Paris Opéra, in 1929, that his second ballet, *Les Créatures de Promethée* (or *Prometheus*, as it is more usually called), inspired by the music of Beethoven, was successfully produced there. It was in *Prometheus* that Lifar began his development of the predominance of the male dancer, especially of the leading *danseur étoile*; and this proved to be a considerable vehicle for the display of his own ever-increasing virtuosity. It was in this ballet, too, that he first began, thus early, to kick against the discipline and restrictions of creating dance movements to fit into a musical score. Though greatly inspired by the lovely music of Beethoven chosen for the ballet and artistically disinclined to omit a note or to alter the *tempo* of any part of it, the difficulties he thus encountered undoubtedly paved the way for his future highly original, but not greatly appreciated, ideas for creating ballets without any music at all in certain cases.

His own first famous example of such strange ballets is *Icare*, which, though it has an entirely academic foundation, has no musical score, the latter being entirely replaced by a percussion orchestra producing rhythms—uncompromisingly described by some critics as plain "noises"—composed by the choreographer himself. While announcing his own preference for ballets with music, Lifar still asserts that certain dance movements, or even certain entire ballets, can be developed and expressed far more freely without music but with the addition of appropriate rhythms only; and, in *Icare*, he exemplified this idea. The ballet, of course, deals with the famous Greek legend of Icarus —the youth who attempted to soar into the sky wearing artificial wings made by his inventive father, Daedalus, and fastened to his shoulders with wax, and of his fatal fall to earth when the heat of the sun melted the wax.

Just before *Icare* was produced by Le Théâtre de l'Opéra in 1935, Lifar published a remarkable book entitled *Le Manifeste du Chorégraphie*, in which he set forth his theory that ballet *could* exist without the aid of music and that certain ballets might be all the better for being released from what he termed such "slavery". This original literary work created as great a sensation as *Icare* itself.

After *Prometheus*, Lifar created, in addition to *Icare*, a great many new ballets, produced at Le Théâtre de l'Opéra. Among these may be mentioned the following: in 1931, *Bacchus et Ariane* (music by Roussel, *décor* and costumes by di Chirico), *L'Orchestre en Liberte* (Roussel), *Prélude Dominical* (Guy Roparz—Paul Colin); 1932, *Sur le Borysthène* (Prokofiev— Larionov); 1934, *Jeunesse* (Ferroud—Godebsky), *La Vie de Polichinelle* (Nabokoff—Pruna), *Jurypary* (Villa Lobos—R. P. de Bois); 1935, *Salade* (Milhaud—Derain), *Icare* (Rhythms orchestrated by J. E. Szyfer, *décor* and costumes P. R. Larthe); 1936, *Bolivar, Harnasie* (Szymanovsky—Irène Lorentowicz), *Promenade de Rome* (Samuel Rousseau—Décaris), *David Triomphant* (Debussy and Moussorgsky, orchestrated Rieti—Fernand Léger), *Le Roi Nu* (Jean Françaix—Pruna); 1937, *Alexandre le Grand* (Philippe Gaubert—P. R. Larthe); 1938, *Oriane et le Prince d'Amour* (Florent Schmitt—Pruna), *Aeneus* (A. Roussel— Moulaert), *Le Cantique des Cantiques* (Rhythms by Lifar, additional orchestral items by A. Honegger—Paul Colin); 1940, *Entre deux Rondes* (Rousseau—Dégas); 1941, *Le Chevalier et la Damoiselle* (Gaubert—Cassandre); 1942, *Adelaide* (Ravel), *La Princesse au Jardin* (Grovlez), *Joan de Zarissa* (Werner Egk —Y. Brayer); 1943, *Noir et Blanc*—later revised as *Suite en Blanc* (Lalo—Bundy, after Nepo).

For the next two or three years, Lifar was absent from the Paris Opéra during the German Occupation; and during this period he became Artistic Director of the New Ballet de Monte Carlo, creating for them several new ballets, among these being *Chota Roustavelli* and other lighter works, concluding with *Dramma per Musica* (Bach—Cassandre) in 1946, his first creation after the Second World War.

On his return to Paris in 1947, and taking up his work once more as *maître de ballet* at the National Academy of Music and Dancing, Serge Lifar quickly revived the flagging interest in dancing at the Opéra, where the *première danseuse*, Yvette Chauviré, had also returned and with whom he danced in *Giselle* with all his former skill and verve. He revived his own *Le Chevalier et la Damoiselle* with great success; and he has since created a number of new ballets. Among these are, in 1948, *Divertissement* (Tchaikovsky—Bouchène), *Guignol et Pandore* (Jolivet—Dignimont), *Les Mirages* (Sauguet—Cassandre), *La Mort du Cygne* (Chopin), *Zadig*—from Voltaire's story *La Danse* —(Pierre Petit—Labisse), *Istar* (Vincent d'Indy), *Escales* (Ibert —Denyse de Bravura), *Animaux Modèles* (Poulenc—Roland Oudot), a new version of *Daphnis et Chloe* (Ravel), a new version of *Pavane pour une Infante Défunte* (Ravel) and *Aubade* (Poulenc). In 1949 came *L'Ecuyère* (on theme by Lifar and Nepo, after Kafka, choreography by Lifar, *décor* and costumes by Nepo, music by Kosma), *Lucifer* (Delvincourt—Yves Brayer), *Naissance des Couleurs* (Lifar choreography in co-operation with Irène Popard, music Honegger), *Septuor* (scenario Francis Blanche, music Jean Lutèce, *décor* Yves Bonnat), *Endymion* (scenario André Doderet, music Leguerney, *décor* Bouchène).

In 1950, Lifar created three important new ballets. On April 19th that year, he produced *L'Inconnue* (music by Jolivet, and *décor* and costumes by Charles Blanc), which proved to be interesting and lyrical; and in this the principal role was danced by Tamara Toumanova. On April 26th, his *Le Chevalier Errant* (music by Ibert, and *décor* and costumes by Pedro Flores) was presented, with Lifar himself as Don Quixote; but the many

distortions from popular incidents in Cervantes' great work did
not please many of the critics. Nevertheless, it is a very elaborate ballet, and much of the choreography is full of brilliance and
beauty. On June 14th, Lifar's eagerly awaited *Phèdre* was produced. The book is adapted from Racine's tragedy by Jean
Cocteau, the music is by Georges Auric, and the *décor* and
costumes are by Cocteau. The role of the tragic heroine was
danced by Toumanova magnificently. Lifar himself danced
Hippolyte remarkably well; and the ballet was very favourably
received.

On April 25th, 1951, this fine choreographer's new ballet,
L'Astrologue dans le Puits (music by Henri Barrault, and *décor*
and costumes by Suzanne Roland-Manuel), was produced. It
is a fantastic subject adapted from one of La Fontaine's Fables.
It was felt, however, that Lifar did not, in this work, show himself as inventive as usual, or make as much of this real fantasy
as he might have done. Later in 1951, Lifar's ballet *Jeanne au
Bûcher* (Claudel—Honegger—Yves Bonnat) was produced at the
Opéra.

In addition to being one of the leading stars of the Diaghileff
Company at the beginning of his career and *maître de ballet*
of the Paris Opéra for so many years since, Serge Lifar has also
appeared with other companies from time to time. In 1930, he
was in a Cochran Revue in London with Nitikina, where Balanchine produced them both in *The Freaks* and in *Night*. In 1933,
he was at the Savoy Theatre, London, with Nikitina and
Doubrovska, in *Promethée*, *L'Après-midi d'un Faune* and *Le
Spectre de la Rose*. In 1937, he shared with Massine the duties
of *maître de ballet* in René Blum's Ballet Russe de Monte Carlo
for nearly a year. Later in 1938, he was again with the Monte
Carlo Company at Drury Lane, where he danced in his own
Icare; and, as mentioned above, during the early 1940's he was
with the New Ballet de Monte Carlo.

He has also achieved a considerable amount of literary work.
In addition to his *Le Manifeste du Chorégraphe*, written in
1935, he published his *Ballet, Traditional to Modern* in 1937.
This has become a popular and useful work, containing as it
does the very original theories of the author, together with
details of his many ballets, in addition to much historical information. It is an elaborate work, psychological and learned;

and it has been very excellently translated into English by Mr. Cyril Beaumont. Other well-known books by Lifar are *La Danse, Carlotta Grisi, Serge Diaghileff, L'Histoire du Ballet Russe,* etc.

While some critics declare Lifar to be, like Diaghileff, too eager a searcher after novelty, that he is inclined to over-elaborate the male roles in certain of his own ballets, and at times shows a lack of continuity, he is more generally considered to be one of the modern world's great choreographers. He has certainly many novel ideas. In addition to the music-less presentation of *Icare,* he made innovations in certain others of his earlier ballets. In *Alexandre le Grand* the dancing was on three planes; in *La Vie de Polichinelle* the *corps de ballet,* instead of forming a background for the soloists, danced in a sort of circus box quite apart; and in *Bacchus et Ariane* were seen two parallel dance actions going on simultaneously. In *Le Cantique des Cantiques* he dwells especially upon what he terms the *recitative,* or mime element in ballet—corresponding to the *recitative* in opera—as opposed to actual solo and combined dances, which he describes as *ariosa* dancing. In his more recent work, however, he has abandoned his more *outré* effects, and has concentrated on perfect beauty of movement.

In November 1951, Lifar's delightful ballet, *Blanche Neige (Snow-White),* was produced at the Opéra (music, Maurice Yvain, *décor* Bouchene); and in April 1953, he created *Fourberies* (Rossini—Roland Oudet). Two other new ballets were also seen in 1953, *Cinéma* (Aubert—Touchagues) and *Variations* (Schubert—Aubin).

Lifar is one of the most prolific of modern choreographers. From being a youthful star in the Russian Ballet of Diaghileff —who always prophesied a brilliant future for him—he became an excellent classical dancer, with a light and effortless elevation and having, likewise, a real dramatic sense in modern roles.

Serge Lifar is very much interested in television; and he has produced many excellent programmes in this medium.

Lydia Lopokova

WHEN TAMARA KARSAVINA WAS A QUICKLY ADVANCING student in the Imperial Ballet School at St. Petersburg, among the juniors there was a merry little round-cheeked girl whose mischievous-looking, bright eyes danced almost as continuously as her clever little twinkling feet. This jolly little person was Lydia Lopokova; and she was the third member of her family to be a student at this famous Ballet School, a sister and a brother having already preceded her—the brother, Andrei, later on became a popular character dancer and teacher under the Soviet régime until his death in Leningrad in 1947. Another brother, F. V. Lopokov, was also connected with ballet. The little Lopokova was a great admirer of the soon-to-emerge star-dancer, Karsavina, into whose monitor-charge she was placed at one time, and who, in her delightful book, *Theatre Street*, thus describes her small charge: ". . . a tiny child with the face of an earnest cherub. Whether she danced or talked, her whole frame quivered with excitement; she bubbled all over. Her personality was manifest from the first, a very lovable one." It certainly then never entered into her pretty little gaily tossing head that at some future date she would appear with her greatly admired friend in London, both as star performers in the world's greatest Russian Ballet Company. No Russian ballerina was then known outside Russia.

Born in Russia on October 21st, 1891, Lydia Lopokova entered the Imperial Ballet Theatre at St. Petersburg at the usual early age—eight years; and here she soon began to attract notice. Michael Fokine was then *maître de ballet* at the Maryinsky Theatre; and he became one of her main teachers. Owing to her small size and daintiness, she was often picked out from the School Classes for small parts at the Theatre—especially in cases where a tiny expert performer was likely to "bring down the house". This was the case when, at the age of ten years, she was chosen as the Page in *The Sleeping Beauty*.

However, as with all other Imperial Ballet students, her training period—which included a good general and musical education as well—was mostly hard work; but she acquitted herself

187

well in every way, finally graduating very successfully in 1909, and so passing on into the Maryinsky Theatre Ballet, where she was soon given small but gradually more important parts, after making her début as the Columbine in *Casse Noisette*.

Although an extremely popular little newcomer, she did not remain long enough at the Maryinsky to become a leading ballerina there; for, within a year of her début, she was invited by Serge Diaghileff in 1910 to join his newly formed Company, already famous after its first Paris season the year before. The great impresario—always on the look-out for " something different "—had quickly realized the advantage of securing for his Company a dancer of the young Lopokova's specially individualistic qualities of overflowing natural gaiety, combined with the perfect technique of a classically trained performer. Under the careful guidance of her former teacher, Fokine—now choreographer, dancer and *maître de ballet* of the adventurous Company—she not only attained to full ballerina status, but quickly became a popular star in her own highly personal style. Always gay and ebullient with mischievous fun, she was particularly successful in the more lively, *soubrette* roles; but she was also able to tackle the more serious classical characters, and was excellent in many of the Fokine ballets. At first she appeared with the Company in Paris; and it was not long before, during the temporary absence of Karsavina—who had to return at intervals to the Maryinsky where she was still a leading ballerina —she had the good fortune to dance some of the latter's principal roles. Among the latter was that of the Firebird in Fokine's famous ballet of that name—a role which, although her appearance in it was lovely, dainty and sparkling, did not suit her own unique qualities so well as the more lively and enchantingly flirtatious part of Columbine in *Le Carnaval*, which, luckily, she was also given at this time to perform and which established her instantly as a popular favourite. After this, she and Karsavina often shared these and other roles; and during the latter's further temporary absences, more lucky chances came the way of this very youthful ballerina.

But Lopokova was always of a somewhat restless disposition, and enjoyed new experiences; and she presently went off to America, where she danced as leading ballerina with Nijinsky, who was at that time touring there.

Lopokova's first appearance in London with the Diaghileff Company did not take place until 1918; but she instantly became a popular favourite whom Londoners took to their hearts at her first performance. Her small daintiness and infectious gaiety appealed to every audience before whom she appeared; and she revealed a new and entirely different aspect of the Russian ballet dancer.

Among the ballets in which she danced gay roles with the Diaghileff Company (in 1918, 1919, 1921, 1926) were *The Good-Humoured Ladies*, *La Boutique Fantasque* (both by Leonide Massine); *Le Carnaval* and *Petrouchka* (by Michael Fokine). As Mariuccia in Massine's *The Good-Humoured Ladies*, she has never been excelled. This is a real *soubrette* role which suited her unique personality to perfection; and her portrayal of this mischievous waiting-maid, with her resourceful tricks and artifices, her flirtatious, tantalizing treatment of her various admirers, old and young, and her unending capacity for poking fun at one and all in this particular part will never be forgotten by those who had the good fortune to see it. As the female *Can-Can* dancer in Massine's *La Boutique Fantasque*, in which she danced with the creator himself, she has also never been surpassed. While performing this amazing high-kicking dance with the utmost abandon and mischievous naughtiness, she never once exhibited the least trace of vulgarity in the manipulation of her frothing, billowing garments, her every frolicsome movement being the spontaneous emanation of her own innate sparkling merriment and irrepressible high spirits. In the flirtatious, coquettish parts of both Chiarina and Columbine in Fokine's *Le Carnaval*, she was equally full of captivating, infectious fun, her perfect and versatile miming being on a par with the perfection of her dancing technique; and the same may be said of her performance as the Ballerina in *Petrouchka*. She kept her dancing technique always up to its highest pitch— Cecchetti, Fokine and Massine were all her teachers during her Diaghileff and later career; and she did not vary from performance to performance, but seemed to bring fresh vitality to each one. In more serious roles, such as those in *Cléopâtre*, the *Firebird*, etc., though these did not suit her own unique personality so well as the lighter characters just mentioned, she yet displayed a real dramatic gift; and in the *divertissements* of the classics, such as in *The Sleeping Beauty*, those of Aurora, Florisse and the Lilac Fairy (she was most tantalizingly charming as the latter), she could equally hold her own. In 1924, she appeared as the Street Dancer in Massine's *Le Beau Danube* —another different type of role in which she was equally brilliant.

Indeed, Lopokova's versatility and excellent miming gifts were such that, later on, for several years she appeared as a "straight" actress on the legitimate stage in London. She played leading parts in Ibsen's *The Doll's House* and *The Master Builder*; also in Shakespeare's *Twelfth Night* and *Lover's Complaint*; but her slight foreign accent somewhat marred the effect of the two latter. She was excellent in the Ibsen plays; and she exhibited a very definite histrionic gift, a soft and well-trained voice, and a real theatre sense—the latter, of course, was to be expected of one so well trained in the Russian Imperial Ballet, where litera- ture, drama and music formed part of the general curriculum, in addition to dancing.

Among the famous dancers with whom Lopokova performed at various times while with the Diaghileff Company were Kar- savina, Danilova, Ninette de Valois, Sokolova, Tchernicheva, Markova, Nikitina, Nemtchinova, Massine, Gavrilov, Dolin, Zverev, Grigorieff, Woizikovsky, Idzikovsky, Slavinsky, Nicholas Legat, Cecchetti, etc. Enrico Cecchetti was *maître de ballet* of the Company at that time.

Lydia Lopokova never returned to Russia; and in 1925 she was married to John Maynard Keynes, the famous economist, who later became Lord Keynes. She and her husband both worked hard for the support and better appreciation of the Arts in this country, and of Ballet in particular. Lord Keynes became a very great and most generous Patron of the Arts; and he was the first Chairman of C.E.M.A. He died in 1946, some five or six years after his ballerina-actress wife had retired from the stage.

After Diaghileff's death in 1929, Lydia Lopokova became interested in the formation of the Camargo Society, her husband becoming its most energetic treasurer whose social influence proved a great asset; and in 1930, she danced under its auspices in the production of Frederick Ashton's *Façade*—with the young choreographer himself and Alicia Markova in the cast—and in various other ballets, including *Rio Grande* (Frederick Ashton), etc. In 1933, she took part in a Gala Performance at Covent Garden in June, in the presence of H.M. Queen Mary, the then Duke and Duchess of York (later King George VI and Queen Elizabeth), and a most specially distinguished audience. The performance included two acts of *Coppélia*, in which Lopokova made a perfectly enchanting Swanilda—this being another of the roles that always suited this charming dancer to perfection and gave great scope for the gleeful and witty *diablerie* of her sunny nature to bubble forth with almost every movement, in addition to exhibiting always her fine technique at its best.

Although Lydia Lopokova had so many brilliant successes to her credit both during and after her reign as a *première danseuse* of Diaghileff's Company, when she established herself as an ever-popular idol of London audiences, she retired from dancing at an early age; and after six years (1933 to 1939) as a "straight" actress, she has not appeared on the stage again. As Lady Keynes, since her husband's death in 1946, she has lived quietly in her own private country home among her friends.

This delightful dancer will always be remembered chiefly for her effervescing good spirits, her quick wit, and the unfailing sparkle of her gay personality revealed more particularly in such roles as the naughty Mariuccia in *The Good-Humoured Ladies*, as Swanilda in *Coppélia* and as Columbine and Chiarina in *Le Carnaval*—all parts that might have been created for her.

Alicia Markova

ONE OF THE FIRST BRITISH-BORN DANCERS TO ATTAIN WORLD-wide recognition and admiration as a perfectly Russian-trained ballerina, Alicia Markova has never lost her high-ranking fame but still holds her own among the most famous names in Ballet to-day.

She was born in London as Alice Marks, one of four charming sisters, all fond of an artistic life and making a very happy family together. Her father was an engineer, and her mother was an excellent singer, with good acting ability, too—so good, indeed, that she was invited to join the George Edwardes' Company, an offer, however, which she had to refuse for family reasons.

Nevertheless, much of Mrs. Marks' own real talent was later to be revived in her bright young daughters; and when the little Alice—though the eldest, always the smallest, daintiest and frailest of them all—very early revealed a remarkable aptitude for dancing, she was determined that such undoubted talent should not be wasted, as in her own case, but should be developed to the utmost extent. She was all the more determined in her resolve because she seemed to see in Alice's small features and way of moving, even as a child, a curious likeness to the severely classical features of Anna Pavlova.

Indeed, this fond notion of her mother's nearly caused possible disaster to the child dancer's early training, as, when she first brought the latter to the famous School of the Princess Seraphine Astafieva and introduced her as "the miniature Pavlova", the great Russian teacher was so annoyed at such temerity that she at first refused to be interested in the small aspirant at all.

However, fortunately for the future ballerina and for Ballet in general, Madame Astafieva, on the child being presented to her notice a second time, quickly recognized the undoubted gifts possessed by the charming little would-be pupil, and then eagerly took charge of her ballet education. The little Alice quickly developed into one of the most remarkably brilliant students in the School, in the exhibition pupils' shows of which she danced even in those early days with the star boy student there at the same time, Patrick Kay—afterwards Anton Dolin, with whom her own name was to be so closely linked throughout her later career.

The still small dancer was only just fourteen when she was seen by Serge Diaghileff in 1925, who, realizing that she possessed the potentialities of a really great dancer, invited her to join his celebrated Company in Monte Carlo. Here, with her name Russianized into Alicia Markova—quite essential in those Russian-Ballet-fan days—and accompanied by a governess, she now continued her training under the famous Enrico Cecchetti,

who proceeded to strengthen her slender limbs in such a way
as to take nothing from her appearance of fragility and the airy-
fairy, gossamer-like quality of her extraordinary lightness and
ballon—always one of her greatest charms.

Even at that early age, there was a fey, elf-like feather-weight
grace about Markova's every movement that has never left
her throughout her brilliant ballet career, but which still
remains an almost unique feature in connection with her every
performance. But, behind that entrancing fragility and lightness of movement is the finely-tempered-steel quality of real
strength put into those delicate limbs and muscles by the gifted,
far-seeing maestro throughout the period this youthful dancer
remained with the great impresario's famous Company, from
1925 to 1929. Incidentally, Alicia Markova was the last great
ballerina to be trained by Cecchetti, who died in 1928.

Diaghileff was too sincere a lover of great dancing and far
too wise to make a "baby-ballerina" out of Markova—though
another might have been tempted to do so with such unexpectedly fine material ready to his hand. Nevertheless, he
permitted her to dance the *pas de trois* from *Le Lac des
Cygnes* on a special occasion at the end of her first year with
the Company. Her first real role danced in public with the
Company, however, was at Monte Carlo, when she gave a
charming performance of the Little Red-Riding-Hood *pas de
deux* in *Aurora's Wedding*. After this, she danced the
American Child in *La Boutique Fantasque*. Later on, too,
she danced in the Blue-Bird *pas de deux* with her former
student-friend, Anton Dolin, already a prominent member of
the famous Company.

The first part she actually created for Diaghileff was that of
the Nightingale in Balanchine's revival of *Le Chant du Rossignol* in 1927—for which role Diaghileff had had her in mind
from first taking her into his Company, seeing in her the ideal
performer for such a part. In that same year she also danced
the part of The Cat in Balanchine's new ballet *La Chatte*. Later
on, she danced in *Cimarosiana*, *Lac des Cygnes* and other
ballets.

At the time of Diaghileff's sadly early death in 1929, Markova
was a fully trained and experienced dancer, almost flawless in
her technique and ready for *prima ballerina* work; and to her,

as to all her colleagues in the Russian Ballet, the loss of the great impresario was a very severe blow.

Fortunately for the young Markova, however, the beginnings of the new British Ballet were gradually being firmly established by the various enterprising Ballet Clubs and Societies either already in existence or in embryo in London and elsewhere; and an entirely new public for Ballet was in process of being created, not only by the "Intelligentsia" of the day but also by artistic and cultured folk everywhere. At first it was "the thing" to go to the ballet; but gradually it became an accepted part of the cultural life of the people. The Vic-Wells Theatre and Company were already a well-established institution.

For a short time, Markova danced with the Camargo Society, with the Ballet Club (1931-33), and as guest artist ballerina with the Rambert Company. With the former she danced in *Façade*, in classics and other ballets; and for the latter she created the role of La Peri in the ballet of that name, written especially around her own personality by Frederick Ashton, then at the beginning of his since remarkably successful career; and, doubtless, her excellent work and keen interest very considerably encouraged the creative genius of this then little-known young choreographer. For the Ballet Rambert, also, she danced the ballerina parts in *Aurora's Wedding*, *Façade*, *Le Lac des Cygnes*, *Foyer de Danse*, *Les Masques*, *Méphisto Valse*, etc.

In 1932, she joined the Vic-Wells Ballet as principal ballerina, dancing the star roles in all their productions from 1932 to 1935, including the classics *Lac des Cygnes*, *Casse Noisette*, *Giselle*, *Coppélia*; the Fokine revivals of *Les Sylphides*, *Le Spectre de la Rose*, *Carnaval*; the de Valois ballets, *The Rake's Progress*, *The Haunted Ballroom*, *La Création du Monde*, *Job*, and others; also in the Frederick Ashton ballets, *Le Baiser de la Fée*, *Façade*, *Rio Grande*, *Les Rendezvous*, *Pomona*, *Lord of Burleigh*, etc.

During her work as *prima ballerina* with the Vic-Wells Company, Markova again had her friend of ballet-school days, Anton Dolin, as her principal partner in classical roles and as colleague in the creation of parts in the many new ballets then being produced by Ninette de Valois and Frederick Ashton. She had as additional partners Robert Helpmann, Harold Turner, Walter Gore and Idzikovski (as guest artist). Later on in her career, Markova has had as partners Serge Lifar, Youskevitch, André Églevsky, Massine, Frederic Franklin and other famous dancers.

In 1935, with the emergence of Margot Fonteyn (always a great admirer of hers) and other excellent dancers in the Company, Markova, having thus seen her young colleagues there safely through their trial stages and already capable of supporting Ninette de Valois and her splendid Vic-Wells undertaking, now left them to stand alone upon their own "light fantastic toes", while she soared away from those historic boards to enjoy the international fame she so thoroughly deserved and which now quickly became hers to take and enjoy.

It was in 1935 that the Markova-Dolin Ballet Company was formed and toured in many places in Great Britain and elsewhere; and these now famous dancers performed in a repertoire of many ballets. Among these were *Giselle, Lac des Cygnes, Aurora's Wedding, Casse Noisette* extracts, *Les Sylphides, Les Biches (House Party)*, the Blue-Bird *pas de deux*, Dolin's own choreographic works, *David, The Nightingale and the Rose, Bolero*, etc.; and various solo dances for both artists.

This first combined Company lasted until 1938, after which the two principals dissolved partnership for a time, so that each might take up the separate engagements so persistently offered them from time to time.

From 1938 to 1941, Markova danced with the Ballet Russe de Monte Carlo, in which Leonide Massine was at that time *maître de ballet*; and with the latter she danced leading parts at Covent Garden and Drury Lane, where the new ballets were Massine's *Seventh Symphony, Gaieté Parisienne, Nobilissima Visione*, and Serge Lifar's *Icare*.

Later on, Markova went with the Company to the United States, where these ballets and others were danced. Then, in 1941, the now-famous ballerina joined the Ballet Theatre Company in New York, with Anton Dolin again as her partner and co-leader; and there she remained for four years, dancing many of her own leading parts in the classics, in Fokine ballets and also in some of the new American ballets given by that Company. In the States she was hailed as the first great British ballerina to be given to the world and was regarded as being artistically the closest successor to Anna Pavlova, with whom she was again constantly compared. In 1945, the Markova-Dolin Group was reformed, and toured America.

In 1946, Markova was invited to travel as guest artist with the de Basil Ballet's American Tour, where she met with great ovations wherever she appeared; and in 1947, the Markova-Dolin Ballet Company was again re-formed, since when these famous dancers have proved themselves to be more deservedly popular than ever before. When they appeared for a season in 1948 as guest artists with the Sadler's Wells Ballet at the latter's new permanent home at Covent Garden, the critics had nothing but praise for them, despite the fact that they had both been absent from this country for nine years. In *Giselle*, in particular, they were acclaimed with especial praise, the years that had passed since their former star days with the old Vic-Wells Company —which they had helped so much to develop—having touched them lightly indeed. Both had gained in nobility and dignity of bearing, the years of experience having brought only the final touches of perfection to their former practically flawless technique. The particular harmony of their work together is dealt with more fully in the notes on Anton Dolin in this book, to which the reader is referred.

Towards the end of 1950, when Dolin became responsible for the formation of the grand Festival Ballet at the Stoll Theatre, London, to give performances there throughout the whole of the 1951 Festival of Britain year, Markova was, of course, his principal ballerina; and the famous pair again danced together in many of the most popular ballets and *divertissements*. Though a number of other famous dancers appeared through-out the Festival Season as guest artists—Toumanova, Riabouch-inska, Danilova, Chauviré, Krassovska, Slavenska, Massine, Frederic Franklin, John Gilpin, Trunoff and others—Markova and Dolin were always greeted with special ovations on their every appearance. They danced, in addition to their usual famous classical roles, in one or two of the new ballets produced by them during the season—in particular, they danced together exquisitely in the second movement of David Lichine's *Impressions*. This wonderful partnership ended in 1952.

Alicia Markova, from the very beginning of her fine career, has always been remarkable for the amazing airy-fairy lightness of her "lifts", so that, as in the case of Pavlova, she seems to float or to soar softly up into the air rather than to spring on rising from the ground, and with a seemingly entire absence of any sort of physical effort on her part. Though she is at her best in classical ballet and sylph-like parts, rather than in strongly characterized roles, she yet combines her perfect technique and romantic style with a sincerely emotional and even magnetic power. She has often been compared with that highly gifted, early Victorian dancer, Marie Taglioni, whom she certainly resembles as regards her fascinating lightness and the fey, spiritual qualities of her style which enable her to portray such a character as that of Giselle with particular sympathy and real beauty. Giselle, by the way, is her own favourite dancing role—this being run closely by Juliet in Tudor's *Roméo et Juliette* and her part in Massine's *Rouge et Noir*. Among her other most famous roles, in addition to Giselle and Juliet, one must name the Princess Aurora in *The Sleeping Beauty*, Odette-Odile in *Le Lac des Cygnes*, *The Dying Swan*, and leading *divertissements* in *The Nutcracker, Les Sylphides, pas de deux* in *Don Quixote*, as being supreme. But where every performance is a dream of beauty, it is not easy to name the most beautiful of all.

Her own movements being always of feather-weight lightness, Markova has a strong dislike of any noise made by the ballet shoes of dancers during a ballet; and she considers that all students should be trained to wear soft shoes. Like many other famous dancers, she has experienced one or two awkward *contretemps* during actual performances. Possibly the most annoying of these was during a performance of *Giselle* at the Metropolitan Opera House in New York, when a stage hand had inadvertently locked the door of the peasant girl's cottage home—thus causing this meticulously prompt and ever-ready ballerina to miss her entrance by a few moments.

In her private life, Markova is very simple, human, genuine, sincere and unspoiled. One of her sisters, Miss Doris Barry, now acts as her personal representative and secretary. Music forms her main outside interest.

Since becoming a free-lance once more, Markova has danced as guest artist with several companies at home and abroad. In Coronation year, 1953, she danced at Covent Garden, her exquisite *Giselle* being one of the highlights of the season.

Though not a writer herself—as is her famous partner, Anton Dolin—she has been the subject of several extremely interesting books. In all of these she is described as holding a quite unique position in the ballet world of to-day; and despite the welcome fact that, at the present time, other very fine ballerinas have now appeared upon the scene to keep her company, she is still regarded by the latter as a wonderful model for them all.

Leonide Massine

LEONIDE MASSINE'S WORLD-WIDE FAME RESTS NOT ONLY ON THE fact of his being one of the greatest choreographers of this century but likewise a magnificent dancer and mime with an amazing range who has continued unsurpassed in certain specially personal roles well beyond the male performer's usually accepted span. He is still the most important and vivid figure in ballet to-day.

Born at Moscow on March 26th, 1896, he received his education and his dramatic and ballet training at the Imperial School for the Theatre in that city. While still there in 1913, at the age of seventeen, he was seen by Serge Diaghileff, then seeking an effective successor to Nijinsky, from whose unexpected defection he was at that time suffering. Though different in every way from the latter, he knew, with his usual unfailing intuition, that the big-eyed, sable-headed youth—well built though of medium size and already revealing a keen intellect in his virile dancing —was exactly right for his purpose. He engaged him on the spot and caused his further training to proceed and be completed with the famous teacher Cecchetti, plus introductions to equally famous painters and musicians of the day. Among the latter were Picasso, Bakst, Larionov, Derain, Bérard, Matisse, Satie, de Falla, Fauré, Stravinsky, etc.—all of whom helped to influence the new dancer's own original creative work.

The first leading role in which Massine appeared was that of the young Joseph in Fokine's *La Legende de Joseph*, given at

Drury Lane, 1914, in which he was an immediate success and proved the great impresario's belief in him.

After this first startling success, so rapidly did the eager youth progress that in 1915 he was already one of the leading dancers in the Company and had become its choreographer. The first ballet he created for the Company was *The Midnight Sun* (*Soleil de Nuit*), to music by Rimsky-Korsakov and *décor* by Larionov, which was produced at Geneva in 1915; his second, in 1916, was *Las Meninas* (music by Fauré, *décor* Socrate and Sert), produced at San Sebastian. Then, in 1917, came his brilliant *Les Femmes de Bonne Humeur* (*The Good-Humoured Ladies*), to music by Scarlatti and *décor* by Bakst, produced Rome; and *Contes Russes* (music Liadov, *décor* Larionov), produced San Sebastian. That same year, at the Chatélet, Paris, the young Massine's first really modernist work, *Parade* (music by Satie, *décor* Picasso), was produced. This marked an entirely new style of ballet on the then fashionable cubist movement and exemplified Diaghileff's insatiable later tendency towards the inclusion of something novel in his repertory. The three last-named ballets were amazingly mature and really dazzling creations for one still so extremely youthful.

For Diaghileff's welcome return to London on the conclusion of the war in 1918, the new and already well-established young choreographer's *Soleil de Nuit*, *Contes Russes* and *Les Femmes de Bonne Humeur* were given at the Coliseum, and were received with great enthusiasm—in particular, the last named, with the gay Lydia Lopokova in her afterwards most famous role as the lively serving-maid, Mariuccia, and Massine himself as the waiter, Niccolo. On the occasion of this London visit, Massine's *Les Jardins d'Aranjuez* (music by Cimarosa, *décor* Sert) was performed.

The following year, in 1919, came the production of Massine's probably two most famous ballets, at the Alhambra in London. These were *La Boutique Fantasque* (music by Rossini, *décor* Derain), and *Le Tricorne* (music by de Falla, *décor* Picasso), and were received with the utmost enthusiasm, being both always regarded since as among his masterpieces. Massine and Tamara Karsavina as the Miller and his Wife in the latter revealed themselves at their highest level, Massine's famous dance, the *Farucca*, in particular, being an amazing performance—as was his light-hearted *Can-Can* with Lopokova in the former. These two performances never ceased to "bring down the house", both then and since.

In 1920, Massine created for Diaghileff *Le Chant du Rossignol* (music by Stravinsky, *décor* Matisse), *Pulcinella* (Stravinsky and Pergolesi—Picasso) and *L'Astuzie Feminili* (Cimarosa—Sert)— all produced in Paris (the latter was later produced as *Cimarosiana*). A revival of Nijinsky's *Le Sacre du Printemps* (Stravinsky —Roerich), with new choreography by Massine, was also produced in Paris this year; and later in 1920, the three former ballets were given in the London Covent Garden season.

For private reasons, Massine now left the Company for a few years. During this period, he danced with Lopokova at Covent Garden in 1922. In 1923, he produced *Togo or the Noble Savage* in a Revue at Covent Garden (with Lopokova, Sokolova, Ninette de Valois and Woizikovsky); and in 1925, he presented *The Rake* and *Crescendo* in the Cochran Revue, *On With The Dance*, at the London Pavilion. In another Cochran Revue at the Pavilion in 1926, he produced with Nemtchinova his own ballet *divertissements The Tub* and *Gigue*. In all these engagements he himself danced.

On his return to Diaghileff's Company in 1925, as guest artist, he created more ballets for the latter. These were *Zéphyr et Flore* (Dukelsky—Braque), produced Monte Carlo in 1925; *Les Mâtelots* (Auric—Pruna), produced Paris, 1925; *Mercure* (Satie —Picasso), produced Paris 1927; *Le Pas d'Acier* (Prokofiev— Jakouloff) Paris, 1927; and *Ode* (Nabokoff—Tchelitchev), produced Paris 1928. The first two were also given at the London Coliseum in 1925; *Mercure* and *Pas d'Acier* were given at the Prince's, London, in 1927; and *Ode* was given at His Majesty's London in 1928. In between these last productions for the Diaghileff Company, Massine also visited America, where for three years he was choreographer at the Roxy Theatre, New York. Later, he presented ballets for the Ida Rubinstein Company at the Paris Opéra, and for the Scala in Milan.

After the death of Diaghileff in 1929, Massine joined de Basil's Ballets Russes de Monte Carlo; and for this Company, and its later groups, he created the following ballets: in 1932, *Jeux d'Enfants* (Bizet—J. Miro); in 1933, *Les Présages* (Tchaikovsky —Masson), *Le Beau Danube* (J. Strauss—V. and E. Polunin and de Beaumont), *Scuola di Ballo* (Françaix and Boccherini—de Beaumont)—all produced Monte Carlo; *Beach* (Françaix—Dufy); *Choreartium* (Brahms—Terechkovitch and Lourié), produced Alhambra, London. In 1934, he created *Union Pacific* (Nabokoff—A. Johnson and Sharaff), produced Philadelphia. In 1935, *Jardin Public* (Dukelsky—Halicka), *Le Bal* (Rieti—di Chirico), both produced Covent Garden, London; and in 1936, *Symphonie Fantasque* (Berlioz—Bérard), produced Covent Garden.

For the René Blum Ballets Russes de Monte Carlo, and its successor Company, he created in 1938, *Gaieté Parisienne* (Offenbach—de Beaumont), *The Seventh Symphony* (Beethoven—Bérard)—both produced Monte Carlo; *Nobilissima Visione* (Hindemith—Tchelitchev and de Beaumont), *Bogatyri* (Borodin—Gontcharova)—produced New York. In 1939, *Capriccio Espagnol* (Rimsky-Korsakov—Andreu); *Rouge et Noir* (Shostakovich—Matisse)—both produced Monte Carlo; *Bacchanale* (*Venusberg*) (Wagner—Dali)—produced New York, and later at Covent Garden. In 1940, *Jurupary* (Villa Lobos—R. P. de Bois), *Vienna 1814* (Weber—Stewart Chaney); *The New Yorker* (Gershwin—R. Irwin)—all produced New York. In 1941, *Labyrinth* (Schubert—Dali); *Saratoga* (Weinberger—O. Smith and A. Colt)—both produced New York. In most of these ballets, Massine himself danced.

For Ballet Theatre, in 1942, Massine created *Aleko* (Tchaikovsky—M. Chagall) and *Don Domingo de Don Blas* (S. Revueltas—J. Castellanos)—both produced Mexico; in 1943, *Mdlle. Angot* (Lecocq—Dobujinsky); and in 1944, *Moonlight Sonata* (Beethoven—Soudéikine)—produced Chicago. From 1945 to 1946, he became Artistic Director of Ballets Russes Highlights, for which he created about fifteen short ballet *divertissements*.

Towards the end of 1945, Massine returned to England and toured in *A Bullet in the Ballet*—a curious mixture of murder-mystery-thriller and ballet combined, adapted from Caryl Brahms and S. J. Simons' diverting novel—bringing Irina Baronova with him as partner; but this material was not generally regarded as being worthy of either dancer's great gifts, despite their lovely dancing in one of the three ballets given, *Reverie Classique*, to music by Chopin. The latter had been produced in New York a short time before. It was, however, a great pleasure to all ballet-lovers when he accepted an invitation to appear, in 1947, as guest artist to the resident Sadler's Wells Ballet Company at Covent Garden, and to revive for them two of his greatest ballets, *Le Tricorne* and *La Boutique Fantasque*; to present his recent popular Ballet Theatre production *Mam'zelle Angot* (adapted from Lecocq's operetta, *La Fille de Madame Angot*); and to create and produce an entirely new ballet later. In the two first named he himself took his original roles, dancing superbly in the famous Farucca in *Le Tricorne* and the Can-Can in *La Boutique Fantasque* with almost the same verve and vigorous virtuosity as of yore. This ballet proved most acceptable with its gaiety, many delightful dances and ensembles and bright music. The new ballet, *The Clock Symphony* (music by Haydn, *décor* by Bérard), dealt with a charming fairy-tale subject, treated by the famous choreographer with great animation and delicate humour; and the magic touch of the master-hand was always evident. It was created especially for the Company, and was produced at Covent Garden on June 26th, 1948. In 1949, he created a new ballet entitled *Suite Bergamasque*, with music by Debussy.

Massine has done much useful work in the film world; and in 1947, he took part in the much-discussed British film *The Red Shoes*; and as the Shoemaker in this production he had a delightful character role that suited him remarkably well.

Another new ballet by Massine (music by Georges Auric, *décor* by Balthus) entitled *Le Peintre et son Modèle*, was produced by Les Ballets des Champs-Élysées at Paris in November 1949. It is for two performers only and the movements are complicated and, at times, even acrobatic. In 1949, also, Massine revived one of his most remarkable ballets for the Marquis de Cuevas' Grand Ballet de Monte Carlo—a work first created in 1944 for the same Company then known as The de Cuevas Ballet International. This ballet dealt with the dramatic love-story of Tristan and Isolde, set to the music of Wagner's opera; and it had elaborate surrealistic *décor* by Salvador Dali. Entitled *Tristan Fou (Mad Tristan)*, it portrays the hideous mind pictures of the ill-starred Tristan driven mad by grief for the loss of his beloved Isolde and haunted by her memory to such an extent that she actually appears before him in a distorted reincarnation—a horrible Chimera in the form of a Praying Mantis making a cannibalistic feast of her one-time lover. This gruesome ballet, while presented in accord with the nightmare-like designs of Dali, has true dramatic feeling, contains many tense moments, and has some fine choreography and miming.

In November 1949, at the Nijinsky Benefit Gala Performances held at the Empress Hall, Earl's Court, London, Massine was one of the several world-famous dancers who appeared there to do honour to the greatest male dancer of this century. His main contribution was his own *Capriccio Espagnol*, in which he danced with Tamara Toumanova. In June that year, he had danced in this same arena with Danilova in his *Le Beau Danube*, when his performance as the Hussar was as brilliant as it had ever been.

Massine is now reviving many of his famous ballets for various companies. In addition to his 1947 revivals of *Le Tricorne*, *La Boutique Fantasque* and *Mam'zelle Angot* for the Sadler's Wells Ballet, he revived his *Le Beau Danube* for L'Opéra Comique, Paris, on January 20th, 1950, and himself danced his own original role of the Hussar. In May 1950, he produced his *Gaieté Parisienne* for International Ballet at the Coliseum, London, in which Mona Inglesby scored a great success as the charming Glove-Seller. In the spring of 1951, he also revived for the same Company his *Capriccio Espagnol*. This was, a little later on, given by International Ballet at a Royal Gala Performance, with *Gaieté Parisienne*, in the Royal Festival Hall during its six-weeks' 1951 Festival Season. Other interesting Massine revivals are also taking place from time to time in many parts of the world.

In the spring of 1951, Massine took part in another film. This was the Michael Power—Emeric Pressburger production in Technicolor of *The Tales of Hoffmann*, set to the delightful music of Offenbach—with the Royal Philharmonic Orchestra, conducted superbly by Sir Thomas Beecham. The choreography was by Frederick Ashton, and the designs by Hein Heckroth. In this film, Massine was particularly fine as Schlemihl in the Venetian episode.

During the season given by Anton Dolin's Festival Ballet at the Stoll Theatre, London, Massine was invited to appear with the Company as an important and popular guest artist. He gave a wonderful performance of the title-role in *Petrouchka*, first with Markova and later with Riabouchinska as the Ballerina.

On May 15th, 1951, the Marquis de Cuevas' Ballet Company presented at the Bordeaux Festival an entirely new ballet by Massine, entitled *Symphonie Allegorique* and set to Sauguet's *Les Saisons*. It provides a series of exquisite moving pictures, very beautifully devised by Massine; and it met with an enthusiastic reception.

Massine has never been of the classical *danseur noble* type. Nevertheless, he excels as a romantic performer, this being revealed in certain of the Fokine ballets and in several of his own creations, notably, the Hussar in *Le Beau Danube*, as the Peruvian in *Gaieté Parisienne*, and as the Miller in *Le Tricorne*. The latter is probably one of his very best roles, revealing him at his top form in virtuosity ballet work. His dancing of the Farucca in this, and his performance as the male Can-Can dancer in *La Boutique Fantasque* have never yet been surpassed. As a mime he is equally remarkable, slipping into "the skin" of his many roles with the utmost ease—especially those of his own creation. His personality on the stage is of the dynamic, arresting kind that holds his every audience; and he has always been able to retain their attention even when standing motionless. He has a vivid sense of style-atmosphere. He has a great sense of humour, and many of his dances of the humorous kind exhibit real wit and *diablerie*.

The many ballets he has created can be listed into several types or classes—and of these there are also variants. There is the romantic story kind, or *ballet d'action*, such as *Le Tricorne, La Boutique Fantasque, Pulcinella, Les Femmes de Bonne Humeur, Les Contes Russes, Le Rossignol*; the ballets of his somewhat later sophisticated period, when such novelties as Cubism and Surrealism were the rage, as expressed in the realistic, constructivist *Pas d'Acier, Parade, Ode*, etc.; his many very fine symphonic ballets, *Choriartium, Nobilissima Visione, Les Présages*, etc; and his more light-hearted creations (usually having a decided romantic tinge), as *Gaieté Parisienne*. Others hardly fit into any of these types, as, for example, *Tristan Fou* and *Aleko*, which are highly dramatic works. Even when his subject is not a beautiful one, or is, indeed, downright ugly, or—

though this seldom happens—when the ballet may be slightly weak in subject, there is always some redeeming incident, or unexpectedly beautiful or original movement which reveals the master touch, the outstanding intellect. In his masterpieces, in his controversial ballets, and in his lighter works, there is always to be found somewhere the magic of beauty and the touch of genius.

In December 1951, Massine created a new ballet for Covent Garden. Dealing with a Scottish folk legend, it was entitled *Donald of the Burthens,* and had music by Ian Whyte and *décor* by Robert Colquhoun and Robert MacBryde.

Massine was first married to the well-known dancer, Eugenia Delarova, from whom he obtained a divorce. He later married Madame Tatiana Milishnokoff, who now assists him with the revivals of his ballets. They have two children, a daughter, Tatiana (Tanya), and a son, Leonide. They both already show a definite gift for dancing.

Pamela May

AS ONE OF THE LEADING BALLERINAS OF THE SADLER'S WELLS Ballet, Pamela May has come into greater prominence since the Company has been established at the Royal Opera House, Covent Garden, as its permanent home. The whole atmosphere of Covent Garden seems to suit her personality, so that her many excellent qualities are now seen to better advantage than ever before. As a classical dancer, she has a remarkably clear line in arabesque, her attack has become stronger and her depth of feeling greater.

Pamela May was born at San Fernando, in Trinidad, 1917. She received her preliminary training from Freda Grant; and later, she studied in Paris, first with Olga Preobrajenska and afterwards with Madame Egorova. Then, in 1933, as a slim, young, fair-haired girl of sixteen, she joined the Sadler's Wells School, whence, in due course, she passed into the Sadler's Wells Ballet

Company, beginning her real dancing career in the *corps de ballet* and gradually working her way up through small roles to leading ones. Her progress was steady, while her work in training was exceptionally thorough; and she gradually emerged as an artist of growing importance and sensitive understanding. She made her début in the *pas de trois* in *Lac des Cygnes*; and soon afterwards she began to dance in most of the productions of the Company.

She has travelled with the Sadler's Wells Ballet on every foreign tour they have taken; and at the beginning of the Second World War, she was with the Company in Holland when the German invading armies marched in and, with her colleagues, made a thrilling escape in a cattle boat. She has also danced with the Ballet in France, Belgium, Poland, Czechoslovakia, Sweden, Norway, Denmark, Austria and Italy; and in the late autumn of 1949, she went with the Company on their now famous and amazingly successful first visit to U.S.A. and Canada, where she received high praises everywhere for the excellence of her work.

Pamela May has danced leading and other roles in *The Sleeping Beauty, Coppélia, Le Lac des Cygnes, Giselle, Casse Noisette, Les Sylphides, Dante Sonata, Nocturne, Symphonic Variations, Horoscope, The Wanderer, The Prospect Before Us, Orpheus and Eurydice, The Haunted Ballroom, Checkmate, Le Carnaval, Les Patineurs, Le Baiser de la Fée, Cinderella, La Boutique Fantasque*, etc. One of her most effective roles has been the Red Queen in the de Valois' ballet *Checkmate*, in which she gave a most sympathetic and touching rendering of this royal weakling. She has also danced the dominating, all-powerful Black Queen in this ballet—an entirely contrasting part. She created the sparkling virtuoso role of the famous dancer, Mlle. Théodore, in de Valois' *The Prospect Before Us*. She also created the role of the Moon in Ashton's *Horoscope*, and of the Fairy Godmother in this same choreographer's full-evening-length ballet *Cinderella*. In *The Sleeping Beauty*, she has danced, in addition to a delightful rendering of the Princess Aurora, the parts of the Lilac Fairy, the Rose Fairy, the Diamond Fairy and the Princess Florisse in the dazzling and difficult Blue-Bird *pas de deux*.

Her Queen of the Wilis in *Giselle* is another outstanding role of Pamela May's, as is also her rendering of one of the girls in *Symphonic Variations*, in which the three female performers are all of equal status as regards their mingled lovely movements —her colleagues being Margot Fonteyn and Moira Shearer. This ballet, by the way, in which there are only six performers —three girls and three youths—is regarded as a great test of endurance, since all the executants remain dancing on the stage, with hardly a pause, from curtain rise to fall.

Pamela May is possessed of good executive ability; she is a member of the Executive Committee of the Royal Academy of Dancing, and is also President of the Old Scholars' Club in connection with that Academy. She has done some excellent work in television. She is an individualist with a definite style of her own; and she has great dignity and nobility of bearing in such roles as Eurydice in *Orpheus and Eurydice*, and the Moon in *Horoscope*—both outstanding performances of hers. At the same time she makes one of the gayest of Swanildas in *Coppélia*, and is quite at home in any *soubrette* part. She is equally delightful as the Lilac Fairy in *The Sleeping Beauty*; and she can be counted upon always to give a finished performance in *divertissements*—in which she excels.

When Pamela May went with the Sadler's Wells Ballet to U.S.A. and Canada in the late autumn of 1949, she was hailed everywhere as a very highly finished ballerina, and her remarkable elevation was especially commented upon. Since her return she has presented all her roles with a more polished and authoritative style even than before; and in the revived performances of *Coppélia* given in March 1950, in particular, she received very high praises for her splendid dancing and miming as the vivacious and tantalizing Swanilda. In Ninette de Valois' new ballet, *Don Quixote*, presented on February 20th, 1950, as the Shepherdess of the Golden Age, she danced radiantly with Alexis Rassine, her Shepherd partner, and added conspicuously to the beauty of that particular scena.

On March 9th, 1950, Pamela May took part in the Grand Gala performance at Covent Garden in honour of the State Visit of the French President and Madame Auriol, at which Their Majesties the King and Queen were present. In May 1950, she went with Margot Fonteyn and Robert Helpmann to La Scala, Milan, to dance in *The Sleeping Beauty*, in connection with the Holy Year celebrations there, where she received an enthusiastic reception with her co-stars.

When the Sadler's Wells Ballet visited the U.S.A. and Canada for the second time at the end of 1950, Pamela May was again one of the principal ballerinas accompanying the party.

In April 1952, she danced in John Cranko's fantastic ballet *Bonne Bouche*, creating the role of a grasping mother ultra socially ambitious for her daughter—a real contrast to her gracious royal mothers in the classics, in which she excels.

Bronislava Nijinska

A YEAR YOUNGER THAN HER FAMOUS BROTHER, VASLAV Nijinsky—that most wonderful dancer of all time— Bronislava Nijinska was born at Kiev, in South Russia, January 8th, 1891, her parents being of Polish extraction. Like her brother, she received her training at the Imperial Ballet School, St. Petersburg, which she entered at the age of nine years, though she had already taken some private lessons with the great Cecchetti. Her main teachers during her eight years' training in the Imperial School were the famous choreographer, Michael Fokine, then *maître de ballet*, Kulichevskaya, Cecchetti and Nicholas Legat; and she was given private lessons by her gifted brother—already a dancer known to have a great future.

In 1908, having passed through the School with great success, she entered the Imperial Ballet, and soon danced important roles in the ballets then being presented at the Maryinsky Theatre. Though blessed with no facial beauty—indeed, she was admittedly quite plain—she always gave the impression of beauty, being unusually graceful and a most excellent and reliable dancer, sensitive and intellectual. She created the role of Papillon in Fokine's *Le Carnaval* when first produced in 1910, and few have excelled her in this dainty part.

She joined the Diaghileff Ballet in its first season in Paris in 1909, and continued among the great impresario's principal dancers during his various seasons in 1910, 1911 and 1912; and in the further Fokine ballets she danced the Puppet Ballerina in *Petrouchka* and a Bacchante in *Narcisse*. She danced in other ballets in the repertoire, and travelled with the Company.

After the Diaghileff—Nijinsky split in 1913, she joined her brother for a time, appearing with him the following year in his ill-fated season at the Palace Theatre, London. During the 1914-18 War she was in St. Petersburg and at Kiev, where she taught in her own Ballet School in her home town; here, also, she realized her special gift for choreography, and began her first small efforts in the art.

In 1921, she rejoined Diaghileff and helped him with his production of *The Sleeping Beauty* at the Alhambra, London; for she had good organizing gifts. She herself danced in the latter production, and in many of the ballets in following seasons. She also arranged the *Casse Noisette* dances given about this time. When Leonide Massine presently left the Diaghileff Ballet, she succeeded him as choreographer to the Company, and became *maîtresse de ballet*. She created some very successful ballets for the Company, several of which almost immediately became famous and popular favourites. These were: in 1922, *Le Renard* (music by Stravinsky, *décor* and costumes by Larionov); in 1921, *Les Noces* (Stravinsky—Gontcharova); in 1924, *Les Biches* (Poulenc—Laurençin), *Les Fâcheux* (Auric—Braque), *Les Tentations de la Bergère*, later *The Faithful Shepherdess* (Monteclair—Gris), and *Le Train Bleu* (Milhaud—Picasso, Laurens, Chanel); in 1926, *Roméo et Juliette*, jointly with Balanchine (Lambert—Miro and Ernst), *Une Nuit sur le Mont Chauve* (Moussorgsky—Gontcharova). She herself danced leading roles in several of her own ballets, and in others.

Nijinska left Diaghileff in 1926 and went to Buenos Aires to become ballet-mistress there. Here she created her charming ballet *Étude* (Bach—Barovsky) and revived several others. Afterwards she returned to Paris to occupy the same position with the Ida Rubinstein Ballet, dancing with the Company and creating a number of new ballets. Among the latter were, in 1928: *Bolero* (Ravel), *La Bien Aimée* (Schubert and Liszt—Benois), *Le Baiser de la Fée* (Stravinsky, *La Princesse Cygne, Nocturne, Les Noces de l'Amour et de Psyche*; and in 1929, *La Valse* (Ravel—Benois) and *Aubade*. For the Russian Opera at

Paris in 1930-31, she arranged the dances for several Russian operas; and for this Company she also created a new ballet *Capriccio*, and revived *Étude*.

Later on, in 1932, Nijinska had her own Théâtre de Danse in Paris, where she revived several of her former ballets, and also created *Variations, Les Comediens Jaloux* and *Hamlet*. For the de Basil Ballet Russe in 1935, she created *Les Cents Baisers* (Baron d'Erlanger—J. Hugo); and in 1936, *Danses Slaves et Tziganes*.

In 1937, Nijinska came to England and joined the Markova-Dolin Ballet as *maîtresse de ballet*, and revived for this Company *Les Biches* (in England produced as *The House Party*) and *La Bien Aimée* (as *The Beloved One*). Later, for the Ballet Polonais, she created several new ballets, the best known among these being *La Légende de Cracovie, Concerto de Chopin* and *Le Chant de la Terre*.

After this, Nijinska spent some years in America; and in 1940, for Ballet Theatre in New York, she revived Dauberval's old classic *La Fille mal Gardée* under the title of *Naughty Lisette*, or *The Wayward Daughter*, with her own choreography, new music by Heitel, and *décor* and costumes by Soudeikine.

In 1942, she arranged for the Ballet Russe de Monte Carlo the dances for *The Snow Maiden* (Glazounov—Aronson); in 1943, for the same Company, she revived her ballet *Étude*, and created a new work *Ancient Russia* (Tchaikovsky—Gontcharova). For the Ballet International, New York, she revived *Bolero* (Ravel arr. Dorati—Ignatiev), and created *Pictures at an Exhibition* (Moussorgsky—Aronson) and *Brahms Variations* (Brahms—Vertès). For Ballet Theatre again in 1945, she created *Harvest Time* (Wieniawski—Gilbert) and *Rendezvous* (Rachmaninov—Gilbert); and also revived for them her *Three Ivans dance* from *The Sleeping Beauty*.

In 1949, Nijinska created for the Marquis de Cuevas' Grand Ballet de Monte Carlo a new ballet in honour of the centenary of Chopin's death which occurred that year. It was entitled *In Memoriam*, and was set to the music of the famous composer's *Fantasia in D Minor*, the *Grand Fantasia on Polish Airs*, and the posthumous *Polonaise No. 2*, all orchestrated by M. Cloez. The *décor* and costumes were by the painter Jean Ribier, who chose soft shades of grey and mauve for the costumes, the backcloth being plain grey velvet curtains. This sad and somewhat gloomy ballet was beautifully danced by the principals of the Company, Rosella Hightower, Éthery Pagava, Ana Cheselka, André Églevsky and *corps de ballet*; and the work, though sombre in character, was harmonious and highly sensitive. Some critics, however, did not consider it at all a satisfactory ballet.

Among Bronislava Nijinska's most famous ballets are the following: *Les Noces*, created for the Diaghileff Company which, strangely enough, was seven years in the making, owing to the many delays caused both to Gontcharova, who designed the *décor* and costumes and to Stravinsky, who composed the music, due to the impresario's frequent changes of plan. When finally produced in Paris, in 1923, though it had an adverse reception to begin with, it became a brilliant success later on—a marvel considering that the three creative artists had mainly worked apart and very fitfully for so long a time. *Les Biches* is regarded by many as her masterpiece, and has become almost as much a "period" piece as any of the Fokine ballets. It was intended as a balletic satire on the popular and then somewhat decadent "house-parties" of that particular period. The dances for the various guests and for the hostess are very cleverly contrived and each is a witty and highly polished item. The same may almost be said of *Le Train Bleu* which, though somewhat snobbish in its treatment of the fashionable Riviera seaside crowd of the day, has likewise continued a popular ballet and is often revived. The *Brahms Variations*—a symphonic ballet; *The Faithful Shepherdess*—a charming seventeenth-century scena; *La Bien Aimée, Étude* and *La Valse* are all lovely ballets, which many would like to see revived at an early date.

Nijinska, as a dancer, was full of grace and understanding; as a choreographer, she was, and is still, an artist with a rich imagination and a vivid creative gift.

Vaslav Nijinsky

A S THE MOST DAZZLING MALE MEMBER OF THE ULTRA-BRILLIANT Diaghileff Company of Russian Dancers, Vaslav Nijinsky reigned supreme for a few short years only; and the tragedy of his early mental collapse still scarcely bears thinking of. It is true that quite a number of other splendid male dancers were his contemporaries in the Russian Ballet world into the midst of which he leapt so lightly—Bolm, Fokine, Mordkin, Kudsov, Semenov, Novikoff, Koslov, even the great maestro, Cecchetti himself, to name but a few; nevertheless, despite the special and general achievements of these wonderful dancers, there was still only the one Nijinsky, who was outstanding among them all. When Nijinsky danced, there was magic in the air, and audiences remained almost breathless until he had vanished from sight.

Vaslav Nijinsky was born in Kiev in 1890; and he came of a dancing and acrobatic Polish family, his parents being performers in a circus, though his mother had been trained at the Imperial Ballet School in Warsaw. At the regulation age of about nine years he entered the Imperial Ballet School in St. Petersburg, where, with the other students, he was taken entire charge of by the State, receiving, without the payment of fees to the latter, his general education and all his physical requirements, as well as a perfect and most complete training in dancing and ballet. Later on he made his début as a fully trained dancer on the boards of the Maryinsky Theatre, passing quickly from the *corps de ballet* to small and then to principal roles.

Even as a boy trainee, Nijinsky was seen to possess unusual gifts as a dancer and soon outshone his immediate male contemporaries. His technique was perfected with the utmost ease; and the extreme lightness of his bounding leaps and his amazing elevation attracted notice long before he appeared upon the stage of the Maryinsky Theatre. The attention of the ballet-master, Michael Fokine—already becoming known as an original choreographer—was soon drawn to the remarkable young dancer; and he began to allot him as partner to Tamara Karsavina, just then also emerging brilliantly from the Ballet School;

and even, on occasion, he was permitted to partner the already established *prima ballerina*, Anna Pavlova. At the School Exhibitions, Nijinsky and Karsavina danced together as principals; and a little later, when they were promoted as finished, fully trained dancers to the Maryinsky, they soon became known as perfectly matched partners.

Fokine tried out several of his own early original choreographic ideas upon the receptive boy-dancer, finding that he reacted to them in an encouraging and helpful manner. Consequently, when, in 1909, Diaghileff was about to take his first Company of Russian dancers to Paris, the wonderful dancing of Vaslav Nijinsky was already well known to him; so he invited him to join his troupe—which Nijinsky gladly did, together with the partner of his more youthful days, Tamara Karsavina, and, for a short time only, the already famous *prima ballerina*, Pavlova.

As is already well known to all students of ballet, Diaghileff's Paris visit created a tremendous *furore*—as did his subsequent visits there and his first descent upon London in 1911. By this time Nijinsky was already regarded as the most wonderful male dancer in the Company—indeed, the finest dancer within living memory and unlikely ever to be surpassed.

With Karsavina, he danced in most of the original Fokine ballets, *Pavillon d'Armide*, *Les Sylphides*, *Le Carnaval*, *Cléopâtre*, *Le Spectre de la Rose*, *Schéhérazade*, *Narcisse*, *Petrouchka*, *Le Festin*, *Le Dieu Bleu*, *Les Orientales*, etc. His most famous successes in the Fokine ballets were: the Rose Spirit in *Le Spectre de la Rose*, the tragic Puppet in *Petrouchka* and the Golden Slave in *Schéhérazade*.

His name will always be more especially bound up with his absolutely unique performance as the Spectre, with his exquisite partner, Karsavina, as the lovely Young Girl just home from her first ball and dreaming ecstatically of her first lover. Never yet has Nijinsky's soaring leap in through the open window from the rose garden beyond, his moment of suspension, or "tarrying", in mid-air, his fairy, gossamer-like alighting beside the sleeping maiden, been forgotten by anyone who beheld it, nor has it ever been equalled since. He seemed actually to be a radiant spirit from another sphere and not a creature of this world at all; and his subsequent floating movements with his ecstatic partner to the lilting strains of Weber's *Invitation to the Waltz* was a dream of enchantment indeed. His final leap back into the garden beyond was even more marvellous still; and it took several men to stop him safely in the wings.

Nijinsky was asked many times how he managed to achieve that moment of suspension and literally to seem to be floating through the air; but, with his slow smile, he usually made some such answer as " I don't know! It just happens! You go up, pause a little, and then come down! " There was nothing hurried about his famous leap through the open window. It was almost slow, as though he came in like a moth from the garden outside, soaring higher and then floating to the ground, which he scarcely seemed to touch—the whole movement apparently absolutely effortless and as light as thistledown.

His amazing elevation was equally remarkable in other famous leaps—such as that of the Golden Slave in *Schéhérazade,* for instance. He could even take additional leaps while still in the air.

Petrouchka—that perfectly constructed ballet, in which Fokine, Stravinsky and Bakst achieved complete unity and harmony in dance, music and *décor*—is universally acclaimed as Nijinsky's most brilliant role, since it provided him with such a splendid medium for the display of his unique gifts as a mime; and his portrayal of the enchanted, shabby puppet so tragically reaching out towards life and love but condemned from the first to the shattering of his eager dreams, was certainly a work of genius. Nevertheless, he was most beloved by one and all as the ethereal *Spectre of the Rose*; and he was constantly besieged—by feminine "fans" in particular—at his dressing-room door by souvenir hunters, who did not hesitate to tear off the shaded petals from his rose-tunic, if they got the chance.

Nijinsky off the stage, and Nijinsky on the stage were two entirely different persons. In his everyday social life, this wonderful dancer was not wonderful at all, but just ordinary and undistinguished. Many who knew him intimately have even declared that he was totally devoid of culture. This, however, could certainly not have been the case, since he had received, at least, an excellent education in the Ballet School.

What was more, he completely understood every role he danced, and the history of the period it belonged to; this implies a good education and a certain amount of high culture.

Others who were his colleagues say that, like Peter Pan, he never quite grew up, but always remained a boy—and a very shy, diffident boy, who was nervous and at his worst in the company of intellectuals. That he was shy and seldom spoke in general company is certainly true; also it is true that he appeared to be ill at ease when he did talk. But that he understood and absorbed what other people said is equally a fact; and he certainly grasped everything he needed to know in connection with his creative work. When Diaghileff took him in hand —for the great impresario was undoubtedly extremely attached to Nijinsky and regarded him as his own particular *protégé* whom he was determined to present to the world in the best possible light—and began to direct his attention to matters of Art and to other cultural interests, he was more than capable of absorbing these as to the manner born. That this was the case was to be seen later, when he came to create his own strange ballets, *L'Après-midi d'un Faune* and *Le Sacre du Printemps*, in which he revealed a surprising knowledge of Ancient Greek Art and Mythology and of the religious lore of Primitive Russia in pagan times. It is true that Diaghileff influenced him greatly and suggested much to him that might not otherwise have come into his mind; but that he was capable of absorbing, carrying out and developing such suggestions and of benefiting by the influence of an ultra-cultured mind is equally true. True, it was noticeable that when he ceased to come under the influence and direction of Diaghileff and was acting entirely on his own initiative, his artistic efforts dwindled accordingly and he seemed to lack much of the inspiration he had formerly shown. Nevertheless, he produced one other really important ballet, *Tyl Eulenspiegel*, after he had parted from Diaghileff.

In his natural appearance, Nijinsky was by no means of the young Greek god type, but was rather roughly built, with none too well-shaped features and limbs; and his eyes had a curiously Eastern slant. But, no sooner did he appear upon the stage than a complete metamorphosis seemed to have taken place. He could assume not only the dress of the character he was to enact, but the features likewise—his make-up being definitely a work of art—in addition to which he appeared to slip into the actual "skin" of a role with the utmost ease. From the moment he appeared upon the stage, he had won his audience, who followed his every exquisite movement with the absorbed fascination only to be accorded to an instantly recognized genius. No matter how apathetic—even dull and uninteresting —he may have appeared on entering his dressing-room, by the time he issued therefrom, it was as though a reincarnation had taken place in the interval and he now was the actual imaginary character he had assumed. The quite ordinary-looking young man, Nijinsky, had vanished and nothing whatever of him remained; but in his place there stood the radiant Spectre of the Rose, or the glamorous Golden Slave-lover of Zobeide, ready to soar lightly or to leap with eager passion on to the stage before the audience awaiting him with bated breath.

Nijinsky was equally successful in all the classic roles he danced; and he made the perfectly courteous *danseur noble* partner. It was, by the way, while he was dancing the part of Albrecht in *Giselle* at the Maryinsky Theatre one time that he caused a small scandal that resulted in his leaving that beloved theatre of his earliest triumphs. Diaghileff had ordered Nijinsky's tunic for Albrecht to be shortened somewhat, considering this might be an improvement. But the sight of this short tunic on the boards of the more conservative Maryinsky was regarded with strong disapproval by the Authorities there, who fined the dancer and reprimanded him severely—with the result that the indignant Nijinsky sent in his resignation. However, Diaghileff—whose fault it really was—felt quite pleased about the incident, since it left the future of Nijinsky now entirely in his own hands, so that he was free to mould the young genius as he pleased.

Diaghileff was never static; and he firmly believed that change and novelty were necessary for the preservation of his Company's high prestige. He was always planning "something different".

Having developed—and, indeed, almost re-educated—Nijinsky into the kind of brilliant dancer never seen before, Diaghileff now began to encourage his *protégé* to become a choreographer. Having himself introduced this unaccountable youth to early Greek Art, he eagerly encouraged him to create a ballet on a Greek mythological subject. The result was *L'Aprés-midi d'un Faune,* with music by Claude Debussy, scenery and costumes by Léon Bakst. It was produced at Le Théâtre du Chatélet, Paris, on May 29th, 1912—where it created a first-rate scandal because of certain actions performed at the finale by Nijinsky as the Child-of-Nature Faun, which displeased the audience. However, with the alteration of the offending finale, the ballet became a successful work; and on being presented shortly afterwards in London, it was accepted there calmly enough. It came, however, as a complete novelty after the gorgeous dramatic work of Fokine—who now left the Company, leaving the impresario's young *protégé* as *maître de ballet* and choreographer.

Nijinsky's second ballet, however, *Jeux* (with music by Debussy and costumes and *décor* by Bakst)—in which the choreographer himself danced as a tennis champion—proved to be much less successful; and after being produced at the same theatre in Paris on May 15th, 1913, and danced a few times only, it was withdrawn.

Another extraordinary ballet for the novelty-loving Diaghileff, however, was created by Nijinsky and produced, at the Chatélet, at the end of the same month, May 29th, 1913. This was *Le Sacre du Printemps (The Rite of Spring),* the book by Igor Stravinsky and Nicholas Roerich, with music by the former and costumes and *décor* by the latter. This ballet certainly created a sensation, owing mainly to its stark ancient primitive Russian theme dealing with pagan religious rites, and to the curiously monotonous, heavily moving, even ugly crouching movements devised for it by Nijinsky—so totally different from anything ever seen before. Even as a novelty, however, and in addition to being most cleverly created by Nijinsky to fit correctly into the primitive period chosen, *The Rite* did not prove a popular ballet, even though true to its period, because of its depressing atmosphere and paucity of beauty and colour.

It was in 1913, soon after the production of *Le Sacre du Printemps,* that the Ballets Russes went on a tour in South America —but without Diaghileff, who had a superstitious horror of the water and always avoided a sea journey, if possible. He permitted his *protégé* to go with the Company, however, and even lent him his own body-servant, Vassily, for the tour; but, strange to say, though he thus appeared to have no forebodings of trouble, his own happy relations with the young dancer now came to an end in a most unexpected manner.

Nijinsky met on board ship and fell in love with an attractive young Hungarian Society girl dancer, named Romola de Pulszky, who had long cherished in secret deep admiration and a passionate attachment for him—with the result that, on reaching Buenos Aires, the pair were married at once. It has been suggested that, though this sudden marriage was undoubtedly a love match, Nijinsky may have considered that such a step might also release him from further entire domination by the great impresario—which domination it is possible he may at times have found somewhat irksome. Be that as it may, however, this totally unforeseen and sudden proceeding came as a tremendous blow to Diaghileff, who had been completely wrapped-up in his young genius-*protégé*; and in angry disappointment, he immediately dismissed Nijinsky from the Company. Nevertheless, Nijinsky appeared the following season in London at the Palace Theatre with a small Company of his own; but he became ill, and the visit was not a success.

In 1916, Nijinsky was permitted to rejoin the famous Company in New York after his release from internment in Austria, whither he and his wife had been sent soon after the beginning of the Great War. Though Diaghileff himself had assisted, with other friends, in securing his welcome release, his presence in the Company was more or less on judicial sufferance. The pair had suffered many hardships during their internment; and it is quite possible that these difficulties as well as the troubles with Diaghileff, may have had a certain share in Nijinsky's subsequent mental breakdown, which soon began to show itself more definitely.

Meanwhile, in 1916, on arriving in New York, Nijinsky danced again with the Diaghileff Company there, performing in *Le Spectre de la Rose* and *Petrouchka*, and in other of his famous roles, with all his former brilliance, despite the fact that he had not danced much from the time of his dismissal by Diaghileff and during his three years of internment—indeed, some critics have declared that he was finer than ever and that he now surpassed his former self.

Soon, he began to work upon the production of his fourth ballet, *Tyl Eulenspiegel*, which deals with a German legendary character of medieval times, to the music of Richard Strauss and with *décor* and costumes by Robert Edmond Jones, the American artist-designer. He had drafted the ballet during his sojourn in Austria as an internee, and now quickly perfected it. It was produced on October 23rd, 1916, at the Manhattan Opera House, New York; and it was a very brilliant production, with Nijinsky giving an amazing performance as Tyl, the rascally, lying, but gay adventurer who plays many lively parts until he ends up on the gallows. The *décor* and costumes were of an exaggerated and highly coloured type, rather like the illustrations in a child's elaborate fairy-tale book, with mysterious perched-up pepperpot-crowned magic castles, and with the dancers wearing fantastic head-dresses with their rainbow-tinted medieval costumes. The whole ballet was gorgeous in the extreme; and never before had Nijinsky attempted to reveal himself in the role of such a gay rogue.

Unhappily, however, this most extraordinary ballet was not seen many times; for it was not very long after its production that the sad mental malady that was the cause of the tragic living death of this amazing dancer-genius began definitely to assert itself. For a year or two longer, he could still do a certain amount of work, and was able to go on a South American tour; and then his mental condition closed in upon him like a dark curtain blotting out the light of reason and memory. Finally, in 1919, this greatest male dancer of modern times was thus compelled to retire altogether from the beautiful world of ballet which he had adorned so brilliantly for so short a time; and nothing but a memory and a legend remained. But what a legend was this!—a legend of everything that was most perfect and most beautiful in ballet.

The well-known book, entitled *Nijinsky*, written by his devoted wife, Romola Nijinsky, tells the sad story of the years that followed since her famous husband's mind became thus disordered, of their long sojourns in sanatoria in Switzerland and elsewhere, of the curious revealing drawings he had produced from time to time, how he was dominated by Diaghileff in his earlier days, and many other matters of considerable interest; and the reader is referred to this book and to the others that have been written about this remarkable master-dancer.

Nijinsky and his wife had one child only, a daughter named Kyra, who, naturally enough, became a dancer and was trained for ballet. She has danced in this country several times, having been with the Rambert Company in 1936, when she performed in *The Planets*, creating the role of The Mortal under Neptune. With this Company, also, that same year, she danced in several other ballets, including *The Mephisto Valse* and *The Spectre of the Rose*, made so famous by her father. A couple of years later, too, she was the *première danseuse* in the popular Cochran Revue *Streamline* at the Palace Theatre. She has also danced in America and elsewhere. She has recently been teaching ballet in Italy.

Nijinsky's sister, Bronislava Nijinska, trained with him in the St. Petersburg Imperial Ballet School, was, like Vaslav, one of the great Russian dancers in Diaghileff's Company, and became a remarkable choreographer. An account of her career immediately precedes that of her brother in this present volume.

On November 21st, 22nd and 23rd, 1949, a series of spectacular Gala Performances were given at the Empress Hall, Earl's Court, London, for the benefit of Vaslav Nijinsky; and on these three brilliant occasions there appeared several of the most famous dancers of to-day to do honour to the most famous of them all. Among these dancers—who were supported by the Ballet Rambert and by Boris Kochno as Artistic Director—were Tamara Toumanova, Yvette Chauviré, Marjorie Tallchief, Leonide Massine, Jean Babilée, George Skibine and Vladimir Skouratoff.

Since 1947, Nijinsky and his wife had settled in this country in the district of Virginia Water, Surrey, where his health partially improved and his clouded periods became less severe. From time to time, he was even able to be taken on short visits to London and elsewhere, mainly to see ballet, in which he still took pleasure. The last occasion on which he was seen and photographed in London was on April 3rd, 1950, when he was taken to Alexandra Palace to see Serge Lifar dance in a rehearsal for a television programme. Later on, however, he became seriously ill and was removed to a London clinic, where he died on April 8th, 1950, at the age of sixty-one—to the sorrow of his friends and the irreparable loss of the entire ballet world.

> The Spectre floats away on soaring leap,
> The perfumed Garden's lure is now in vain,
> The Roses bow their heads in homage deep,
> But Memory's magic pictures still remain!

Éthèry Pagava

◎◎

THIS SLIGHT, SYLPH-LIKE AND EXTREMELY YOUTHFUL DANCER has come into prominence as a serious performer of great intelligence and charm at an incredibly early age. She was born in Paris on December 13th, 1932; and her parents hail from the Caucasus. Her father is Prince Levan Pagava, of Georgia; and her grandfather was the first President of Georgia (1919-21). She comes of a musical family, one of her uncles being a composer who has occupied the position of orchestral conductor with the Marquis de Cuevas' Grand Ballet de Monte Carlo.

Éthèry Pagava has lived most of her short life, when not travelling, in Paris; and her only dancing teacher has been Madame Egorova. She began to learn dancing when five-and-a-half years of age; and when she was only six years old she danced her first role in a *Ballet de la Jeunesse* with the now-famous dancer, George Skibine, also very youthful at that time. A few months later, she danced with Serge Lifar at a Nijinsky Benefit Gala at the Louvre. Following this, she danced in several of Lifar's Concerts in Paris; and by the time she reached the age of twelve years, she had already danced many times with Janine Charrat and Roland Petit. At her first recital she performed entirely in dances she had composed herself.

From the age of twelve to fourteen years, she danced regularly with Roland Petit at his Friday performances at the Théâtre Sarah Bernhardt; and latterly with the full Ballets des Champs-

Élysées. Among the ballets she now appeared in were *Le Rossignol et la Rose*, *Le Déjeuner sur l'Herbe*, *Les Forains*, etc., with Jean Babilée and other members of the Company.

Then, desiring to study more continuously and without too many interruptions, the young girl dancer now left the Ballets des Champs-Élysées and worked hard every day with Madame Egorova, though she still danced at occasional concerts and recitals with Janine Charrat, Renée Jeanmaire and Vladimir Skouratoff.

At the age of fifteen years, she joined the Marquis de Cuevas' Grand Ballet de Monte Carlo; and she has remained with this Company until the present day. During this still quite short period, she has performed in the ballets of Serge Lifar, George Balanchine, Bronislava Nijinska, Leonide Massine and David Lichine; and she has already had considerable valuable experience, as her delicate and sensitive personality has been closely studied and used very carefully to the best advantage. She has danced leading roles in *Roméo et Juliette*, *La Fille mal Gardée*, *Constantia*, *Night Shadow*, *Barocco Concerto*, *L'Anniversaire d'Infante* (*Birthday of the Infanta*), etc.

As with many other budding ballerinas, Éthèry Pagava had always longed to dance *Giselle*, for which important part she had, so far, been considered too young, though her technique approached the necessary standard. Then, quite without warning, came her wonderful chance. During the visit of the Grand Ballet de Monte Carlo to Manchester in 1948, it happened that the Company's brilliant American ballerina, Rosella Hightower, was taken ill and was unable to dance *Giselle*, which had been billed to be performed the next evening; and, rather than disappoint the public by putting on another ballet, Éthèry Pagava was given the famous part. She learned it in one day. From ten o'clock next morning until 1 p.m. she studied and practised Act 1. Then, as it was a matinée day, she had to take her usual parts in the performances that afternoon, dancing in *Lac des Cygnes* and in *Constantia*. The matinée over, she returned to the study of *Giselle* from five o'clock till 7 p.m. That same evening she danced the whole ballet before a delighted audience; and her *Giselle* was a great success. She danced the ballet three times during that Manchester visit; and now it is her great ambition to dance it again at some not too distant date, but with full preparation and adequate rehearsals. When this happy day arrives, there is every likelihood that this still very young dancer will give a really fine rendering of that much-coveted role, for she has the right temperament for it.

Her fey, ethereal sensitivity and dramatic feeling have already been revealed in her lovely rendering of the Sleepwalker in Balanchine's *Night Shadow*—in which she was partnered by Skibine; and her work is maturing with her every performance. In 1949, she appeared in Nijinska's ballet *In Memoriam*, created to commemorate the centenary of Chopin's death. Then, in the summer of that year, she had an important role in the revival of Massine's *Tristan Fou*, in which she danced the emotional Isolde with sympathetic understanding. In this her partners were André Églevsky as the distraught Tristan, with Marjorie Tallchief as the terrible Chimera of the Queen of Cornwall imagined in the maddened brain of that ill-starred hero. In 1949, also, she danced very successfully in a number of television programmes with Rosella Hightower, André Églevsky and other members of the Grand Ballet de Monte Carlo during their visit to Paris.

On August 4th, 1950, the latter Company produced, at Monte Carlo, George Skibine's first ballet, *Tragedie à Verone*, set to Tchaikovsky's Fantasy Overture and having *décor* and costumes by Delfaux. This ballet deals with the evergreen tragic subject of *Romeo and Juliet*; and in it Éthèry Pagava danced the gentle Juliet with exquisite grace, softness of line and deep romantic feeling. The role suits her fresh youthfulness to perfection; and she won the highest praises for her really lovely presentation. In October 1950, also, she danced very beautifully one of the charming variations in John Taras' *Le Bal des Jeunes Filles*.

That a brilliant future awaits this clever and always delightful dancer, there seems not the slightest doubt.

David Paltenghi

T HIS FINE, VERSATILE DANCER-MIME WAS BORN AT BOURNE-
mouth in 1919, and comes of a Swiss family. Though at
first intended to follow the family profession of *hotêliers*,
he developed such a strong tendency towards dancing and the
drama that he abandoned the former and took up the latter as
his life's career. He studied dancing first at the Margaret Saul
School, and later continued his ballet training with Antony
Tudor, Molly Lake, Idzikovski, Madame Volkova and Madame
Rambert.

At the age of eighteen, he joined the London Ballet Company
at Toynbee Hall, under Antony Tudor, its founder, who gave
him his first chance in *The Planets* (Tudor—Holst—Stevenson),
in which he danced Mortal under Venus; and after this, he
remained with Tudor, dancing in all the works given. When
the London Ballet was amalgamated with the Rambert Company in 1940, he continued with the latter and became, later on,
one of that Company's principal male dancers. With the Rambert Company he danced the Lover in *Jardin aux Lilas*, Second
and Third Dancer in *Dark Elegies, pas de deux* in *Gala Performance*, Mars in *The Planets*, Death in *Death and the Maiden*,
Mephisto in *Mephisto Valse*, the Personage in *Les Masques*,
Hercules in *The Descent of Hebe*, Grandfather in *Peter and the
Wolf*, Mr. Tebrick in *Lady into Fox*, the Waiter in *Bar aux
Folies-Bergère*, etc.

In 1941, David Paltenghi joined the Sadler's Wells Ballet,
remaining with this famous Company for six years and dancing
in almost all its productions; and starting again from the beginning, he gradually worked his way up to the sharing of principal
roles with Robert Helpmann and creating others of his own.
Among his more important roles with the Sadler's Wells Ballet
were: The Prince, or hero, in revivals of the classics, *The Sleeping Beauty*, *Le Lac des Cygnes*, *Casse Noisette*, *Giselle* (Hilarion)
and *Coppélia* (Dr. Coppélius); in the Fokine ballets, Eusebius
and Pierrot in *Le Carnaval* and the young Poet in *Les Sylphides*;
in the Frederick Ashton ballets, the Hussar in *Apparitions*, a

Saracen Knight and St. George in *The Quest*, all male parts in *Façade*, Winter in *The Fairy Queen*; he also danced in *Les Patineurs, Nocturne, The Wedding Bouquet, Dante Sonata*, etc. In the Ninette de Valois ballets, he danced Elihu in *Job*, and had good roles also in *The Rake's Progress, Orpheus and Eurydice, The Prospect Before Us, Promenade* and *The Haunted Ballroom* (The Master of Tregennis). He likewise danced leading roles in Robert Helpmann's ballets—Claudius and Hamlet in *Hamlet*, Brother and Comus in *Comus*, the Official in *Miracle in the Gorbals*, the Producer in *Adam Zero*.

Becoming intensely interested in the vast possibilities and development of films and television, Paltenghi left the Sadler's Wells Company to take up this new work, though still mainly with emphasis on ballet. He has completed a number of films, chiefly being responsible for the choreography of these, though he has also acted in some. Among the latter may be mentioned *The Queen of Spades*, and the mime-play in Sir Laurence Olivier's film version of *Hamlet*. He has also danced in television; and, more recently, has been the commentator in the successful educational programme, *Ballet For Beginners*, in which, as the pleasantly informative narrator, he explained very lucidly the examples and demonstrations being shown. In "straight" stage work he has produced a Revue; and he was also the choreographer of Noel Langley's musical play, *Cage Me A Peacock*. In 1949, he became guest artist with the Rambert Ballet on its return from Australia, where its top ranks had become somewhat depleted; and he still returns to the Sadler's Wells Ballet when required for special purposes. He has concentrated more recently on artistic progress in films, television and production work.

David Paltenghi is a remarkably fine ballet-mime, and his work in dramatic roles is notable. His performance as the Official in Helpmann's *Miracle in the Gorbals* was the most outstanding feature in that most extraordinary ballet; and his presentation of this dominating character—strong, yet revealing a weaker side in his jealousy of the Stranger lest the latter's advent should lessen his own power and prestige, and his sudden yielding to the Prostitute's temptation with its consequent remorse and self-contempt—suggest that, possibly, many a playwright may regard him as a definite loss to the "straight" stage.

In *Adam Zero*, too, in which he takes the role of a stage Producer, he gives such a vivid picture of the reliable, dependable director shepherding his wavering flock of performers in the way they should go—he must again arouse envy when seen by some harassed theatrical impresario, since he appears to be the ideal calm and collected producer the latter always hopes to find, but so seldom does.

Quite apart from this particular type of perfect miming, however, David Paltenghi has always shown himself to be a sensitive and highly intelligent dancer, with considerable charm, in addition to revealing a complete grasp of the essentials of mime for balletic purposes. Whether in roles dealing with ordinary everyday life, or in the portrayal of characters of a classical or more picturesque type, he is equally to be depended upon to give a finished and carefully defined performance.

When, in February 1950, the Ballet Rambert went on a six-weeks' tour of Germany—under the auspices of the British Council—David Paltenghi went with them as guest artist; and on his return at the end of March he created for the Company a new ballet, entitled *The Eve of St. Agnes*. This has music by César Franck (orchestrated by Geoffrey Corbett), and *décor* and costumes by Roger Furse; and it was presented by the Company at Bath on August 31st, 1950. It proved to be a promising first ballet, showing a real theatre sense and careful handling of his subject and dancers. The medieval atmosphere was well sustained.

Paltenghi's second ballet, *Prismatic Variations* (music, Beethoven's Variations on a Waltz by Diabelli; *décor* and costumes by Vivienne Kernot), was of the abstract kind, and did not very happily suit the music, though its idea was a good and original one. It dealt with the breaking up of a prism into primary and secondary colours, which revolve around a leading dancer representing Light, and it was somewhat complicated in treatment. It was given its *première* by Ballet Rambert at the King's Theatre, Hammersmith, on October 23rd, 1950.

For Ballet Workshop at the Mercury Theatre, Paltenghi created his third ballet, given on April 8th, 1951. It was entitled *Scherzi Della Sorte*, and has music by Monteverdi, and *décor* and costumes by Leslie Hurry. It had a good dramatic plot dealing with the foretelling of a man's fate by the cards—the main characters being the King and Queen of Diamonds and the Knave of Clubs. It showed some ingenious invention.

On May 24th, 1951, Paltenghi's fourth ballet was given by the Rambert Company at the Bath Assembly. With the appropriate title of *Fate's Revenge: or The Rebellion in the Upper Rooms* (music by Peter Tranchell, *décor* and costumes by Ronald Ferns), it dealt with an incident in Bath during Regency times; and it met with a good reception. That year he was also commissioned by the Arts Council to prepare a ballet for the Canterbury Festival, in connection with the Festival of Britain. This was *Canterbury Prologue* (music Fricker, *décor* Burra).

In 1953, Paltenghi was choreographer for Walt Disney's film *The Sword and the Rose*, in which he presented that difficult Elizabethan dance *The Volta*—taught to the stars by himself.

Anna Pavlova

THE ONE AND ONLY PAVLOVA! HOW OFTEN ONE HEARS THE phrase; and how true it is! The great Russian novelist, Doestoevsky, once said: "The world will be saved by Beauty"; and there is no doubt that Pavlova brought beauty into every part of the world she visited—not only by the absolute and seemingly effortless perfection of her dancing and her ineffable grace—but also by her rare gift of inner spirituality unconsciously felt by all who ever beheld her wonderful performances.

Anna Pavlova was born in St. Petersburg on January 31st, 1882, her parents being very poor and her father dying two years later. She was so frail and delicate that at first it was feared she could not be reared. Fortunately for the world, however, her devoted mother brought her safely through her early physical struggles; and when she was four years old she was sent to live with her grandmother in the then delightful little country village of Ligova—now a considerable town.

In Ligova, the little Anna lived very happily and gained greatly in physical strength; and here she also developed a real love of nature which remained with her throughout her much too short life. The flowers and birds of the meadows and woodlands became her friends and meant much to her.

On one of her visits to St. Petersburg, her mother took her to the Maryinsky Theatre to see a performance of the wonderful Petipa-Tchaikovsky ballet *La Belle au Bois Dormant* (*The Sleeping Beauty*); and this so enraptured and fired the imagination of the eight-year-old child that she then and there resolved to become a dancer herself. Already she had danced like an elf in the country meadows and woodlands; but now, in imagination, she could see herself on the boards of the Maryinsky Theatre, and she longed to be trained there—a truly prophetic vision.

However, to her disappointment, she found that she had to wait until she was ten years old before she could become a candidate for admission to the famous Imperial Ballet School which was maintained by the Imperial Court and the tests for which were very severe. The two years of waiting passed slowly enough; but at the end of that time, the little Anna passed all the tests successfully and was admitted as a student to the Ballet School, there to begin the regulation six years' training.

At the Ballet School the students were entirely cared for by the Imperial Governors, living for the most part as boarders and receiving an excellent general education—which included the study of music and languages—in addition to ballet and dramatic training. They were even supplied with food and clothing—a plain uniform dress being compulsory for day wear, while the necessary costumes for ballet practice were likewise provided. The ballet training itself was of the highest order and the most severe in modern civilization, though it was then entirely unknown outside Russia.

The students, however, though they worked hard, were very happy and loved their work; and they suffered no real privations, even though they saw but little of outside juvenile life and lived more or less as a small but privileged community complete in itself. They were well fed, and their physical condition was meticulously cared for. In addition, as Imperial State students, they had no fees of any kind to pay.

Anna Pavlova soon proved herself to be one of the most apt, sincere and talented of all the students of her particular generation—she was already an established *première danseuse* at the Maryinsky Theatre when Tamara Karsavina, Lydia Lopokova and Lydia Kyasht made their débuts there. Her teachers were at first Oblakov and Ekaterina Vasem; later on she became a member of the classes presided over by Paul Gerdt—the latter a dancer and teacher of the highest order, who took a special pride in the training of the gifted young Pavlova, quickly recognizing in her a coming great artist. Later on, when her actual student days were over, she studied under the famous maestro, Enrico Cecchetti, with whom she continued to practise throughout her brilliant career until his death in 1928. She also took occasional courses of lessons with other famous teachers —among whom were the Milan ballerina, Beretta, Eugenia Sokolova and Christian Johannsen.

Anna Pavlova passed out from the Imperial Ballet School at the age of seventeen years with high honours and the status of First Dancer; and even at her school-leaving début, she attracted the special attention of all and stood out from her student colleagues as a dancer with a certain brilliant future before her. From that time onwards, she never once looked back, but went on from success to success.

During her early years at the Maryinsky Theatre, Marius Petipa was the principal *maître de ballet*; and naturally she danced in all his ballets—*The Sleeping Beauty, Lac des Cygnes, La Bayadère, Paquita, King Candaules, Harlequinade* and many others. At the Maryinsky, also, she danced in *The Daughter of Pharaoh, The Fairy Doll, Casse Noisette, La Source, Esmeralda, Bluebeard, Camargo, Coppélia, The Corsair, The Awakening of Flora, Eunice, Chopiniana*, etc. Another *maître de ballet*, Ivan Clustine, was there also in her time; and later on, this choreographer created or adapted several personal ballets for her, among these being the popular *Gavotte Pavlova, Russian Dance, Chopiniana, The Fairy Doll, Raymonda, The Péri, The Frescos of Adjanta, Dionysus, Valse Triste, The Undines, Minuet, Dance of the Hours* and others.

In due course at the Maryinsky, Pavlova danced the leading ballerina roles in all the Petipa and other ballets presented there. She created a wonderful impression in 1903 when she

229

first danced *Giselle* (Coralli, music by Adam); and from that time to the present day most critics are unanimous in declaring that she has never been equalled in this famous role. With her unique gift of spirituality, in addition to the perfection of her seemingly effortless technique, she was, undoubtedly, the greatest of all Giselles.

The ballets in which Pavlova danced as *prima ballerina* of the Maryinsky Theatre are too numerous to mention here; and she remained at this theatre—with occasional visits to Moscow —until 1908. It was in the years immediately preceding and succeeding that year that new influences had been growing up in the Russian Ballet—those of Isadora Duncan and of Michael Fokine. Serge Diaghileff had likewise appeared upon the scene.

Pavlova was greatly interested in the new movements, and she danced in several of the early Fokine ballets at the Maryinsky; and when, in 1909, Diaghileff took his first Company of Russian dancers to the Théâtre du Chatélet, Paris, she was one of them, dancing principal roles with the already famous young Nijinsky. She also danced with Diaghileff's Company again in Paris in 1911.

But Pavlova no longer wished to be bound by the routine and restrictions of Company life under an impresario; and greatly though she admired Diaghileff and Fokine and appreciated the work they were doing for modern ballet, she felt that her own best work would lie elsewhere—she preferred to reveal her beautiful Art to the best advantage in a Company of her own. She had the real missionary spirit; and she desired to bring beauty not only into vast cities, but also into small towns and unimportant places where great artists had never been before.

Already, between her two seasons with Diaghileff, she had taken a small Company into several of the capitals of Europe, her partner being Adolf Bolm on her first visit; and on her second visit she had two partners, Bolm and Nicholas Legat. On her first visit to London in 1910, she appeared at the Palace Theatre with Michael Mordkin as her partner; and here she met with a tremendous success, her beauty and grace being positively breathtaking, while the perfection of her own and her Company's work proved a revelation to her enthusiastic audiences.

For five consecutive years Pavlova danced during the summer

seasons at the Palace Theatre, London; and though she was more than once there throughout the subsequent famous Diaghileff London seasons, her own audiences never dwindled, and she was always received with great ovations. She also danced at Covent Garden and at Drury Lane.

By this time, Pavlova was world famous and had developed her own individual type of programme, which differed entirely from that of Diaghileff's Company. The latter usually presented two or three complete Fokine or other ballets, with no intermediate solo pieces; whereas Pavlova's programmes consisted of a series of short separate items, or *divertissements,* some of these being supported by the *corps de ballet* and others given as solos or as *pas de deux,* etc. A famous *pas de deux* was *L'Automne-Bacchanale,* arranged by her partner, Mordkin, to music by Glazounov. Each separate item, however, though often quite simple, was perfectly performed; and the music and *décor* for each was equally perfect. Occasionally, a very short complete ballet was included; and sometimes an entire classic, such as *Giselle,* or a scene from one of the classics, would also be given. Always, however, there were some separate *divertissements,* such as her popular *Oriental Impressions,* faultlessly performed by the Company. Pavlova's own most famous solo dances were *The Californian Poppy, The Dragonfly, The Butterfly, Valse Caprice* (Rubinstein), *Christmas, Rondine*—all with choreography by herself—and the most famous of all, the immortal *Dying Swan,* arranged for her by Fokine to Saint-Saens' ethereally lovely music. The latter exquisite gem was a perfect poem in movement—or, rather, every movement was a separate poem in itself. Her exquisite presentation of the royal bird in its last moments of life created in the rapt beholders a strange sense of ultimate peace. She made the inevitable act of dying appear so beautiful that one could contemplate one's own last moments on earth with an equal calm contentment and hope. A complete silence that could be felt always reigned for a few moments before the almost sacrilegious applause burst forth. Her youthful absorption in the beauties of nature, engendered by her early years spent in the country, remained with Pavlova throughout her life—hence her own choreographic works dealing with nature subjects, and her short but perfect little ballet, *Autumn Leaves* (Chopin—Castro). She always had a passion for flowers and birds, and never could see enough of either. She would never rest until all the flowers showered upon her at performances had been placed in water.

Having founded her own Company, Pavlova took it all over the world; and she was always received everywhere with real joy. Her every audience loved her. That was part of the secret of her amazing career. By the magic of her own personality, she brought happiness and peace to all who beheld her, in addition to the admiration she excited by means of her always perfectly finished technique and the grace of her every dancing movement. Many honours were showered upon her; and she was a welcome guest in many of the Royal Palaces of Europe and in Presidential and Official residences in the Western Hemisphere.

As was inevitable, Pavlova has frequently been compared with such great dancers of the past as Marie Taglioni and Fanny Elssler—a somewhat futile proceeding, since the dancing of our present age is much more fully developed than in the time of these early nineteenth-century dancers. Each age has its own criterion of perfection. To describe Pavlova as a "second Taglioni" is merely absurd. Had she been really like Taglioni, she would not have been Pavlova.

Pavlova had a great love for London, and between her frequent world tours she always returned thither to rest. She bought a beautiful old house at Hampstead, Ivy House—once the home of the famous English landscape painter, Turner—and had her furniture brought thither from St. Petersburg, adding to this her collection of souvenirs from her travels in many parts of the world. Ivy House made a delightful haven of rest for her; and the lovely flowery garden that surrounded it was a constant joy to her. She had a charming aviary in her greenhouse; and flamingos and swans were to be seen in the ornamental lake she had built. The swans were a gift from some of her English friends, presented to her in gratitude for her ever-memorable rendering of *The Dying Swan*. She was many times photographed with Jack, her tame pet swan; also with her several beloved dogs and cats. When not in her garden, Pavlova was often to be found in her studio, drawing, painting or modelling, for all of which arts she had a natural gift, though completely untaught. For modelling, in particular, she had a real talent, which she might well have developed had she not chosen instead to be a dancer. Her statuettes of dancers were exquisite.

Although she loved Russia dearly, Pavlova was never able to return thither after the revolution in 1917; but she was so grieved for the distressed and destitute state of the unhappy Russian refugees in Paris that she did everything in her power to help them, not only from her own private resources but also by means of vast entertainments and charitable performances. She established a permanent home for the children of Russian refugees; and she also sent large sums of money for the relief of the destitute in Russia.

Pavlova recruited most of her own *corps de ballet* from among the young English dancers in whom she became interested. Well-known names among these English recruits are Ruth French, Hilda Boot (afterwards Hilda Butsova), and Algeranoff, now chief character dancer with International Ballet. She also recognized the budding talents of the young English choreographers with whom she came in contact from time to time; she was especially interested in the original work of Frederick Ashton and had already commissioned him to create a ballet for her when her tragic death occurred.

The members of her Company were all well-trained and excellent performers—for Pavlova would permit no "ragged edges" in the work of her *corps de ballet*; even the smallest and simplest item in any of her presentations had to be rendered as perfectly as possible.

Her dancing partners were always picked and splendid dancers. After her Maryinsky Theatre and Diaghileff Company partners—the famous Fokine, Gerdt, Nicholas Legat, Nijinsky, Bolm, Kosloff—her standard as regards partners had remained fixed at the highest possible level; consequently, she always sought out the best colleagues available for her London seasons and foreign tours. Among these were Adolf Bolm again, Michael Mordkin, Laurent Novikoff, V. Tikhomirov, A. Volinin, Zjukov, Svoboda and P. Vladimirov. Among her musical directors were N. Tcherepnine, Theodore Stier, Alexander Smolens, L. Wurmser, E. Kurts, Hermann Finck, Baranovitch, A. Goldschmidt and E. Schicketans.

Pavlova was helped greatly throughout her dancing career by her husband, Victor Dandré, who devoted himself entirely to her interests and to easing the many burdens imposed upon her, not only by her position as the world's greatest dancer, but also as the owner of such an important Ballet Company. He managed all her business affairs, smoothed her difficulties, arranged her numerous tours, and acted as her personal secretary.

Alas! Despite his untiring efforts on her behalf and his constant personal care of her, he could not prevent her sadly untimely end in middle life, at the height of her dazzling career. Her death occurred on January 23rd, 1931, at The Hague in Holland, after an illness, caused by a chill, lasting scarcely a week.

The whole artistic world was completely stunned by the sudden and unexpected death of Anna Pavlova, the greatest of all dancers—and not only the artistic world, but also the world of ordinary everyday folk, who felt that they had lost something wonderful in their lives—someone they had loved and, unconsciously, almost worshipped, someone on a plane all by herself.

When gazing upon this radiant figure—as the present writer was privileged to do—and following her every movement so generously charged with a soft and exquisite grace, one seemed as though transported to another sphere, where only perfection reigned. Quite apart from the peerless beauty of her dancing, it was as though one had caught a fleeting glimpse of the divine. Cecchetti, the beloved teacher of her maturer years, once truly said of her: "I can teach her everything connected with dancing, but Pavlova has that which can only be taught by God"—surely an everlasting tribute to, and acknowledgment of, the miracle that was Anna Pavlova!

Roland Petit

⊚⊚

T HAT VERSATILE YOUNG FRENCH DANCER AND CHOREOGRAPHER, Roland Petit, is a Latin of the Latins. He was born in Paris in 1924, his mother being an Italian and his father a Parisian owning a small restaurant-café in the rue Montmartre. The young Roland was born the possessor of an intensely artistic temperament, revealing a dynamic personality from the first. He was light, careless, impetuous, living only to express his own ideas, and difficult to fit into ordinary everyday life. He was always impatient—even intolerant at times—eager to create, to make an impression on the world, a sensation in Art. That he has abundantly succeeded nobody can deny—but it has required the great determination and the strong will-power with which he was undoubtedly born.

Very early he showed a special joy in dancing, in design, and a surprising originality in the creation of dances. Consequently, he was entered as a student at the Paris Opéra, to be trained in ballet; and he remained there until he was twenty years of age, going forward after his training period as a professional dancer in that famous theatre. Though always brilliant, he was never an easy pupil, caring more to go his own original way in Art rather than submit to humdrum routine. He was for ever rushing after new ideas and influences, pursuing them passionately for a time, then discarding them for something he considered better still. Even though in those early days he did not always understand the " thing " he was chasing, he still had the instinctive inborn feeling that it was the one and only " thing " for him to do at that particular moment.

Nevertheless, he stuck to his artistic training and became a remarkably fine dancer, with unusual elevation and great virtuosity. He put the whole of himself into his performances, dancing almost with fury and with every fibre of energy he possessed, plus the confident zest of the embryo showman. Yet, though sure of his own powers, he was always deeply sincere in his search for perfection in his art.

His passion for creation, however, never left him for a moment; and though, on completion of his prescribed training, he danced at the Opéra for a time, he felt the classical atmosphere there too cramping for his bursting energy. He needed more scope for his inventive powers; and he left soon after his twentieth birthday in 1944. He had already done a certain amount of choreographic work from the early age of seventeen, in collaboration with Janine Charrat, and had seen his work performed; and he now determined to follow up and to enlarge upon these boyish efforts, since his taste and creative powers had developed considerably. It happened that Les Vendredis de la Danse had just been formed, and he joined this already successful venture; and thus began his real choreographical life.

Petit's first ballet for Les Vendredis was *Le Rossignol et la Rose*, to music by Schumann, produced at the Théâtre Sarah Bernhardt, which attracted considerable attention and proved that his work was already surprisingly mature. This fact became a certainty with his next ballet, *Les Forains* (book by Boris Kochno, music by Henri Sauguet, and *décor* and costumes by Christian Bérard), a simple but very beautiful work regarded ever since as a little gem and a perfectly constructed work of its kind. It was produced at the Théâtre des Champs-Élysées on March 2nd, 1945. Later that same year there now came into existence the Ballets des Champs-Élysées, backed financially by the father of Roland Petit; and the latter became its leading choreographer. The Director of the new Company was Boris Kochno; among the first group of dancers were Jean Babilée, Janine Charrat, Irène Skorik, Solange Schwarz, Nathalie Philippart, Gordon Hamilton, Danielle Darmance, Paul Gnatt, Alexandre Kalioujny and Ana Nevada. The last four were temporary members only. Here, too, Petit encountered difficulties, but overcame them all by the sheer force of his genius, which now burned within him as a flame.

The ballets he created for the Ballets des Champs-Élysées were the following: *Les Amours de Jupiter* (theme Boris Kochno, music Ibert, *décor* and costumes Jean Hugo), *Le Déjeuner sur l'Herbe* (theme Irène Lidova, music Lanner, *décor* and costumes Marie Laurençin), *La Fiancée du Diable* (theme Kochno, music Hubeau, *décor* and costumes Jean-Denis Malclés), *Le Jeune Homme et la Mort* (theme Jean Cocteau, music Bach, *décor* and costumes Wakhevitch-Karinska), *Le Bal des Blanchisseuses* (theme Boris Kochno, music Vernon Duke, *décor* and costumes Stanislas Lepris), *Le Rendezvous* (theme Jacques Prévert, music Kosma, *décor* and costumes Mayo), *Treize Danses* (music Grétry, *décor* and costumes Christian Dior).

One of the most remarkable of the above-named ballets was *Le Jeune Homme et la Mort*, a very dramatic, if somewhat gloomy, work for two performers only, marvellously portrayed by Nathalie Philippart and Jean Babilée. It is full of tragic beauty. *Les Amours de Jupiter*, though sensual in theme, contains some of Petit's finest and most inventive choreography. *Le Déjeuner sur l'Herbe* has a charming pastoral scene; *La Fiancée du Diable* has a highly fantastic and romantic subject, with some excellent solos and *pas de deux*; and *Le Bal des Blanchisseuses* is lively and amusing—a somewhat rare quality seldom shown by Petit; *Treize Danses* is not up to his usual high standard.

In November 1948, Roland Petit, still eager to be under no other management than his own, left the Ballet des Champs-Élysées to form his own Company in which, as sole Director, principal dancer and choreographer his undoubted genius would have entirely free play. The new Company, known as Roland Petit's Ballets de Paris, had its opening performance at the Marigny Théâtre (its headquarters); and, so far, it has met with a real success. Among its fine dancers have been: Renée Jeanmaire, Colette Marchand, Nina Vyroubova, Janine Charrat, Joan Sheldon, Jane Laoust, Roland Petit, Vladimir Skouratoff, Milorad Miskovich, John Gilpin, Gordon Hamilton, Serge Pérrault, Oleg Briansky, Teddy Rodolphe and Stanley Hall.

The new ballets created by Roland Petit for his own Ballets de Paris are: *Les Demoiselles de la Nuit* (music by Jean Françaix, *décor* and costumes by Léonor Fini), produced Marigny Théâtre, Paris, May 20th, 1948, with Margot Fonteyn as guest artist from Sadler's Wells Ballet. *Que le Diable l'Emporte* (music by Rosenthal, *décor* and costumes by Derain), produced Marigny Théâtre, Paris, May 20th, 1948. *L'Oeuf à la Coque* (music by Maurice Thiriet, *décor* and costumes by Stanislas Lepri), produced Prince's Theatre, London, February 16th, 1949. *Carmen* (music by Bizet, *décor* and costumes by Clavé), produced Prince's Theatre, London, February 21st, 1949. *Pas d'Action* (music by Wagner), produced London, March 10th, 1949.

Among these, *Carmen* was outstanding, and is probably the most excitingly dramatic ballet ever seen upon any stage at any period. It seethes with the intensity of passion, its final tragedy is inevitable, it is often sordid and tawdry; yet there are moments of real charm and beauty. It is a free adaptation of Merimée's novel, and by no means a copy of the *Carmen* opera. The dancing and acting of Renée Jeanmaire as Carmen was superb; and Roland Petit a remarkably fine Don José. This ballet is regarded by many as a masterpiece of its kind.

Les Demoiselles de la Nuit gives the adventures of a romantic young poet (Roland Petit) among the Cat-Girls in the mansion of the Ginger Cat Baron (Gordon Hamilton), where he falls in love with Agathe the dainty White Cat and finally perishes with her. On its first production in Paris, Margot Fonteyn, as the Company's guest artist on this occasion, danced and mimed delightfully. So clever was her performance, indeed, that her creation of Agathe the White Cat is regarded by many as one of the highlights in her brilliant career. This very original and most fantastic ballet gave its performers many opportunities for the display of high-power dancing, as well as clever miming.

Among other new ballets produced by the Roland Petit Company are William Dollar's *Le Combat* (music Banfield, *décor* Laure), Janine Charrat's *Theme and Variations* (music Tchaikovsky) and *Adame Miroir* (music Milhaud, *décor* Delfaux); and Ashton's *Le Rêve de Léonor* (music Britten, *décor* Fini), produced Prince's Theatre, London, April 15, 1949. The latter ballet created quite a sensation, owing to its exaggerated, fantastic treatment, but was not a really successful work, despite the charm of Benjamin Britten's music and of many of Ashton's beautiful dances.

In February and March 1950, Roland Petit took his Company on a very successful tour of the United States and Canada, where they gave four ballets only in each city visited: *Le Rendez-vous*, *Le Combat*, *Carmen* and *L'Oeuf à la Coque*. On their return to Europe, Petit produced at Covent Garden, May 5th, 1950, the new ballet he had been invited to create for the Sadler's Wells Ballet. Entitled *Ballabile*, this amusing ballet has music by Emmanuel Chabrier and *décor* and costumes by Antoni Clavé. On July 11th, 1950, he created and produced at the Marigny Théâtre, Paris, a delightfully humorous ballet entitled *Musical Chairs*, with music by Georges Auric and *décor* and costumes by Georges Geffroy. It deals with the subject of the famous old parlour game of that name, with very ingeniously contrived choreography, and is a really brilliant and novel little work.

On September 25th, 1950, Petit presented at the Marigny Théâtre another new ballet, *La Croqueuse de Diamantes*, which many regard as one of his most entertaining creations. For this, dialogue and singing are included, the lyrics being by Raymond Queneau to the lively and invigorating music of Jean-Michel Damase; and the *décor* and costumes are by Wakhevitch. The story, though based on a theme by Alfred Adam, has been adapted by Petit himself; and it is full of wit and verve in its ballet form, the choreography being most inventive and exactly suited to the fantastic fairy-tale subject. It showed off surprisingly well the fine dancing and miming powers of Renée Jeanmaire— for whom it was mainly created—and is an excellent medium for the first-rate work of the other members of the Company.

After the finish of his 1951 spring season in Paris, Petit and his Ballets de Paris went off to Hollywood to make films for Howard Hughes.

While some of his ballets are inclined to be somewhat over-weighted by sex, Roland Petit has sufficient delicacy to avoid real offensiveness, even when a definitely suggestive scene is in progress. Strong drama is certainly his main *forte* at present, as evidenced by *Le Jeune Homme et la Mort* and *Carmen*. He can, however, as easily and effectively present a delightful picture of simple, calm, lyrical beauty, such as is to be enjoyed in *Les Forains*; and it is to be hoped that this lovely little ballet will not be the last of its kind from the same source.

In 1953, this fine dancer-choreographer was seen again in London in three of his new ballets: *Ciné-Bijou* (Pierre Petit— Beaurepaire), *Le Loup* (Dutilleur—Carzou), and *Deuil en 24 Heures* (Thiriet—Clavé) . . . all were of great interest.

Roland Petit has already reached great heights as a chore-ographer of truly amazing originality and power; and as a virtuoso dancer he is remarkable. He is still in his early twenties; and, for one of his rare gifts, an assured and brilliant future seems certainly to await him.

Marie Rambert

⦿⦿

MARIE RAMBERT, FOUNDER OF THE BALLET CLUB AND OF the Ballet Rambert, may be regarded as the first real pioneer of modern British Ballet, since her brave little Company was already in existence when Ninette de Valois' great and adventurous plans were still in an embryo form. Both these now famous benefactors of the ballet were keen, hard workers and indefatigable strugglers; and though the latter has certainly enjoyed more good fortune, the name of Marie Rambert will also never cease to be held in the highest honour and her splendid untiring work will always be spoken of with sincere gratitude by all ballet lovers in this country. Despite stupendous difficulties, she helped to keep the torch of ballet steadily burning here at its almost darkest hour and thus prevented its total eclipse following the stunning effects of the sudden death of Serge Diaghileff. Many of our present leading British dancers, choreographers and stage designers owe their success and well-deserved positions in the ballet world of to-day to her initiative and to the excellent training and unfailing encouragement given them in their early days by this clever and always optimistic teacher-producer who first discovered and guided their latent talents.

An excellent all-round dancer, though never herself a top-line executant—she began her dancing career at rather too late an age for this—she loved dancing and ballet with a sincere and burning passion; so much so, indeed, that, instead of submitting to any kind of frustration, she determined to make dancers of other people and to present them to the world as fine examples of her own Terpsichorean dreams. She was a born teacher and could always bring out the best in any promising pupils and inspire them with her own enthusiasm.

But the creation of dancers was merely a part of her ambition. She also desired to create choreographers and designers and to present the ballets she had encouraged them to produce, and finally to form her "creations" into a Company instinct with her own dynamic personality.

All these ambitions have been fulfilled, after twenty-five years or more of struggles and disappointments; and to-day the Ballet Rambert is not only fully established but is recognized as a Company distinguished by its artistic development and its continuously high standards. What is more, all its members are fired with the enthusiasm and the sincerity of their beloved leader; and from the beginning they have always regarded themselves as one happy family—indeed, their motto might always have been that of Dumas' famous Musketeers, "One for all, and all for one!"

Born in Poland's capital, Marie Rambert received her own training in Warsaw and in Paris; and for some years she specialized as a teacher of the Dalcroze System of Eurhythmics, in which, as a valuable aid to the development of the body in preparation for every form of dancing, she has always been a firm believer. She first came directly into touch with Russian Ballet when she was engaged by Serge Diaghileff to teach the Dalcroze System to the members of his Company—for this great impresario was always eager to give his dancers the best continuation training possible while working for him. It was for this reason he engaged the famous ballet-master, Cecchetti, who, while he was also glad to retain him as a great character dancer, held daily classes even for his star performers and kept his entire Company at the highest standard.

Consequently, while teaching Dalcroze Eurhythmics in the Diaghileff Company, in addition to dancing therein herself, this enterprising young dancer from Warsaw also took lessons from Cecchetti, and studied the whole Russian system of training and of ballet production.

On coming to London, therefore, later on, she was well equipped to set up her own School of Ballet—which she proceeded to do, forming it on the strictly classical lines she had so thoroughly absorbed during her recent tuition with the famous maestro, Cecchetti; and the very young English students she gathered round her gradually began to acquire a first-class style and to reveal the soundness of their training. Having by this time become married to Ashley Dukes, the playwright and theatrical producer, the scope of her endeavours began to increase rapidly. Her husband bought and converted an old parish hall into a charming *bijou* theatre, the now famous little Mercury Theatre at Notting Hill Gate; and here her Dancing

School and ever-growing Company of youthful dancers now found a permanent home where they could be "tried out" on a real stage under actual theatre conditions.

In 1931, Marie Rambert founded the famous Ballet Club, which met at week-ends for special ballet performances in the little Mercury Theatre; and here, jointly with the Camargo Society—founded the year before by P. J. S. Richardson, editor of *The Dancing Times*, Arnold Haskell and others—many excellent ballet performances were given, with visiting stars, such as Markova, and even Karsavina and Woizikovski, as guest artists, to provide special glamour for the ever-increasing and always most enthusiastic audiences.

On one of Karsavina's guest artist visits to the Mercury, she chose Harold Turner—then one of Madame Rambert's most finished and well-trained male dancers—to be her partner in Fokine's lovely ballet *The Spectre of the Rose*; and when, a little later on, she went on a Continental tour, she invited this very youthful dancer to accompany her as her partner and to take Nijinsky's famous role—an honour which Harold Turner has always regarded as the greatest "highlight" in his fine career.

For a short time, in 1934, Nijinsky's daughter, Kyra Nijinsky, danced with the Ballet Rambert, when she created the role of Mortal under Neptune in Antony Tudor's *The Planets* (music by Gustav Holst, *décor* and costumes by Hugh Stevenson). During this visit, also, she danced The Young Girl in *The Spectre of the Rose*, Marguerite in Ashton's *Mephisto Valse* (music by Liszt, *décor* and costumes by Sophie Fedorovich) and in other ballets.

Alicia Markova became the regular ballerina of the Company and remained as such for about four years. During this time she danced not only classical ballerina parts, but also created most of the leading roles in the new ballets then being produced by Frederick Ashton, Susan Salaman, Andrée Howard and others. In addition to providing this additional "glamour" for Madame Rambert's group of dancers, her ballerina work at the little Mercury Theatre proved a very useful experience for the already established Diaghileff dancer, enlarging her scope and giving her constant practice, in readiness for her later work as ballerina to the Vic-Wells Company and for her future career in general.

During the earlier ballets performed by the Company, Madame Rambert frequently danced leading roles in them herself. One of these was *Our Lady's Juggler*, with choreography and *décor* by Susan Salaman, to music by Respighi and produced in 1930; and she danced in many other ballets for some considerable time.

The smallness of the little Mercury's stage somewhat restricted the scope of the ballets produced, these tending to be what might be termed "chamber" ballets; and the Rambert Dancers were the first Company to produce such "chamber" ballets and to make them popular. As time went on, however, occasional engagements at larger theatres became essential, in order to accustom the young Company to performing on a full-size stage —especially in connection with the great classical ballets, for which Madame Rambert has always had a real passion and which she regards as providing the necessary background and basis for all dancing. Her recent production of *Giselle*, by the way, has been acclaimed by an important critic as being "a perfect evocation of the Romantic Period and coming nearest in spirit to what the original production must have been". In this production, Sally Gilmour was the "wraith-like" Giselle, to Walter Gore's finely danced and convincingly mimed Albrecht. and to Joyce Graeme's inhuman majesty as Myrtha, the Queen of the Wilis.

The Company's first full-size stage venture occurred when the young choreographer, Frederick Ashton's, first ballet, *A Tragedy of Fashion*, was produced at the Lyric Theatre, Hammersmith, in the Revue *Riverside Nights*, on the invitation of Sir Nigel Playfair. So great a success was this first outside performance that the Ballet Rambert now undertook frequent engagements at other theatres, among these being The New and The Lyric at Hammersmith many times more. The Company was thus firmly launched and became well known and popular, not only in its own *bijou* Mercury Theatre—which was constantly visited by balletomanes from all over London— but also in other theatres. Later on, too, the Company began to tour the provinces; and in more recent years it has visited most of the pleasure resorts in the South of France, and, in 1947, it made a remarkably successful tour of Australia—the first British Company to visit that far-off continent.

During the Second World War, the Rambert Ballet suffered considerably from the call-up of dancers and from production difficulties of many kinds; and though it joined forces for a short time with the London Ballet—a group formed by Antony Tudor at Toynbee Hall, and later taken over by Harold Rubin for his Arts Theatre—it eventually had to disband, and its members became scattered and worked with other companies and groups for a time. Towards the end of the war, however, the Arts Council—then known as C.E.M.A.—came to the rescue, and the Ballet Rambert was re-formed under its auspices, and has been able to hold its own and to continue its fine work ever since; and during more recent years it has reached a very high standard in dancing and production.

The Company has given highly successful seasons at Sadler's Wells Theatre and at Covent Garden Opera House, The King's and Lyric, Hammersmith, the Arts Theatre and also in other theatres; and its provincial tours have proved equally popular. Its members have danced at the Festival Theatre at Cambridge, and have also provided the *corps de ballet* background at several huge Gala Ballet Performances at Earl's Court and at the vast Harringay Arena in London. They performed this service most admirably at the special Gala Performance held for three days at the Empress Hall, Earl's Court, during November 1949, for the benefit of the world-renowned male dancer, Vaslav Nijinsky, at which the famous dancers Leonide Massine, Tamara Toumanova, Yvette Chauviré, Jean Babilée, George Skibine, Vladimir Skouratoff and Marjorie Tallchief were the Continental stars.

Marie Rambert, though she has not specialized in choreography herself, has yet proved a most able teacher of this difficult art to others; and whenever she has discovered among her students or fully trained dancers a tendency towards ballet creation, or to the art of *décor* and scenic design, she has never failed to bring it to fruition.

Among the male choreographers she has "discovered" and whose works have been first produced for her Company are Frederick Ashton, Antony Tudor, Frank Staff, Walter Gore and David Paltenghi; and among her female choreographic discoveries are Susan Salaman, Wendy Toye, Andrée Howard. Frederick Ashton created for Madame Rambert *A Tragedy of*

Fashion, Leda and the Swan, Le Petits Riens, Mars and Venus, Capriol Suite, La Peri, The Lord of Burleigh, A Florentine Picture, Façade, Mercury, The Lady of Shalott, Foyer de Danse, The Tartans, Pavane pour une Infante Défunte, Mephisto Valse, Valentine's Eve. Frank Staff's Rambert creations are: *Czernyana,* revival of *The Tartans, Peter and the Wolf,* revival of *Pavane pour une Infante Défunte,* second version of *La Peri, Enigma Variations, Czerny 2, Un Songe.* Antony Tudor's best-known ballets for the Rambert Company are: *Cross-Gartered, Lysistrata, Les Masques, The Planets, The Descent of Hebe, Le Jardin aux Lilas, Dark Elegies, The Judgment of Paris, Gala Performance, Soirée Musicale, Paramour, Atalanta of the East, Pavane pour une Infante Défunte, Mr. Roll's Quadrilles.* Walter Gore's ballets for this Company are: *Valse Finale, Paris Soir, Cap Over Mill, Bartlemas Dances, Confessional, Simple Symphony, Mr. Punch, Plaisance.* Among Walter Gore's later ballets for the Company are *Concerto Burlesco, Winter Night, Kaleidoscope, Antonia.*

Susan Salaman created for this Company *The Tale of a Lamb, Circus Wings, Our Lady's Juggler, Le Rugby, Le Cricket, Le Boxing, Waterloo and Crimea, The Garden, The Mermaid* (with Andrée Howard).

Andrée Howard's best-known ballets for the Company are: *The Mermaid* (with Susan Salaman), *Alcina Suite, Cinderella, The Rape of the Lock, La Muse s'Amuse, Death and the Maiden, Croquis de Mercure, Lady into Fox, Fête Étrange, Carnival of Animals, The Fugitive, The Sailor's Return.*

In 1934, Ninette de Valois' *Bar aux Folies-Bergère* was created for and first produced by this Company; in 1937 a second version of *Cross-Gartered* was arranged by Wendy Toye; and in 1943, Elsa Brunelleschi's *Flamenco* was created and presented.

David Paltenghi's work as a choreographer began only in very recent years, his first ballet for the Rambert Company being created for and produced by them on their return from the very successful Australian Tour in 1949. On August 31st that year, his *The Eve of St. Agnes* was given during their visit to Bath. He followed this with *Prismatic Variations* in October 1950; and in May 1951, presented at the Bath Assembly Festival, came his ballet *Fate's Revenge, or Trouble in the Upper Rooms,* a special

Regency piece. During the Festival of Britain year, 1951, also, the Company presented his *Canterbury Prologue*, commissioned by the Arts Council for the Canterbury Festival celebrations.

Most of these now well-established choreographers have also produced works for other Companies. Antony Tudor has been with the American Ballet Theatre Company for several years; and Frederick Ashton is now chief choreographer of the Sadler's Wells Ballet. They all owe, however, the production of their earlier works and choreographic development generally to the training and encouragement given them by Madame Rambert.

Among the well-known dancers trained and produced at the little Mercury Theatre by Madame Rambert may be mentioned: the late Pearl Argyle, Andrée Howard, William Chappell, Harold Turner, Paula Hinton, Maude Lloyd, Margaret Hill, Walter Gore, Sally Gilmour, Mona Inglesby, Diana Gould, John Gilpin, Elizabeth Schooling, Joyce Graeme, Alexis Rassine, Antony Tudor, Peggy van Praagh, Belinda Wright, Celia Franca, Leslie Edwards, Prudence Hyman, Pauline Clayden, etc. Among artistic designers who have been first introduced into ballet work by Madame Rambert and are now well known are William Chappell, Sophie Fedorovich, Nadia Benois, Hugh Stevenson, Susan Salaman, Andrée Howard, Ronald Wilson, Harry Cordwell, etc.

When not touring at home or abroad, or appearing at various of the larger London theatres, Madame Rambert gives a season of suitable smaller ballets at her own little Mercury Theatre. On the Company's return from Australia in the spring of 1949, she presented a very successful season of these more intimate chamber-ballets, the show being entitled *Ballet at Eight*, when several Ashton and Tudor revivals were given.

Madame Rambert declares that her whole career has been a "voyage of discovery"; and, indeed, it has always been, and still is her joy to "recognize talent, whether it be in a dancer, choreographer, designer or musician, to do all in her power to help it to find an outlet". That she has succeeded beyond the shadow of a doubt is certainly true; one has only to think of Frederick Ashton, Antony Tudor, Walter Gore, Andrée Howard and Sally Gilmour—to name but a few at random— who have all justified the faith and helpful interest she has shown in them since first they came within her generous orbit. The world of modern ballet has much for which to thank her; and it is good to know that she is still the ruling genius of a really excellent all-round Company.

In the Coronation Honours of 1953, Madame Rambert received the well-deserved award of C.B.E.

Alexis Rassine

A NATURAL CLASSICAL DANCER OF EXCELLENT TECHNIQUE, Alexis Rassine has gradually emerged as a leading *danseur noble* with the Sadler's Wells Ballet. He comes of a Russian-Lithuanian family, and was born at Kovno in 1919; but he is of South African nationality, having passed most of his early life in South Africa. He received his first dance training in Capetown; and later on he went to Paris to study with Madame Olga Preobrajenska.

In 1938, he came to London and joined the Ballet Rambert for a short time, with which Company he made his preliminary début and danced in several ballets. He then joined the John Regan Ballets des Trois Arts, making his début with that Company by dancing the leading male role in John Regan's ballet *Chanson Choréographique* at the Lyric Theatre, Hammersmith, in 1939; and he also danced in other ballets there. He then joined the Arts Theatre Ballet for a short time, leaving this Company later to dance the Spectre in *Le Spectre de la Rose* and other leading roles with the Anglo-Polish Ballet.

In 1942, while still only twenty-three years of age, but with considerable practical experience behind him, Alexis Rassine joined the Sadler's Wells Ballet, and has remained with that Company until the present day. Under the continuous training, practising and strict discipline involved as a member of the Sadler's Wells Ballet, the policy of which is all-round Company perfection rather than the turning out of star performers, Rassine has now corrected some of his earlier faults—a tendency to somewhat erratic work on occasions, and even a certain physical weakness, and he has now acquired a remarkably brilliant technique in solo work and a *ballon* and elevation that make his Blue-Bird *pas de deux*, for instance, a joy to behold. With his slight, but well-built physique, his grace and fluidity of movement, he has all the requirements of the *danseur noble*; and it is in such classical roles that he excels.

His versatility in dramatic roles is still somewhat limited in range—though his recent performances as Albrecht in *Giselle* leave little to be desired, this part suiting him remarkably well. Indeed, his restrained acting of this romantic, noble youth has seldom been bettered, while the virtuosity of his technique is frequently dazzling. He has rather recently revealed that certain *demi-caractère* roles are particularly well within his grasp. An example of this was seen early in 1947, when Leonide Massine revived for the Sadler's Wells Company at Covent Garden his ever-popular ballet *La Boutique Fantasque*. In this revival, one of the best of the mechanical doll performances was given by Rassine as the Snob, in which role the slender elegance of his super-dandy's smart appearance and the superciliousness of his amazingly rhythmic movements were a revelation—and brought back to older members of the audience nostalgic memories of the great Idzikovsky as the original creator of that delightful part. Quite apart from its many amusing touches, it was a little gem of exact timing—and exact miming.

In addition to his virtuosity as the Bluebird in *The Sleeping Beauty*, he also gives a particularly sparkling performance in the *pas de trois* in *Lac des Cygnes*. He was really delightful, too, as the Seagull in Ashton's *Les Sirènes*. In Helpmann's charming Chinese ballet, *The Birds*, he gave a truly bird-like and tender performance as The Dove. He has little to learn in the matter of execution, and his future progress as an established *danseur noble* seems assured.

Among Rassine's leading roles have been: Prince Siegfried in *Le Lac des Cygnes*, Albrecht in *Giselle*, Franz in *Coppélia*, Harlequin in *Le Carnaval*, Spectre in *Le Spectre de la Rose*, the Poet in *Les Sylphides*; and he has also given good performances in *The Gods Go a-Begging*, *Les Patineurs*, *Adam Zero*, *Miracle in the Gorbals*, *The Quest*, *Les Rendezvous* and many other ballets. His romantic portrayal of one of The Lovers in *Miracle in the Gorbals* and the charm of this happy couple's absorbed dance was a grateful and comforting interlude in that most gloomy work, and it left a pleasant and truly cheerful memory of youthful love in beautiful movement.

In 1949, Rassine made a successful appearance in a television programme at Alexandra Palace, with Moira Shearer as his partner in *Le Spectre de la Rose*, in which his dancing was admirable.

When the Sadler's Wells Ballet made their highly successful first visit to U.S.A. and Canada in the late autumn of 1949, Alexis Rassine went with them as one of their leading classical male dancers and was greatly admired for his elegant partnering of the ballerina in the popular classics; also for his finished technique—in particular for his virtuosity performance as the Bluebird in *The Sleeping Beauty*. Early the following year, he created the part of the Shepherd of the Golden Age in Ninette de Valois' new ballet, *Don Quixote*, produced on February 20th, 1950, in which he and his charming Shepherdess, Pamela May, danced a very beautiful *pas de deux*, regarded as one of the highlights of that particular scena. On March 9th, 1950, he took part in the Grand Gala Performance at Covent Garden in honour of the State Visit of the French President and Madame Auriol, at which Their Majesties the King and Queen were present.

In June 1950, Rassine took part in a particularly successful television ballet performance from Alexandra Palace, with various members of the Sadler's Wells Ballet and the Sadler's Wells Theatre Ballet, among whom were Beryl Grey, Gerd Larsen, Avril Navarre, Anne Negus, Rowena Jackson, Brian Shaw, Kenneth Macmillan and John Field. Once again, this accomplished *danseur noble* revealed his grace and skill in several very finely performed solos.

At the end of 1950, he accompanied the Sadler's Wells Ballet on their second, and even more successful, visit to U.S.A. and Canada, and again won admiration with his co-stars for the excellence of his work. On his return early in 1951, he again appeared with the Company at Covent Garden and took up his many good roles as a leading dancer.

In Frederick Ashton's grand Coronation ballet of 1953, *Homage to the Queen*, Rassine danced one of the Cavalier *danseur noble* roles with brilliance.

Tatiana Riabouchinska

A S WITH HER TWO FAMOUS DE BASIL COLLEAGUES—TAMARA
Toumanova and Irina Baronova—Tatiana Riabouchinska
leapt into sudden stardom practically overnight on her
first appearance with the de Basil Ballets Russes de Monte Carlo.
Unlike her fellow stars in style, she was never their rival, nor,
indeed, the rival of anyone else, because her individuality was
so entirely different from that of any other dancer. From the
beginning of her similarly meteoric career, she has exhibited a
subtle, fey-like quality and understanding of youthful, un-
sophisticated simplicity extremely rare—a quality which,
though it may have appeared natural enough at the time of her
extremely youthful début, has, curiously enough, remained with
her ever since. She still seems to be nearer the World of Faery
than of ours; and she has always possessed a style of her own.
Yet she cannot be described definitely either as a *soubrette*—
though her light gaiety is unfailing—nor quite as a character
dancer. She is just Riabouchinska, the dancer who is different.
She has a light and wonderful elevation, with a thistledown
quality about it; and her sensitivity is of a similar delicately
elusive kind. While never in active competition with her two
youthful but more dazzling early colleagues as a dancer of the
great classical roles, her technique has always been irreproachable and she has always fitted perfectly into the exquisite ballet
scenes of which she formed so important a part.

Tatiana Riabouchinska, though born during the Russian
revolutionary period, was never called upon to endure such hardships as fell to the lot of her future Star-colleagues. Her parents
were well-to-do—her father, indeed, was a rich merchant, well
known in Moscow for his generous encouragement of the Arts.
Forced to become *emigrés* during the Civil War, the family
remained in exile; but, having ample resources, they did not
suffer want in any way. It was not surprising that the little
Tatiana early revealed a passion for dancing, since, on her
mother's side, she was later to be the third dancer in the family.
Her mother, as a former dancer herself, naturally encouraged
her small daughter to dance almost as soon as she could walk,

carefully training the latter's baby steps in the traditional Russian ballet manner.

In due course, the family removed to Paris, in order that the budding dancer might be trained there. Madame Riabouch-inska placed her gifted child first with the well-known teacher, Volinine, and afterwards with the Maryinsky Theatre ex-baller-ina, Madame Kschesinskaya, then conducting an excellent ballet school in the French capital, where the pupils were taught by her on the grand system of the old Imperial Russian Ballet Schools. It was, therefore, from these two famous teachers that the small new arrival received her very excellent training. Madame Kschesinskaya quickly recognized the latent powers hidden beneath the shy and sensitive little girl's somewhat gawky exterior, and the ethereal, unusual grace likely to emerge as a definite asset; and she set to work to bring out her every quality and to encourage her belief in herself. In this good work she was constantly supported by Madame Riabouchinska —herself a woman of great business ability, in addition to her dancing gifts and knowledge of theatre life, which latter stood her in good stead later on when travelling around with her young daughter.

Such excellent progress did Tatiana make that, while still just in her early teens, she was invited to join Balieff's *Chauve Souris*; and for a short time she toured with this popular show. Then, in 1932, George Balanchine, recruiting talent for Colonel de Basil's newly formed Ballets Russes de Monte Carlo, invited the young Riabouchinska to join that Company instead; which she did with the full approval of her enterprising mother, who travelled around with her prodigy daughter and attended to all her business and physical needs.

Having already secured from the equally famous studio of Olga Preobrajenska the two other young dancers, Tamara Toumanova and Irina Baronova, Colonel de Basil proceeded to advertise his trio of "Baby Ballerinas" for all they were worth, and presented them as principals in most of his ballets, pinning all his hopes upon them as a tempting novelty in this first great revival of real Russian Ballet since the death of Diaghileff, the famous pioneer. This seemingly rash experiment proved to be a tremendous success, and the young ballerinas—already well trained and able to carry out the roles entrusted to them, though none was over fourteen years of age—created a real furore wherever they went. They were at first placed under the immediate supervision of the already famous dancer, Alexandra Danilova, chief ballerina of the Company, than whom they could not have had a more finished example constantly before their eyes; and they quickly went on from success to success.

They first appeared in London in 1933 at the Alhambra, where they were the sensation of the four months' season there; and from then onwards until 1937, they danced with the Company each successive year at Covent Garden. They also visited New York several times, always returning to the de Basil headquarters in Monte Carlo at the end of the various tours.

As stated above, the young Riabouchinska's sensitive, almost fey personality made her the ideal dancer for certain roles, particularly those requiring the portrayal of a very young girl; and among the more important parts she danced with the Company—and afterwards with Educational Ballets—may be mentioned the following as outstanding: The Child in Massine's *Jeux d'Enfants* (always one of her best parts even in succeeding years); Frivolity in Massine's *Les Présages*; the Golden Cock in *Coq d'Or* (another of her most dazzling roles); the American Child in Massine's *La Boutique Fantasque*; the Girl Lover in Fokine's *Paganini* (with Rostoff as her partner, and later with Skouratoff and with David Lichine); the Young Girl in Massine's *Le Beau Danube*; the Girl in Lichine's *Graduation Ball*, in which her performance of the *Perpetuum Mobile* was a joy to behold. She danced in several of the Fokine ballets, her portrayal of the airy-fairy Papillon in his *Le Carnaval* and in *Les Sylphides* being exquisitely perfect.

During the Second World War, this always delightful dancer was in America, where she danced with the Original Ballets Russes (De Basil's) in 1940. It was during this period that she danced so brilliantly in *Graduation Ball*. She married David Lichine, the choreographer of this charming ballet; and under his expert and critical guidance, she steadily improved and developed still further her own unique natural style and personality. She has never cared to dance in a great variety of roles, but has always preferred to develop and to polish to the utmost those which seem to be more particularly her own, and in which she is inimitable.

Riabouchinska came with the Marquis de Cuevas' Grand Ballet de Monte Carlo for its season in London in June 1949; and again she danced the part of the Young Girl in Massine's *Le Beau Danube*, revealing once more the indubitable fact that she is still unsurpassed in this charming character, in which innocence and a certain amount of will power are definitely and delightfully mingled. She also danced in *Les Sylphides*, in which her famous arm movements—always one of her best features—were shown to greater advantage than ever. During this season, her husband David Lichine's new ballet, *Infanta*, was given and met with an excellent reception. Later that same season, yet another new Lichine ballet, *The Enchanted Mill*, was given its first production at Covent Garden.

In December 1950, when the full-length performance of *Giselle* was first given in a television programme from Alexandra Palace, Riabouchinska danced the title-role, supported on this occasion by Celia Franca as the Queen of the Wilis, Tutte Lemkow as Albrecht and David Paltenghi as Hilarion, with other members of the Ballet Rambert.

During the 1951 Festival of Britain celebrations, Riabouchinska danced as a guest artist with Anton Dolin's Festival Ballet at the Stoll Theatre. Later, she stayed on with the Company with her husband, David Lichine, who became its resident choreographer. Here she received a very glad welcome return to London, and delighted her every audience. In *Le Beau Danube* she was as perfect as ever as the Young Girl Fiancée. Another wonderful performance was her ballerina-puppet in *Petrouchka* —in which she danced with Massine in the title-role and Trunoff as the Blackamoor. In her husband's new ballet, *Harlequinade*, created for this Company, she danced Columbine with John Gilpin as Harlequin, with all the mischievous charm expected of her. With John Gilpin, too, she danced the Young Girl in *The Spectre of the Rose*—a Dream, indeed! As was her dancing with Gilpin in *Les Sylphides*. She also danced the Sugar-Plum Fairy in *The Nutcracker*; and in Lichine's second ballet for the Company, *Impressions*—in the latter she had to dance a remarkably speedy, even hectic, *pas de deux*, again with John Gilpin.

Tatiana Riabouchinska is extremely interested in her husband's choreographic work, and delights in the preparation and presentation of each of his new ballets. She danced with him as guest artists with Ballet Theatre in Ballet Theatre's American tour of 1952-53 in *Graduation Ball* and *Les Sylphides*.

Whenever Riabouchinska appears on the stage she instantly creates a special sense of personal atmosphere belonging to herself alone; and never does she cease to delight her gladly welcoming audience in her performance—brilliant in its quiet perfection—until she vanishes from sight once more with the light, gossamer-like movements of a being from some enchanted land.

Nicolai Sergueeff

WHEN NICOLAI SERGUEEFF CAME AWAY FROM RUSSIA IN 1919, he brought with him, like Aladdin from the Magic Cave, a "lamp" that should shed light upon the correct presentation of the Russian classical ballets in other lands. This "lamp" was his own unique knowledge, and his own sole record, of how these beautiful works of art were actually produced when Russian ballet was at the height of its ancient glory; and he has caused this dazzling "light" to shine on many momentous occasions since he came to this country.

No other male dancer, or ballet official, ever to come out of Russia was better qualified to speak of Russian classical ballet of the old régime than Sergueeff. Born in St. Petersburg in 1876, he was educated and trained at the Imperial Ballet School there; and among his teachers were Nicola Balkoff and the famous Marius Petipa, the creator of *The Sleeping Beauty, Le Lac des Cygnes, La Bayadère, Raymonda, Barbe Bleu,* etc.

Sergueeff worked under Petipa for many years; and when, at length, the great master retired, he succeeded him as *régisseur-general* of the Imperial Maryinsky Theatre. He was the last man to hold this important post before the Russian Revolution.

Among Sergueeff's own famous pupils and contemporaries

were Anna Pavlova, Michael Fokine, Leonide Massine, David Lichine, Nicholas Legat, Tamara Karsavina, Lydia Lopokova, Oboukhoff, etc. It was during his work as teacher and *régisseur* of the Maryinsky Theatre that Sergueeff realized more than anyone else the absence of written records of the famous—and irreplaceable, in many cases—classical, as well as the contemporary newer ballets then in the repertory; and he set himself the stupendous task of remedying this highly important omission.

He first of all made himself well acquainted with the system of Dance Notation, or Dance Shorthand, that had been invented by the Russian doctor Stepanoff; and then he began the long and laborious job of making exact records of the most famous classical and current ballets then being performed. It took him the whole of his twenty years of service to copy these authentic versions of about the same number of celebrated works; but each was a complete record of every step, movement, grouping, stage direction or other detail of the intention of the choreographer, composer, artist, etc., concerned.

Then came the Revolution, and no more work of this kind could be done; but when Sergueeff himself finally came away from Russia in 1919, he brought these unique records with him, plus a considerable quantity of music as well. In 1921, he met Serge Diaghileff in Paris; and the famous impresario, delighted to come across him again, brought him to London to reproduce *The Sleeping Beauty* he was then about to present at the Alhambra. Sergueeff, however, did not remain long with Diaghileff; and when his contract had ended, he went to Riga, in Latvia, where he set up a Company of his own and produced Act IV of *La Bayadère*, *La Fille mal Gardée* and *Paquita*, all from his own valuable records. In 1925, he was invited by Olga Spessivtseva (Spessiva) to produce *Giselle* for her at the Paris Opéra; which he did.

This ballet had previously been a failure; but Sergueeff's exact reproduction of it now proved such an immense success that he, himself, as producer, was awarded the medal of L'Académie Nationale de Musique et de Danse.

On returning to Riga, after this happy event, finding not sufficient financial support for his own Ballet Company, Sergueeff joined the newly established Russian Opera Company, with which he made a world tour, and gave scenes from classical ballets as well as operatic ballet interludes, acting as ballet-master to the Company. When this Company was disbanded, Sergueeff came to England in 1934, and produced *Giselle* for the Camargo Society and, later on, for the Vic-Wells Company, with Spessiva, Markova and Dolin as principals at various times. For the Wells, he also produced *Lac des Cygnes*, *Coppélia* and *Casse Noisette*, from his original records.

Differences having arisen with Sadler's Wells, Sergueeff joined International Ballet in 1940; and he remained closely associated with this Company. In connection therewith not only did he produce during the succeeding years the great classics in full-length form, *Le Lac des Cygnes*, *Coppélia*, *Giselle* and *Casse Noisette*, but he also arranged some scenes from *La Bayadère* which, though delays in production have unavoidably taken place, it is still hoped may be presented in due course. He also arranged *The Polovtsian Dances from Prince Igor* from Fokine's ballet of that title; and he put various other classics and Fokine ballets in process of preparation. In addition, he became chief instructor at the International School of Ballet which has been set up in connection with this Company —of which Miss Mona Inglesby is Founder and Director. The latter charming ballerina and her entire Company received the greatest assistance and valuable instruction in all their productions from Nicolai Sergueeff, and found his highly specialized knowledge and unique experience of the utmost significance.

Nicolai Sergueeff remained the only man outside Russia in possession of the exact records of the Imperial Russian Classical Ballets—too few of which have yet been seen in our country, or in America. That there is now the likelihood of a growing demand for these—since the immense popularity of the full evening-length classics recently given by the Sadler's Wells Ballet in U.S.A.—seems more than possible. It would, indeed, be a real ballet thrill if a few more rubs of Nicolai Sergueeff's "Magic Lamp" should result in the presentation of a dazzling performance of, say, *Raymonda*, *La Peri*, *Barbe Bleu* or *La Bayadère* (in its entirety)—given exactly as in the wonderful days of the Imperial Russian Ballet, with the same tradition, the same steps, the same feeling!

Even though some of our ultra-moderns might mutter contemptuously under their breath "Museum Piece!", the experiment might be well worth trying, the result surprising. The fact remains that when the Sadler's Wells Ballet visited the U.S.A. in 1949, ultra-modern New York swallowed the full evening-length *Sleeping Beauty* whole at one glorious mouthful and loved every moment of it! And Nicolai Sergueeff had many more such glorious mouthfuls, just waiting to be swallowed. But, alas! he died in the spring of 1951. It is to be hoped that the fine Company he helped so greatly to develop will be able at some not too distant date, with the aid of its accomplished and ever-enterprising ballerina-director, to present some of these long-hoped-for revivals of Imperial Maryinsky ballet thrills.

Moira Shearer

ALTHOUGH MOIRA SHEARER FIRST BECAME RENOWNED FOR HER charming performance in the popular film *The Red Shoes,* she was at that time not entirely the finished ballerina then somewhat prematurely acclaimed by all and sundry. Nevertheless, in "straight" ballet she had already made very definite strides towards that enviable, but difficult-to-attain, status which she has now definitely reached. As with Margot Fonteyn, her famous and brilliant Sadler's Wells colleague, there was never any doubt about her eventually becoming a true *ballerina-assoluta*, if not enticed away from the completion of the arduous and many years' training necessary, plus a sufficiently continuous experience in the traditional and most exacting classical roles essential to put the finishing touches and polish upon each of her performances. Fortunately for ballet, however, she has been able to resist the too early offers and the glamour of Hollywood; and the completion of her dance training has, consequently, proceeded on normal lines.

Moira Shearer comes of a Scottish family and was born at Dunfermline in Fifeshire in January 1926. Here she lived until she was six years old, when her father, a civil engineer in the Colonial Service, had to spend some years in Rhodesia, and his wife and child accompanied him thither. The latter was already a clever little dancer, even at that early age; and a short time later, her parents having made the acquaintance in Ndole—a small place not far from the Belgian Congo—of a former member of Diaghileff's Company, who had also been a pupil of the famous Cecchetti, she was thus able to begin her first dancing lessons under an experienced, Russian-trained teacher.

When the little girl was eight years old, her parents came to England, and Moira was naturally eager to continue her dance training; but a good general education being regarded as the first essential—although already well grounded—she was sent for the next two years to an excellent school in Scotland. Here she continued her studies intensively and conscientiously, being especially interested in music, literature and the Arts generally, and not neglecting to "keep up" to pitch the dancing instruction she had so far received.

At the age of ten, she came to London with her parents, who, having been advised by their Diaghileff-trained friend in Africa to take the child to the famous Russian teacher, Nicholas Legat, arranged an interview with him. Legat was already old, however, and at first felt unable to cope with so young a student; and consequently, he sent her to the Theatre and Dancing School of Flora Fairbairn, with whom she took lessons for a few months. After this, the old Russian teacher, interested in the good progress made by the talented child, agreed to take her into his own studio for main ballet training. Very soon afterwards, however, Legat died; and his youthful and most promising new pupil continued her studies with his widow, Nicolaeva Legat, with whom she remained for four years.

A most attractive child, with her well-formed limbs, her "crowning-glory" of bright, red-gold hair, and the delicate pink-and-white complexion that goes with the latter, the young Moira Shearer was always a distinctive and noticeable student—above all, however, she was enthusiastic and ambitious about her work and eager to become well educated in every possible way. She had many opportunities for trying out stage appearances, since both Miss Fairbairn and Madame Legat believed in holding frequent shows for their students; and little Moira Shearer always received her full share in the various exhibition dances given—indeed, she quickly revealed the pleasant fact that, in addition to advancing satisfactorily in her dancing training, she likewise possessed a natural gift for mime.

As soon as she reached the age of fourteen years, she joined the Sadler's Wells Ballet School in 1940; but, within six weeks of this longed-for event, the exigencies of the Second World War necessitated her evacuation to Scotland—to her great disappointment. Nevertheless, she kept up her regular dancing exercises; and in 1941, temporarily, she joined the newly formed International Ballet Company, where she continued her training and experience under the excellent guidance of Mona Inglesby, that Company's star ballerina. While with this Company, she created with much charm the pretty little part of the Guardian Swallow in Mona Inglesby's own amusing and most delightful ballet, *Planetomania*.

When permitted to return to London in 1942, she took up her training work once more in the Sadler's Wells School, where her true career began and whence she passed on eventually to the Sadler's Wells Ballet—where she has remained to the present day. Here, as with all students graduating to the senior Company of this now world-famous Ballet, despite the fact that she had already danced small and even occasional leading classical parts in the School, she had to begin in the *corps de ballet* and gradually work her way forward from lesser to more important roles.

Although her unusual colouring and vivid personality have, doubtless, been useful assets, they would have carried no weight at all in the Sadler's Wells Ballet had not her good dancing ability, miming, dramatic sense and musical sensitivity been of the ever-increasing high standard always demanded by its famous Director, Ninette de Valois—who, by the way, is frequently described as the "Diaghileff" of that splendid all-British Company. Here, an attractive-looking dancer is never pushed forward merely on account of a charming appearance. She must also have fully benefited by the excellent training she has received, and be fully competent not only in the necessary technique required, but also possess a high intelligence to enable her to grasp the inner meaning of the story and character to be danced.

Fortunately, it happened that the youthful Moira was a very sincere and conscientious student, not only of the technical part of her training, but, thanks to her thoroughly good general education, had also a well-trained mind, plus a lively Celtic imagination that made her sensitive to the romantic stories so often associated with ballet. The result was that whenever a small role was entrusted to this bright-haired, wide-eyed young dancer, she entered into the character with real understanding and zest and made of it a perfect little item that exactly fitted into the story's whole.

Some of these small parts, later on, were actually created around her personality by Frederick Ashton, the Company's well-known choreographer. The more important role of Pride in Mr. Ashton's ballet *The Quest*, was developed with her in mind; and this most difficult and sophisticated part she danced in 1943, at the age of seventeen, with complete understanding and with a self-possession truly remarkable in so youthful a performer—also revealing real dramatic ability.

Before and after this, she danced in practically every production of the Company, in the ballets of Ninette de Valois, Frederick Ashton, Robert Helpmann and Andrée Howard—in addition to the classics and the few Fokine ballets then in the repertoire. Thus, gradually, she came to the immediately secondary parts; and finally she arrived at the stage when she was permitted to be "tried-out" in principal ballerina roles.

After dancing in *The Sleeping Beauty* the parts of the Fairy of the Crystal Fountain, the Florestan *pas de trois*, the Lilac Fairy and Florisse, there came her début at Covent Garden as the Princess Aurora, on March 2nd, 1946, in which she exhibited a surprisingly assured and graceful technique and a radiant charm that captivated her critical audience—for the audiences at this new home of the ballet watch their favourite artists as they emerge from the ranks with intensely critical understanding, though with much sincere affection.

That same year she danced Swanilda in *Coppélia*, and Odette—and a little later Odette-Odile—in *Lac des Cygnes* (leading up to the latter most exacting of the classic roles by first dancing the Leading Swan and the *pas de trois*). In all these classical roles she proved herself equal to the occasion, gradually improving her technique and miming with every performance, and revealing definite signs of the future ballerina-to-be.

Among the ballets in which she had danced before this great event, and also later in her career, were the following: *Le Carnaval* (valse, *pas de trois*, Chiarina, Columbine), *Les Sylphides* (valse, prelude, mazurka, *pas de deux*), *Orpheus et Eurydice* (Peasant *pas de deux*), *Les Patineurs* (*pas de deux*), *The Gods Go a-Begging* (The Serving-Maid), *The Quest* (Pride), *Promenade* (*pas de trois*, *pas de deux*), *Le Spectre de la Rose* (The Young Girl), *Casse Noisette* (Sugar-Plum Fairy), *The Birds* (The Nightingale), *Festin de l'Araignée* (The Butterfly), *The Haunted Ballroom* (Ursula), *Façade* (valse, polka, tango), *Miracle in the Gorbals* (A Lover), *The Rake's Progress* (The Dancer), *The Prospect Before Us* (Mdlle. Théodore), *Dante Sonata* (Child of Light), *The Wise Virgins* (A Wise Virgin), *The Wanderer* (The Lovers' *pas de deux*), *A Wedding Bouquet* (Julia), *Apparitions, Comus, Hamlet,* etc.

In 1946, she also danced and acted the gay part of Lady Kitty in Ashton's *Les Sirènes*; and she was one of the three equal-part female dancers in the same choreographer's intricately beautiful *Symphonic Variations*; and the Nymph of the Spring in *The Fairy Queen*. In 1947, in Massine's revival of *La Boutique Fantasque*, she danced with success the famous *can-can* with the equally famous choreographer himself as her partner; and she also danced the *Jota* in his *Le Tricorne* and created The Aristocrat in his *Mam'zelle Angot*. In 1948, she gave her first performance of the classical role of *Giselle* with much charm and dramatic feeling; and she also danced the Ballerina in Ashton's *Scènes de Ballet*. In 1948, too, she created the principal part of The Princess in Massine's new ballet *The Clock Symphony*, The Young Wife in Ashton's *Don Juan*, and the name part in the same choreographer's first full-evening-length ballet *Cinderella*. In this latter she gave a very lovely performance, taking the role—which she shared alternately with Violetta Elvin—originally allotted for creation to Margot Fonteyn who was unable to appear in that role until later in the season owing to an accident she incurred while dancing in *Don Juan*. Her own favourite roles, by the way, are Giselle, Odette-Odile in

Le Lac des Cygnes, The Young Girl in *Le Spectre de la Rose* and Aristocrat in *Mam'zelle Angot.*

Among Moira Shearer's famous partners may be mentioned Leonide Massine, Robert Helpmann, Frederic Franklin, Frederick Ashton.

It was in 1947 that she was invited to take the main ballerina part in the much-discussed Arthur Rank film *The Red Shoes,* in which she had as colleagues Leonide Massine, Robert Helpmann and Ludmila Tcherina. Opinions differ as to the virtues or otherwise of this now world-renowned film-ballet, but there was never any doubt about the delightful portrayal of the charming wearer of the red shoes and of her beautiful dancing throughout, despite the fact that her dramatic powers were not at that time quite equal to the almost melodramatic work required of her. Her dancing, nevertheless, was a joy to behold.

Her brilliant success in *The Red Shoes,* however, has done nothing to spoil this always quiet and modest young dancer; nor does it appear likely to divert her from her life's ambition—to become eventually a great ballerina. She has declared her intention of perfecting her training and her portrayal of principal and less-important ballet roles with the Sadler's Wells Company at Covent Garden, in addition to which she has ambitions towards the legitimate drama later on—to which end she has received special instruction in "straight" dramatic work.

Naturally enough, she has received many tempting film offers since her initial success in this medium of Art; and when she went with the Sadler's Wells Company to U.S.A. and Canada in the late autumn of 1949, she received many more. Indeed, she found herself an even more popular "film star" on the other side of the Atlantic than at home. While the Company—with whom she shared with Margot Fonteyn and her other colleagues a most enthusiastic reception—was playing to overcrowded and wildly enthusiastic audiences at the Metropolitan Theatre in New York, *The Red Shoes* film celebrated its first year of continuous performances on Broadway; and its Titian-haired heroine was invited to a grand luncheon in celebration of this event, being received with great acclamation.

She has now appeared in a very successful television programme at Alexandra Palace, in which she danced beautifully as The Young Girl in *Le Spectre de la Rose*, with Alexis Rassine as her partner, with whom also she danced in the *Casse Noisette pas de deux*, in March 1949.

On February 25th, 1950, Moira Shearer was married to Ludovic Kennedy at the Chapel Royal, Hampton Court Palace. She interrupted her honeymoon to return for a few days in order to take part in the Grand Gala Performance at Covent Garden on March 9th, in honour of the State Visit of the French President and Madame Auriol, at which Their Majesties the King and Queen were present.

When Balanchine's magnificent work, *Ballet Imperial*, was produced by him at Covent Garden, London, April 5th, 1950, she several times danced the leading ballerina role with much charm and real brilliance.

In May 1950, she was invited to the Marigny Theatre, Paris, by Roland Petit to dance the part of Carmen in his remarkable ballet based on Bizet's famous opera of this name, during the temporary absence of Renée Jeanmaire. who had created the part so brilliantly. This was a role, however, which did not suit the non-Latin temperament of this essentially British dancer, although her personal beauty and exquisite dancing were much admired by her Parisian audiences.

When the Sadler's Wells Ballet paid their second visit to U.S.A. and Canada towards the end of 1950, Moira Shearer was again one of the principal ballerinas accompanying them; once more she was received everywhere with great delight and admiration. On returning to England in February 1951, she again danced at Covent Garden in the revival of Ashton's *Cinderella*, taking the title-role as before; and she was acclaimed by all as a fine ballerina.

It was on April 18th, 1951, that the *première* of Moira Shearer's second film took place. She had devoted herself entirely to ballet work since *The Red Shoes* was produced. The new film was *The Tales of Hoffmann*, produced by Michael Powell and Emeric Pressburger at the Shepperton film studios. The music is, of course, from Offenbach's famous opera, played by the Royal Philharmonic Orchestra under Sir Thomas Beecham. The *décor* and costumes are by Hein Heckroth. Shearer takes the role of Olympia, the mechanical doll, with whom Hoffmann, wearing magic spectacles, falls in love. Unfortunately, singing is included, the voice parts being sung "off" by operatic singers, while the dancers make appropriate movements with their mouths to synchronize—in addition to miming and dancing. Some of the performers manage this difficult feat better than others—notably Robert Helpmann as the unlucky hero's Evil Genius; but in the case of the mechanical doll, the continuous opening and closing of the mouth tends to become monotonous and even absurd. Despite this tiresome fact, Moira Shearer danced the part with real brilliance. She was a joy to behold in an interpolated Dragonfly ballet—also in a sylph-like *pas de deux* with Edmond Audran danced to the luscious strains of the popular Barcarolle. Among her co-stars in this film were Robert Helpmann, Leonide Massine, Alan Carter, Michel de Lutry and Ludmila Tcherina (choreographer Frederick Ashton, though Massine also created one of the dances).

Among her later films are: In 1952-53, *The Story of Three Loves* (choreographed Ashton, music Rachmaninoff) and *Jealous Lover*. In 1954 she was starred in the film *The Man who Loved Redheads* (from Terence Rattigan's play *Who is Sylvia*). Nevertheless, Moira Shearer does not intend to desert her first love, straight ballet; and she will continue to shine as a guest ballerina on the famous and historic boards of Covent Garden's Royal Opera House.

Two books about Moira Shearer have already been written. One of these is a Ballet Album with a Biographical Study by Rose Tenent, published by the Albyn Press; and the other is a Biography of her by Pigeon Crowle, published by Faber.

George Skibine

O NE OF THE OUTSTANDING MALE DANCERS OF TO-DAY IS George Skibine, a leading dancer in the Marquis de Cuevas' Grand Ballet de Monte Carlo.

Though born in the neighbourhood of Kharkov in Russia, in the year 1920, of a Russian father and a Belgian mother, George

Skibine has lived most of his life in France and in America. He was educated in Belgium and Paris, and secured an Honours Bachelor Degree in Art. Then he began to study ballet, training with Preobrajenska, Lifar, Vladimiroff and Vilzak at various times. His father had been a dancer in the famous Diaghileff Russian Ballet; and for a time the young Skibine worked with him and also did some "straight" dramatic work and danced in various shows in Paris.

Soon deciding to make ballet his life's career, however, he joined the René Blum Ballet de Monte Carlo in 1938, where he quickly rose to the rank of a solo performer, dancing in Nijinsky's *L'Après-midi d'un Faune* and in most of the other ballets in that Company's repertoire. He went with the Company to America; and there, later on, he joined Colonel de Basil's Original Ballet Russe, in which he danced, among other works, Schwezoff's *The Eternal Struggle*. This was in 1940; and in 1941, he became a member of Ballet Theatre in New York, where he danced leading roles in most of the classical ballets.

From 1942 until the end of the Second World War, he served in the United States Army Intelligence Branch. On his return, he danced for about a year with the Markova-Dolin Company; and later in 1946, he rejoined Colonel de Basil's Original Ballet Russe. With this Company, in addition to special *pas de deux* from the classics, he danced the more important roles in some of the newer ballets, notably in William Dollar's *Constantia* and in Edward Caton's *Sebastian*.

Then, in 1947, when the Marquis de Cuevas founded his Grand Ballet de Monte Carlo, Skibine joined it as one of the principal dancers—a position he still holds at the present time.

When the Grand Ballet de Monte Carlo first visited London in 1948, it was not then in very good form so far as the general work of the Company was concerned; but George Skibine himself received excellent notices from the critics, who recognized in him a dancer of splendid and firmly established technique and a mime of real intelligence and imagination. In particular, he was praised for his performance in Balanchine's *Night Shadow*, in which he was really admirable as the Poet, as was his partner, the very youthful Éthéry Pagava, as the Sleepwalker. Again, as the Poet and sole male dancer in Fokine's *Les Sylphides*, he was commended for his perfect technique and welcome lack of effeminacy—which so many young male dancers reveal in this highly romantic role. In the *Don Quichotte pas de deux*, too, with Tamara Toumanova as his partner, it was declared that he " danced superbly ".

In their next season at Covent Garden in 1949, the Company had improved amazingly, and its many star performers were hailed with enthusiasm; and among them, George Skibine again received the most encouraging commendations. This time he gave a remarkably moving and romantic performance as Albrecht in *Giselle*, with Toumanova in the title-role; and as the Hussar in Massine's *Le Beau Danube* he was equally out-standing. In the new Lichine ballet, *Infanta*, he created the difficult part of the frustrated Dwarf with remarkable sympathy and skill, again with Toumanova as the lovely Princess he adores.

With Marjorie Tallchief—to whom he had been married in 1947—he received equal praise for his fine dancing in Nijinska's *Les Biches*, in Balanchine's *Concerto Barocco*, and in Massine's *Capriccio Espagnol*—his performance in the latter being re-garded as the most effective characterization of any item in the ballet. He also danced leading roles in Taras' *Design with Strings* and in Ana Ricardo's *Del Amor y de la Muerte (Of Love and Death)*—in the latter he danced the Torero.

On October 2nd, 1950, Skibine's first complete choreographic work was produced by the de Cuevas Company at the Théâtre des Champs-Élysées, Paris. Entitled *Tragedie à Verone*, it deals very tenderly, yet skilfully, with the tragic but beautiful story of Romeo and Juliet. It met with much success, and Skibine was highly praised for his first creation. He himself danced the role of the romantic Romeo with deep understanding, grace and verve; and his Juliet was the sweet and gentle Éthèry Pagava, who gave a lovely performance. The music of this ballet is Tchaikovsky's Fantasy Overture; and the *décor* and costumes are by Delfaux.

Skibine is much interested in the development of television as a ballet medium; and early in 1951, he appeared in a very successful performance from the B.B.C. Studios.

During the 1951 Spring Tour of the Continent by the Cuevas' Company—now known as the Grand Ballet du Marquis de Cuevas—Skibine was the *premier danseur*, André Églevsky, who formerly held that position, having left the Company some months previously to join the New York City Ballet.

George Skibine shows every sign of becoming at an early date one of the finest male dancers of modern times. In particular, he has the main attributes of the classical *danseur noble* of the old Russian School—almost faultless technique and style, romantic dignity and intelligent feeling for, and understanding of, each role entrusted to him. He is a vigorous and intelligent exponent of the modern up-to-date ballet.

Skibine's second ballet, *Annabel Lee* (Schiffmann—Delfaux), was produced in 1951; and in 1952 came his third work, *Prisoner of the Caucasus* (Kachaturian—Doubujinsky).

Michael Somes

MICHAEL SOMES IS ESSENTIALLY A MODERN-TYPE DANCER; and he is more particularly successful in roles that have been specially evolved around his particular personality. Despite his splendid physique and a build reminiscent of the youth of Ancient Greece, he did not at first so readily fit into a classical role as one expected to be the case. He is extremely musical; but he prefers to dance to a difficult complicated modern rhythm rather than to the more conventional music of the classical masters. Nevertheless, despite his own personal preferences, he has now developed into a remarkably fine *danseur noble*, and partners Margot Fonteyn, the famous *ballerina-assoluta* of the Sadler's Wells Ballet, in all her classical roles with the utmost grace and chivalrous ease.

Born at Horsley in Gloucestershire in 1917, Michael Somes was brought up in an atmosphere of music, his father being a musician. Even when only four years old, he showed a definite tendency towards dancing; and as soon as possible he began to take dancing lessons with a teacher at Taunton, where, in due course, he passed the preliminary examinations of the Royal Academy of Dancing. At the age of fifteen years, he studied with Katharine Blott of Weston-super-Mare. Here he won a Scholarship for the Sadler's Wells Ballet School, being the very first boy to gain that distinction; and thus he was enabled to take up dancing as a career.

The young student graduated into the Sadler's Wells Ballet in 1935. During his years of training, and afterwards, he was fortunate in being able to work under such famous teachers as Ninette de Valois, Judith Espinosa, Idzikovsky, Sergueeff, Volkova, Volinine, Pruzini, Plucis, Phyllis Bedells and Margaret Craske. He first appeared in the Sadler's Wells *corps de ballet* in *Casse Noisette, Les Rendezvous, Job* and other ballets then being produced; and later on he was given small and then leading roles in *Les Sylphides, Pomona, Checkmate* and *Le Carnaval*, quite early dancing the Blue-Bird *pas de deux* from *The Sleeping Beauty*.

It was in 1938 that Michael Somes first created a role—that of the Young Man in Ashton's ballet *Horoscope*, a part that suited his temperament and style exactly. In connection with this ballet he tells an amusing story of how, on one occasion when dancing with his partner, Margot Fonteyn, his costume—the upper part of which was composed of a wide-meshed coarse net —became entangled with hers. Unable to extricate themselves, they managed, with difficulty, to finish their *pas de deux*, then left the stage (which they were not supposed to do just then) and got hurriedly disentangled by someone in the wings before resuming their performance. Another ballet that suited this young dancer excellently was *Dante Sonata*, also created by Ashton, in which he appeared in 1940. That same year he danced in *Le Lac des Cygnes* and in Ashton's *The Wise Virgins*. In another Ashton ballet in 1941, *The Wanderer*, he fitted unusually well into the role allotted to him.

During the Second World War, Michael Somes served for four years with H.M. Forces; but on his return to the Sadler's Wells Ballet, he worked hard to make up for this long interruption to his career. Whereas before his enforced absence he had varied considerably from performance to performance, he now became far more reliable as a classical partner, and developed very quickly into one of the Company's most promising male dancers.

Among the many ballets he has danced in since his return in

1945 have been *Giselle, The Sleeping Beauty, Le Lac des Cygnes, Casse Noisette, Job, Symphonic Variations, Scènes de Ballets, Hamlet, Miracle in the Gorbals, Les Sirènes, The Fairy Queen, Mam'zelle Angot, Cinderella.*

Some critics consider his most outstanding performance has been in Ashton's *Symphonic Variations*, in which six dancers—three girls and three men—take part, all chosen for their musical sensitivity, in addition to the beauty of their technique and in which all fit into a perfect pattern and have an equal part to dance. The other two original men dancers were Brian Shaw and Henry Danton, the three girls being Margot Fonteyn, Moira Shearer and Pamela May, the Company's leading ballerinas. This graceful ballet, with its original performers, appeared in a television programme on May 23rd, 1947, with complete success.

In Frederick Ashton's charming version of *The Fairy Queen*, in 1946, Michael Somes partnered Margot Fonteyn in a marvellous *pas de deux*, in which, as the swallow-like Spirits of the Air, they had to skim, almost to fly, down a fairy glade from one end of Covent Garden's enormous stage to the other; and this beautiful dance, exquisitely performed by both dancers, was praised by all as one of the really dazzling "highlights" of this remarkably fine production.

In *Miracle of the Gorbals*, Somes took the role of the Stranger, a seriously dramatic part in striking contrast to his lively Captain Bay Vavaseur in *Les Sirènes*. In *Mam'zelle Angot*, he had another amusing and lively part, that of the Caricaturist, in which he made a splendid partner for Moira Shearer as the Aristocrat.

Michael Somes was among the principal male dancers who went with the Sadler's Wells Ballet on their famous first tour to the United States and Canada in the late autumn of 1949; and he received excellent criticisms—in particular for the quiet perfection of his performance in *Symphonic Variations* and for his fine leaps and splendid technique as Prince Siegfried in *Le Lac des Cygnes*. That he has been steadily developing into a finished all-round artist during the past few years is definitely evidenced by his now skilful and chivalrous partnering of the ballerina as the debonair Prince Charming in Ashton's first full-evening-length fairy ballet, *Cinderella*—in which he was praised in New York and elsewhere.

In 1949, Michael Somes did some excellent work in television at Alexandra Palace, when he danced the "Leo" solo from *Horoscope*, and appeared in other items in a programme with Margot Fonteyn and Harold Turner.

On March 9th, 1950, he took part in the Grand Gala Performance at Covent Garden in honour of the State Visit of the French President and Madame Auriol, at which Their Majesties the King and Queen were present.

Michael Somes has already made his début as a choreographer. On March 28th, 1950, he created for the Sadler's Wells Theatre Ballet his first ballet, *Summer Interlude*, produced at the Sadler's Wells Theatre. The music for this work consists of sixteenth-century Italian tunes orchestrated by Respighi; and the *décor* and costumes are by Sophie Fedorovich. It has a slight and simple story about a pair of Italian peasant girl and boy lovers whose romantic idyll is interrupted by a more sophisticated group of modern bathing folk; and it has a youthful, spring-like charm about it that is delightfully refreshing. It is hailed as a very promising first choreographic attempt, providing some excellent dancing for young performers in gay and pretty costumes—and a welcome relief from the sordid dullness that has lately crept into so many modern ballets.

On April 5th, 1950, Michael Somes won a further success by creating one of the leading roles in George Balanchine's splendid personal production of *Ballet Imperial* at Covent Garden—a beautiful work which had not previously been seen in this country. His skilful dancing in this difficult ballet was remarkably fine.

On April 5th, 1951, Michael Somes danced a role that may well become one of the best of his career. This was in Frederick Ashton's *Daphnis and Chloe,* a new and original version of the fascinating subject chosen nearly forty years ago by Fokine, and which proved to be one of that great choreographer's most beautiful and successful ballets. Ashton tackled the fine old legend boldly and skilfully, using the same lovely music of Maurice Ravel, but with *décor* and costumes by John Craxton (Fokine had Bakst as his designer). Despite criticism from those who saw the Diaghileff production, its present-day audience received it with delight. Michael Somes danced the difficult and exacting role of Daphnis remarkably well and with a good sense of atmosphere; and his passages with Margot Fonteyn as Chloe were beautiful indeed. His miming was dramatic and convincing.

He has since danced brilliantly the leading roles in *Sylvia* (September 1952), in the revival of *Apparitions* (1953), and in Ashton's splendid Coronation ballet, *Homage to the Queen* (1953).

Jack Spurgeon

ⓄⓄ

DESPITE THE FACT THAT HE DID NOT BEGIN TO DANCE UNTIL HE was round about twenty years old, Jack Spurgeon has certainly very quickly made up for lost time; and for several years he was the premier classical male dancer with International Ballet.

He is a Londoner; and when he had overcome a certain amount of parental opposition to his choice of a profession, he began his dancing career at once. He trained first at the Italia Conti School, and also studied under Nicholas Legat, Olga Preobrajenska, Anton Dolin and Vera Volkova. At various times throughout his career he has been associated with many outstanding figures in the ballet world, among these being Alexandra Danilova, Tamara Toumanova, Mona Inglesby, Bronislava Nijinska, Moira Shearer, Leonide Massine, André Églevsky, Frederic Franklin, Youskevitch, Woizikovsky, Harold Turner and Walter Gore.

Having finished his training, Jack Spurgeon received several engagements with well-known Companies, among these being one headed by Woizikovsky, Madame Nijinska's National Polish Ballet, Ballets des Trois Arts and the Anglo-Polish Ballet. He has also toured with the René Blum Ballet Russe de Monte Carlo. Amongst the roles he danced with these Companies may be mentioned those of Harlequin in *Le Carnaval*, South-Wind in *Biroska*, Gold in *Midas*, the Hero in *Perseus*, the Warrior Chief in *Prince Igor Dances*, the Blue-Bird in *The Sleeping Beauty*, *The Spectre of the Rose*, etc.

Jack Spurgeon served in H.M. Forces throughout the whole period of the Second World War; but despite his long years of absence, his work had not suffered unduly, and soon after his return, he became principal classical dancer with International Ballet, dancing the leading roles and partnering the Company's chief ballerina, Mona Inglesby. His outstanding classical roles have been Prince Siegfried in *Lac des Cygnes*, Albrecht in *Giselle* and Franz in *Coppélia*. Other roles he has danced have been in *Le Carnaval*, *Les Sylphides*, *Twelfth Night*, etc. He has also more recently danced very excellently the role of the Sailor in the modern ballet, *Sea Legend* (choreography Dorothy Stevenson, music Esther Rofe, *décor* and costumes John Bainbridge) created for the Company by the Australian choreographer, Dorothy Stevenson, then dancing with International Ballet. In the latter's grand complete production of *The Sleeping Beauty*, he took the classical role of the Prince, which he danced with much dignity and feeling. The fact, too, that he makes such an excellent Franz in *Coppélia*, proves that this acknowledged classical dancer is versatile and able to cope with character roles, while his fine performance in *Sea Legend* reveals his scope in modern works.

Towards the end of 1949, Jack Spurgeon left International Ballet and became a member of the faculty of The School of Russian Ballet opened in December of that year, of which, at its inception, Madame Nadine Nicolaeva-Legat was its principal Artistic Adviser. At the official opening, Alicia Markova and Anton Dolin declared the School open. A few months later, Madame Legat withdrew from the School. The first patron of the latter was Vaslav Nijinsky, followed, after the death of the great dancer, by Romola Nijinsky. In July 1951, Madame Mathilde Kschesinskaya (Princess M. Krasinsky) became its Artistic Adviser.

In 1952, Jack Spurgeon was dancing with the Original Ballet Russe Company, and in their production of *The Golden Cockerel*, his clever miming as the Astrologer was excellent.

Frank Staff

THAT WITTY AND RESOURCEFUL CHOREOGRAPHER, FRANK Staff, hails from South Africa, having been born at Kimberley in 1918. He first studied dancing in South Africa with Helen Webb and Maude Lloyd—the latter having trained with Madame Marie Rambert and been a leading dancer with the Ballet Rambert.

At the age of sixteen, he came to England to complete his training as a student at the famous Rambert School at Notting Hill Gate. He danced for a time with the Sadler's Wells Ballet but returned to the Ballet Rambert, where he soon became a good all-round dancer with the Company, for whom he created a number of roles, among these being: Cupid in Ashton's *Cupid and Psyche*, the Bread Boy in *Harlequin in the Street*, Sir Plume in *The Rape of the Lock*, the Trapezist in *Circus Wings*, Sir Andrew Aguecheek in *Cross-Gartered*, the Virtuoso in *La Muse s'Amuse*, Danse Tendresse in *Croquis de Mercure*, the Anarchist in *Paris Soir*, etc. Later on, he danced leading roles with the Company, such as the Faun in *L'Après-midi d'un Faune*, the Waiter in *Bar aux Folies-Bergère*, Harlequin in *Le Carnaval*, Prince in *Cinderella*, Death in *Death and the Maiden*, Mercury and Hercules in *The Descent of Hebe*, Popular Song and Dago in *Façade*, Hilarion in *Giselle*, Lover in *Le Jardin aux Lilas*, Prince in *Lac des Cygnes*, Sir Lancelot in *The Lady of Shalott*, Faust and Mephisto in *Mephisto Valse*, Juggler in *Our Lady's Juggler*, Mercury in *The Planets*, mazurka in *Les Sylphides*, Spectre in *Le Spectre de la Rose*, etc. He was always especially good as a character dancer.

It was just four years after entering the ballet world that Frank Staff began to try his hand at the creative work of choreography, in which he received great encouragement from Madame Rambert, who was always eager to discover new talent in this difficult art. His first work was to prepare, in 1938, new choreography for two ballets already in the Company's repertoire; these were *The Tartans* (music by Boyce, *décor* and costumes by William Chappell), and *La Péri* (Dukas—N. Benois), which were quite successful. Then came his first entirely original creation produced at the Duchess Theatre in 1939 by the Ballet Rambert in connection with the Ballet Club. This was *Czernyana*, a most diverting and witty satire on ballet of the day. The music was an adaptation of the famous Czerny Piano Exercises, so well known to the Victorians; and the *décor* and costumes were by Eve Swinstead-Smith. It made an instant hit with its very original humour and clever adaptation to ballet technique.

The following year, 1940, Staff produced an even more delightful ballet at the Arts Theatre, Cambridge. This was the evergreen *Peter and the Wolf*, which became very widely popular. The music was Prokofiev's *Symphonic Tale for Children*; and the *décor* and costumes were by Guy Sheppard. This charming ballet deals with a humorous fairy-tale; and appealing, as it does, to children and adults alike, it has become a favourite for all time. The subject is taken from an old Dutch legend; and it is interesting to note that the Dutch Scapino Ballet Group for Children in Amsterdam has made use of the same story as a ballet in their repertoire, and find it equally popular with their juvenile audiences. The Dutch version also has music by Prokofiev; with choreography by Albert Mol.

Frank Staff's next ballet, *Enigma Variations* (Elgar—Guy Sheppard), produced at the Arts Theatre, Cambridge, that same year, did not meet with a similar popular success. After this he created the choreography for *The Seasons* (Glazounov—Chappell) for the London Ballet; but his war service now followed. On his return in 1945, he created *Un Songe* (Lekeu—Ronald Wilson). In 1945-46, too, he was also choreographer and dancer in *The Tales of Hoffmann*, and in the musical plays *The Glass Slipper* and *Perchance to Dream* (Ivor Novello). He danced again with the Rambert Company at various times until 1946; and then he undertook a tour in South Africa with Elizabeth Schooling, the dancer whom he had then married. On his return, he danced again with the Rambert Company; and when Andrée Howard's ballet, *The Sailor's Return*, was produced in 1947, he created the part of Harry and made an excellent impersonation. Later that year, too, he accompanied the Rambert Ballet on their most successful Australian tour, which lasted until the spring of 1948, though he did not complete the tour.

On his return from Australia, he was invited to join the Metro-

274

politan Ballet as resident choreographer; and for this Company he created two very successful ballets. The first of these—which he produced in 1947, before joining the Company—was *Lovers' Gallery* (the music for this being Lennox Berkeley's *Divertissement in B flat*, and the *décor* and costumes by George Kirsta), which deals with the coming to life of pictures in a gallery and provides scope for some interesting dancing, but which, though witty and bright, is somewhat slight in treatment. His second ballet for this Company, however, *Fanciulla delle Rose* (Arensky—Guy Sheppard), presented in 1948, is a much more important work. It deals with the theme of a young girl about to offer a wreath of roses to a statue of the Virgin being beset by the Seven Deadly Sins in human form, which snatch the flowers from her one by one, leaving her the bare frame-work only as her offering. It provided some lovely dances for the young girl, created by Svetlana Beriosova, who gave a wonderful performance; and Frank Staff himself danced most effectively in this ballet as one of the Deadly Sins.

When the new Arthur Bliss—J. B. Priestley opera, *The Olympians*, was presented at Covent Garden on September 29th, 1949, Frank Staff took over the dancing role of Mercury from Robert Helpmann—who performed it on the first night only on the eve of his departure with the Sadler's Wells Ballet to U.S.A. and Canada; and, with his companion Olympian, Venus (Moyra Fraser), he mimed the part with an originality and witty brilliance that added much charm to the whole performance. The choreography was by Pauline Grant.

Later in 1949, Frank Staff was appointed ballet-master and choreographer to the new Permanent Ballet being installed at the Empire Theatre, London, where ballets were to be given as part of the daily programme, in addition to films. His first ballet in this new connection was entitled *Yester-year*, and met with considerable success. It dealt delightfully with the three types of ballet seen in this country during the present century—the Adeline Genée period, the Russian period, and the Symphonic ballet of to-day. Unfortunately, his second ballet, *Amphytryon 50* (with music by Bach), was not so successful, as its Ancient Greek subject seemed somewhat obscure and unknown to the cinema audience beholding it. But Staff had a large *corps de ballet*, and some fine principal dancers, plus an excellent orchestra; and he soon found it quite possible to present exactly the right type of delightful ballet to fit into the Empire programmes, and to give variety and high-class performances. He created several new short ballet-scenas for these Empire shows—one of these being a very lively one on the familiar *Punch* theme, with special music by Melachrino. Another was *Showboat-Time*, based on the American *Frankie and Johnny* story. He also adapted and curtailed several other equally good subjects, interspersing these with shortened versions of and *divertissements* from *Les Sylphides*, *Swan Lake* and other classics. Many good dancers came to him from various companies to lead these little " pocket" ballets—among them being Annette Chappell, Leo Kersley, Jeanne Artois and others. The effort of devising and rehearsing four small ballet shows daily, however, is a very strenuous undertaking; and after several busy months of this hectic life, Staff decided to leave the Empire— his work there being taken over by Alan Carter. After this he worked and danced with the Ballets des Champs-Élysée, and during their 1951-52 season, he created for the Company a very successful ballet, *Romanza Romana* (Pierre Petit—Karinska).

Frank Staff always revealed an excellently original invention in his choreographical work; and that he has a real gift for dealing with a fantastic subject was clearly demonstrated by his effervescent, sparkling *Czernyiana*—by the way, he produced a second ballet on this intriguing subject in 1941, entitled *Czerny 2*. His *Peter and the Wolf* was a fine example of his merry journeyings into the improbable Land of Fantasy. That he also has a softer and deeper side is evidenced first by his *Un Songe*, and more recently by his thoughtful presentation of the young girl in *Fanciulla delle Rose*, whose treatment is full of sympathy and beauty. He is both witty and poetical; and he is a choreographer to watch, who will most certainly bring forth a really great ballet before long. Meanwhile, we are grateful for *Peter and the Wolf* and for *Czernyiana*; also for the excellent pioneer work he has done at the Empire.

Maria Tallchief

THOSE TWO REMARKABLY FINE VIRTUOSO DANCERS, MARIA AND Marjorie Tallchief, have become leading performers at a pleasantly early age. Both still in their early twenties, they are already star members of their respective Companies.

These clever dancing sisters are of Osage Indian stock on their father's side—hence their black hair, soft dark eyes, and unusually svelte figures—their mother being of Scottish-Irish extraction. They were educated in Canada; later Maria graduated at Beverley Hills, California. She was also trained as a pianist. Both sisters were keen on dancing from their earliest days; and each received an excellent ballet training. They studied first with Ernest Belcher in California, then they went to New York, where their main teachers were Bronislava Nijinska and David Lichine. Later on, Maria also studied with George Balanchine.

Having completed their training and enjoyed a certain amount of early dancing experience together, the two sisters decided to part company in order that each might develop more closely her own individual personality and continue her future career separately and independently.

Maria Tallchief began to be noticed more particularly when she joined the American Ballet Russe de Monte Carlo in 1942, where she gained much valuable experience. Her first role was in Nijinska's *Chopin Concerto*. Later, as the Fairy in Balanchine's lovely *Le Baiser de la Fée*, she dazzled her New York audiences with her already sparkling technique and her charming personality. Among other ballets she danced in with this Company were Balanchine's *Danses Concertantes*, *Night Shadow* and *Ballet Imperial*; Fokine's *Schéhérezade*; Balanchine's *Le Bourgeois Gentilhomme*; and in Massine's *Gaieté Parisienne*—in which she danced the *Can-Can*—she revealed herself as a quickly developing virtuoso dancer.

She left the Ballet Russe to dance as guest artist with the Paris Opéra Ballet, when the latter Company visited New York in the spring of 1947, dancing in Balanchine's *Apollo, Baiser de la Fée*, etc. Later on that year she joined Ballet Society of New York.

In the spring of 1948, when Ballet Society gave an All-Balanchine programme, she danced in this famous choreographer's *Symphonie Concertante*, and gave a beautiful performance in the leading role. She also danced leading roles in his *Four Temperaments*, *Symphony in C*, *Capricorn*, *Orpheus*, etc. In the latter she danced with real sympathy as Eurydice. During the spring of 1949, she danced as guest artist with Ballet Theatre in Tudor's *Lilac Garden*, in the Blue-Bird *pas de deux* in *Aurora's Wedding* and in the dazzling *pas de deux* in *Don Quixote*.

At the end of this engagement, she became leading ballerina in Lincoln Kirstein's New York City Ballet—which had now been merged with Ballet Society—of which George Balanchine was Artistic Director; and with this Company she still remains. Here she has danced leading roles in most of the ballets produced, including Balanchine's *Divertimento*, *Four Temperaments*, *Symphony in C*, *Symphonie Concertante*, *Serenade* and *The Prodigal Son*; in Jerome Robbins' *The Guests*; and in other ballets.

Maria Tallchief was married to George Balanchine in 1946; and the latter has been largely instrumental in guiding and moulding her into exactly the right dancer able to interpret the principal roles in his own ballets, but also to give equally fine performances in other difficult works.

For instance, the amazing success and sensation of the early winter 1949 season of the New York City Ballet was the appearance of Maria Tallchief in the famous Fokine-Stravinsky ballet, *The Firebird* (with new choreography by Balanchine and gorgeous *décor* and costumes by Marc Chagall), in which she gave a brilliant performance in the title-role—a role which fitted her perfectly. Her quick, spontaneous, almost flying movements at times gave the impression of dancing flames; and her truly amazing virtuosity left all beholders gasping. Yet, withal, there was also to be seen the softness essential to this lovely creation of Fokine's—once the favourite role of that exquisite dancer, Tamara Karsavina, who first danced it years ago. Her partners as Ivan Tsarevich, dancing alternately, were Francisco Moncion and Nicolas Magallanes. The latter was also her partner in Balanchine's new ballet presented that same season, *Bourrée Fantasque*. Just before this brilliant season began, this fine young dancer was guest artist in Lucia Chase's Ballet Theatre.

The greatest interest was aroused when she appeared at Covent Garden, London, during the New York City Ballet's summer season in 1950; and it was her scintillating *Firebird* that thrilled her audiences most. She was, however, almost equally admired for her fine performances in *Palais de Cristal*, Balanchine's several beautiful symphonic ballets, and his splendid *Orpheus*. Her Eurydice was beautiful. In 1951, she was outstanding in revivals of *The Fairy's Kiss* and *Apollo*—also in Balanchine's new ballets *Scotch Symphony* and *Metamorphoses* in 1952.

Her wonderful performance in *Firebird* (*L'Oiseau de Feu*) has definitely placed Maria Tallchief in the front rank of American ballerinas.

Marjorie Tallchief

WHEN THE TWO TALLCHIEF SISTERS, MARIA AND MARJORIE, decided each to create and develop her own dancing career independently of the other,[1] Marjorie Tallchief joined Ballet Theatre in New York, where she gained much varied experience and remained for three seasons. She danced in most of the ballets in that Company's repertoire, both in minor and, later, in leading roles. On leaving Ballet Theatre in 1946, she appeared with the Original Ballet Russe; and here, among other roles, she danced very successfully the difficult part of Myrtha, Queen of the Wilis, in *Giselle*, when Alicia Markova was the heroine and Anton Dolin partnered the latter as Albrecht. She danced Myrtha alternately with Rosella Hightower.

It was not, however, until Marjorie Tallchief joined the Marquis de Cuevas' Grand Ballet de Monte Carlo in 1947 that she sprang into real prominence as an excellent virtuoso dancer. With this Company—of which she is still a member—she has had many opportunities of distinguishing herself. She has

[1] See preliminary paragraphs in immediately preceding biographical sketch dealing with Maria Tallchief.

danced most successfully in Edward Caton's *Sebastian*, in which she portrays one of the Prince's sisters; and in Serge Lifar's *Noir et Blanc*, she dances a leading role remarkably well. In John Taras' *Design with Strings*, she is also excellent.

It is, however, as the Girl in Blue in Nijinska's *Les Biches* that she proves herself so brilliant a performer—this role being regarded by many critics as one of her very best parts. It certainly suits her ultra-modern style to perfection; and she performs the wonderful *Adagietto* solo in this ballet almost flawlessly. She also dances Diana in Lifar's *Aubade* with the correct classical coldness of the chaste goddess, giving a really fine performance. In Balanchine's *Night Shadow*, she portrays the Coquette with exactly the right touch of callous seductiveness, miming and dancing extraordinarily well. In Lichine's *Infanta*, she has some interesting *entr'acte* dances, which she gives with much grace and vigour. In Massine's curious ballet *Mad Tristan*, she is outstanding, dancing the role of the terrible Chimera of Isolde imagined in the distraught brain of that grief-maddened hero with a dramatic and almost bloodcurdling effect —an amazing performance. Yet, in the Balanchine ballets she is equally successful in entirely contrasting roles—in particular, she dances the leading role in his *Concerto Barocco* with George Skibine with remarkable grace, her every movement seeming entirely effortless.

Early in 1950, the Grand Ballet de Monte Carlo had a very successful tour in Germany, visiting Berlin, Hamburg, Munich and many other important cities; and it was during this tour that Marjorie Tallchief danced Odile in *Lac des Cygnes* for the first time. This seductive role suits her extremely well, and it shows off her astonishing virtuosity at its very best, the famous thirty-two *fouettés* being a mere nothing to her; while her subtle attempts to "vamp" the deceived Prince Siegfried proves her excellence as a mime. She still continues at times to dance the Queen of the Wilis; and she has certainly made of the cold, remorseless Myrtha a fine study of mime and faultless dancing.

Marjorie Tallchief has a very strong and definite personality, and she creates artistic interest in all her roles; and her technique is equally strong and steady, her elevation, in particular, being wonderfully high and effortless. She was married in 1947 to George Skibine, one of the outstanding male dancers of the

De Cuevas Company; and he is now her frequent partner in many important *pas de deux* and principal roles.

With the latter in the late autumn of 1949, she took part in the Nijinsky Benefit Gala Performances held at the Empress Hall in London. Here, again, she danced Myrtha, Queen of the Wilis, in *Giselle*, with her usual regal demeanour, her fine interpretation of the role, and her splendid dancing being greatly admired.

During the de Cuevas Company's several Continental tours —they also visited the Edinburgh Festival—Marjorie Tallchief gained many fresh laurels and more firmly established herself as a brilliant and versatile ballerina. In particular, she was outstanding in *Night Shadow* and in the famous *Don Quichotte pas de deux*, in both of which she was partnered by her virtuoso husband, George Skibine (q.v.). This brilliant pair, in the faultlessly performed *pas de deux*, never fail to receive enthusiastic applause. In Skibine's beautiful ballet *Annabel Lee* they were equally fine as sad and tragic lovers requiring a softer approach.

Tamara Toumanova

ⓥⓥⓥ

ALTHOUGH IT IS EASY TO IMAGINE THAT TERPSICHORE AND VENUS must both have been present at the birth of Tamara Toumanova and that they generously showered their own especial gifts upon her, there seems little doubt that the goddess Fortune did not smile upon her in her earliest years, which were full of hardships. She was born during the Russian Civil War—actually her birth took place in a rough cattle wagon in which her mother and father—a wounded Russian officer— were escaping with other refugees to Siberia. The *émigrés* eventually reached Shanghai, where they remained for seven years.

The little Tamara—a child of remarkable beauty—revealed an unmistakable gift for dancing from her earliest years; and after having been taken to see Anna Pavlova on one of the latter's visits, she was fired with the desire to become a dancer, too, spending most of her time practising all the dance steps she knew and making up dance stories of her own. When she was still only seven years old, her parents, proud of their beautiful child's budding talents, determined to have her properly trained; and so they gave up their present security and moved to Paris, risking all for the sake of the little Tamara's future, in which they firmly believed. Recklessly, but wisely, they plunged for the best and placed their eager small daughter in the studio of Madame Olga Preobrajenska, who was so deeply impressed by the great potentialities of her new pupil that she readily enough overcame all financial and other difficulties in the way.

The little Tamara advanced in her studies at an amazing pace and immediately began to attract attention. At the age of nine years she appeared at the Paris Trocadère as a small guest artist at a Pavlova Gala, where her miniature-like beauty and already surprising technique "brought down the house". Here, again, she was inspired by a further glimpse of the great Pavlova, who this time visited the studio and prophesied a great career for her youthful admirer.

After this, though still so extremely young, she began to accept minor engagements to appear at fashionable parties and concerts, and even to give little dance recitals of her own—the fees she earned for these performances being of the greatest assistance to her struggling parents—indeed, in another couple of years, she was keeping herself almost entirely, while still studying hard and conscientiously with Madame Preobrajenska.

With this hard-working child prodigy in the Preobrajenska studio was another promising student, Irina Baronova, whose name was presently to become linked with hers as a similar "Baby Ballerina", as they both came to be called. Later, with the addition of Tatiana Riabouchinska, they became a very famous trio.

Toumanova, however, was the first of the three to become known, owing to the constant necessity for her to earn fees to help out the family exchequer. At the age of eleven years, she made her first ballet début at the Opéra as a guest artist in *L'Éventail de Jeanne*; and after this, she continued to accept more and more concert and private engagements, working much too strenuously for one so young. She was always in great demand because of her attractive appearance, charming, small

figure—she never appeared to go through an "awkward" period
—in addition to the ever-increasing and astonishing virtuosity
of her dancing.

Then, at last, came a change. George Balanchine, the well-
known choreographer, visited the studio one day, and, instantly
perceiving an important "find" in the lovely young Toumanova
—then thirteen years of age—invited her, then and there, to
join Colonel de Basil's Ballets Russes de Monte Carlo, for which
he was then seeking new members. This was in 1932; and she
now quickly became a star, dancing leading roles in *Cotillon*
and *Concurrence*, created especially for her by Balanchine. She
also danced in the classics and in certain of the Fokine ballets.

Balanchine had also recruited for the new Company the
equally youthful Irina Baronova and Tatiana Riabouchinska;
and, as stated above, these three exquisite young dancers—all
Russians and trained on the Russian principle by Russian
teachers and ex-Maryinsky Theatre ballerinas—came to be
spoken of everywhere as "de Basil's Babes" or as "Baby Ballerinas", since none of the three was over fourteen years of age.
Fortunately, however, they quickly "lived down" these tiresome
nicknames, and each developed and won her own public in her
own individual way. All three had entirely different main
characteristics, though Toumanova and Baronova danced
similar roles, especially in the classics, and are sometimes regarded as rivals in this respect—very much as were Taglioni
and Ellsler in a former generation. Riabouchinska, however,
was never the rival of either, since her very distinctive temperament always marked her out more especially for certain particular roles.

When the de Basil's Ballets Russes de Monte Carlo first
appeared at the Alhambra Theatre, London, in 1933, for a four
months' season, Toumanova had left the Company for a short
period to dance with Edward James' *Les Ballets*, then being
presented by Balanchine at the Savoy; but she rejoined de Basil
before the end of the Alhambra season, which was an immense
success. Later that same year, Toumanova and the other two
members of her trio went with the Company to New York;
and S. Hurok, in his racy book, *Impresario*, gives a most amusing description of the arrival and reception of these already
famous "baby ballerinas", all accompanied by anxious mothers,

and all wearing well-worn "little girl clothes", with faces devoid of make-up—adding that when they came the following year and on future occasions, they all wore fur coats and were smartly turned-out in every way as befitted well-established, world-famous ballerinas.

Toumanova remained as a star ballerina with the de Basil Company for five years, and danced in most of the modern ballets by Balanchine, Massine, Lichine, Nijinska, Lifar, etc. Among these may be mentioned *La Concurrence, Cotillon, Jeux d'Enfants, Le Beau Danube, Scuola di Ballo, Le Tricorne, Les Présages, La Boutique Fantasque, Les Femmes de Bonne Humeur, Union Pacific*, etc. She also danced in the classics, *Lac des Cygnes, Le Marriage d'Aurore*, etc.; and in various Fokine ballets, *Petrouchka, Schéhérazade, Cléopâtre*, etc.

During the Second World War, Toumanova was in America, where she danced with various companies; and she also made some films at Hollywood. She married the well-known film producer, Casey Robinson.

In 1948, Toumanova joined the Marquis de Cuevas' Grand Ballet de Monte Carlo, and danced in Lichine's new ballet *Un Coeur de Diamond*, in which George Skibine was her partner. She came with the Company in 1949 to London for their season at Covent Garden, where she received a great welcome, after her long absence since 1938, by an audience now recognizing in her a great dancer in her prime, fully matured and having, as one critic stated, "a Russian ballerina's nobility of style". During this season she danced brilliantly in *Lac des Cygnes, Les Sylphides, Giselle, Don Quichotte, Casse Noisette*; and in these famous classics she revealed again the steady and extraordinary virtuosity for which she has always been famed, together with a wonderful balance in *bravura* items, where her ever-mounting speed was at times breath-taking.

While some critics are inclined to cavil at such a truly amazing virtuosity, all are unanimous in proclaiming this beautiful dancer as one of the most truly brilliant ballerinas of the post-Diaghileff period. Her finished and dramatic performances as *Giselle* with the Company in Paris in 1949 led to her being awarded by Le Cercle de Journalistes Critiques de la Danse, their *Grand Prix* for the best interpretation of this famous role. Her partner on this occasion was André Églevsky.

At the Nijinsky Benefit Gala Performances held at the Empress Hall, London, in November 1949, Toumanova was one of several world-famous dancers who appeared there to do honour to the greatest male dancer of modern times. She danced in *Capriccio Espagnol* with Leonide Massine, and in *Giselle* and the *Don Quichotte pas de deux* with George Skibine.

After the finish of the late 1949 season, Toumanova left the Marquis de Cuevas' Company and went back to her home in America for a holiday. In the spring of 1950, she returned to France to dance as principal ballerina at the Paris Opéra. Among the classics, she danced in *Giselle*, *Coppélia* and *Swan Lake*, in all of which she gave lovely performances—though at times sacrificing the lyrical side to her astonishing virtuosity. She also appeared in present-day ballets, and created roles in some new works. Among the latter were Serge Lifar's *L'Inconnu* and his long-awaited *Phèdre*. *L'Inconnu*, which provided her with an interesting role, was dedicated to her by the famous choreographer. In *Phèdre*, produced on June 14th, Toumanova rose to the occasion magnificently, and danced Racine's tragic heroine with real dramatic power and beauty; and Lifar had provided a wonderful and difficult solo for her, in which virtuosity and tragic sentiment were combined.

In 1952, Toumanova was guest artist with Dolin's Festival Ballet, London, and was brilliant as ever in *Casse Noisette* and the *Don Quixote pas de deux*; and in 1953, she starred in the film *Tonight We Sing*, impersonating Pavlova and dancing several of the latter's famous solos, notably *The Dying Swan*.

Antony Tudor

LIKE SEVERAL OTHER NOW FAMOUS DANCERS AND CHORE-ographers of the present day, Antony Tudor's ambitions were first turned towards ballet by seeing a performance by the incomparable Anna Pavlova and her Company.

This was in 1928, when he was already nineteen years of age; and at that time he had no practical knowledge of dancing, but was engaged in clerical work, being intended by his parents for a business career in London—where he was born on April 4th, 1909. However, the beauty of ballet having entered his soul on that obviously fateful occasion when he first beheld Pavlova, it remained with him for ever; and now, fired by the desire to make this lovely art his real career, he began to study dancing in every spare moment he could snatch. He placed himself under the wise guidance of Madame Marie Rambert, who encouraged and helped him in every possible way; and he also took special additional lessons in ballet work from her two first-class dancers, Harold Turner and the beautiful Pearl Argyle.

The young enthusiast made good progress, but not quite quick enough for his eager ambition because of the hampering calls of his daily business life. Consequently, when Madame Rambert—who had quickly recognized and appreciated his natural gifts—presently invited him to become secretary of her newly founded Ballet Club and to dance in the ballets at her little Mercury Theatre at Notting Hill Gate, while continuing his training, he gladly accepted and recklessly threw up his safe business job—somewhat to the preliminary dismay of his family. However, the latter's fears proved groundless; for the keenly determined and naturally artistic young ballet student now advanced by leaps and bounds and, in a very short time, was dancing leading roles in many of the ambitious and well-presented performances of the Rambert dancers. Having been born with a definite musical sense and a fertile imagination, it was not long before he was fired by the further desire to create new ballets. In this ambitious purpose he was warmly encouraged by Madame Rambert, always on the look-out for choreographic talent among her student-dancers.

Consequently, in 1931, just three years after beginning his ballet training, Antony Tudor created his first ballet, *Cross-Gartered*, which was produced by the Ballet Club at the Mercury Theatre. It dealt with the famous baiting of Malvolio in *Twelfth Night*, to music by Frescobaldi and with *décor* and costumes by Bocquet and Burnascini; and it had a very good reception, with the young choreographer himself dancing the leading role.

Tudor created a number of ballets for the Rambert Company and became their chief choreographer, when Frederick Ashton left to join the Sadler's Wells Company in 1935. These ballets were: in 1932, *Mr. Roll's Quadrilles* (to old music, and with *décor* by Susan Salaman); *Lysistrata* (music Prokofiev, *décor* William Chappell). In 1933, *Les Masques* (music Poulenc, *décor* Sophie Fedorovich); *Pavane pour une Infante Défunte* (music Ravel, *décor* Hugh Stevenson); *Atalanta of the East* (music Szanto and Seelig, *décor* Chappell). In 1934, *Paramour* (music Boyce, *décor* Chappell); *The Planets* (music Holst, *décor* Stevenson). In 1935, *The Descent of Hebe* (music Bloch, *décor* N. Benois). In 1936, came his now famous and very lovely ballet *Lilac Garden* (*Jardin aux Lilas*) with music by Chausson and *décor* by Hugh Stevenson. In 1937, *Dark Elegies* (music Mahler, *décor* N. Benois); and *Suite of Airs* (music Purcell, *décor* N. Benois). In all these ballets, Tudor danced himself, usually in leading roles; and though never a great classical *danseur noble*, he became an excellent all-round general performer. He also danced in many other ballets besides his own with the Ballet Rambert, among his principal roles in these being: Mazurka in *Les Sylphides*, Vieux Marcheur in *Bar aux Folies-Bergère*, the Baron in *Rape of the Lock*, Pavane in *Capriol Suite* and Suitor in *Récamier*. Among the best roles he danced in his own ballets were Malvolio in *Cross-Gartered*, Serpent in *Adam and Eve*, Husband in *Lysistrata*, Neptune in *The Planets*, Hercules in *The Descent of Hebe* and The Man She Must Marry in *Jardin aux Lilas*. The latter is still the role that suits him particularly well, the ballet itself having remained his most popular work. Indeed, these early ballets of Antony Tudor were surprisingly matured and well constructed, and revealed from the first his vivid imagination, psychological tendency and natural sense of form, plus an undoubted musical gift.

In 1937, Antony Tudor formed a Company of his own, known as The London Ballet (this was first known as Dance Theatre and was partly directed by Agnes de Mille, who, however, presently withdrew), in which he was assisted by Hugh Laing, a fine young dancer also trained by Marie Rambert. They gave occasional performances at Toynbee Hall. For this Company, Tudor created in 1937 *Gallant Assembly*, with music by Tartini, in which he danced the leading role; and in 1938, came *The*

Judgment of Paris (music Weill, *décor* Laing), *Gala Performance* (music Prokofiev, *décor* Stevenson), *Soirée Musicale* (music Rossini-Britten, *décor* Stevenson). These now equally popular and frequently performed ballets were given by the Rambert Company at the Mercury Theatre. Among the dancers in these London Ballet productions were several now well known in connection with the Sadler's Wells and other Companies: Peggy van Praagh, Maude Lloyd, Gerd Larsen, Pauline Clayden, David Paltenghi and Hugh Laing.

Tudor also created for the Camargo Society (danced by the Rambert Company) in 1932, *Adam and Eve* (music Constant Lambert); and his *Dark Elegies* (Mahler—N. Benois) was produced at the Duchess Theatre in 1937, before being given at the Mercury. He also produced *Castor and Pollux* for the Oxford University Opera Club in 1934; and he was choreographer for the incidental dances in the operas *La Cenerentola* (Rossini), *Schwanda the Bagpiper* (Weinberger), *Koanga* (Delius) and *Carmen* (Bizet) during the Covent Garden Opera Season of 1935; and in 1937 he created and produced his ballet *Gallant Assembly* at the Oxford Playhouse.

The fame of Antony Tudor as a really inspired and original choreographer was now firmly established, and the news of his many artistic ballet successes had already reached America. When, therefore, his new enterprise had to be abandoned at the beginning of World War No. 2 in 1939, he gladly accepted an invitation from Ballet Theatre of New York to work for them as choreographer, dancer and artistic director. He took with him Hugh Laing as one of his principal dancers.

Among the new ballets Tudor has created for Ballet Theatre are: *Pillar of Fire* (music Schoenberg, *décor* Jo. Melziner), produced Metropolitan Opera House, New York City, April 8th, 1942; *Dim Lustre* (music R. Strauss, *décor* Motley), produced Metropolitan Opera House, New York City, 1943; *Romeo and Juliet* (music Delius, *décor* Eugene Berman), produced Metropolitan Opera House, New York City, April 6th, 1943; *Undertow* (music William Schuman, *décor* Raymond Breinin), produced Metropolitan Opera House, New York City, 1945; *Shadow of the Wind* (based on poems by the Chinese poet, Li Po—music Gustav Mahler, *décor* Jo. Melziner), produced Metropolitan Opera House, New York City, 1948; *Time-Table* (music

Aaron Copland's *Music for the Theatre, décor* James Stewart Morcom). This was first presented by American Ballet Caravan in 1948, and revised a few months later for Ballet Theatre's spring programme in 1949. He also arranged revivals of *Aurora's Wedding* and Fokine's *Petrouchka* and *Les Sylphides*; also revivals of his own ballets *Judgment of Paris* (1940), *Lilac Garden* (1940) and *Gala Performance* (1941).

Of his new and highly original ballets for Ballet Theatre, *Pillar of Fire* has probably aroused the most attention and admiration. As with *Jardins aux Lilas*, it is of the psychological type of ballet which he has made more particularly his own. It deals with the frustrations in love of the middle one of three sisters and of her final redemption and restoration to happiness through conflicting emotional and mental suffering. The balletic treatment is excellent and entirely satisfactory throughout; and it is a work of real depth and importance and at once placed Tudor among the top-ranking choreographers of to-day. Both Tudor and Hugh Laing danced the leading male roles with the utmost sympathy, while the gifted American ballerina, Nora Kaye, was superb in her rendering of Hagar, the frustrated sister who loves, loses and returns to happiness. His beautiful psychological study of the evergreen romance of *Romeo and Juliet* considerably added to his reputation on both sides of the Atlantic, despite its somewhat crowded action and the fact that the music hardly fits so dramatic a theme. *Dim Lustre* is of a much lighter character, though still psychological, in which the two participants, by means of a stolen kiss and a transient touch of the hand, set their memories back to a past moment of delight which, however, leaves them all too soon. *Undertow* probably delves into Freudian realms more deeply still, as it deals with a hyper-sensitive hero so frustrated in his infantile love for his mother that he later seems doomed to hate the women to whom he is at first attracted. It is an intensely dramatic, but somewhat morbid and gloomy work. *Shadow of the Wind* is a much more elaborate ballet, containing six episodes, all widely different in character, but somewhat confusing in their detail. It has magnificent scenery, and contains several balletically lovely and poetic incidents. One of his later works, *Time-Table*, strikes an entirely new note, and centres around the many small meetings and partings of various war-time couples on a small country railway-station in 1917—girls parting from their soldier-lovers, casual flirtations among other birds-of-passage, and so on. It is a realistic modern scene, with here and there a touch of pathos and a final glimpse of real happiness in the reunion of a returning soldier with his faithful, waiting sweetheart, who has remained in the background until that moment. This ballet was produced by the New York City Ballet in January 1949. It was first given under the title of *Despedida* by American Ballet Caravan; but it was entirely revised by Tudor for the New York City Ballet. The music is Aaron Copland's *Music for the Theatre*; and the *décor* and costumes are by J. S. Morcom.

When Ballet Theatre came to London for its first season at Covent Garden in 1946, the Tudor ballets, *Pillar of Fire, Romeo and Juliet, Gala Performance, Undertow* and *Lilac Garden*, were included in the repertoire and attracted much notice, owing to the fact that this choreographer was English, had been trained in the Rambert Ballet, and had gained much added lustre to his name during his seven years' absence in America. Curiously enough, despite the universal interest in and great admiration for the wonderfully dramatic and psychological quality of *Pillar of Fire* and for the tense tragedy of *Undertow*, it was realized that the beautiful, though highly emotional *Lilac Garden*, and the gay, satirical *Gala Performance* still appealed most to the majority of ballet lovers over here and, although among his earlier creations, still remained his most popular ballets. It was also seen that, in the former, his own dancing of his original role of The Man She Must Marry—also that of Hugh Laing, dancing *his* original role of Caroline's Lover —still left nothing to be desired. *Lilac Garden*, indeed, is a little masterpiece—though perhaps more French than English in conception—and, in the opinion of many critics, has not yet been surpassed in its own particular *genre* by its creator. Other critics, however, consider that *Pillar of Fire* is his most inspired work, with *Dark Elegies* and *Lilac Garden* coming second and third.

In the latter part of 1949, Antony Tudor accepted an engagement to become ballet-master of the Stockholm Opera Ballet for the winter season, and to produce Fokine's masterpiece, *Petrouchka*, for the Company there. For the Swedish Company, too, he arranged to create two new ballets, both to music by Prokofiev—the first to that popular modern composer's *Symphonie Classique*, and the other to his *Third Piano Concerto*.

He returned to New York in the late spring of 1950; and on May 8th that year, he created and produced for Ballet Theatre a new ballet entitled *Nimbus*, which had music by Louis Gruenberg (his *Concerto for Violin and Orchestra*), décor by Oliver Smith, and costumes by Saul Bolasni. This is a quite simple but delightful little ballet—perhaps less psychological than most of his others. It concerns the dream, on a hot summer night, of a romantic young work-girl who wakes and makes her way to her tenement dwelling's cool roof-top, and there meets her dream-lover in the flesh. He makes love to her, and they dance together happily; and then she leaves him as her hour for work begins. A slight subject, but cleverly treated. The main idea is to show the contrast between the girl's voluptuous dream-dance and the less exciting one in real life—so Freud is not absent, after all.

In 1951, however, Tudor created a much more brilliant work, which was produced by The New York City Ballet on February 28th. This deals with the ever-popular, romantic subject of *The Lady of the Camellias*, and is set to the lovely music of Verdi (from some of his lesser-known operas), with designs and costumes by Cecil Beaton. In February 1952, Tudor created another important ballet for New York City Ballet, *La Gloire* (music Beethoven, décor Longchamps), dealing dramatically and psychologically with a Bernhardt-like character who dreams of similar greatness.

Antony Tudor, as the creator of the modern psychological ballet, is its greatest and most successful exponent to date. He is also noted for the beauty and expressiveness of his choreography and for his clever adaptation of classical steps and forms to present-day subjects. Though not so prolific in his output as some of his contemporaries, each of his creations reveals the polish and careful thought of an understanding and loving creator. That even greater things may be expected of him in the future, there seems not the slightest doubt. Meanwhile, he has reached an enviable position among those clear-thinking, original-minded choreographers of to-day who are recognized as being really important. His influence upon the now quickly developing ballet of America has been considerable; and the excellence of his work is, in particular, greatly appreciated among American artistic and intellectual ballet-lovers.

Harold Turner

Ⓥ Ⓥ

HAROLD TURNER IS ONE OF THE MOST EXPERIENCED AND THE most virile of all our British male dancers of to-day, in addition to being a remarkably finished and imaginative executant. Indeed, he may be regarded as one of the few remaining present-day male exponents of the true classical Russian method of dancing, such as obtained in Diaghileff's Company—not that he was ever a trainee there, however, but because he gives that impression, being such a firm believer in the old Imperial Russian Ballet system.

Born in Manchester, December 2nd, 1909, Harold Turner, while still a youth, had his preliminary dance training with Alfred Haines, a well-known Manchester teacher. In 1927, he had already won prizes in the Stage-Dancing Section of the "All-For-Dancing" Exhibition in Manchester. Then, at the suggestion of Leonide Massine and Anton Dolin, he came to London to complete his training with Madame Rambert and to join her Company—of which he later became principal dancer for several years.

While with the Rambert Company—where he danced in ballets with Anton Dolin—he had the amazing good fortune to be chosen as partner to the great Russian dancer, Tamara Karsavina—a further Russian ballet education in itself. He was still only twenty-one years of age when Karsavina—then an occasional guest artist with the Rambert Company—quickly recognizing his virile strength and other excellent qualities, selected him first of all to dance with her in *Le Spectre de la Rose*, which she was giving in a performance at the Arts Theatre in 1930; and so brilliant was he in this famous Nijinsky role that she retained him as her partner in various other ballets at the Lyric, Hammersmith. Afterwards, too, he accompanied her on important tours she made in this country and also in Germany. When these tours ended, Karsavina joined Madame Rambert in a special season at the Lyric, Hammersmith; and again Harold Turner was her partner and chief male dancer for the season—a position he continued to hold in the Company's further performances at the Mercury Theatre and elsewhere.

With the Rambert Company, the young dancer had many opportunities for perfecting his remarkably fine technique, and for developing his own strongly personal style. He created many important roles in new works on their first presentation by this Company; and he also danced leads in classics and other established ballets. Among these may be mentioned the Lover in *Le Jardin aux Lilas*, Harlequin in *Le Carnaval*, the Juggler in *Our Lady's Juggler*, Mars in *Mars and Venus*, Pavane in *Capriol Suite*, Cupidon in *Les Petits Riens*, Player in *Le Rugby* and other leads in *The Tartans, Passionate Pavane*, the Blue-Bird *pas de deux* and other roles in *Aurora's Wedding, The Sleeping Beauty*, etc.

In 1932, Harold Turner joined the Sadler's Wells Ballet, where the sureness of his technique and his excellence in character studies developed still further. Frederick Ashton's *Les Patineurs*, in particular, provided a perfect means for revealing his fine technical virtuosity—in fact, it seemed almost to have been created for him. In this gay little piece, his brilliant variation as the Blue Skater is something to remember. His real gift for *demi-caractère* roles proved a great asset to the Company —especially in such difficult parts as Satan in *Job*, and, later, the Rake himself, in *The Rake's Progress*, to name but two; and there have been many others. He had principal roles in *Apparitions, Checkmate*, etc.

He has twice left Sadler's Wells temporarily to dance with other Companies and thus to gain more varied experience. In 1940, he joined the Arts Theatre Ballet; and when Mona Inglesby founded her International Ballet in 1941, he became her *premier danseur* for a while, dancing in her own ballet, *Planetomania*, and in the *Prince Igor Dances*. He created the part of Death in Inglesby's splendid production of *Everyman*; and he also danced in his own ballet, *Fête Bohème*, produced by her Company.

As a choreographer, Harold Turner has not yet had any very outstanding success, though four of his ballets have been produced: *May Collin* and *Serenade* by the Arts Theatre Ballet when he was dancing with that Company in 1940; *Fête Bohème* by the International Ballet in 1941; and *Shore Leave* in 1944, given by the Anglo-Russian Merry-Go-Round.

After his war service in the R.A.F., Harold Turner returned to the Sadler's Wells Ballet, where he danced a number of leading parts, including the Miller in the grand revival of Massine's *Le Tricorne* at Covent Garden, 1947—and in the revival of *La Boutique Fantasque* at the same time he danced the famous *Can-Can* and the *Tarantella* with real verve and excellent technique. He also danced again the difficult part of Satan in the revival of *Job* in the following year with great dramatic forcefulness. In the magnificent *Sleeping Beauty* performances he has again danced the Blue-Bird; and in this Company's *Lac des Cygnes* presentations he has danced Prince Siegfried with much grace and easy dignity. In Ashton's *Fairy Queen*, he danced the Mandarin in the Chinese scena; and in the revival of *Checkmate*, he danced the Red Knight remarkably well. He also had an interesting character role in Ashton's amusing Edwardian ballet, *Les Sirènes*, in which he took the dignified part of the Eastern Potentate.

On June 25th, 1948, in Massine's delightful ballet, *The Clock Symphony*, he created the role of the Baron, one of the princely insect suitors of the lovely Dragonfly Princess (Moira Shearer). This elaborate and colourful ballet takes place in the gorgeous palace of the Insect King; and as one of the rejected suitors, he danced and mimed with great spirit.

Harold Turner went with the Sadler's Wells Ballet on their famous first visit to U.S.A. and Canada in the late autumn of 1949; and wherever he went he won very high praises—especially for his remarkably dramatic performance as the Rake in *The Rake's Progress*. During the Canadian tour, Turner gave several lectures to the Canadian Dance Teachers' Association, to the Boris Volkoff Ballet School, and at the Winifred Wickman Studio. For these talks he usually took with him four members of the Company to give special movement and dance illustrations to mark his various points. So successful were these talks that he was invited to return the following summer vacation in 1950, and to give another series of lectures.

When, on February 20th, 1950, Ninette de Valois' new ballet

Don Quixote was produced at Covent Garden, Harold Turner created the role of the Barber with outstanding excellence.

He also took part in the Grand Gala Performance at Covent Garden on March 9th, 1950, in honour of the State Visit of the French President and Madame Auriol, at which Their Majesties the King and Queen were present.

This versatile dancer-mime has already done good work in television programmes. His first essay in this new medium was in May 1949 when he took part in a programme at Alexandra Palace with Margot Fonteyn and Michael Somes, with Frederick Ashton introducing the various items. His own particular high spots were his performance of the fine solos in *Les Rendezvous* and *Rio Grande*, when he revealed his really acrobatic powers in virtuoso dancing and made viewers realize that the former is one of the best examples still of choreographic work for a first-class male dancer. One may look forward with real interest to further television ballet work from this good all-round dancer.

He is greatly interested in teaching and in production work; and as he possesses a natural gift for engineering—and is particularly keen on anything to do with electricity—good stage and lighting effects can be depended upon when he is in charge of a dramatic performance of any kind. He has recently begun teaching at the Sadler's Wells Ballet School.

During 1950, Harold Turner created the choreography for a short documentary film for the Crown Unit Studios. It was first shown in February 1951, and was made for the National Wool Textile Export Corporation and the Board of Trade, to arouse interest at home and abroad in the wool industry. It was entitled *The Dancing Fleece*, and Turner made of the subject a charming little ballet, illustrating the various processes of wool manufacture from the raw fleece to the final finished materials made up into beautiful costumes designed by Norman Hartnell. His choreography was cleverly worked out; and he gave a fantastic touch to his story by transforming dancing puppet-girls into woolly lambs and sheep.

During the summer of 1951, he was one of the group of dancers chosen by Margot Fonteyn and Robert Helpmann to accompany them on a short provincial tour; and he had some good roles in the programme—notably, he gave an amazingly fine performance as Harlequin in an excerpt from *Le Carnaval*.

During the Festival of Britain London celebrations, Harold Turner performed daily throughout the summer season in the Open-Air Amphitheatre in Battersea Park, where a most delightful ballet was presented. Entitled *Orlando's Silver Wedding*, it was adapted from Kathleen Hale's series of children's books dealing with the adventures of *Orlando, the Marmalade Cat*. The choreography was by Andrée Howard, the music by Sir Arthur Bliss, and the *décor* and costumes designed by Kathleen Hale herself. Harold Turner took the role of the redoubtable Marmalade Cat with great dexterity and humour, and gave a really splendid performance, full of wit and fantastic movement—as did also his co-star, Sally Gilmour. These two clever and entertaining artists were an inimitable pair, and gave joy to children and adults alike.

In January 1952, Harold Turner was responsible for the dances included in Jean Anouilh's *Thieves' Carnival* at the Arts Theatre.

Harold Turner is married to that charming dancer, Gerd Larsen.

Ninette de Valois

THAT NO SINGLE INDIVIDUAL HAS DONE MORE FOR BRITISH Ballet than Dame Ninette de Valois, D.B.E., will be readily endorsed by every ballet lover in this country. When this famous Director and Founder of the Sadler's Wells Ballet took her Company, in the late autumn of 1949, to the United States of America and Canada for the first time, she and they created such an unprecedented furore because of the high standard of their work and of their personal charm that they were hailed as true ambassadors who raised the prestige of their country to a greater height than it had ever reached before—not only culturally, but also for their amazing dollar-earning capacity, which far exceeded expectation. This was a truly wonderful achievement which could never have come about had it not been for the artistic sense and unfailing business ability, the solid hard work over many years, and the constant belief in a great idea of this one quite small woman—small in stature, but great in brain and in artistic capacity.

An Irishwoman, born in Dublin as Edris Stannus, this embryo "Diaghileff" never expected to become, first, an excellent dancer in that great man's world-famous ballet, and, later, an equally excellent choreographer, teacher and impresario. Even as a child, however, she showed great determination and made the best possible use of her undoubted gifts. She studied dancing almost as soon as she could walk; and, when a child of ten, she came with her parents to England where she was able to continue her training on a much wider scale. A small, graceful, attractive child, she quickly became known as a juvenile dancing prodigy, appearing in pantomimes and children's plays under the name of Ninette de Valois.

Her father, a Colonel in the Army, having been killed during the First World War, his young daughter found it more necessary than ever to make a name for herself in her chosen career. After travelling for a time with a troupe of juveniles, she settled in London, and here received many interesting and important junior engagements, now dancing in Lyceum pantomimes and in musical shows of various kinds. She became *première danseuse* of the Lyceum pantomime in 1914-15, and continued to be engaged as such in each succeeding season until 1918, when she became *première danseuse* in the Beecham Opera Company at the Palladium. Later on still in 1922, she danced with Leonide Massine and Lydia Lopokova at Covent Garden and also at the Coliseum.

In 1923, she joined the Diaghileff Company as a soloist. This was a momentous decision for her, as she did not join the Company with the idea of becoming one of the famous impresario's star ballerinas—she was already a well-known and greatly admired "star" in London—but rather for the opportunity of learning how to manage a great company of dancers and how to produce ballets. The ballets she danced in while a soloist in the Diaghileff Company were: Fokine's *Narcisse, Daphnis and Chloe, Petrouchka, Papillons, Le Carnaval, Les Sylphides, Cléopâtre, Prince Igor, Schéhérazade* and *Thamar*; in Massine's ballets *Soleil de Nuit, Les Femmes de Bonne Humeur, Les Contes Russes, La Boutique Fantasque, Le Tricorne, Chout, Cimarosiana.* She also appeared in the revivals of Petipa's

Le Lac des Cygnes and *Le Mariage d'Aurore*; and in the Nijinsky ballets *Le Sacre du Printemps* and *L'Après-midi d'un Faune.* She likewise created roles in Bronislava Nijinska's *Les Biches, Les Fâcheux, Les Tentations de la Bergère, Le Train Bleu* and *Les Noces*; in Massine's *Zéphyr et Flore*; and in Balanchine's *Le Chant du Rossignol.*

By this time, Ninette de Valois was an individualist with definite ideas of her own; and she was also possessed by a wonderful dream—though she did not then know whether it would ever be realized—of bringing into being a great Company of British dancers, a Company which should have its own ideals.

Consequently, she learned all she possibly could during the two years she danced with the Diaghileff Company—even going so far, latterly, as to disapprove of certain tendencies she regarded as adverse which its famous Director was then beginning to show. Among these, she felt, was a seeking after novelty for novelty's sake, a tendency which did not appeal to her.

Consequently, when she left Diaghileff in 1925, although she continued to take good engagements as they occurred—she danced with Dolin at the Coliseum and in *The Whitebirds Revue* in 1927, and in the Covent Garden season in 1928—she kept her precious private dream in view. From 1928-30, she became choreographic-director of the Festival Theatre at Cambridge, the Old Vic, and at the Abbey Theatre, Dublin. She had already started her own School of Dancing in London under the title of "The Academy of Choreographic Art"; and this soon began to succeed. With the formation of the Camargo Society in 1930, opportunities arose for her to arrange under its auspices, performances with her own dancers.

After producing in 1928 her own ballet, *Rout*, with the aid of the Camargo Society, she revealed herself as an original and really fine choreographer by producing her now well-known *Job* (book by Geoffrey Keynes, based on William Blake's illustrations to The Book of Job; music by Vaughan Williams, and *décor* and costumes by Gwendolen Raverat), given at the Cambridge Theatre, July 8th, 1931; and this was followed by her *La Création du Monde, Cephalus and Procris* and *The Origin of Design. Job* is still regarded as one of her finest ballets and has been revived many times since, the dramatic role of *Satan* hav-

~~ing been rendered by several now famous male dancers, notably~~
Robert Helpmann, Anton Dolin, Harold Turner, etc.

Meanwhile, the little troupe of British dancers she had trained
were also performing at the Old Vic in the operas being given
there by Lilian Baylis; and, on the invitation of the latter, these
two great women of the theatre now joined forces with splendid
results to the benefit of both—and of Ballet in particular. De
Valois closed her own already successful School and brought
her students to the Old Vic, where full ballet performances began to be given alternately with opera and Shakespearian plays.
The new Sadler's Wells Theatre being completed about this
same time, this theatre was also taken over by Lilian Baylis; and
thus, the Vic-Wells Ballet was born—just in the nick of time,
so far as Ninette de Valois' ideas for British Ballet were concerned. The great Serge Diaghileff had died in 1929; and by the
time Colonel de Basil with his newly constructed Ballet Russe
de Monte Carlo appeared in London in 1934, the Vic-Wells
Ballet was already well established on firm foundations and
could hold its own as a permanent institution, despite such a
brilliant, but temporary, counter attraction.

Thus, de Valois began to realize her life's dream of directing,
teaching and training a real British Ballet Company, with its
own British choreographers, scenic designers and occasional
composers; and many new ballets were gradually produced, together with revivals of the classics and of other famous works.

At first, of course, there were no sufficiently good soloists for
the major roles; so Alicia Markova and Anton Dolin (the latter
intermittently) were engaged and danced with the Company
from 1933 to 1935.

When these two stars left, there arose the knotty question
of replacing them. The Company's wise and ever-optimistic
Director decided that her well-trained Company *could* now
stand upon its own legs, or at least should be given the chance
to do so; and she watched the gradual emergence of her new
soloists with hopeful pride. Among these emerging soloists
were Margot Fonteyn, Pamela May, Julia Farren, June Brae,
Beryl Grey, Ursula Moreton, Wenda Horsburgh, Moira Shearer,
Celia Franca, Margaret Dale, Peggy van Praagh, Mary Honer,
Elizabeth Miller, Moyra Fraser, Pauline Clayden, Joan Sheldon
and others. Among the male dancers were Robert Helpmann,

Frederick Ashton, Harold Turner, Gordon Hamilton, Leslie Edwards, David Paltenghi, Alexis Rassine, William Chappell, Michael Somes, Brian Shaw, Alan Carter, John Hart, Henry Danton, John Field, Leo Kersley, etc.

Not all these dancers, of course, could be considered then as principals; but most of them became well known as good, reliable soloists and have frequently danced leading parts. Several are outstanding and have become famous.

Among this fine list, two of the male dancers have become well-known choreographers, Frederick Ashton and Robert Helpmann; and William Chappell has become known as an artist and scenic designer. Celia Franca has become known as a choreographer, several of her ballets having proved great successes.

Ninette de Valois herself has proved to be a very fine choreographer to the Company, having created some thirty ballets, or more, though a few of these may be considered as *divertissements* only.

Among her earlier ballets may be mentioned the following: in 1928, her first ballet, *Rout*; in 1931, *The Creation of the World, The Jew in the Bush, Fête Polonaise, Italian Suite, Cephalus and Procris, Job*; in 1932, *Douanes, The Nursery Suite, The Scorpions of Ysit, The Origin of Design, The Jackdaw and the Pigeons, Narcissus and Echo, Dances Sacred and Profane*; in 1933, *The Birthday of Oberon, The Wise and the Foolish Virgins*; in 1934, *The Jar*. Of these, the most important one was *Job* (music by Vaughan Williams, *décor* by Gwendolen Raverat) which, although created at this early period, has always been considered a masterpiece. With this exception—and perhaps, also, that of *The Creation of the World*—her really important ballets began to appear in 1934, when she created for the Rambert Company *Bar aux Folies-Bergère* (Chabrier—William Chappell). Then, for the Vic-Wells Ballet came, in 1934, *The Haunted Ballroom* (Geoffrey Toye—Motley); in 1935, *The Rake's Progress* (Gavin Gordon—Rex Whistler); in 1936, *The Gods Go a-Begging* (Handel—Hugh Stevenson), *Barabau, Prometheus, The Emperor's New Clothes*; in 1937, *Checkmate* (Arthur Bliss—E. McKnight Kauffer); in 1940, *The Prospect Before Us* (William Boyce—Roger Furse); in 1941, *Orpheus and Eurydice* (Gluck—Sophie Fedorovich); in 1943, *Promenade* (Haydn—Hugh Stevenson).

Most of Ninette de Valois' ballets contain good plots, with easily followed stories; and she presents every essential detail with the utmost care. She has an excellent musical sensitivity and knowledge of music, and holds the degree of D.Mus. She has been particularly happy in being well served by her chosen composers, among whom may be mentioned Emmanuel Chabrier, Arthur Bliss, Geoffrey Toye, Vaughan Williams, Gavin Gordon; and the classical composers William Boyce, Haydn, Handel and Gluck. Among her artists for *décor* and costumes may be named William Chappell, E. McKnight Kauffer, Hugh Stevenson, Gwendolen Raverat, Sophie Fedorovich, Roger Furse, Motley and the late Rex Whistler.

Among de Valois' great productions have also been the wonderful, full-evening-length famous classics, *Le Lac des Cygnes*, *Coppélia*, *Giselle*, *Casse Noisette* and *The Sleeping Beauty*, all produced with meticulous care and regard for every essential detail and with due emphasis on the performance of minor roles, always so important in these particular ballets. She has always believed in concentrating on as perfect a whole as possible, rather than on a few star performers, and, with her, undoubtedly, "the ballet is the thing". Hence her admiration for Michael Fokine, among whose ballets she has produced *Les Sylphides*, *Le Carnaval* and *Le Spectre de la Rose*.

When the Second World War broke out in 1939, Ninette de Valois managed to keep her ballet going, despite depleted ranks owing to war service. She and her members even carried out in 1940 a long-promised tour in Holland, where they danced to crowded and delighted houses. While in Holland, however, the German invasion of that country took place, and the trapped visiting dancers had to depart at great speed from Rotterdam for home, only just managing to make their escape to the waiting boats as the German tanks roared in—and they lost, or left behind, much of their luggage and scenery, including the entire lay-out (scenery, costumes, scores) of six ballets. This was a great misfortune; but having luckily saved their lives, they immediately set to work to "make do" with such material as they had left.

During one of the London "blitzes", their beloved Old Vic was demolished; and as the operatic and Shakespearian work of that famous theatre was now continued at Sadler's Wells, the

de Valois Company—now known as the Sadler's Wells Ballet
—gave their performances at the New Theatre, where their
devotees still followed them in enthusiastic crowds and where
many of their most famous ballets were first produced.

Then, at the conclusion of the war, a very happy change took
place; and the Sadler's Wells Ballet was invited to take up its
residence at Covent Garden Opera House—the scene of so many
former glorious operatic and ballet triumphs. This was a
crowning triumph for its Director, Ninette de Valois, who, in
the New Year Honours of 1947, was honoured by the King with
the decoration of C.B.E. in recognition of her splendid work
for British Ballet. At the opening night of their new permanent home at Covent Garden, too, her Company was likewise
honoured by the presence of Their Majesties the King and
Queen; and the ballet given on this auspicious occasion was the
full-length performance of the Petipa-Tchaikovsky Fairy Ballet
The Sleeping Beauty, with Margot Fonteyn in the *prima
ballerina* role of Princess Aurora, her partner being Robert Helpmann as the Prince.

Not only has Ninette de Valois seen her cherished dream of
establishing and directing a really fine British Ballet come true
and has seen it permanently housed in one of the world's most
famous theatres, but she has also watched the growth of the
Company's first-class British Ballet Training School in Colet
Gardens, W.14, where a general education and training for the
ballet for girls and boys aged 9-16 can take place. This Ballet
School—for which Scholarships may be secured—is under her
own direct personal supervision; and it prepares students for
the Royal Academy of Dancing Examinations. She is also a
vice-president of the latter academy—of which Her Majesty
Queen Elizabeth is Patroness and Dame Adeline Genée is President. The Sadler's Wells Ballet School, too, now has a "junior
Company", known as the "Sadler's Wells Theatre Ballet",
which functions at Sadler's Wells Theatre, where ballet performances are given alternately with operas. Thus there is a
constant supply of "comers-on" to replenish the ranks of the
parent Company at Covent Garden from time to time. The
public performances of the Sadler's Wells Theatre Ballet have
now reached a very high standard; and the Company there
makes frequent provincial tours. It has also produced some

excellent choreographers, as well as dancers, principal among whom may be mentioned Celia Franca, John Cranko, Alan Carter, Anthony Burke. Several of the young dancers trained there, too, have already become well known. Among these may be mentioned Nadia Nerina, Elaine Fifield, Maryon Lane, Pauline Harrop, Patricia Miller; Leo Kersley, David Blair, Stanley Holden, David Poole, Pirmin Trecu, Eric Hyrst, Kenneth Macmillan, Michael Hogan.

Since "moving-in" to Covent Garden, Ninette de Valois has continued her wonderful work for the Company with the same concentration and real devotion as in the former days of struggles and disappointments; and though the latter are no longer so frequent as of yore, she still regards perfection only as her goal. In private life she is the busy wife of an equally busy London doctor—she is Mrs. A. B. C. Connell.

Possibly, her greatest feat of organization was the arranging for the transportation by air, and the several overland journeys afterwards, of her bevy of dancers and orchestra performers, attendants, dressers, etc.—about sixty-five individuals altogether, to say nothing of scenery and costumes—to the United States of America and Canada in the late autumn of 1949. This was a real triumph, as was also the Company's brilliant success on the other side of the Atlantic—a triumph indeed and one well fitted to be included in this present unfinished "success story" of a great dream brilliantly realized.

On February 20th, 1950, a new choreographic work by their energetic Director was produced for the Sadler's Wells Company at Covent Garden. Entitled *Don Quixote*, it has music by Roberto Gerhard, *décor* and costumes by Edward Burra; and it met with an enthusiastic reception. This was the first new de Valois ballet since *Promenade* in 1944; and it is a major work.

On March 9th, 1950, at another grand Gala Performance by the Sadler's Wells Ballet given before Their Majesties the King and Queen at Covent Garden in honour of the State Visit of the French President, Monsieur Auriol, and Madame Auriol, Madame de Valois was decorated by the President with the Legion of Honour.

In the late autumn of 1950, her Company made their second visit to U.S.A. and Canada, which was more extensive and even more successful than the first one—financially, artistically, and to the further enhancement of British prestige. In the spring of 1951, she went on a lecture tour to Yugo-Slavia, and extended this in order to visit Salonica, Athens and Turkey before returning home.

Revivals of several of the finest de Valois ballets have been given at Covent Garden since the Company took up residence there. These were: in 1947, *Checkmate*; in 1948, *Job*; in 1949, *The Rake's Progress*; in 1950, *The Haunted Ballroom*; in 1951, *The Prospect Before Us*.

On May 15th, 1950, the Company celebrated its twenty-first birthday; and in honour of this auspicious event a lively Gala Performance was given at Sadler's Wells Theatre, its former home, when Princess Margaret honoured the occasion by her presence. The popular de Valois ballet, *The Haunted Ballroom*, was given, with Margot Fonteyn, Robert Helpmann and Pamela May taking their original roles. A scene from *The Rake's Progress* was performed. The highlight of the evening, however, was Ashton's *Wedding Bouquet*, in which Ninette de Valois herself took her original part of Webster. Ashton's *Façade* was also given; and several of the original creators of roles in the various ballets took part. Congratulations were offered and speeches made; and it was a very happy occasion for the founder of the ballet and her colleagues.

In the New Year's Honours List, 1951, Ninette de Valois appeared as a Dame of the British Empire, the highest title that can be bestowed upon a woman in this country. She had already been created a C.B.E.; and this new and more important honour was in further recognition of the almost incredible achievement of building up a splendid all-British Ballet which is admired by lovers of this beautiful art all over the world. That such a crowning of her remarkable life's work, achieved by her enduring courage in overcoming the constant difficulties that have beset her, and her unfailing belief in a great idea, was never better deserved, has been endorsed by all the friends and admirers of Dame Ninette de Valois.

Short sketches of Dame Ninette de Valois' life and work are to be found in many books on Ballet; and she has herself contributed to the literature of this ever-increasingly popular art by her own interesting and important book *Invitation to the Dance*.

General Index and Appendices

General Index

306

Appendix 1

The Ballets

mentioned in this book

311

Appendix 2

The Dancers

mentioned in this book

(There are full biographical sketches of those names in capital letters)

Appendix 3

The Music

Composers, musicians and conductors mentioned in this book

◎◎◎

Appendix 4

The Artists
and designers mentioned in this book

Appendix 5
The Choreographers
mentioned in this book

335